INDOOR RELIEF

by

Opal Gibson

*A diary of the life and times of a
London Workhouse*

First Edition

Front cover
Swaffield Road Workhouse

Frontispiece
Workhouse at Wandsworth 1810

ISBN 0 9552 444 0 4

Published by Opal Publications
6 Manor Road, West Wickham, Kent, BR4 8PS
First published 2006
© Opal Gibson

Designed and printed by Litho Direct Colour Printers Ltd. Brighton. Tel: 01273 563111

Dedicated to my Mother and Father

INTRODUCTION

Swaffield Road Workhouse was architect designed on a large scale, built in 1886 and cost £100,000. There were many purpose-built workhouses built in London around that time, they were known as the "Metropolitan Workhouses".

It was managed by a Master, Matron, Assistant Master and Assistant Matron also Office Staff, though overall control was by the Guardians.

The Workhouse was not the first to be built in Wandsworth. The first one was built in 1810. It was built on a site with Alms houses. There are not any known records of this establishment. The second one was built in Garratt Lane. It was not in existence for very long and after it closed it was thought to be converted into a public house. The third one was St John's Workhouse and Infirmary on East Hill which was built in 1838. When Swaffield Road was built it took most of the able bodied inmates and St. John's became an Infirmary.

The book has been written chronologically, the chapters in decades and within the decades, the subject headings have also been written chronologically. It shows the transition from Workhouse to Institution to Residential Home.

It is hoped that this book will be a window on the Wandsworth Union that existed for 86 years which had caring and compassion within the norm for that era.

During its lifetime inmates entered through the Swaffield Road Gatehouse, many several times. For the aged and those who did not have a surviving relative, "Indoor Relief" really did become "home".

THE WANDSWORTH UNION

The Wandsworth Union consisted of the following establishments:

The Swaffield Road Workhouse.

St James's Branch Workhouse,

The Intermediate Schools.

St John's Infirmary.

The Tooting Home.

Also the following Committees:

The Visiting Committee for the Swaffield Road Workhouse and for the St James's Branch Workhouse.

The Finance Committee.

The Works Committee.

The Boarding Out Committee.

The Intermediate Schools Visiting Committee.

The St John's Infirmary Committee.

The Tooting Home Committee.

The Gardening Committee.

The Clothing Committee.

The Collectors Cases and Settlement Committee.

The Battersea Dispensary Committee.

The Combined Relief and General Purposes Committee.

The Rota Committee.

The Forms of Contract Committee.

The Indoor Accommodation Committee.

The Outdoor Relief Committee.

ACKNOWLEDGEMENTS

Joy Farrow, without whose assistance and expertise this book would not have been produced.

Joyce Walker, MBE, for all her helpful advice.

Jenice Jeffers.

Joan and Kenneth Dippie.

Nigel Terrell for all his help with the computer and proof reading.

BIBLIOGRAPHY

A Victorian Workhouse by John Barwell.

The London Metropolitan Archives.

The Wandsworth Local History Library.

The Images of England - Wandsworth by Patrick Loobey.

The London Encyclopaedia by Ben Weinreb and Christopher Hibbert.

Wandsworth Past by Dorian Gerhold.

The Guildhall Library.

Bromley Reference Library.

Victoria by Richard Poulton.

The Land Registry.

The Town Planning Office, Wandsworth Town Hall.

The Wandsworth Borough News.

Young's Brewery.

Yesterday's Britain - Readers Digest.

The Compact Edition of the Oxford Dictionary.

CONTENTS

CHAPTER 1: *The Early Years - 1900*

Workhouse at Wandsworth.

Sketch'd 1810.

The first Poor Law Act was passed in 1601. From that time onwards workhouses appeared all over the country. They had to run on minimum cost; hence if you wanted a roof over your head and food, without any money, you had to work for it.

Workhouses were a charge on the Parish. They were kept unpleasant deliberately to keep numbers down. The general opinion was that if you were poor, did not have any work, or somewhere to live it was your own fault. Today we know differently. It is well documented through the centuries of how awful the workhouses were.

In 1834 changes were made. The Poor Law Reform Act allowed parishes to join together and form Poor Law Unions. This meant that workhouses could work together with better management and more importantly become efficient.

The passing of time had also been a great factor. Lessons had been learned regarding segregation of inmates and the conditions that they were expected to live in.

A separate section of the workhouse was the "Casual Wards". It had its own Relieving Officer, and their own quarters. It had a kitchen, dining room, utility rooms, sleeping cubicles, stone breaking yards and oakum picking sheds. They were for men and some women who were able bodied who wanted food and shelter and to come and go as they pleased. Only men did stone breaking, some men did oakum picking but the women did most of it. Some of the men were married and their wives and children would be in the workhouse.

Stone breaking was the breaking of "Guernsey Spalls" (large round stones) into small stones that would pass through a two-inch sieve. This would be used in the building trade. Oakum was rope that had been creosoted. It had to be teased out so that it could be used as caulking in the ship building industry.

In the main part of the Workhouse Medical Officers were appointed as well as Ward Assistants, Nurses and eventually Teachers for the children.

There was a large laundry, which did have employed women running it, but female inmates did the work. Male inmates would do some of the very heavy work.

An employed, skilled mattress maker ran a mattress shop, with male inmates as assistants.

The kitchens had employed cooks and assistants. Male and female inmates did the unskilled work; they also did all the scullery work.

There was a large Needle Room with employed staff. Some female inmates, who were good with a needle and were reliable, worked there.

The workhouse had a Landau and a Brougham, probably bought second-hand. There was a large coach-house and stables. Coachmen were employed to look after the coaches and the horses.

There was a large furniture store. This enabled inmates to keep furniture for when they were able to leave the workhouse with a job, find somewhere to live and settle back into the community once more.

A large school block was built for the children. It had to cope with children of all ages. There was a nursery for the under three year olds. The older children went out to schools. Compulsory Education became law in 1870.

The site was divided into male and female quarters. Families who were admitted were separated with the children going into the school block. There was a time set aside for relatives to meet one another.

ADMINISTRATION

As in any large institution there had to be rules and regulations. The inmates were expected to look after themselves as much as they could. To rise in the morning when called and go to meals at designated times.

If permission was given for 'leave' either alone or with a relative they would have to return by a given time. An official request preceded the permission for 'leave', because the inmates were in the care of the Guardians. The Master and Matron also needed to know how many inmates were on site in case of fire, for catering, and could not have large numbers wandering the streets and perhaps getting lost.

The Guardians met once a fortnight. They had a visiting committee that did the rounds of the workhouse. They chose all different parts of the workhouse on each visit. The Master did not know where they would go. They made their report at the next Committee meeting. They would talk to the inmates and report back any complaints the inmates made.

There was always an increase of inmates during the winter months, understandably so. Swaffield Road was always full, and in the autumn needed to transfer quite a lot of inmates ready for the winter intake. In August 1892 they started to make preparations to transfer as many as possible contacting workhouses as far away as Bloomsbury.

Over the past few years, demands on the workhouse accommodation had gradually changed. The following report is revealing:

WANDSWORTH AND CLAPHAM UNION

Extract from the Report made by N. Herbert, Esq., Assistant Local Government Inspector, on the Workhouse of the above Union, after a visit on the 7th July, 1893:-

Although 50 Aged Women were transferred to the St. Giles' Workhouse, this Workhouse during the past winter has been overcrowded.

On January 14th and 15th there were 650 Inmates (the certified accommodation allows for 627).

A few years ago there were no Infirm cases at this Workhouse, but at my visit to-day 83 Men and 60 Women were classed as such.

Since my last visit, a Dormitory on the first floor of "C" Block on the Female side, certified for 60 Beds, is now used as a Day and Night Ward. There were 45 Beds in this Ward, but it appeared to me that should this Ward continue to be used as a Day and Night Ward, there should not be more than 36 Beds, in order that a part may be set aside for the old people to sit in during the day.

A Dormitory on the first floor of "B" Block, on the Male side, is also used as an Infirm Ward. This Ward is certified for 34 Beds; there should not be more than about 18 Beds in this Ward, but at my visit there were 25.

The Boys' Wards, certified for 18 Beds, contained 23 Inmates. In the Girls' Wards, certified for the same number, there were 27 Children. One Girl, named Ada Rowe, had suffered from Opthalmia, and upon making enquiries of the Attendant she stated that the Child had "crusts" round the eyes in the morning. It appears to me unwise to overcrowd this part of the workhouse.

Inmates were issued with uniform clothing on entering the workhouse. All possessions and clothes issued were stamped with the workhouse stamp. They were not to be sold or lost. If a new item was needed the old one had to be handed in.

The Committee had been asked for guidance regarding storage of inmates own possessions:-

That your Committee had under consideration the question of the condition of the Inmates own Clothing, and, with reference thereto, gave the following directions: -

1) *For each Bag of Clothing to be labelled with the Name and Date of admission of the Inmate to whom it belongs.*

2) *For the whole of the packages to be overhauled every Six months, and those in which Moths, &c., may be discovered to be baked and properly cleansed.*

3) *For steps to be taken to Fumigate the Store containing the Clothing when necessary.*

In August 1892 Tobacco was issued to certain male inmates. There was also an order that any misconduct would render the issue suspended and the matter reported to the next workhouse committee meeting or the visiting committee. This threat might seem very harsh, but it was necessary because of fire precautions.

That it was referred to your Committee to consider the Order issued by the Local Government Board with reference to an allowance of Tobacco for certain Inmates, with power to give directions, and in pursuance of this, your Committee gave directions as follows, viz.:-

(a) That in accordance with the Resolution of the Guardians, passed on the 18th August last, one ounce of Tobacco be given weekly to the Male Inmates over 60 years of age.

(b) That under the Order of the Local Government Board, men who may be employed in -

    (a) Cleansing a drain, or

    (b) Clipping the inside of Boilers,

    be also supplied with one ounce of Tobacco weekly.

(c) That the Tobacco be distributed weekly on Sunday mornings, and that no Inmate shall be entitled to the same until the second Sunday after the last admission.

(d) That smoking be permitted out of labour hours, and from 10am to 10.15am, from 3pm to 3.15pm in the Yards, also in the Day-rooms after supper.

(e) That the Aged and Infirm Men be permitted to smoke at any time in the Day-rooms and Yards assigned to that class only.

Leave of absence from the workhouse was quite strictly controlled. In 1894 inmates could have leave on Sundays, together with their children to visit family or friends. A total of 30 inmates of each sex were allowed out at any one time. They had to return by 7.45pm. By 1900 the Master requested that this be altered to alternate Sundays and second Wednesdays in the month only. This was with a view to doing away with the numerous issuing and receptions of clothing into Stores, and interfering with labour in Workshops.

In July 1895 the Guardians made provision for female inmates to have three months "leave", with their children left in the care of the workhouse and chargeable. The idea behind this scheme was to give time for the single women with (or without) children a chance to find work and accommodation. They had to report to the Enquiry Officer at the workhouse every month. Records do not show how successful this scheme was.

In 1895 the Christmas Day visiting committee recorded: -

"We visited the workhouse this day; found everything satisfactory. We tasted the food supplied which was ample and very well prepared and of good quality."

In 1896 the Master gave the male inmates permission to use the dining hall for reading. The dining hall was divided in half, one side for the men and the other for the women. The women were given reading space but it was not the other half of the dining hall!

At one time the police tried to send four boys aged 14 to 16 to the workhouse. They were accused of Felony. They were not accepted. The Master stated that the workhouse was not the proper place for Felons.

A telephone extension between the General Office, the Porter's Lodge and Battersea Exchange was installed. It cost £4.00. With the workhouse becoming even busier, instant communication was seen to be imperative.

In July 1894 overcrowding was becoming a serious problem. The number of Aged and Inform was rising fast. The Infirmary was full and the workhouse was not built for Aged and Infirm Inmates. The following letters show the problems only too clearly:-

It was MOVED by Mr Turner, Seconded by Mr Millar, and Resolved - That the offer of the Guardians of the Poor of St Giles and St George, Bloomsbury be accepted and that 30 additional Inmates be sent to their Workhouse as soon as possible.

34. The Board proceeded to consider the following letter (No. 139), from the Local Government Board, viz:-

No. 69,743 A.   LOCAL GOVERNMENT BOARD, WHITEHALL, S.W.,
1804   25 July 1894

SIR,

I am delighted by the Local Government Board to acknowledge the receipt of your letter of the 19th instant, informing them that the Guardians of the Wandsworth and Clapham Union have adjourned the consideration of the provision of additional accommodation for Infirm Inmates, until they receive the Board's decision with reference to the alteration in the constitution of the Union, as suggested in the Resolution forwarded with your letter of the 25th June.

The Board direct me to refer to their letter of the 18th of August, 1893 and to state that they adhere to the opinion expressed in the letter, and are not, therefore, prepared to entertain the question of dividing the Union. They may accordingly urge the Guardians to proceed, without further delay, with the necessary measure for relieving the congestion both in the Infirmary and the Workhouse; and they think that the requisite provision can probably best be secured by the erection of separate buildings for the Aged and Infirm on the Swaffield Road Site.

I am, Sir,

Your obedient Servant.

(Signed) W.E. KNOLLYS

Assistant Secretary.

Clerk to the Guardians of the
Wandsworth and Clapham Union

Note: The consideration of this letter was on the 2nd August adjourned for Four weeks, on the 30th August again adjourned for Four weeks, and on the 27th September adjourned until to-day.

The Clerk submitted the following letter from the Local Government Board, which has been received since the last Board meeting, viz.:-

No. - A   LOCAL GOVERNMENT BOARD
1894   WHITEHALL, S.W.,
                                                                           4th October 1894

SIR,

I am directed by the Local Government Board to advert to their letter of the 25th July last, and to enquire the result of the further consideration by the Guardians of the Wandsworth and Clapham Union of the accommodation for the Indoor Poor of the Union.

I am at the same time to forward, for the information of the Guardians, the accompanying extracts from Reports made by the Board's Assistant Inspector, Mr Herbert, upon the Workhouse and Infirmary, and to point out that the facts referred to therein show the need for increased accommodation for the Sick and Infirm, which the Board have urged the Guardians to provide.

I am, Sir,

Your obedient Servant,

(Signed) W.E. KNOLLYS,

Assistant Secretary.

Clerk to the Guardians
Of the Wandsworth and Clapham Union.

11 October 1894

[ENCLOSURE.]

71,126a

1894

WANDSWORTH AND CLAPHAM UNION

Extract from the Report made by N. Herbert, Esq., Local Government Inspector, on the Workhouse Infirmary of the above Union, after a visit on the 6th July, 1894.

On January 25th, 1894, the Medical Superintendent reported:-

"During the past few weeks we have had considerable pressure on our space, the highest number dieted on one day being 672 on the 19th instant.

Six cases of Erysipelas have developed in the Institution since December 20th.

At my visit there were 530 Inmates, but at the same time there were 27 Patients at Sandgate, and 42 at Margate. These latter cannot be transferred to the Infirmary, owing to the wards having to be cleaned. With regard to this matter the Superintendent reported on April 26th, 1894:-

I beg to remind the Guardians that I have already reported the accommodation for 100 Patients will probably be needed at Margate or Sandgate during the carrying out of the cleaning and painting operations decided to be done at the Infirmary. It will be remembered that last year we were unable to carry out this work, owing to the crowded condition of the establishment.

In my last report I referred to the insufficient Nurses' accommodation, and also to the storing of combustible material in the basement.

The Laundry arrangements are very unsatisfactory. At the present time the foul linen is washed in the Infirmary, and the other linen at the Workhouse.

Upon calling the Matron's attention to the state of the Laundry, she said that the number of women was too small.

Upon making further inquiries, I found that the total number employed in the Laundry was nine, that the number of articles washed weekly was 9,000, in addition to which the linen from the Workhouse (consisting of about 6,000 articles weekly) had to be sorted by the Staff at the Infirmary Laundry.

This is the only Infirmary, situated at a distance from the Workhouse, where the linen is washed at the Workhouse.

With regard to the Sanitary arrangements, the supply pipes to the W.C.'s are in direct connection with the drinking water-tanks, and the same pipes also supply water to taps from which drinking water is sometimes obtained.

84,421 A
1894

WANDSWORTH AND CLAPHAM UNION

Extract from the Report made by N. Herbert, Esq., Assistant Local Government Inspector, on the Workhouse of the above Union, after a visit on the 1st August 1894.

The workhouse is quite inadequate. What is much wanted is separate accommodation for the Infirm.

This Workhouse is over certified, see my last Report.

On January 12th, 1894, there were 691 inmates, with accommodation or barely 600. In addition, about 120 old people were farmed out at that date, at great expenses, at the Beach Rocks Convalescent Home, and at Perry's Sanatorium. The Infirmary was also overcrowded.

Every part of the Workhouse has been overcrowded since the date of last Report. At my visit the Mothers' and Infants' Block was crowded, and beds were made up in the corridor on the Female side.

It was MOVED by Mr Turnor, Seconded by Mr Millar, and Resolved - That the matter stand adjourned until the Second Meeting of the new Board, to be elected in December next

It was MOVED by Mr Muspratt (pursuant to notice), and Seconded by Mr Osborn - That the Resolution of adjournment of the question of erecting separate Buildings in Swaffield Road, for Aged and Infirm, passed at the Board meeting on 11th October, be rescinded.

After considerable discussion the MOTION was put to the Vote, and declared by the Chairman to be lost.

The foregoing MOTION having been lost, Mr Muspratt could not proceed with the following MOTION standing in his name - "That, considering the great and rapidly increasing population of all the Parishes in this Union, and the great increase of the work and responsibility thrown on the Guardians, and that there is great need that the Parishes should, as soon as possible, be separated - it is not advisable that a new and expensive building, which cannot afterwards be converted into an Infirmary, should be erected in the Parish of Wandsworth' the Guardians therefore decline to erect the proposed Buildings, for Aged and Infirm Patients, on the Swaffield Road site, in the Parish of Wandsworth.".

The Local Government Board were realising the cost of difficulties arising in the Workhouses. It was important to keep the rates coming in, so it was decided to apply for a Rate Collector at the next Conference.

APPOINTMENT OF RATE COLLECTOR

The Guardians of the Poor of the Wandsworth and Clapham Union, and the Churchwardens and Overseers of the Parish of St Mary, Battersea, are prepared to receive Applications for the Appointment of a Rate Collector for No. 2 District of the Parish of Battersea.

Candidates, who must not be less than 25 year of age, or over 40 years of age, must be fully competent to keep the Books and Accounts, and to discharge efficiently the other duties prescribed by the Local Government Board.

The person appointed will receive a salary from the Guardians of £100 per annum, rising by annual increments of £5 to a maximum of £125 per annum for the collection of the Poor Rate; and also from the Churchwardens and Overseers, for the Collection of the Local Rate, a salary of £100 per annum rising by annual increments of £5 to £125 per annum. In case the number of Collections in the District exceeds 2,500, an additional sum of £10 per annum in respect of each 100 collections up to 3,000 will be paid by the Churchwardens and Overseers out of the Local Rates.

The person appointed will have to effect in some approved office two Policies of Guarantee of £500 each to secure his faithful services, and he will be required to devote his whole time to the duties connected with the collection of the Poor and Local Rates.

The Appointment will be subject to the approval of the Local Government Board, and to the person appointed undertaking to consent to any alteration in the District being made which may be considered necessary for facilitating the Collection of Rates.

Applications must be sent in not later than 12 o'clock noon, on Friday, the 28th September 1894, upon forms which may be obtained upon application to Mr. Henderson, Clerk to the Guardians, Union Offices, St John's Hill, S.W., or by forwarding to him a stamped directed envelope of foolscap size.

Personal canvassing is strictly prohibited, and will be deemed a disqualification of any Candidate.

By Order,

(Signed) ALFRED N. HENDERSON,

Clerk to the Guardians

(Signed) W. MARCUS WILKINS

Clerk to the Churchwardens and Overseers

17th September 1894

The Local Government Board was concerned that the only qualification a Guardian had was that of a property owner. So the following circular was issued:-

I am directed by the Local Government Board to state that in view of the important changes made in the system of the election of Poor Law Guardians by the Local Government Act of last Session, and of the fact that many of those who have been elected as Guardians have had no previous experience in the administration of the Poor Law, the Board deem it desirable to bring under the special attention of the Guardians certain points connected with Workhouse administration.

It is undoubtedly the case that since Workhouses were established under the Poor Law Amendment Act, 1834, the circumstances connected with the administration of relief, and the character of those for whom accommodation in Workhouses has to be provided, have so materially changed, that arrangements originally adequate and in accordance with the spirit of the times have ceased to be so. It may be pointed out that whilst Workhouses were in the first instance provided chiefly for the relief of the able-bodied, and their administration was therefore intentionally deterrent, the Sick, the Aged, and the Infirm, now greatly preponderate, and this has led to a change in the spirit of the administration, although it is still based on the General Consolidation Order of 1847. The Board feel sure that the Guardians will bear in mind this change in the character of the Inmates who are under their charge.

The Board direct me to remind the Guardians that, subject to the Rules and Regulations of the Board, the Guidance, government, and control of the Workhouse and of the Officers and Servants, and the Inmates, are placed in the hands of the Guardians, and that the responsibility for the management of the Workhouses and the welfare of the Inmates rests with them and the Officers under their control.

VISITING COMMITTEES. Under a General Order issued in January, 1893, authority was given to every member of a Board of Guardians to visit the Workhouse at any reasonable time that he might think proper, but this does not affect the duty of the Guardians to appoint one or more Visiting Committees from their own body, or the duty of the Committees so appointed to carefully examine the Workhouse, to inspect the reports of the Chaplain and Medical Officer, to examine the stores, to afford, as far as practicable, to the Inmates an opportunity of making complaints, and to investigate any complaints which may be made to them, and from time to time to write such answers as the facts may warrant to certain questions in a book provided by the Guardians for the purpose. The manner in which these duties should be performed is very clearly set forth in a circular letter which was issued by the Poor Law Board on the 6th January, 1868, which the Board trust will have the careful attention of the Guardians.

There are, however, two points to which the Board would specially refer. The Committee should bear in mind that surprise visits are of great value to enable them to ascertain the real character of the administration of their Workhouse, and if they ordinarily meet at fixed intervals they should be careful that visits of this nature are also made. It is also important that opportunities should be given to the Inmates of the Workhouse to make any communication they may wish to members of the Committee, without any Officers being present at the time.

By the Order of January, 1893, above referred to, the Guardians were expressly empowered, from time to time, to appoint, in addition to the Workhouse Visiting Committee, a Committee or Committees of ladies, whose duty it should be to visit and examine those parts of the Workhouse in which the female Inmates and the Children are maintained, and to report to the Guardians any matters which may appear to the Committee to need attention. The Board consider that the appointment of such committees has been attended with great advantage.

CLASSIFICATION. As regards the classification of the Inmates of Workhouses, the regulations specify the classes to which separate wards or buildings and yards are to be assigned; but the Guardians are also directed, so far as circumstances will permit, to further sub-divide any of these classes, with reference to the moral character or behaviour, or to the previous habits of the Inmates, or to such other grounds as may seem expedient. This is a matter to which Guardians should give careful consideration.

It seems desirable once more to call attention to the arrangements that should be made for married couples, as misconception appears still to exist as to their separation in the Workhouses. The Poor Law Act of 1847 provides that where any two persons, being husband and wife, both of whom shall have attained the age of 60 years, shall be sent into any Workhouse, such two persons shall not be compelled to live separate and apart from each other, and by the 39 & 40 Vict. c. 61 it is further provided that the Guardians may permit any married couples to live together, either of whom shall be infirm, sick, or disabled by any injury, or above the age of 60 years.

THE SICK AND INFIRM. The altered character of the Inmates of the Workhouse in the present day, which has been previously referred to, has brought the question of these Infirmary wards and the arrangements that should be made for the care of the sick into special prominence.

The due performance, by the Medical Officer of the Workhouse, of the duties attaching to his office, is, of course, of paramount importance in ensuring proper administration in the sick wards, and amongst the principal of these duties is that of advising the Guardians, by written reports, upon the dietary of the Inmates, the drainage, ventilation, warmth, and other arrangements of the Workhouse, and as to every defect which he may observe in the arrangement of the Infirmary and sick wards, and as to the performance of their duties by the Nurses of the sick. The Guardians should be careful to see that the reports required from him by the General Consolidated Order, and by the General Orders of April 4th 1868, and August 24th, 1869, are regularly laid before them. The Half-yearly statement required by the last-named Order the Board consider of especial importance. Care should also be taken that the requirements of the General Consolidated Order, by which the dietaries of the sick and of the young children are placed entirely under the control of the Medical Officer, are complied with. The proper use of bed cards in every case the Board deem of much importance; it is a safeguard, both to the Nurses and their Patients that all directions of the Medical Officer should be given in writing. It is desirable that these cards should, in a great measure, show the history and treatment of each case, and they should be carefully preserved.

It is, no doubt, the case that the majority of the Boards of Guardians have under the advice of the Board, and at the instance of their Inspectors, improved the system of nursing in the Workhouses, and that in many Workhouses an adequate standard of efficiency has been attained. But, notwithstanding this, there are many Workhouses where the present nursing arrangements have not been brought to the standard of modern requirements, and the Board must strongly urge on the Guardians that this matter should receive their most careful consideration.

The Board, in a circular letter issued some year since, referring to the nursing arrangements in Workhouses, stated as follows: -

"The office of Nurse is one of very serious responsibility and labour, and requires to be filled by a person of experience in the treatment of the sick, of great respectability of character, and of diligent and decorous habits. Such person cannot discharge the duties of the office singly, but must have the *assistance of others of both sexes; and there is scarcely less need of the same qualities in the persons who are to be the assistants than of those required by the chief Officer. Hence It is necessary that the Nurses should be adequately remunerated, and that they should be appointed after a strict investigation of their qualifications for the office. But the Board consider it of the highest importance that the assistants to the Nurse should also be paid Officers. By appointing paid assistants the Guardians will have an opportunity of selecting persons whose qualifications for the office can be properly ascertained, and they will also be able to hold such Officers responsible for negligence or misconduct, as in the case of the superior Officers of the Workhouse. Where Pauper Inmates are directed to act, as Assistant Nurses there is no stimulus to exertion, no test of capacity, and no responsibility for negligence. The Board therefore recommends that the Guardians will, as far as possible, discontinue the practice of appointing Pauper Inmates of the Workhouse to act as Assistant Nurses in the Infirmary or sick ward."*

The difficulty of obtaining such Nurses as those referred to has, in some instances, been assigned by Boards of Guardians as a sufficient reason for not complying with these recommendations. But whatever may have been the case in the past, in view of the general advance that has taken place in recent years in the provision for training Nurses, no such difficulty should now arise, and the Board think it desirable to draw the attention of Guardians generally to the enclosed memorandum of the Board's Inspector, Dr Downes, dated April, 1892, with reference to the general question of nursing arrangements in Workhouses, which has been already forwarded by the Board to the Boards of Guardians of many Unions, where the nursing arrangements have been insufficient.

The Guardians should be satisfied that the nursing staff by day and by night is in numbers fully equal to the proper nursing of the sick, and they should give their most careful consideration to any representations which may be made to them on the subject by the Medical Officer of the Workhouse in the discharge of his prescribed duty. They should also be careful when they make appointments of Nurses that the persons appointed are, by training and experience, fully equal to the responsible duties, which they have to discharge.

Whilst the Board are not prepared to lay it down as a rule that the case should Pauper Inmates act as attendants in sick wards, as clearly distinguished from Nurses, they consider that their services should only be used with the approval of the Medical Officer, and under the closest supervision at all times of paid Officers.

In the larger Workhouses the Infirmaries have, in many cases, been placed under separate administration from the Workhouse proper, with very beneficial results; but in cases where the buildings form part of the same establishment, the Master and Matron necessarily remain the chief Officers of the whole establishment, and primarily responsible for its administration and discipline. It seems to the Board important that this should be understood, as their experience shows that the improvement that is taking place in the character of Workhouse nursing from the employment of trained Nurses, occasionally leads to objections being raised to the legitimate exercise of the authority of the Master and Matron in the arrangements connected with the sick wards.

The Board consider that so long as these establishments are constituted as at present, the Nurses should be responsible to the Medical Officer for the treatment of the Patients, but should clearly understand that in other matters they must defer to the authority of the Master and Matron.

IMBECILES. The proper care of Imbeciles retained in Workhouses is a matter, which should receive the special attention of the Guardians. It is important that they should, as far as practicable, have means of suitable employment, that adequate provision should be made for their exercise and recreation, that simple means should exist to ensure their personal cleanliness, that their food should be sufficient and properly served, and that the Officers in charge of them should be careful and kindly, and the buildings and appliances be of such a character as to minimise the risks of injury.

THE CHILDREN. With regard to the Children in Workhouses, the Board note with satisfaction to what a large extent those still maintained in Workhouses are sent out for education to public elementary schools, and they are clearly of opinion that, where it is practicable, Boards of Guardians should adopt this course. It may also often be possible for arrangements to be made for the Children to attend the Sunday Schools of their own denomination. The Board attach such importance to all Children maintained in Poor Law Institutions being given opportunities for mixing as far as circumstances will admit, with other Children.

Special care should be taken that a sufficient part of each day is set apart for recreation only, that the Children should be allowed to take exercise frequently outside the Workhouse premises, and that they should be encouraged in healthy games of all sorts.

The Board need hardly point out that all Children in Workhouses should be under the charge of Officers, either industrial trainers or caretakers, and should not be left to the charge of Adult Paupers.

The Medical Officer should frequently and individually inspect all Children.

There are questions connected with the Boarding-out and Emigration of orphan and deserted Children, which will, doubtless, receive the careful consideration of the Guardians. The Board do not propose to refer to them in detail on the present occasion; they would only urge upon Guardians the importance of always remembering that they stand in loco parentis to such Children, and that whether they are retained in the Workhouse, or in a district or separate school or cottage homes, or are sent to a certified school, or are boarded-out or emigrated, it is on the Guardians that the responsibility for their welfare primarily rests.

HOURS FOR GETTING UP, MEALS, &C .As regards the hours to be observed by Inmates of Workhouses for getting up, meals, work, &c., the Board think it unnecessary to make any alteration in those prescribed in existing regulations. They attach much importance to uniformity in this matter, but they would draw attention to the point, which appear to be frequently overlooked, that these hours do not apply to the Infirm Inmates or the young Children. It rests with the Master and Matron, subject to the direction of the Guardians, to fix the hours of rising and going to bed or Inmates infirm through age, or from any other cause, and for Children under seven years of age, and for those Inmates the meals are to be provided at such times, and in such manner as the Guardians may from time to time direct.

CLOTHING. It appears desirable to refer to the question of the clothes to be supplied by the Guardians to Inmates of the Workhouse. The clothing to be worn by the Inmates is to be made of such material as the Board of Guardians may determine, and in their instructional letter of February 5th, 1842, the Poor Law Commissioners called attention to the fact that this clothing need not be uniform either in colour or material. The Board would specially suggest that the clothing worn by Inmates when absent on leave from the Workhouse should not be in any way distinctive or conspicuous in character.

LIBERTY. As regard the power which Guardians possess of authorising the Master to allow an Inmate to quit the Workhouse and to return after a temporary absence only, it appears to the Board that in the case of Aged and Infirm Inmates, so long as they are well-behaved, and do not abuse the liberty given to them, it is desirable so far as it can be done without undue interference with the discipline and management of the Workhouse, that permission to leave the Workhouse should be given without reasonable limits. Of course, should it be found in any particular instance that the permission was abused, exception should be made, but the Master of the refusal of leave on this ground should keep a careful record.

DIETARIES. With reference to the important question of dietaries, it is to be observed that whilst the Guardians are empowered, subject to the sanction of the Local Government Board, to fix the amount and nature of the food which shall be given to the Inmates generally, it is the duty of the Medical Officer to order such food as he may consider requisite for the sick. With regard to the Inmates in health, a memorandum was drawn up by the Board's Inspector, Dr. Downes, in 1893, setting forth the general principles which should guide Boards of Guardians in framing dietaries for this class, and in any case when the Guardians may be proposing to revising the dietaries, the Board will be happy to furnish them with copies.

ESCAPE IN CASE OF FIRE. The security of the Inmates in case of fire is a matter which, whilst it applies with special force to the sick and helpless, should receive the careful consideration of the Guardians as regards all Inmates of the establishment, and the Guardians should satisfy themselves that adequate means of escape from all wards are available, and that the means are ready to hand of extinguishing any fire at its first outbreak.

APPOINTMENT OF OFFICERS. The Board must impress upon the Guardians the grave responsibility, which rests upon them as regards the selection of the Officers employed in the Workhouses. They cannot do better than refer to the letter of the Poor Law Commissioners of February 5th, 1842, in which they said: -

"The Commissioners are satisfied that good temper, joined in firmness and self-command, will enable a skilful teacher to manage Children with little or no corporal punishment. The frequent use of corporal correction is the common resource of teachers, who, through idleness or other defect, are incompetent to acquire command over Children by a knowledge of their characters and by gentle means.... The observations made above with reference to the management of Children are equally applicable to the treatment of Adults. Warmth of temper and passionate conduct generally betray a consciousness of want of firmness. The discipline of a Workhouse has to be maintained by an undeviating adherence to rules, and a steadiness which defies provocation, while it deliberately enforce obedience to orders by legal and authorised means. The Master of a Workhouse is answerable for the general order of the whole establishment, and minute personal attention on his part can alone detect and remedy defects in the discipline and cleanliness of the house. The temper and discretion required for the discharge of his duties, and the confidence necessarily placed in his integrity, make it essential that the greatest care should be exercised in the choice of that Officer. The Master, too, is in some degree dependent on the aid afforded him by the other Officers of the establishment.... And as want of harmony between the principal Officers of the establishment cannot fall to impair their efficiency and disturb the general discipline of the house, the Commissioners are desirous of inculcating the necessity of the utmost forbearance and command of temper in their mutual relations"

In conclusion, the Board desire to point out that all experience shows that whether a Workhouse is well or ill administered, depends to a large extent upon the personal interest, which the Guardians take in the matter. The work is often arduous, and the constant attention to small details, which is absolutely necessary for efficient administration, may impose a heavy tax on the time and patience of the Guardians' but the Board feel sure that they may rely on those who take upon themselves the office of Guardian discharging their duties with a due sense of the responsibility which the position involves.

I am, Sir,

Your obedient Servant,

(Signed) HUGH OWEN

Secretary

The Clerk to the Guardians.

1891 Census

14

Registration District *Wandsworth*

Registration Sub-district *West Battersea*

ENUMERATION BOOK

For the undermentioned Institution.

Name *Wandsworth and Clapham Union Infirmary*

Description

Where Situated *St. John's Hill*

This Institution is situated within the Boundaries of the

Civil Parish of	Municipal Borough of	Municipal Ward of	Urban Sanitary District of	Town (Village or Hamlet, &c.) of	Rural Sanitary District of	Parliamentary Borough or Division of	Ecclesiastical Parish or District of
Battersea		*No 3 4*				*Battersea*	*St John*

Note.—Draw the pen through such of the words of the headings as are inappropriate.

1891 Census

The Guardians requested a 'call over' of all inmates under 60 years old, with a view to freeing the workhouse of those able to work in the community. It caused a lot of work considering there were about 600 inmates at that time. This 'call over' happened from time to time. Inmates would often be in poor health on entering the workhouse. Regular meals and medical attention meant that some inmates could be brought back to better health and be able to face a return to the community. The following reports show some of the problems the workhouse had to cope with: -

That your Committee received the following Report on the Sub-Committee appointed to make a "Call over" of Inmates in the Workhouse under 60 years of age, viz.: -

14th May 1896.

Present: Mr Rogers (in the Chair), Mrs. Gray, Messrs. Osburn and Plumridge.

Reporting -
That:

16 were Single Women pregnant with first Child.
4 had previously had Children.
1 Single Woman with one Child.
9 Women with more than one Child.
Total 30

9 Demented cases.
12 Mentally and Physically incapable.
8 Weak intellect.
Total 29

2 Deaf and Dumb.
3 Cripples.
14 Physically Incapable.
7 Helpless through Ill-health, or want of energy, &c.
Total 26

5 Deserted.
5 Inebriates.
Total 10

11 able to support themselves
8 should remain for various causes
Total 19

114

19th May, 1896.

Present: Mr Rogers (in the Chair), Mrs. Gray, Messrs. Digby, Kidman, Osburn and Plumridge.

Reporting -
That your Committee interviewed 84 Male Inmates, and found that:

10 were idle and worthless.
9 capable of earning their living outside.
Total 19

7 Demented.
9 Mentally and Physically incapable.
3 Weak Intellect.
Total 19

2 Deaf and Dumb, or Blind.
10 Cripples.
21 Physically disabled.
3 Helpless and no energy.
Total 36

5 Inebriates.
5 to remain employed at useful work.
Total 10

84

Recommending -

That the following be allowed out of the Workhouse, leaving their "Families chargeable, viz: -

RECOMMENDED BY SUB-COMMITTEE TO BE ALLOWED OUT	LEAVING CHARGEABLE	COMMENT
Bennett, William	Wife and 3 Children	To be allowed out.
Crawford, Walter	2 Children	No recommendations
Donegan, John	4 Children	To be allowed out.
Hooper, Henry	3 Children	To be allowed out.
Munson, Walter	1 Child	No recommendation.
McLoughlin, Patrick	2 Children	No recommendation.
Robinson, Joseph	1 Child	To be allowed out.
Powell, Frederick	Wife and 5 Children	No recommendation.
Tranter, Henry	2 Children	To be allowed out.
Bridge, Emma	1 Child	No recommendation.
Fryer, Emma	2 Children	To be allowed out.
Freeman, Laura	4 Children	To be allowed out.
How, Edith	3 Children	To be allowed out.
Harmsworth, Sarah	1 Child	No recommendation.
Soper, Frances	1 Child	To be allowed out.
Tull, Eliza	1 Child	To be allowed out.

Your Committee recommend -

That the Male Inmates recommended by your Committee to be allowed out, be so allowed out of the Workhouse for 14 days, leaving their Families chargeable, and that they report themselves weekly to the Enquiry Officer.

Inmates were often moved from one workhouse to another. Apart from the demand for space, it is not understood why they were moved. Could it be a change of scenery? As the following report and letters show, they always wanted to keep the inmates that were fit and useful!

That your Committee considered the Report of the Committee, and a visit to St Giles' Workhouse.

The Medical Officer, as directed, submitted a Return of the Aged Female Inmates of the Workhouse, summarised as follows, viz.:-

Total No. of Women	76	
Physically fit for Transfer	50	Of these 36 have already been sent to St Giles' for periods ranging from One to Three years.
Physically unfit for Transfer	26	Of these, Nine have already been sent to St Giles' for periods ranging from One to Three Years.

At present about 20 Aged Women are engaged at useful work in the Laundry, cleaning Officers' Rooms, and Needlework

That your Committee received the following letter from the Matron of the Workhouse, viz.:-

> Union Workhouse
> Wandsworth, S.W.,
> October 14th, 1896

To the Workhouse Committee

LADIES AND GENTLEMEN,

The Medical Officer having been requested to submit to you a List of all Inmates fit to be transferred to St Giles' Workhouse, I beg most respectfully to be allowed to make some observations on the subject.

First. - There will be some on that List who are usefully employed in attending to the subordinate Officers' rooms, assisting in instructing the young Girls in bed-making and general cleaning, going to and from Anerley and Norwood Schools in charge of Children, and doing light work in the Laundry by their own choice.

Secondly. - There are many Inmates who are not suited to the foregoing duties, and others who are not disposed to exert themselves to do the work required to be done daily. On these grounds, I beg to draw your attention to the disadvantage of anything like an indiscriminate transfer, or which would include those Inmates who are of great assistance here.

In making selections of persons to be submitted for the Medical Officer's approval I have always been actuated by a sense of duty, feeling that I am compelled under any circumstances, to retain here sufficient Women of the "useful" class to maintain the necessary order of the Establishment.

I am,

Ladies and Gentlemen,

Your obedient Servant,

(Signed)M. HODGE,

Matron

That your Committee also received a letter from the Guardians of St. Giles', enquiring whether the Guardians intended to utilise the accommodation set apart for Inmates from this Union.

That your Committee gave instructions for the remainder of the Inmates at St. Giles' who desire to come back, and have been at St Giles' over Twelve months, to be brought back, and for the number there to be made up to 80, as far as possible from the Inmates now in the Workhouse who have not been at St. Giles' Workhouse during the past Six months.

The invoice Accounts are interesting. Christmas Quarter, December 1896:-

Invoice account (Christmas quarter):-

		WORKHOUSE £	INFIRMARY £
Amery & Sons	Repairs to ambulance &c	15.00.06	
Arding & Hobbs	Fibre	7.10.00	
Avery W & T	Adjusting Weighbridge	3.00.00	
Bacon & Co.	Crockery	17.01.00	16.16.00
Bells Asbestos Co.	Covering Pipes	20.00.11	5.17.06
Berry, Z.D. & Sons	Repairs to Heaters		
Blatch, H F	Tea	73.06.08	40.00.00
Blott, T W	Meat	142.14.00	148.09.05
Boswell W G	Veterinary Surgeon	0.13.00	
Burleigh T	Binding Books &c		9.18.10
Burroughs, Wellcome & Co.	Medicines		19.03.00
Calvert F & Co.	Carbolic soap	9.13.03	23.05.06
Carter & Co.	Yeast	9.03.06	
Cartwright & Sons	Clothing	172.08.05	169.03.06
Clarke John	Cheesemongery	166.07.04	336.12.11
Coulson, F V	Fish	15.12.02	107.17.11
Dairy Supply Company	Milk	86.05.09	319.15.05
Dixon, J & Sons	Keeping Garden in Repair		04.17.06
Doyle & Son	Adjusting Scales	1.01.00	2.19.00
Dunkley, William	Organette	2.00.06	
Farmiloe, T & W	Paints &c	15.02.06	5.04.01
Farwig, J F & Co.	Fire - bars		4.04.00
Fellowes, F & Co	Wood tyres	3.03.00	
Gatti & Stevenson	Ice		13.03.00
Green, J F	Wood truck &c	12.19.06	
Goldman, R & M	Haircutting & shaving		11.02.06
Grove, E	Uniforms	10.13.08	22.06.05
Hampton, W	Manure	3.05.00	
Hendra & Son	Fire bars	8.04.05	
Idris & Co.	Mineral waters &c		35.19.02
Jennings, G	Lavatory basin	0.14.00	
Johnson, G	Repairs to lifts		6.19.00
Knight, J & Sons	Soap	35.10.00	21.16.00
Leach Brothers	Brandy		3.06.00
Little, W J	Building Materials	7.14.06	0.16.06
Longford Wire Company	Horse-hair	20.10.08	
Lotery, H & Co.	Drapery	77.09.08	102.17.05
Marriage, Neave & Co.	Flour	172.07.00	
Marter, F W & Co.	Timber	63.05.05	
Masson, Scott & Co.	Repairs to machinery	1.10.08	
Mayhew & Son	Flour	174.18.00	
Merry, J	Grocery	21.1.11	19.19.00
Medhurst, R W	Oilman's goods	28.09.01	35.03.05
McDougall Brothers	Disinfectants		5.00.00
Miller, R	Shoeing horses	2.01.06	
Moore, W	Flour	158.13.00	
Munt Brothers	Repairs to organ	1.15.00	

		WORKHOUSE £	INFIRMARY £
Neal, R	Brooms	0.04.00	
Pfeil & Co.	Engineer's sundries	20.19.02	
Pocock Brothers	Boots and leather	37.14.04	21.15.00
Powell, J W	Tobacco	39.03.03	1.08.02
Private Wire & Telephone Co.	Repairing Electric bells		2.02.00
Pratt Brothers	Carpet	17.03.01	
Rawlings & Sons.	Removing rubbish	5.00.00	
Shand, Mason & Co.	Fire alarm	9.10.00	
Smith, G M	Brushes	17.11.09	10.09.09
Southwark & Vauxhall Water Co.	Water	116.15.00	112.07.05
Stevenson & Co.	Tea and cornchandlery	78.15.04	37.02.00
Sullivan, A	Horse provender	20.03.06	
Sutton, G	Potatoes and vegetables	47.11.00	76.17.02
Wade, J L & Co.	Asbestos	2.00.06	
Wallis, T & Co.	Marking ink	1.04.06	
Wandsworth & Putney Gas Co.	Gas	165.06.01	
Ward, A	Baskets		7.06.00
Watts, J	Poultry	5.13.07	35.06.00
Webb, A	Repairs to harness	2.12.00	
White & Sons	Mineral Waters	1.07.00	
		2,150.15.01	1,797.06.04

The amount of work caused by the inmates and the policy of the workhouse to attend to these demands caused the guardians to realise that a Settlement Clerk and Relieving Officer would have to be appointed.

The following are a list of the duties referred to, viz.:-

DUTIES OF SETTLEMENT CLERK AND GENERAL RELIEVING OFFICER AND ASSISTANT

I. SETTLEMENT WORK

a) To see and take examinations of all Persons admitted to the Workhouse and Infirmary, as to their places of settlement.

b) To make personal enquiries into such settlement.

c) If not settled in this Union, to prepare and obtain Justices' Orders for their removal to other Unions or Parishes.

d) To remove all such Persons to their different places of settlement.

e) To make enquires as to all Order of Removal of Paupers obtained by other Unions or Parishes for their removal to this Union; to ascertain if the Orders are correct.

II. POLICE COURT WORK

To obtain Warrants or Summonses, and conduct proceedings at Police Court against Persons for desertion or neglecting to maintain their Wives or Families.

III. REMOVAL, &C., OF LUNATICS

a) To give notice and obtain the attendance of Magistrates to certify in all cases of Lunatics.

b) To obtain vacancies in Asylums for Lunatics.

c) To remove all Lunatics to Asylums.

d) To remove all Lunatics from Asylums on their recovery or other case of discharge.

e) To remove all Imbeciles (Children or Adults) to Asylums of the Metropolitan Asylums Board.

IV. MISCELLANEOUS

a) To keep in touch with the Parent or Parents of Children in Schools and other Institutions, who are not residing within the Union, and to periodically bring such cases before the Guardians.

b) To keep a record of the names and addresses of all relatives outside the Union who apply to visit Children at the District and other Schools, and forward a copy of the same to the Superintendent of the School.

c) To visit and report as to situations obtained for Apprentices and Children sent to service when instructed to do so.

d) To prepare Indentures of Apprenticeship, and to arrange for the attendance of the Master before the Board, and the due execution of the Indentures.

e) To report on cases of Children admitted to the Workhouse and Infirmary who are eligible for Boarding-out.

f) To find Homes, and remove Children to the care of different Boarding-out Committees.

g) To remove Paupers to Certified Schools, Convalescent Homes, and other Institutions.

h) To keep the Registers of Persons in Asylums, Schools and other Institutions.

i) To make such enquiries as he may be required by the Guardians by their Clerk.

The following is a list of the Books, which have to be kept by the Settlement and Removal Officer and Assistant, viz: -

a) Book containing the Removal, Police Court proceedings and enquiries, ordered by the Guardians, showing results of each case.

b) Paupers@ Examination Book.

c) Register of Orders of Removal made on other Unions, showing the result of each case.

d) Register of Orders of Removal made on this Union, showing the result in each case.

e) Register, showing the Warrants and Summonses, ordered to be taken out by Guardians, showing the result of each case.

f) Register of Persons allowed out of the Workhouse and Infirmary leaving Children chargeable, showing the result in each case.

g) Receipt and Expenditure Book.

h) Register of Apprentices.

i) Diary.

j) Registers of Persons in Asylums, Schools, and other Institutions.

Your Committee are of opinion that the Staff engaged for the performance of these duties in the past has been totally insufficient, and they recommend that the following appointments be made: -

a) A General Relieving Officer, at a salary of £200 per annum, the salary apportioned as follows: £150 to position of General Relieving Officer, and £50 as an Assistant Clerk for Settlement work, with dinner daily, except on Sundays.

b) An Assistant Relieving Officer, to deal with School Cases, &c., at a salary of £120 per annum, with dinner daily, except on Sundays.

c) An Assistant Relieving Officer for Removing Lunatics, &c., at a salary of £100 per annum, without dinner.

d) An Assistant Relieving Officer for removing Persons to their places of settlement, and making enquiries as directed by the General Relieving Officer, at a salary of £100 per annum, without dinner.

The details of the duties of these Officers were fully explained to your Committee, and they are quite satisfied that such Officers are absolutely necessary, and they would mention that they had before them the Staff of the neighbouring Parish at Lambeth, where five Officers are appointed to do these duties, at an annual cost of more than £100 per annum than that proposed for this Union.

Having regard to the extremely satisfactory manner in which Mr Haggis has carried on the work during the past three months, the Committee unanimously recommended that he be appointed the General Relieving Officer, and that Mr Tidcombe be appointed the Assistant Relieving Officer, at a salary of £120 per annum.

The workhouses would work together to help one another. In 1897 Swaffield Road was overcrowded. An application was made to Mitcham Workhouse to see if they could take 50 inmates that were aged and infirm. Swaffield Road did not have an Infirm Ward. St John's Infirmary was full and could not take any more. The inmates coming into Swaffield Road were becoming predominantly aged.

The workhouse had a Chapel which was used by all denominations. Divine Service was held on a Thursday. At one time the Church Army held an Eight Day Mission there.

Such were the rules of the workhouse Religious denominations had to be correct. The following letter shows how thorough they had to be:-

With reference to paragraph No. 9 of the forgoing Report of the Workhouse Committee, submitted the following explanation by the Rev. J. Cooney, viz.:-

32 Santos Road
Wandsworth
8th January 1898

SIR,

In compliance with your request, I have the honour to observe with reference to the complaint forwarded by the Lord Mayor to the Secretary of State,

(1.) *That the Boy, William McDonald, was admitted to the Workhouse, in custody of the Police, on the 13th July, not on the 26th September, as declared in his written statement.*

(2.) *That, according to the Creed Register, he declared himself on admission to be a Roman Catholic.*

(3.) *That up to that time he was unknown to me.*

(4.) *That during his detention in the Workhouse he showed his knowledge of the Catholic religion, passing the usual tests.*

(5.) *That during his detention his father, whom I visited, stated that the Boy was a Roman Catholic; so did his mother; and it will be observed that the father, in his written statement, says that the Boy was baptised a Roman Catholic.*

The Surrey Needlework Guild donated garments regularly. In 1898 they donated 70 garments. Records do not show who they were for, but one can guess they were for the children.

Education for the young children in the school block was becoming difficult because of the number of them. The boys had a class in the morning and the girls in the afternoon. Older children were sent to Anerley and Norwood Schools. A small organ called an Organette was purchased for the school, it had six tunes. The old piano they had was sold.

Inmates who had children in the Anerley and Norwood Schools were allowed to go and visit their children. There was a problem arising, they went into a Public House on the way back and got drunk. It must have been a great temptation for the inmates, but the practice had to be stopped. Records do not show how they had the money to go drinking.

Inmates were quite quick to make a complaint and it did not always benefit them. Here is an example. It can be understood how trying they could be, especially as they would return to the workhouse again soon.

The Clerk submitted a letter from the Local Government Board, enclosing copy of a letter received from Patrick McLaughlin, an Inmate of the Workhouse, complaining that he was not allowed to leave the Workhouse without taking his two Children with him. Your Committee recommend that the Local Government board be informed that a Committee, which was recently appointed to enquire into cases of this kind, could not recommend that Patrick McLaughlin be allowed to leave the Workhouse without his Children, because of his intemperate habits. With regard to his not being allowed to take his discharge from the Workhouse on two occasions until 1.15 and 12 o 'clock respectively, this was on account of his Children having to be fetched from the School at Norwood.

In March 1899 a desk telephone was purchased for the Master's Office. It was becoming obvious that the Master had to be in touch instantly with events.

A Tailor was appointed in October 1894. His name was Thomas Ash and his wage was 30 shillings a week. At the same time a Singer Tailors Sewing Machine was purchased. A room would have had to be found for him to work in and the workhouse would have their own Tailor. This was economically sound sense, as there were over 300 men in the workhouse.

Boots for the men were ordered by the dozen. At one time four dozen were ordered and when they came in they were not as sample. They had been stamped with the workhouse stamp, so could not be returned. The guardians were angry and held the Master responsible, the boots should have been referred and returned. The Master was warned that this must not happen again.

The guardians decided that the women over 60 years of age should have an additional petticoat when out during the winter months. Together with the coats that were about to be ordered they would be much warmer. It also came to the committee's attention that women under 60 years of age were not issued with a nightdress, and that it should be remedied immediately. It is difficult to understand why the differential between the under 60s and over 60s was made in the first place.

There were three drivers who requested an extra pair of trousers annually, most of their work was outdoor work and the request was reasonable, their trousers would have hard wear, and a coachman asked for a silk hat annually. Records do not show if this request was granted.

BUILDINGS

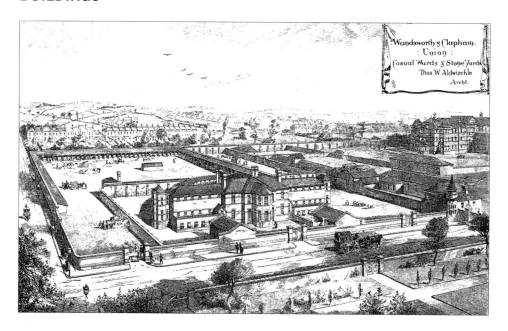

Fire precautions had needed updating in the workhouse. A new Rubber Lined Canvas Fire Hose Pipe was purchased for £3.12.00. Improvements had been carried out as the following report states: -

Fire Brigade Station,
Balham High Road, Tooting, S. W.,
23rd September 1892.

WORKHOUSE - WANDSWORTH AND CLAPHAM UNION
SIR,

I beg leave to inform you, that I have periodically during the Third Quarter 1892, drilled the Male and Female Staff in these buildings in the use of the various Fire Appliances, and am pleased to say with satisfactory results.

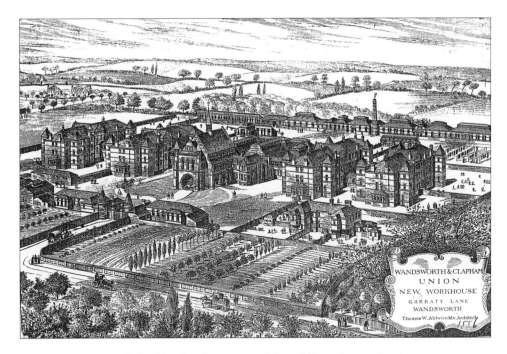

WANDSWORTH & CLAPHAM
UNION
NEW WORKHOUSE
GARRATT LANE
WANDSWORTH
Thomas W. Aldwinckle, Architect

I have inspected the Fire Appliances, and found them in good order.

I also beg to mention that I forwarded a report in December, 1891, drawing your attention to the unsatisfactory pressure of water obtained from the Hydrants attached to these buildings for fire purposes, and offered suggestions to remedy the defect.

Since I submitted my Report to your consideration upon the subject of water pressure, I have found a very great improvement.

On my attendance for Fire drill on the 21st July last, and subsequent occasions, the pressure of water has been quite sufficient to reach any part of the buildings in the event of fire. I have ascertained from Mr Hodge, the Master, that no alterations have been made to the water arrangements inside the buildings, therefore the additional pressure of water has been given by the Southwark Water Company's mains.

Should the present pressure of water be maintained there is no occasion to carry out the suggestions offered by me in the Report referred to, as I consider the present water-pressure sufficient in the event of fire.

I append the under-mentioned water pressure, as taken by Mr. Thomas Aldworth, the Engineer to the Union, viz.: -

Date	6 A.M.	12 NOON.	6 P.M.	8 P.M.	10 P.M.
1892					
September 12	---	---	---	30 lbs	35 lbs
September 14	40 lbs	25 lbs	20 lbs	26 lbs	40 lbs
September 15	40 lbs	26 lbs	30 lbs	35 lbs	48 lbs
September 16	45 lbs	31 lbs	40 lbs	42 lbs	45 lbs
September 17	45 lbs	21 lbs	30 lbs	27 lbs	35 lbs
September 18	40 lbs	0 lbs	30 lbs	35 lbs	30 lbs
September 19	40 lbs	18 lbs	25 lbs	35 lbs	30 lbs
September 20	45 lbs	21 lbs	28 lbs	25 lbs	40 lbs

By now there is constant demand on the Engineer's Department for maintenance around the workhouse. Some modification to the Engineer's shop for efficiency must take place. The Master reported as follows:-

I beg to submit a plan and specification, designed to replace the present Engineer's shop; the approximate cost will be £170. At present, the Carpenter's shop is also used as a storage for painting materials; the room, however, being too small for this purpose, the result being inconvenience and noticeable disorder.

It is suggested that the adjoining Engineer's shop could be utilised as a Painter's shop, the paints stored there, and the painting and polishing of the various joinery and cabinet-work, made by the Inmate labour of the House, be better proceeded with. This workshop has the disadvantage of being some distance from the Engineer's department, and to erect a structure opposite the Engine-room and Boiler-house (there being a suitable site), as a Fitter's shop, would economise time and centralise the work of the Engineer, and, by the substitution stated, provide the much needed Painter's shop.

The specification has been prepared by the Superintendent of indoor labour, Mr Hicks; and the plan by him and the Engineer, Mr Aldworth.

Your Committee having inspected the plan and the site, and perused the specification, RECOMMEND that, subject to the approval of the Local Government Board, the work be carried out by direct labour, under the superintendence of Mr Hicks, the Superintendent of indoor labour.

By 1896 there were parts of the workhouse that needed maintenance or improvement. The Laundry was one of them. Drying conditions needed improvement. Equipment required repairs and some equipment replacing. There was extra strain on the Laundry now as St John's Infirmary and he Tooting Home washing was also done at Swaffield Road. Extra staff were needed and this was taken into account when costing the relative institutions.

That Mr Martineau, J.P., on behalf of the Sub-Committee appointed to consider the matter of an improvement in the Laundry Drying Apparatus, reported to your Committee upon schemes which were receiving consideration, and authority was given for the Engineer of the Workhouse to make some further inquiries, and also to report as to the position of certain drains

Your Sub-Committee further recommend that application be made to the Local Government Board to sanction the balance of Loans raised for the Erection, &c., of the Workhouse, amounting to £228, being applied towards the cost of the proposed alterations to the Laundry Drying Apparatus.

Your Committee adopted the foregoing Reports, and they recommend the same to the Board for approval and adoption.

The Huge Dining Hall required cleaning the Ventilation attention. Three meals a day were served to 600 inmates every day, the smell of cooked food, if not ventilated throughout, would give a permanent smell in there.

The Scullery also needed cleaning. This was where all the dirty work was done, but the walls etc., should still be clean. Records do not show who did this work but it was probably done by workhouse maintenance.

The Oakum Sheds in the Casual Ward needed improved ventilation. The smell of creosote must have been overpowering. It was not surprising that the Medical Office of Health was involved.

That the Clerk submitted a letter from the Sanitary Committee of the Battersea Vestry, with reference to alleged over-crowding in the Oakum Shed, and also as to the total number of Inmates being in excess of the certified accommodation. The Medical Officer also reported that the Establishment had this morning been visited by the Medical Officer of Health for the Wandsworth District, who would report upon his visit. Your Committee instructed the Clerk to inform the Sanitary Committee of the Battersea Vestry that, in February last, the Guardians gave instructions that only 70 persons were to be employed at one time in the Oakum Shed, and that further accommodation has been set apart so as to prevent over-crowding, and that they also be informed of the visit of the Medical Officer of Health for the District in which the Workhouse is situated.

The East Wall of the Stone Breaking Yard would have to be raised. Inmates had been caught climbing over it! The men were free to come and go as they pleased. What was the point of climbing over the wall? If they thought they would just go out for the morning, it was a useless exercise, as they could not do the amount of work to earn their food. The Master decided it had to stop. The wall was to be raised and authorised materials (3000 bricks) to be purchased and the work was to be done by inmate labour.

The stables also needed attention. The Ventilator needed replacing. The yard where the horses were washed and groomed needed a Veranda 21 feet wide and 18 feet long so as to provide shelter for the horses.

The Coach House was to be extended to the line of frontage of the Furniture Store. It had three folding doors, these were to be re-used.

The Guardians, Master and Matron were always mindful of Fire and Fire Escapes. Stairs and exits were checked for obstruction regularly. It was not surprising that additional means of escape were considered in June 1896. A staircase was to be constructed at the south end of "A" block and staircases to be constructed from the Lavatories on the West side of "B" and "C" blocks. "D" block was to have a Ladder escape to be placed at the Dormitory window. The childrens block had adequate means of escape.

The laundry is a very hard working section of the workhouse, the wear and tear on machinery is enormous. A report by the Laundry Sub-Committee follows:-

The Sub-Committee obtained a price for Baker & Company's A.4 washing machine for £69.15s and for a galvanised iron boiling trough from Bradford & Company for £12.10s and they recommend the same be ordered subject to the best discount to be obtained and fitted up as soon as practicable and that the repairs to the present Machine and Trough be done if on subsequent examination they be found worth it. The estimate for repair of present Washing Machine is £11.10s, no estimate at present for repair to boiling Trough

However, the Wringer also is not working properly either so the Committee have further discussion, and then refer back to the Sub-committee. As stated any hold up of machinery not in use causes inconvenience to many institutions so they have to be careful to make the correct decisions. The following report shows they want to do the best financially.

18th May 1896.

The Laundry Sub-Committee met, and, in response to matters referred to them, inspected the Wringer, which it is complained does not do its work thoroughly' and this is the case. They recommend a powerful Spring be substituted for the present dead weight, as likely to improve its efficiency.

They found the present Boiling-bank leaking, and the woodwork worn away; the iron fittings appear good, and could be used again. They recommend that new wood sides and bottom be fitted to it.

They found the Rotating Washer to be in a bad state of repair throughout. They recommend repairs to be doe, if found to be the most effective and economical proceeding.

Owing to the great inconvenience that will be caused in the Laundry by being without the Boiling-tank for a week at least, and the Washer for a longer time, they strongly recommend that new ones be purchased, of the best and newest type in each case, which will cause but little hindrance, and the old ones be repaired as recommended, and put down either at the Workhouse or Infirmary, as they may be required.

They suggest, if the Committee agree to this idea, that the matter be referred back to the Sub-Committee for Estimates, and to report before action is taken.

The Guardians decided that the Lying-In Ward would benefit from having four perambulators. They were purchased at a cost of £1.16s.6d each. In the good weather the babies and mothers would enjoy the fresh air walking round the grounds.

BOARDING OUT

"Boarding Out" children was a way of reducing the number of children in the school block as well as giving them a better chance in life. The following recommendation explains quite a lot: -

With reference to the Committee's recommendation as to Boarding-out Children within the Union, the Clerk stated that there was no Boarding-out Order issued to Metropolitan Unions and Parishes under which Children could be Boarded-out within the Union.

Whereupon it was Resolved -

a) *That steps be taken to Board out in the Country so many of the young Children now in the Workhouse as may be eligible.*

b) *That, where possible, Children be given up to the care of their friends, and Out-relief granted where required.*

c) *That it be referred to a Committee of the Guardians, consisting of the following, viz.:- Mrs. Gray, Messrs. Osburn, Rogers and Wade, to visit the Workhouse and see if arrangements could be made to use the rooms adjoining the receiving wards, so that the same could be utilised for the better accommodation of some of the Children, and that such Committee have power to act in the matter.*

Many boys were apprenticed to different Trades. One particular boy, Edwin Ash, was apprenticed to a Farrier of Woking Village. He had been there two years when his report stated:

"Doing very well, has saved 33 shillings. If he had 1000 boys to choose from he could not have had a better lad".

Praise indeed!

There was a Training Ship, 'Exmouth', that took many boys aged 13 to 14 years. From the training ship they were transferred to Ocean going ships.

A Farm colony in Lingfield was also a favourite place for apprenticeships; the cost to the rate payers was 7 shillings a week.

A Chimney Sweep contacted the workhouse and offered to take two boys into his service. Records do not show which area the boys would be working in; it must be presumed it was in the Country.

A considerable number of children emigrated to Canada under the "Boarding-Out" scheme. It is not recorded as to whether the children were actually adopted or just fostered, but they were all welcomed and treated as one of the family. A Mr Robert Wallace from the Marchment Home Belleville, Ontario, Canada, visited 52 children in all and sent the following reports back to the Guardians.

30th January 1896
REPORTS, re Children Emigrated to Canada

Name of Child Emigrated	Year of Emigration	Date of Report	Residence	General Remarks as to Conduct, Position and Prospects.
Dulbey, Annie	1890	18 October (1895)	James Boldrick, Canifton, Ontario	Annie seems more settled and contended than she used to be. She is saving a little money, and has a great inclination to spend or give away all she has. Mr. And Mrs. Boldrick give her every comfort, and treat her as a daughter. Attends Church and Sunday-school.
Jackson, Christopher	1893	21 September (1895)	Thomas J. Lee, Lindsay, Ontario	Christopher is well and healthy, but does not grow much. Went to School five months last winter, and got on well with his lessons; also continues to attend Sunday-school and Church. Mrs Lee said he is a good boy in most respects, but lately has once or twice had to speak to him about being cheeky.
Cox, Henry	1893	14 September (1895)	Thomas Keates, Wesleyville, Ontario	Henry is in good health and has grown well, but has not improved in character; is as slow as ever, requiring about twice the time to do a thing as is needed. Is also bad-tempered and dull at School, and became so unruly that he had to be kept from Church.
Worley, Albert John	1889	24 September (1895)	Richard Storey, Bailieboro, Ontario	Albert has grown quite a bit since last year. I heard he had a wonderful appetite, and after taking dinner with him I consider the statement correct. Not very bright, but faithful and trusty over the work he can do. Receives 32 dols. For this summer and hopes to save 25 dols. As he will not need to spend much. Mr. Storey likes him, and would not care to part with him.

Freeman, George	1894	16 September (1895)	Thomas F James, Solina, Ontario	Mr James has not been well, so had another boy to help George. Unfortunately he had a bad influence over George, who became quite saucy and unsatisfactory; but has behaved a little better lately. Made fair progress at School during winter. Wages this year 30 dols. Goes to Church and Sunday-school.
Jackson, Harry	1893	July (1895)	William R Atchison, Perth	Harry has grown considerably during the the past year. He is a stout, healthy little fellow. He is inclined to be stubborn, but is improving, Mr. And Mrs. Atchison take a great interest in training him aright. He goes to School nearly all the time, and is in the Part II Book. He has a good home, and kind "Pa" and "Ma"; he is the only child.
Harrington, Edward	1894	July (1895)	Joseph A. Code, Smith's Falls	Edward just came home from hoeing turnips with his shirt-sleeves turned up above his elbows, English fashion. He has made a fair start in growth now, is stout, and is much improved in appearance. He says he is pleased with his place, and thinks Canada is a much better place than England. Mrs. Code says Edward is a good, steady, trusty boy, and they have no complaint whatever. Attends Church and Sunday-school regularly. He is now in the 4th Book.
Smith, John Robertson	1889	4 July (1895)	John Alfred Brown, Moscow, P.O., Ontario	John appears to be a smart, active lad, not big, but strong and healthy. Mr. Brown says he could not wish for a better boy, and if Johnnie stays with him he will do for him as if he were his own son. Goes to school, in 3rd Book. Getting quite handy with the horses. Everyone speaks well of John
Neville, Thomas	1890	27 June (1895)	William McCullough, Kingsford, Ontario	Tommy is a healthy-looking lad, not very tall for his age. He is doing fairly well, and is to get wages next year. He is contented, and likes his place. Goes to School in winter, in 2nd Book, not smart or quick to learn his lessons, but is getting useful on the farm.
Heath, Alice	1890	5 July (1895)	Joshua Switzer, Desmond, Ontario	Alice is getting to be quite a fine, tall girl. She has a good home, is thought a great deal of by Mr. And Mrs. Switzer, and is in everyway treated as one of the family. Goes to School regularly, in 3rd Book; also Church and Sunday-school.
Crowe, Arthur	1889	9 July (1895)	William A Hickerson, Shannonville, Ontario	Arthur thinks he is getting stronger than he used to be, he does not seem fit for hard work. He has a comfortable home and says he is quite content to do a little for his clothes and board. Goes to Church and Sunday-school.
Stonebridge, William	1895	25 June (1895)	S. D. Taylor, Shannonville, Ontario	I went out to the field to see Willie. He was hoeing corn, and looked very happy. He has a good home and likes it. He is quick to learn and beginning to be very useful. Attends Church and Sunday-School.

CASUAL WARDS

The Casual Wards were the busiest area of the workhouse in respect of movement of inmates. In February 1898 the Medical Officer felt he had to object to the new regulations issued by the guardians. The following report makes it very clear: -

17TH February 1898

Re: REFUSAL OF CASUALS

"Board's Order, dated the 12th inst., states that they are to be refused admission after the Wards are full (the nearest Casual Ward is Fulham, which is some distance for an applicant to walk), and that Aged Persons, and those unable to travel, are to be accommodated in the Receiving Wards of the Workhouse.

I beg to state that the Receiving Wards are often fully occupied with ordinary admissions, consequently cannot be depended on for that purpose. There is an opportunity of converting six compartments, appropriated to the Women in the Casual Wards, for the use of the Men.

Persons admitted by me are supposed to be cases of necessity, and such as should remain in the House, or be transferred to the Infirmary, and reported to the Guardians.

Without presuming to be dictatorial, permit me to respectfully state that to admit Casuals into the Workhouse Receiving Wards, in the state in which they often present themselves, is most detrimental and dangerous to the sanitary condition of the Wards and Persons therein and their language, habits, &c., would be very painful for Children there to be subjected to.

My career in office being nearly at an end, and the present regulation being in force for some years past, I respectfully appeal to the Guardians to allow their order on this contentious complicated subject to remain in abeyance until I leave.

(Signed)J. H. Hodge."

The approach to the Workhouse in the early 1900's

The Casual Wards were inspected by the Local Government Board and the following is an extract from their Report: -

EXTRACT FROM ASSISTANT INSPECTOR'S REPORT.

The Superintendent informed me that the Guardians had given him instructions that no applicant was to be turned away so long as he was sober

Owing to the inadequate accommodation, the habitual vagrants take advantage of these instructions, and as there are not enough task cells for all, they are in the habit of waiting until the Wards are full before demanding admission, knowing there would be no task on detention for the late comers; individuals of the class referred to have gone so far as to ring the bell to ask if he Wards were full, and then hung back until they were. To meet this the Superintendent reserves some of the cells for the more able-bodied.

From the return below it will be seen that since September 1st, 1897, relief has been given to 393 more men than the Wards were built to accommodate.

Week ending	No. of Men Accommodated In excess of certified Accommodation	Week ending	No. of Men Accommodated In excess of certified accommodation
1897		1897	Brought forward 227
Sept. 1	1	Dec. 1	31
Sept. 8	9	Dec. 8	11
Sept. 15	5	Dec. 15	5
Sept. 22	24	Dec. 22	6
Sept. 29	41	Dec. 29	20
Oct. 6	11	1898	
Oct. 13	26	Jan. 5	11
Oct. 20	15	Jan. 12	3
Oct. 27	28	Jan. 19	25
Nov. 3	9	Jan. 26	14
Nov. 10	25	Feb. 2	8
Nov. 17	21	Feb. 9	14
Nov. 24	12	Feb.16	27
	Carried Forward 227		Total ... 392

The applicants in excess of the certified number are provided for in the Day-room, they are given a blanket, and are allowed to sleep on the floor.

The Day-Room accommodation is adequate for the legitimate requirements of the Wards, but not for a weekly excess average of 15.

The task of work is from 7 to 10 cwt. Of stone (7 cwt. Being the minimum), or 4 lbs. Of oakum.

The sliding scale for the stone task for Men is open to the objection that the loafer can take advantage of it, and do only a small amount of work.

These Wards are mostly frequented by country casuals, very few of whom are seen in the other Metropolitan Casual Wards. Many of the applicants are very dirty and return periodically, and some admit that they go there to be washed and fumigated.

Prosecutions for neglecting or refusing to do a task of work seldom occur. This is probably due to the Superintendent's time being fully occupied, and he is therefore reluctant to take before a Magistrate, Casuals who do not perform their tasks.

The Superintendent of the Casual Wards was questioned, and stated that he considered the reason the large numbers were in excess of the accommodation was in consequence of allowing Casuals to sleep on the floors after the beds were occupied, and letting them out next morning without doing the task of work.

That the Committee, after inspecting the Casual Wards, do not suggest any enlargement of the Wards, but recommend, with a view to stopping the practice of able-bodied men waiting till the beds are filled before applying for admission.

a) That notices be put up in the rooms and on the gate of the building, that on and after the 30th March, "no person will be admitted after the Wards are full," it being left to the discretion of the Officer as to admitting any person whom he considers advisable to do so.

b) That the present task of "breaking seven to ten cwt. Of stone," be altered to breaking "ten cwt. Of stone."

The clothes of the inmates in the Casual Ward are dealt with quite harshly. The following letter will explain how efficiently!

CASUAL WARD

WANDSWORTH AND CLAPHAM UNION

January 10th, 1896

Dear Sir,

In reply to your letter of this morning, I have great pleasure in giving a full detail of the manner of dealing with the clothing of the Casuals. Wet or verminous.

Wet clothes. - After supper, and before the bathing takes place, the Officer on duty requests the Men (as they undress) to put their wet clothes down the shoot for drying, when the bathing is finished, the clothes are placed in the disinfector and thoroughly dried.

Dry clothes. - When dry clothes are placed down the shoot it is considered that they are verminous, and treated as such.

Rugs. - When the beds are all occupied, should there be any Men sheltered in the Day-room, not less than two rugs are issued in the first instance, and where necessary, three or four are given. Any Man having no shirt to sleep in is provided with a woollen one for the night.

If there be more clothes than can be conveniently dried at one time, the Assistant Superintendent attends to it during the night; this applies to Casuals admitted late, or sheltered on the floor of the Day-room.

The Day-room is kept well heating during the night.

I am, Sir,

Your obedient Servant,

(Signed)RICHARD BUTT.

The Clerk to the Guardians of the Wandsworth and Clapham Union.

CLOTHING

Inmates wore uniform dress in the workhouse. Now there was to be a change of attitude for dress when out on leave. This would mean they would not be recognised by the public so easily, also it would be good for them psychologically. It was left to the Master and Matron to consider the best plan for carrying out the proposal. The report was as follows:-

7 December 1892

Present: - Mr Bugler (in the Chair), Messrs. Kidman, Millar, Turnor, and Wade

Reporting:-

That the Master submitted Samples of Materials, &c., which had been obtained by him.

Recommending -

(1.) That the Sixty Coats and Sixty Vests directed to be purchased be obtained from Mr. E Grove, as per pattern cloths selected by your Committee, at the following prices, viz.;-

Coats	*12s.6d each*
Waistcoats	*4s. each*

(2.) That the Sixty Overcoats directed to be purchased, be also obtained from Mr E Grove, as per pattern cloths selected by your Committee, at 14s. 6d. each.

(3.) With regard to the Neckerchiefs, that Eight dozen be ordered for the use of the Men and Women, as per sample approved by your Committee, of Messrs. Dobinson, Sewart & Co., at 6s. 3d. per dozen.

(4.) That the Forty-eight Shawls be obtained from Messrs. Dobinson, Stewart and Co., as per samples approved by your Committee, at 5s. 3d. each.

(5.) That Bonnets for the Women, and Ribbon for trimming the same, as required, be ordered of Messrs. Dobinson Stewart & Co., as per samples approved by your Committee, at the following prices, viz.:-

Black Shapes	*15s. 6d per dozen*
Brown Shapes	*18s. 11d per dozen*
Ribbons in assorted Colours	*5½d. per yard*

(6.) That the Ten patterns of Bower's Regatta Dress Material, selected by your Committee, be adopted. (This Material is the existing Contract with Messrs. Dobinson, Stewart & Co.)

DIETARY

Workhouse food had a bad name. Cooking large quantities makes it difficult to make tasty meals as they are known today. The food at Swaffield Road was as good as economic constraints allowed. Through the years improvements were gradually being made.

In 1893 the price of a 4lb loaf made in the Workhouse cost 4d. The Outdoor Stone Yard had extra bread on Saturdays, cost 5/-, that was a lot of bread. Perhaps it was extra for Sunday as well.

Records show that all food given was calculated in ounces and pints (or part of). This must have made serving food quite laborious. Inmates were classed and according to their class received the relevant amount. There were eight classes including the children. It is difficult to imagine how they knew who was which class in the dining hall. Perhaps different classes sat at certain tables.

(See DIETARY TABLE)

Suet Pudding was made with salt added. This was to change. A sauce was made instead with 2lbs of Treacle to half a pound of flour made up to one gallon. This must have been a welcome change.

In 1895 some inmates were sent to work at Tooting College, gardening. They took their food with them and they had their allowance of bread reduced from 12 ounces to 6 ounces and had 8 ounces potato added. This must have been more sustaining for them.

Easter was celebrated by the inmates having a hot cross bun on Good Friday.

Dr Downes suggested an improvement in the diet of the children aged 2 - 5 year old. They were to have an increase in their milk, from a third to a half pint, so important for their growth.

Cooking methods were attracting attention in the kitchen. "There was not any provision for Steam-cooking fish, except placing it along with potatoes in the steam oven and that a separate Steam Oven be provided". A Steward was asked to procure prices. This extra oven could be used for steam puddings as well as anything else and would undoubtedly improve the quality of the cooking overall.

In 1895 there were changes for the inmates at Dinner time. For the first time rice was served instead of potatoes on Thursday. There were not any complaints recorded so the inmates must have enjoyed the rice. It was only for one day a week and there were other changes as well as the following report shows.

(2.) *That the Suet Pudding and Rice Pudding Dinner to Adult Inmates (i.e., from 16 to 60 and upwards), on Thursdays, be discontinued, and that, in future, the Dinner on Thursdays be as follows:*

Men over 60 - 8 ozs. Vegetables or Rice, and 16 ozs. Meat Pie
Women over 60 - 8 ozs. Vegetables or Rice and 14 ozs. Meat Pie
Men over 16-60 - 8 ozs. Vegetables or Rice, ad 16 ozs. Meat Pie
Women from 16-60 - 8ozs. Vegetables or Rice, and 16 ozs. Meat Pie

(3.) *That the ingredients of the Meat Pie be as follows:-*

To the Pound -

Raw Meat (without Bone)	*4ozs.*
Flour	*7ozs.*
Fat	*1oz.*
Salt and Pepper	*¼oz.*

(4.) *That the Dinner of Suet Pudding on Thursdays for Children be substituted by similar quantities of a Pudding to be made of the following ingredients:-*

7 ozs. Flour
1½ ozs. Suet
2 ozs. Sultanas
1oz. Sugar
(The Sweet Sauce hitherto served with the Suet Pudding to be discontinued).

Day	Classes	Breakfast	Additional for Classes 1a, 2a, 3a, 4a and Children	Dinner	Supper	Additional for Classes 2b, and 4b only	Alternative Foods to be issued in the event of failure of the ordinary supply on any day
SUNDAY	1 and 1A Men	8ozs bread, 1pt tea, ½oz margarine		4½ozs roast beef, 4ozs bread, 12ozs vegetables	8ozs bread, 1pt tea, ½oz margarine	At the discretion of the Medical Officer	8ozs bread, 3ozs cheese, 1pt coffee
	3 and 3A Women	6ozs bread, 1pt tea, ½oz margarine		4ozs roast beef, 4ozs bread, 12ozs vegetables	6ozs bread, 1pt tea, ½oz margarine		6ozs bread, 2ozs cheese, 1pt coffee
	2 and 2A Men	8ozs bread, 1pt tea, ½oz margarine		4½ozs roast beef, 4ozs bread, 12ozs vegetables	8ozs bread, 1pt tea, ½oz margarine		8ozs bread, 3ozs cheese, 1pt coffee
	4 and 4A Women	6ozs bread, 1pt tea, ½oz margarine		4ozs roast beef, 4ozs bread, 12ozs vegetables	6ozs bread, 1pt tea, ½oz margarine		6ozs bread, 2ozs cheese, 1pt coffee
	2B Men	6ozs bread, 1pt tea, ½oz margarine		4ozs roast beef, 4ozs bread, 12ozs vegetables	6ozs bread, 1pt tea, ½oz margarine		8ozs bread, 2ozs cheese, 1pt coffee
	4B Women	4ozs bread, 1pt tea, ½oz margarine		3½ozs roast beef, 4ozs bread, 12ozs vegetables	4ozs bread, 1pt tea, ½oz margarine		6ozs bread, 1ozs cheese, 1pt coffee
	5 Children, 3 to 8	5ozs bread, 1pt tea, ½oz margarine		1½ozs roast beef, 4ozs bread, 12ozs vegetables	5ozs bread, ½pt milk		4ozs bread, 1ozs cheese, ½pt cocoa
	6 Children, 8 to 16	6ozs bread, 1pt tea, ½oz margarine		2½ozs roast beef, 4ozs bread, 12ozs vegetables	6ozs bread, ¾pt tea, ½oz margarine		6ozs bread, 1ozs cheese, ¾pt cocoa
MONDAY	1 and 1A Men	4ozs bread, 1½pt porridge	4ozs bread, 1½ozs cheese	3½ozs boiled mutton, 4ozs bread, 6ozs vegetables	8ozs bread, 1pt broth		8ozs bread, 3ozs cheese, 1pt coffee
	3 and 3A Women	6ozs bread, 1pt cocoa, ½oz margarine	4ozs bread, 1½ozs cheese	3ozs boiled mutton, 4ozs bread, 4ozs vegetables	6ozs bread, 1pt tea, ½oz margarine		6ozs bread, 2ozs cheese, 1pt coffee
	2 and 2A Men	8ozs bread, 1pt cocoa, ½oz margarine	4ozs bread, 1½ozs cheese	3½ozs boiled mutton, 4ozs bread, 6ozs vegetables	8ozs bread, 1pt tea, ½oz margarine		8ozs bread, 3ozs cheese, 1pt coffee
	4 and 4A Women	6ozs bread, 1pt cocoa, ½oz margarine	4ozs bread, 1½ozs cheese	3ozs boiled mutton, 4ozs bread, 4ozs vegetables	6ozs bread, 1pt tea, ½oz margarine		6ozs bread, 2ozs cheese, 1pt coffee
	2B Men	6ozs bread, 1pt cocoa, ½oz margarine		3ozs boiled mutton, 4ozs bread, 4ozs vegetables	6ozs bread, 1pt tea, ½oz margarine		8ozs bread, 2ozs cheese, 1pt coffee
	4B Women	4ozs bread, 1pt cocoa, ½oz margarine		2½ozs boiled mutton, 4ozs bread, 4ozs vegetables	4ozs bread, 1pt tea, ½oz margarine		6ozs bread, 1ozs cheese, 1pt coffee
	5 Children, 3 to 8	5ozs bread, ½pt milk	2ozs plain cake	1½ozs boiled mutton, 4ozs vegetables	5ozs bread, ½pt tea, 1oz jam		4ozs bread, 1ozs cheese, ½pt cocoa
	6 Children, 8 to 16	3ozs bread, ½pt milk, ¾pt porridge, ½oz sugar	2ozs plain cake	2½ozs boiled mutton, 2ozs bread, 6ozs vegetables	6ozs bread, ¾pt tea, 1½ozs jam		6ozs bread, 1ozs cheese, ¾pt cocoa
TUESDAY	1 and 1A Men	4ozs bread, 1½pt gruel	4ozs bread, 1½ozs cheese	6ozs hashed meat, 4ozs bread, 12ozs vegetables	4ozs bread, 1½pt porridge		8ozs bread, 3ozs cheese, 1pt coffee
	3 and 3A Women	6ozs bread, 1pt coffee, ½oz margarine	4ozs bread, 1½ozs cheese	5ozs hashed meat, 4ozs bread, 8ozs vegetables	6ozs bread, 1pt tea, ½oz margarine		6ozs bread, 2ozs cheese, 1pt coffee
	2 and 2A Men	8ozs bread, 1pt coffee, ½oz margarine	4ozs bread, 1½ozs cheese	6ozs hashed meat, 4ozs bread, 12ozs vegetables	6ozs seed cake, 1pt tea		8ozs bread, 3ozs cheese, 1pt coffee
	4 and 4A Women	6ozs bread, 1pt coffee, ½oz margarine	4ozs seed cake	5ozs hashed meat, 4ozs bread, 8ozs vegetables	4ozs seed cake, 1pt tea		6ozs bread, 2ozs cheese, 1pt coffee
	2B Men	6ozs bread, 1pt coffee, ½oz margarine		6ozs hashed meat, 4ozs bread, 4ozs vegetables	6ozs seed cake, 1pt tea		8ozs bread, 2ozs cheese, 1pt coffee
	4B Women	4ozs bread, 1pt coffee, ½oz margarine		5ozs hashed meat, 4ozs bread, 4ozs vegetables	4ozs seed cake, 1pt tea		6ozs bread, 1ozs cheese, 1pt coffee
	5 Children, 3 to 8	5ozs bread, ½pt milk	2ozs seed cake	2ozs hashed meat, 4ozs vegetables	4ozs seed cake, ½pt tea		4ozs bread, 1ozs cheese, ½pt cocoa
	6 Children, 8 to 16	6ozs bread, ¾pt milk	2ozs seed cake	3ozs hashed meat, 2ozs bread, 6ozs vegetables	6ozs seed cake, ¾pt tea		6ozs bread, 1ozs cheese, ¾pt cocoa
WEDNESDAY	1 and 1A Men	4ozs bread, 1½pt porridge	4ozs bread, 1½ozs cheese	16ozs meat pudding, 6ozs vegetables or rice	8ozs bread, 1pt rice milk		8ozs bread, 3ozs cheese, 1pt coffee
	3 and 3A Women	6ozs bread, 1pt milk	4ozs bread, 1½ozs cheese	14ozs meat pudding, 6ozs vegetables or rice	6ozs bread, 1pt tea, ½oz margarine		6ozs bread, 2ozs cheese, 1pt coffee
	2 and 2A Men	8ozs bread, 1pt tea, ½oz margarine	4ozs bread, 1½ozs cheese	14ozs meat pudding, 6ozs vegetables or rice	8ozs bread, 1pt tea, ½oz margarine		8ozs bread, 3ozs cheese, 1pt coffee
	4 and 4A Women	6ozs bread, 1pt tea, ½oz margarine	4ozs bread, 1½ozs cheese	12ozs meat pudding, 6ozs vegetables or rice	6ozs bread, 1pt tea, ½oz margarine		6ozs bread, 2ozs cheese, 1pt coffee
	2B Men	6ozs bread, 1pt tea ½oz margarine		10ozs meat pudding, 4ozs vegetables or rice	6ozs bread, 1pt tea, ½oz margarine		8ozs bread, 2ozs cheese, 1pt coffee
	4B Women	4ozs bread, 1pt tea, ½oz margarine		8ozs meat pudding, 4ozs vegetables or rice	4ozs bread, 1pt tea, ½oz margarine		6ozs bread, 1ozs cheese, 1pt coffee
	5 Children, 3 to 8	2ozs bread, ½pt milk, ½pt porridge, ½oz sugar	2ozs plain cake	8ozs meat pudding, 4ozs vegetables or rice	5ozs bread, ½pt tea, 1oz jam		4ozs bread, 1ozs cheese, ½pt cocoa
	6 Children, 8 to 16	3ozs bread, ½pt milk, ¾pt porridge, ½oz sugar	2ozs plain cake	12ozs meat pudding, 4ozs vegetables or rice	6ozs bread, ¾pt tea, 1½oz jam		6ozs bread, 1ozs cheese, ¾pt cocoa
THURSDAY	1 and 1A Men	2ozs bread, 1½pt porridge, 1oz sugar	4ozs bread, 1½ozs cheese	4½ozs cold or tinned meat, 4ozs bread, 12ozs vegetables	8ozs bread, 1pt broth		8ozs bread, 3ozs cheese, 1pt coffee
	3 and 3A Women	6ozs bread, 1pt cocoa, ½oz margarine	4ozs bread, 1½ozs cheese	4ozs cold or tinned meat, 4ozs bread, 8ozs vegetables	6ozs bread, 1pt tea, ½oz margarine, 2ozs onions or 4ozs lettuce (WIS)		6ozs bread, 2ozs cheese, 1pt coffee
	2 and 2A Men	8ozs bread, 1pt tea, ½oz margarine	4ozs bread, 1½ozs cheese	3½ozs cold or tinned meat, 4ozs bread, 6ozs vegetables	8ozs bread, 1pt tea, ½oz margarine, 2ozs onions or 4ozs lettuce (WIS)		8ozs bread, 3ozs cheese, 1pt coffee
	4 and 4A Women	6ozs bread, 1pt tea, ½oz margarine	4ozs bread, 1½ozs cheese	3ozs cold or tinned meat, 4ozs bread, 4ozs vegetables	6ozs bread, 1pt tea, ½oz margarine, 2ozs onions or 4ozs lettuce (WIS)		6ozs bread, 2ozs cheese, 1pt coffee
	2B Men	6ozs bread, 1pt tea ½oz margarine		3ozs cold or tinned meat, 4ozs bread, 4ozs vegetables	6ozs bread, 1pt tea, ½oz margarine, 2ozs onions or 4ozs lettuce (WIS)		8ozs bread, 2ozs cheese, 1pt coffee
	4B Women	4ozs bread, 1pt tea, ½oz margarine		2½ozs cold or tinned meat, 4ozs bread, 4ozs vegetables	4ozs bread, 1pt tea, ½oz margarine, 2ozs onions or 4ozs lettuce (WIS)		6ozs bread, 1ozs cheese, 1pt coffee
	5 Children, 3 to 8	5ozs bread, ½pt cocoa, ½oz margarine	2ozs seed cake	1½ozs cold or tinned meat, 4ozs vegetables	5ozs bread, ½pt milk, 1oz onions or 2ozs lettuce (WIS)		4ozs bread, 1ozs cheese, ½pt cocoa
	6 Children, 8 to 16	6ozs bread, ¾pt cocoa, ½oz margarine	2ozs seed cake	2½ozs cold or tinned meat, 2ozs bread, 6ozs vegetables	6ozs bread, ¾pt milk, 1oz onions or 2ozs lettuce (WIS)		6ozs bread, 1ozs cheese, ¾pt cocoa
FRIDAY	1 and 1A Men	6ozs bread, 1½pt gruel	4ozs bread, 1½ozs cheese	10ozs fish, 4ozs bread, 12ozs vegetables or rice	4ozs bread, 1½pt porridge		8ozs bread, 3ozs cheese, 1pt coffee
	3 and 3A Women	6ozs bread, 1pt cocoa, ½oz margarine	4ozs bread, 1½ozs cheese	8ozs fish, 4ozs bread, 8ozs vegetables or rice	6ozs bread, 1pt tea, ½oz margarine		6ozs bread, 2ozs cheese, 1pt coffee
	2 and 2A Men	8ozs bread, 1pt cocoa, ½oz margarine	4ozs bread, 1½ozs cheese	8ozs fish, 4ozs bread, 12ozs vegetables or rice	6ozs plain cake, 1pt tea		8ozs bread, 3ozs cheese, 1pt coffee
	4 and 4A Women	6ozs bread, 1pt cocoa, ½oz margarine	4ozs plain cake	8ozs fish, 4ozs bread, 8ozs vegetables or rice	4ozs plain cake, 1pt tea		6ozs bread, 2ozs cheese, 1pt coffee
	2B Men	6ozs bread, 1pt cocoa, ½oz margarine		6ozs fish, 4ozs bread, 4ozs vegetables or rice	6ozs plain cake, 1pt tea		8ozs bread, 2ozs cheese, 1pt coffee
	4B Women	4ozs bread, 1pt cocoa, ½oz margarine		6ozs fish, 4ozs bread, 4ozs vegetables or rice	4ozs plain cake, 1pt tea		6ozs bread, 1ozs cheese, 1pt coffee
	5 Children, 3 to 8	5ozs bread, ½pt milk	2ozs plain cake	4ozs fish, 3ozs bread, 6ozs vegetables or rice	4ozs plain cake, ½pt tea		4ozs bread, 1ozs cheese, ½pt cocoa
	6 Children, 8 to 16	6ozs bread, ¾pt milk	2ozs plain cake	8ozs fish, 3ozs bread, 8ozs vegetables or rice	6ozs plain cake, ¾pt tea		6ozs bread, 1ozs cheese, ¾pt cocoa
SATURDAY	1 and 1A Men	2ozs bread, 1½pt porridge, 1oz sugar	4ozs bread, 1½ozs cheese	3ozs bacon, 4ozs bread, 12ozs vegetables or rice	8ozs bread, 1pt rice milk		8ozs bread, 3ozs cheese, 1pt coffee
	3 and 3A Women	2ozs bread, 1pt porridge, 1oz sugar	4ozs bread, 1½ozs cheese	3ozs bacon, 4ozs bread, 8ozs vegetables or rice	6ozs bread, 1pt tea, ½oz margarine		6ozs bread, 2ozs cheese, 1pt coffee
	2 and 2A Men	8ozs bread, 1pt tea, ½oz margarine	4ozs bread, 1½ozs cheese	3ozs bacon, 4ozs bread, 12ozs vegetables or rice	8ozs bread, 1pt tea, ½oz margarine		8ozs bread, 3ozs cheese, 1pt coffee
	4 and 4A Women	6ozs bread, 1pt tea, ½oz margarine	4ozs bread, 1½ozs cheese	3ozs bacon, 4ozs bread, 8ozs vegetables or rice	6ozs bread, 1pt tea, ½oz margarine		6ozs bread, 2ozs cheese, 1pt coffee
	2B Men	6ozs bread, 1pt tea ½oz margarine		3ozs bacon, 4ozs bread, 4ozs vegetables or rice	6ozs bread, 1pt tea, ½oz margarine		8ozs bread, 2ozs cheese, 1pt coffee
	4B Women	4ozs bread, 1pt tea, ½oz margarine		3ozs bacon, 4ozs bread, 4ozs vegetables or rice	4ozs bread, 1pt tea, ½oz margarine		6ozs bread, 1ozs cheese, 1pt coffee
	5 Children, 3 to 8	2ozs bread, ½pt milk, ½pt porridge, ½oz sugar	2ozs seed cake	1ozs bacon, 4ozs vegetables or rice	5ozs bread, ½pt tea, ½oz margarine		4ozs bread, 1ozs cheese, ½pt cocoa
	6 Children, 8 to 16	3ozs bread, ½pt milk, ¾pt porridge, ½oz sugar	2ozs seed cake	2ozs bacon, 2ozs bread, 6ozs vegetables or rice	6ozs bread, ¾pt tea, ½oz margarine		6ozs bread, 1ozs cheese, ¾pt cocoa

At a Meeting of the Board of Guardians of the Wandsworth and Clapham Union, held on the day of   1900 in accordance with the requirements of the Workhouse Regulation (Dietaries and Accounts) Order, 1900, that the following DIETARY TABLES for the Paupers of the respective Classes and Disabled in the Workhouse of this Union be adopted.

Wandsworth Infirmary and Workhouse, East Hill, c. 1912, which was opened in 1838 under the Poor Law Reform Act of 1834. In 1866 there were 523 inmates, of which 224 were on the medical officer's books with only two illiterate nurses administering the medicines. An earlier workhouse stood on East Hill, just above Tonsley Hill. The workhouse moved to Swaffied Road in 1886 and the building on East Hill remained as an infimary only, named St John's Hospital. Part of the buildings survices and has now been converted into flats.

(5.) *That the allowance of Bread for Supper to the Adult Inmates (ie., from 16 to 60 and upwards), be decreased as follows, viz.:-*
For men, from 6ozs to 5ozs. For women, from 5ozs to 4ozs.

(6) *That the Adult Inmates (i.e., from 16 to 60 and upwards) do receive at 3 o'clock each afternoon, 1½ ozs. Bread, ½ pint of tea and ¼ oz. of margarine.*
Your Committee having considered, seriatim, the several proposals contained in the foregoing report recommend as follows:-
That the Ingredients of the Oatmeal Porridge be, in future, 16 ozs. Of oatmeal and 7 pints of Water, with 1 pint of New Milk (added after the Porridge is made) to a gallon of Porridge.

With regard to Recommendation (2.) of the Sub-Committee's Report

That the recommendation to discontinue the Suet Pudding and Rice Pudding Dinner to Adult inmates on Thursday be adopted, and that, in future, the Dinner on Thursday be as follows:-

Men over 60 - 8 ozs. Vegetables or Rice, 14 ozs. Meat Pudding.
Women over 60 - 8ozs. Vegetables or Rice, 14 ozs. Meat Pudding
Men from 16 to 60 - 8 ozs. Vegetables or Rice, 16 ozs. Meat Pudding.
Women from 16 to 60 - 8 ozs. Vegetables or Rice, 14 ozs. Meat Pudding.

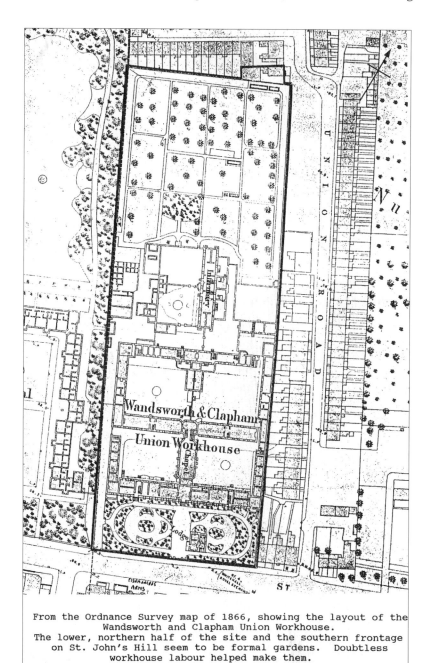

From the Ordnance Survey map of 1866, showing the layout of the
Wandsworth and Clapham Union Workhouse.
The lower, northern half of the site and the southern frontage
on St. John's Hill seem to be formal gardens. Doubtless
workhouse labour helped make them.
-38-

Also in 1895 it is discovered that the Reverend Patrick Watson supplied the employed men from the Stone-Yard their dinners at his Mission Hall. The following letter explains his problems:-

The Vicarage
Earlsfield, S.W.,
February 14th, 1895.
Dear Sir,

DINNER TIME OF MEN EMPLOYED IN STONE-YARD
May I respectfully ask you to consider the following application as urgent; and to deal with it to-day.

I supply, in my Mission Hall at Wardley, Free Dinners to all Men on their first day in the Stone-yard, and as much Soup and Bread as they desire for the sum of one penny to the others.

Today we had about two hundred to feed. I also supply Free Dinners to two hundred Children from Garratt Lane and Waldron Road Schools.

The difficulty is, that all the four hundred have to be supplied with food between 12 and half-past 1. The rush is now so great as to create confusion, and to make the Men, the Children, my voluntary Workers, and everyone connected with the kitchen, more uncomfortable.

If you could alter the Men' dinner hour from 12.30 to 12 o'clock, the difficulty would entirely disappear, and both Men and Children could have their food in comfort.

I therefore earnestly and respectfully request that you will be good enough to grant me this favour forthwith.
I am, Sir,
Yours faithfully.
(Signed) PATRICK WATSON

PS: Assuming that you kindly comply with this suggestion, I would give your Men their Dinners first, and keep back the Children's Dinners until 12.30, which would suit both parties, I think, as the little ones would not have to hurry over their food.

To the Chairman of the Guardians,
Wandsworth and Clapham Union
It was MOVED by General Boddam, Seconded by Mr Penfold, and Resolved - That the application contained in the foregoing letter be complied with, and in future the Stone-yard be closed for Dinner time from 12 o'clock noon to 12.30.

In March 1898 a visiting committee member suggested increasing the amount of dry tea used to make the inmates tea. The following letter was the Local Government Board reply:-

32945
1898

LOCAL GOVERNMENT BOARD
WHITEHALL, S.W.,
22nd March 1898.

Sir,
I am directed by the Local Government Board to acknowledge the receipt of your letter of the 11th instant, with reference to the proposal of the Guardians o the Wandsworth

and Clapham Union, that the amount of dry tea to be used in preparing each gallon of tea beverage, for the Inmates of the Tooting Home, should be increased from one and a half to two ounces.

I am directed to state that the Board are advised that if tea of a reasonably good quality is provided, and due care is taken to ensure that the beverage is properly made, the present formula for its preparation should suffice.

I am, Sir,
Your obedient Servant
(Signed) W.E. KNOLLYS,
Assistant Secretary

Clerk to the Guardians
Of the Wandsworth and Clapham Union

RESOLVED - That the matter be referred back to the Workhouse Committee for further consideration and report.

The chart of the weekly dietary shows that the Master, Matron and Officers lived very well.

The Board of Guardians decided to alter the dietary of the inmates. This must have caused a lot of work for the kitchen staff generally. There were always some alterations, but this major one really was an upgrade to their food intake.

In 1896 the Committee authorised the purchase of one bushel of linseed. Quite why the decision was made is not recorded, it was to be crushed and put into the meal for general use. The order was not repeated even though there were not any complaints by the inmates.

In December 1897 the committee deemed it necessary to make alterations regarding the Bakery. The following report shows how:-

That the Committee have held two meetings and have fully considered the question referred to them, and RECOMMEND -

(1.) That in future the Baker be not allowed to receive any money and yeast money from the Contractors.

(2.) That the flour be contracted for to be supplied in 14lb bags, belonging to the Guardians, and that it be stated in the form of contract that the pitch money will have to be paid by the Contractors; by this arrangement it is estimated a saving of 5d. per sack will be effected.

(3.) That 300-140lb. Bags be purchased, and that price be obtained from Mr. Wooderson, of Wandsworth, Mr Smith, York Road, and Messrs. Carr, Thames Street.

(4.) That the bread in future be made in small loaves of 1lb and 5ozs. For the Inmates of the Workhouse, and the necessary tins, &c., purchased, the Committee at the end of a month to again report as to the working of the new arrangement.

(5.) That the Local Government Board be asked to sanction an allowance of bread being served to the Inmates in two portions.

(6.) That German or French yeast be used in making the bread and that prices be obtained from -

Mr Wilkins, St Mary Axe.

Messrs. Carter & Co., Hammersmith.

(7.) That, in reference to the wages of the Baker, the Committee find that the work has considerably increased by reason of the opening of the Tooting Home, and as the Baker will not receive in future the sack and yeast money which he estimates at 5s. weekly, your Committee make the following recommendations, viz.:-

(a.) That the salary of Mr Gill, Baker, be increased to £2.2s per week and dinner.

(b.) That a second hand be employed, at wages of 30s. per week and dinner.

(c.) That Inmates employed in the Bakehouse receive a meat dinner daily and one pint of tea. The tea to be in addition to the ordinary diet.

(Consideration of this paragraph was adjourned by the Workhouse Committee.)

For Queen Victoria's Diamond Jubilee Celebrations the paid staff had an extra day's holiday and the inmates had a bag of special pastries costing 3d.

In February 1898 one ton of potatoes delivered were not up to standard. A replacement order was not up to standard either. They were returned to the contractor and the Master purchased a replacement from the market and charged it to the contractor. This was the beginning of an era when goods were not supplied as per sample, and was going to cause the workhouse a great deal of difficulties. Second rate supplies were not going to be tolerated. The workhouse was feeding large numbers of people and the orders were vast and to the contractors the profits were high if they could get away with second rate quality. The workhouse would not tolerate poor quality. Contractors lost their contracts!

The workhouse made all the fruit cakes for the Tooting Home. They requested the ingredients such as fruit, eggs, and sugar. Margarine was used in the cakes at first but the workhouse decided to use dripping instead, they had quite a lot from the meat, and must have made a very good moist cake.

A lot of the younger female inmates disliked porridge and said as much. They were offered 5 ounces of bread, 1 pint tea and half an ounce of margarine instead.

In October 1899 male inmates were allocated cocoa for breakfast instead of tea. At the same time it was decided that aged male inmates were to be given Mutton instead of beef for dinner occasionally. No reason was given for this variety and it can be questioned why not the female inmates as well?

It had also been decided that all the men employed were to have a mid-day meal, records do not show if they had their meal with the Officers!

Tea was still expensive in the 1890s. It was about two shillings and seven pence a pound. That would have made an ounce of tea about 2pence. Compared to bread, one of our staple foods, it was very expensive. The cost of a two pound loaf was 2 pence. Interestingly Thomas Lipton, the grocer who had 300 shops, entered the tea trade to supply a cheaper tea at one shilling and seven pence. However, the suggestion by the visiting committee member did succeed in the Board increasing the dry tea to one and three quarters of an ounce! The gallon of tea had a pint of milk and 6 ounces of sugar added, no doubt the inmates became accustomed to the brew!

(a) That a tea infuser, similar to that at the Infirmary and Tooting Home, be supplied to the Workhouse, and that the present dietary be increased to one and three quarter ounces of tea, 6oz. Sugar, and 1pt. Milk to the gallon.

(b) That the Master submit a list of Women over 50 years of age employed at cleaning, scrubbing, sewing, &c., with a view to giving them afternoon tea.

With regard to recommendation "b" the Master submitted a list of four names, and your Committee instructed the Master to furnish a list of all the Women between 50 and 60 years of age, showing how they are employed.

Some male inmates that could be relied upon were working as "Messengers" at Relief Stations. In 1899 they were allowed "dry materials" to make tea and were to have vegetables with their dinner.

At Christmas time there was a lot of extra baking to do and often a temporary baker was engaged to help in the preparations.

In March 1900 a Plant for making Soda-water was bought for £55.4.9d. This was a large outlay, but it would be used to make soda-water for the Master, Matron and Officers of the workhouse instead of buying ready made bottles which would have been more expensive. The Plant would have been operated by an inmate.

	Bread	Uncooked meat (including bone)	Poultry	Soup or Fish	Bacon	Potatoes	Other Vegetables	Cheese	Fresh Butter	Tea, or Coffee, or Cocoa	Loaf Sugar	Moist, or Caster Sugar	Milk	Eggs	Mustard, Pepper, Vinegar, Salt	Pickles and Sauces	Pastry and Cake	Mineral Waters, Ginger Beer or Lemonade	Jam and Marmalade
	Lbs	Lbs	Lbs		Lbs	Lbs		Lbs	Lbs	Oz	Lb	Lb	Pts	No					
Master	7	7	1 Fowl or Duck	Daily	1	7	Daily	½	¾	14	1	½	7	8	As required	As required	Daily	As required	¾
Matron	7	7	1 Fowl or Duck	Daily	1	7	Daily	½	¾	14	1	½	7	9	Ditto	Ditto	Ditto	Ditto	½
Male Officer	7	7	1 Fowl or Duck	1lb Fish	1	7	Daily	½	½	8	½	½	7	4	Ditto	At discretion of Master	1lb Pastry or milk pudding daily, alternatively	*At discretion of Master	½
Female Officers			1 Fowl or Duck	1lb Fish											Ditto	Ditto	1lb Pastry or milk pudding daily, alternatively	Ditto	½

ENTERTAINMENT

Entertainment came in many forms.

The Magic Lantern Show given by different groups was very popular with the children. One was even given on Christmas Day in 1898.

The inmates always enjoyed singing, listening to a choir, especially Carols at Christmastime.

There were concerts from the Stormont Hill Friends, Ye Olde Boyes Minstrel Tramps and a "Happy Evening for the People" for the over 60s and the children. Quite how the two age groups were entertained at the same time is difficult to imagine.

For two years running adults and children attended a performance of a pantomime at the Shakespeare Theatre, Clapham. This theatre opened in 1896 for dramatic productions and was converted for cinema performances in 1925. Unfortunately it was damaged during 1940 and demolished in 1957. Those attending a pantomime would have had to walk to and from the theatre from the workhouse.

Local groups and societies were very good offering their "charity work". The inmates, both adults and children, benefited from a great deal of empathy, as the groups returned time and again.

Christmas trees were donated along with new sixpences for the children. One constant group of people who donated money were from the publication called "Truth". It can be imagined how excited the children were to have a new sixpence. In those days a sixpence would buy quite a few items.

Books and periodicals were donated from the Kyrle Society. They also donated pictures which were not framed. Stretchers for the canvases and frames were made at the workhouse.

A piano was also donated to the workhouse; it was probably put in the dining hall where there was a stage. It must have been a great asset for the concert parties.

The children also had two chair swings, scrap albums and picture books donated.

HOLIDAYS

There was a lovely gesture by a Reverend & Mrs Hamilton in August 1894. To take six blind inmates to a Home for two weeks holiday. A Miss Rex was meeting the cost of their visit:

"7 Union Crescent,
Margate,
1st August, 1894

Dear Mr Milligan,

I did mention to you some days ago when I had the pleasure of meeting you, something about a "holiday place of rest for the Blind" at St. Leonards.

I have the offer from a lady, which I make to you and to your colleagues on the Board at Wandsworth, that is, of sending six Blind persons from the Workhouse to this "Home" for a fortnight in September next.

I may mention that the cost of their keeping there is nil, to the Guardians, and through the kindness of one or two personal friends, my Wife and I are able to meet their travelling expenses.

The only favour I would ask you and the Guardians to grant, is the use of the Ambulance to bring them to and from Clapham Junction, permission to use the Workhouse Clothes while on their visit, and a change of linen with them for the fortnight.

They will be met at St. Leonards. I am willing, however, to pay the expenses of an officer to travel with them, and deliver them up. Miss Rex, I am sure, would be very willing to accompany them, if you think right.

With kind regards,
I am,
Yours very faithfully,
(Signed)G. F. HAMILTON

P.S. - Perhaps you would kindly bring the matter before the Board to-morrow, and let me know your decision through the Clerk."

It was MOVED by Mr. Turnor, Seconded by Mr. Penfold, and Resolved - That the Rev. G F Hamilton's offer be accepted with thanks, and that it be left in his hands to make the necessary arrangements.

MEDICAL

The doctor wrote a report to the committee about the condition of the inmates on entering the workhouse, as follows: -

(8.) That the following report was made by the Medical Officer, viz: -

"I beg again to call the attention of the Committee to the cases which are continually being sent here, in all ill and unfit state for walking, by the Relieving Officers. They state that the Relieving Officers tell them that they cannot give orders for the Infirmary, but that they must come to the Workhouse, and ask to see the Doctor at once, and he will send them to the Infirmary. I submit that, before sick people are sent for such a distance, as carrying out the Relieving Officers' orders, must necessarily entail, they should be submitted to the District Medical Officers, who have equally with myself, the right of sending people into the Infirmary. The present course if in many cases, and especially at this time of the year, fraught with great danger to life.

(Signed)A. E. DODSON"

There should have been more cooperation between Relieving Officers in the Union. There was not any follow-up memorandum, on record. As the committee was involved it is almost certain changes were made.

An aged woman was sent from Bolingbroke Hospital. She was quite unable to stand and even had to be lifted up in bed. Also a man aged 50 was suffering from gout and unable to walk. He had been sent from a lodging house; he should have gone to an infirmary. If the Master had been on the telephone they would not have been admitted.

Nursing the sick took on a new significance in 1892. In the past inmates who seemed capable were given the task. If inmates did not come in sick they at some time became sick. The workhouse did have nurses but not many and the nurses they did have used to delegate jobs through pressure of work. As the following report shows, things were about to change: -

NURSING IN WORKHOUSE SICK WARDS
EXTRACT FROM MEMORANDUM OF DR. DOWNES, INSPECTOR OF THE LOCAL GOVERNMENT
BOARD, DATED APRIL, 1892.

It may be well to draw the attention of the Guardians, who have not as yet ceased to employ Pauper assistants in the sick wards, to the following considerations: -

There is great and increasing difficulty in finding among the Inmates in health persons of good character, sufficiently able of body or fit in mind, to act as Nurses. To commit the care of the sick to Paupers is, therefore, frequently to entrust them to unsuitable person, having little at stake, without interest in their work, and practically irresponsible. Skill is obviously not to be expected of such persons; but, beyond the sum of suffering which lack of knowledge implies in such matters, experience of Pauper nursing has unhappily not seldom exemplified the evils which indifference, cupidity, and want of forbearance may entail.

The employment of Pauper Inmates in sick wards is, in a variety of ways, costly.

If fit for such employment, they should be fit to earn their own living, and a proof of this is often afforded by the discharges which are taken when the extras and indulgences of the sick wards are no longer forthcoming.

The removal of wards-people usually sets free a number of sick beds, having a money value, which may be estimated on average at £100 per bed.

The waste and misappropriation of food, which is commonly so large an item of infirmary expenditure, is largely dependent on the employment of Pauper helps, whose interest is selfishly concerned in its continuance.

The want of proper care of appliances is no small item of cost. It is not unusual, for example, to find a costly water-bed spoiled through want of knowledge.

It may be observed, also, that Guardians will rarely obtain the full value of their paid Nurses' service, so long as there remains opportunity or excuse for these Officers to delegate their duties to Inmates.

Humanity and economy alike dictate that the sick poor in Workhouse sick wards should receive nursing treatment not less efficient than that which is now afforded in general hospitals, and in well-administered cottage hospitals.

In Workhouse where Pauper nursing is dispensed with, it is usually found that the majority of paid Nurses and assistant Nurses to the average number of occupied sick beds should be from about one to fifteen to one to ten, this allowance including night Nurses and Nurses off duty.

The actual provision must largely depend on the size of the Infirmary, and the character of the cases, but it should be remembered that, although the sick are mostly chronic, a large number are of such kind as to require constant care and attention.

In January 1895 the Medical Officer requested a Probationary Ward for new admittances, for 14 days occupation with a view to preventing the introduction of infectious diseases to the workhouse. This was sound common sense considering the large numbers of inmates in the workhouse. This request would have had the Committee's approval though the records do not show it.

The workhouse was not prepared for the number of aged and infirm inmates. St John's was the Infirmary, but it was full. So a special nurse was to be appointed to look after them at £26.00 per annum, with board, lodging, washing and uniform. Her name was Edith Lance.

The lying-in ward became even busier. The midwife was often up two or three nights running; they had recorded 124 births in recent months and needed a midwife for night duty. The lying-in ward had only pauper supervision when the midwife was off duty. This state of affairs had to be remedied. What also caused further problems was the number of Puerperal Fever cases. Once again the Committee had to act on increasing the nursing staff.

Concerns regarding the lying-in ward were the responsibility of the medical officer. Complaints had obviously been received, which were always followed up to prompt Dr Dodson to write such a strongly worded letter.

"New Workhouse
Wandsworth, S.W.,
14 October 1898.

SIR,

In reply to the letter from the Local Government Board, of the 1st August last, and which was at yesterday's Workhouse Committee, referred to me for report, I beg to state that ever since the opening of the Lying-in Wards here, the provisions of Articles 1 and 2 of the General Order have been strictly observed. Rules were then drawn up for the guidance of the Midwife, and the first of them is as follows: -

"The Midwife and the Nurse of "D" Block (who is the appointed Deputy) "must arrange leave of absence, so that both are not away from the Workhouse at the same time", &c.

I am unaware of any infraction of this rule since the Workhouse Lying-in Ward has been opened. No inmate has ever done the duties of Nurse, nor have the Wards at any time been "under pauper supervision."

Article No. 2. - No Inmate has ever been employed as cleaner in the Lying-in Ward, or in any other capacity, without my approval, and always under the supervision of a paid Officer (the Midwife).

With reference to the paragraph stating that there have been "repeated outbreaks of puerperal fever in the Midwifery Wards," I beg to submit statistics of the cases of childbirth since the commencement. From these it will be seen that the total number of cases confined up to the 29th of last month is 1, 469. In 1894 we had an outbreak of puerperal fever, which was fully reported upon by me at the time, and subsequently inquired into by Dr. Downes, the Medical Inspector of the Local Government Board. From that time until July, 1896, we had no case of puerperal fever, but on the 9th of that month, a Woman (Hartnell) was admitted from Battersea in labour, from a house in which her Mother had a short time before died of puerperal fever. By isolation, and sending the Midwife for a holiday, we prevented any bad effects from the case. From that day to this no further case has occurred.

Considering that more than 50 per cent, of the cases come in, in labour, in a filthy state (many suffering from infectious disease), from filthy homes and the most insanitary surroundings, and that more than half the cases are Girls with their first

Child, I personally consider that we have had a much greater immunity from puerperal fever than might be expected, and proves that nothing is wanting on the part of all Officers concerned to gain satisfactory results. As Medical Officer, and having personally attended every case of operative Midwifery since the Lying-in Wards were first opened, I am not cognisant of "repeated outbreaks of puerperal fever in the Midwifery Wards."

I am, Sir,
Yours faithfully,
(Signed) ARTHUR E DODSON

To the Clerk to the Guardians of the
Wandsworth and Clapham Union.

The workhouse was inspected from time to time, as were the other London workhouses. In August 1899 a report was received from a Local Government Inspector about the nursery.

This nursery is part of the lying-in ward. It was most necessary that hygiene be of a high standard.

"WANDSWORTH AND CLAPHAM UNION

EXTRACT from the report made by Miss Stansfeld, Assistant Local Government Inspector, on the Workhouse of the above Union, after a visit on the 1st day of July 1899.

I have inspected the Nursery of the Workhouse. The Midwife being on leave, the Children's Head Nurse was taking her place. The assistant Nurse (non-resident) was in charge of the Nursery.

I found 26 children, 17 of whom were under two years of age, and the Nurse informed me that there are sometimes 35 Children in the Nursery. It is evident that with such a number, many of whom are "Ins and Outs", there must often be a risk of infection, which may be dangerous to the Patients in the Lying-in Ward, while the Nurses' continual presence in the Nursery is necessary for the discipline of the nursing Mothers, and the maintenance of the order and management in the Nursery, upon which the health and well-being of a number of very little Children depend.

A ward Kitchen is greatly needed. At the time of my visit I found the Lavatory, which is particularly small, being used by 15 of the Children. Foul linen is also kept there. The hand-basin, in which the Mothers wash, contained tea things waiting to be washed.

More accommodation is needed for the Nursery line, and it is not desirable that the milk for the Mothers and Children's use should be kept in a cupboard in the passage.

The bathing accommodation in the Night Nursery is, in my opinion, insufficient. The one large bath is used for Mothers only, the Children being washed in zinc troughs at the other end of the Nursery. The Children look fairly well.

There appears to be no night supervision in this Nursery. The head Nurse sleeps in an adjoining room.

The Clerk was instructed to acknowledge the letter, and point out that the question of accommodation for the class of Children referred to has been adjourned, pending the proposed dissolution of the North Surrey School District."

The guardians decided not to act on the inspector's report because the London area were in the process of forming their own Inspectorate as the North Surrey District were readjusting theirs. However, it does show that the lying-in ward and nursery needed a lot of attention although the children "looked fairly well".

In September 1899 the school block was in crisis. They had Scarlet Fever, Chicken Pox and Measles there. A large number of children were very ill, no movement of children could take place, and the whole of the School block was in isolation. When the crisis was over there was general concern about the accommodation in the School block. The following report was from the Medical Officer: -

"The condition of things in the School Block is very serious. The Male side, built for 18 Boys, contains 24 Boys and two Adults, while five more are sleeping in the Temporary Ward, near the gate. On the Female side, built for 18 Girls, there are now 28 Girls and two Adults, while two Children are detained in the Receiving Ward. This state of things is prejudicial to health, and several of the Children are poorly, and the Nurse is overworked. Only about half of the total number of Children can receive instruction, as the School-room will not accommodate them."

In those days if you were disabled in anyway you were more often than not described very bluntly. The Feeble minded went to a home for the Feeble Minded, cost to the rate payers, seven shillings a week. If you were crippled you went to a home for Cripples. It was not meant to be cruel.

TRANSPORT

The workhouse's own transport department was very busy. Coachmen were paid 4s3d per day, they had to look after the Laudau and Brougham and the horses. In the 1893s shoeing of the horses cost 15s per horse. The bread van needed a thorough overhaul, repair, paint and varnish. The laundry van also needed repairs, (a new one would cost £52.10s) as did the ambulance. New wheels for the ambulance would cost £19. Glews Patent Rubber Tyres. The ambulance also needed disinfecting.

The three drivers were so busy at this time the stable work was being neglected. The Committee wanted answers. The drivers simply told the Committee that they could not be in two places at once! They were driving the ambulance, laundry van, bread van, Laundau, Brougham and bus and were fully occupied! The Committee authorised the appointment of a groom, it was, however, agreed reluctantly.

By 1897 there was a considerable movement of inmates and children to different institutions, which was becoming costly as they had to hire conveyances. The following reports show how they were going to improve their own means of transport.

REPORTING

That your Committee have very carefully considered the question of the provision of Conveyances for removal of Patients, and in connection therewith have visited several carriage establishments, and they now

RECOMMEND

(1.) That a Bus be built (to carry 12 inside and 2 out), at a cost not exceeding £120, and that sketches and prices be obtained from the following Firms, viz.:-

Messrs. Halford and Nalder, Newington Butts, S.E.

Messrs. Morgan & Co., Long Acre, W.C.

Mr. H. Pickett, 2 Mansfield Road, N.W.

Messrs. Redhouse and Son, 186 Goswell Road, E.C.

(2.) That a Landau be purchased, at a cost not exceeding 50 guineas, and that it be referred to your Committee to make the purchase.

In making the above recommendations, your Committee are of opinion that a very great saving will be effected, as the Conveyances can be used in the removal of the following:

(a.) Patients to Lunatic and Imbecile Asylums,

(b.) Inmates (settlement cases) to other London Workhouses,

(c.) Children to Railway Stations when going to Convalescent Homes, &c.,

(d.) Children to District Schools at Anerley, for whom Railway Fares have at present to be paid,and the amount of about £20 monthly now paid for Hire of Conveyances will practically cease.

If the above recommendations are adopted, your Committee consider that it will be necessary to purchase another Horse and Harness.

That your Committee received the Report of the Sub-Committee with reference to Conveyances, as follows, viz.:-

April 15th 1897.

Present: - Messrs. Digby, Kidman, Penfold and Wade.

We beg to Report that, acting upon the instructions given by the Board, we invited from several Firms particulars and prices of second-hand Landaus, to which three replies were received: one stating they had none; one stating they had one at 65 guineas; one at 75 guineas; and one at 105 guineas. Another Firm stating they had one at 75 guineas; and one at 40 guineas. Your Committee viewed three fine vehicles, and are satisfied with the one offered by Messrs. Alford and Alder, Newington Butts, as the most suitable one for our purpose. This Laudau is an exceedingly good one, never been painted since new, only had twelve months' wear, and your Committee got them (after a lot of persuading), to take off 5 per cent., bringing it down to £65. Your Committee unanimously recommend that this one be purchased for £65, and that the Clerk informs Messrs. Alford and Alder at once, by wire, as this one is not likely to remain in stock many days, and that steps be taken to amend the Board's order, not to exceed 50 guineas.

Your Committee also saw at Messrs. Alford and Alder's a double set of Harness, nearly new, cost 35 guineas, offered for 16 guineas. Your Committee recommend that the Board offer £12, as we shall be wanting Harness, when using a pair of Horses in the Landau.

WORK

Messengers work was of course mostly outside. In 1892 the Master decided that they should have waterproof capes. They cost 8s each and he ordered four.

In 1893 the Guardians decided that a Committee be appointed to consider whether some more profitable and satisfactory employment could be found for the able-bodied inmates than that of Oakum picking. Records do not show that the Committee was actually appointed, as in 1896 it was found that 90 men were in the picking sheds when only 70 were authorised. It did show that the Committee were beginning to change their attitude to long established practices. By November 1898 the work by then was abolished and separating Telephone and Ships Cables was substituted for men under 60 years of age.

Although many inmates were not skilled in any particular trade, some were. It was decided to make a list of those who had a trade on entering the workhouse. It was also decided to teach trades as well. The work was to be carried out by paid instructors.

The winter of 1897 was very cold and wet. The laundry had to employ a Laundress at 4s. a night to look after the "drying horses" in order to keep the laundry functioning at the normal rate.

Stone breaking continued with regular adverts for Guernsey Granite Spalls, 1500 tonnes at a time. Admission to the Stone Breaking Yard was not allowed after 9.30am. No one could leave except under special reasons, but they could ask to see a doctor. 7-10cwt of stone had to be broken per day was issued by the Local Government Board. Another form of work was wood chopping. The wood was bought by the "Fathom", the measure was the width of a man's reach with both arms outstretched, from finger-tip to finger-tip. The wood would be cut into 14 inch lengths and tied into bundles. They were sold for 3s.3d. per hundred bundles to shopkeepers and 3s.6d. to private purchasers. At one time there were 1000 circulars advertising bundles of wood for sale. Male inmates aged 65 and physically fit were given this work.

The Needle-room mended linen from the St. John's Infirmary apart from all the work for their own linen. Certain machines in the laundry were inclined to tear the items in the wash. Dresses must have been made at one time, perhaps for the children, as a Goffering Machine was put up for sale. This machine made plaits and ruffles.

Wandsworth was a good area for those wanting work. It had long been a light industrial area. Most of the industry was sited along the river Wandle for obvious reasons. There had been a lot of windmills and watermills in the past but at the time of Swaffield Road's existence there were only two - a paper mill and a flour mill. Young's Breweries was in Garrett Lane (and is still there today) and Wandsworth was also well known for hat making.

Hat making was very skilled work. Woollens had to be cleansed, bleached, scoured and thickened in a mill. The person who did this was a 'Fuller'. The people who made the hats were called 'Hurrers'.

The leather industry was doing very well too; the wealthy all having coaches and horses. They also had large houses round Wandsworth Common and needed staff to run the households.

The building industry was booming. Different Institutions were being constructed. New Asylums and Hospitals needed staff who needed houses. Wandsworth Bridge was also rebuilt at this time, a new Iron Lattice Girder Bridge of five spans. It must have given a lot of work to a great many men during its construction.

The Master visited other Workhouses in 1898 to enable him to make a comparison in efficiency and variety of work at Swaffield Road. It seems that they did fairly well. The report makes interesting reading:-

To the Chairman, Ladies and Gentlemen of the
Wandsworth and Clapham Board of Guardians,

SIR, LADIES AND GENTLEMEN,
Having recently visited certain of the Metropolitan Workhouses, I beg to submit to you the following observations thereon.

The Workhouses visited were:- The Holborn Union Workhouse, situated at Mitcham (numbering over 1,000 Inmates); the Strand Union Workhouse at Edmonton (with over 1,000 Inmates); the Edmonton Union Workhouse, which is adjacent to that of the Strand Union (with 600 Inmates); and the Bethnal Green Workhouse (with 1,700 Inmates).

The object of these visits was to ascertain the nature of the employment pursued by the Aged and Able-bodied Men, with a view of submitting to your consideration any occupation enforced at these Workhouses, likely, by its nature or utility, to claim your attention.

At the Mitcham Workhouse I found more variety of employment engaged in than in the others named; the occupations of the Aged and Able-bodied Men comprising as-making, tailoring, carpentry-work, shoemaking, mat-making, smith work, upholstery, bookbinding, corn grinding, gardenwork, wood-chopping and bundling and painting. The average number of Men engaged in the skilled trades in the various departments appeared not to exceed a dozen. One Man was employed in upholstery (making of kneeling mats and of flock cushions for forms, &c.,); one as a French polisher, and two as book-binders. Much of this work could be done by skilled labour only.

I observed that the greater number of Men - Aged and Able-bodied - were employed in wood-chopping and bundling. The number in the wood shop exceeded 100.

Their circular saws were driven by steam power, which would considerably augment their output of firewood, ensuring uniform production of sawn wood, and facilitating the chopping and bundling. Their sales of firewood weekly I understood to be £35, the price per 100 being 3s.2d. and 3s.6d.

Oakum-picking is generally engaged in at the Bethnal Green Workhouse by the Aged and Able-bodied Men, together with their employment in the usual domestic routine of the House. No fixed task is exacted from the Aged and Infirm Men, but their employment is enforced.

At the Edmonton Workhouse the employment for the Aged and Able-bodied Men is mainly that of wood-chopping, turning of circular saw, oakum picking, of field and garden work. Their mechanics are usefully employed in their respective trades, with the usual drawback of limited numbers.

The Strand Union Workhouse exhibited a departure from the usual work performed by the able-bodied. The work here assigned them was that of separating the inner copper wire from the rubber and hemp comprising telephone cables, also the division of the wire and fibre in marine grapnel-rope. The wire, fibre and rubber are separately packed and charged to the contractor, at the rate of 15s. per ton. The wire from the grapnel-rope is exported to the Chinese, who convert it into tea-chest nails. The fibre is by a chemical process made into brown paper - after its reception by the contractor -

and the copper wire and rubber extracted from the telephone cable is again of commercial value.

I beg to recommend to the consideration of the Board, the substitution of this work for that at present enforced of certain of the able-bodies class here - oakum picking. These are either youths or young men, not sufficiently robust to be employed at stone-breaking.

Oakum-picking is only useful as an alternative to sheer idleness; it is generally employed in the Metropolitan Workhouses, thus avoiding idleness, and the carrying out of the orders of the Local Government Board, vide Articles 102, 112, and 208, No. 6, which enact the compulsory employment by the Master of the Workhouse of all adults in proportion to their capacity. The only general employment to supersede oakum-picking for the Aged and Infirm Men appears to be that of wood-chopping and bundling.

Other than these two employments, no other occupation common to unskilled labour - apart from the domestic work of the House - is pursued, so far as I am aware, in any of the Metropolitan Workhouses.

I beg to append a summary of the various employments in which the Men are engaged in your Workhouse, together with the numbers so employed - wood-chopping and bundling, 18; carting wood, 2; Gardening, 8; tailor, 1; shoemakers, 8; bakers, 3' mat-makers, 1; mattress-maker, 1; carpenters, 3; cleaning windows, 1; hydrant burnishing, 1; clerk (occupied), 1; boys' attendants, 2; receiving ward scrubbers, 2; kitchen work, 19; laundry workers, 6; messengers, 19; workers proceeding to Tooting House daily, 12; workers at Infirmary, 3; domestic workers, 30; infirm, 24; engineers; work, 5; carpenters, 3; ditto labours 1; painters, 7; sweepers, 3; bricklayers, ; oakum picking, 102. Total, 275.

The conclusion is forced upon me, by the results of these visits to the large and important Metropolitan Workhouses mentioned, that the different occupations engaged in at your Wandsworth workhouse is as varied and, with the exception of the Mitcham Workhouse, equally useful as those pursued in the Workhouses mentioned.

I have the honour to be,

Your obedient servant

(Signed) H. ALDRIDGE
Master

CHAPTER 2: *Part of the Community - 1910*

The local community must have been intrigued by the inmates coming and going from the workhouse. They were probably messengers, gardeners or inmates just going out with relatives or friends. They looked well fed and seemed quite at ease returning to the workhouse. The Brougham and Landau must have also raised a few eyebrows and not a few questions.

Information about the running of the workhouse must have filtered out from the staff and through the Churches. The Churches were incredible supporters and the inmates, both adult and children, benefited greatly. There were other benefactors who regularly donated time, effort and money to the inmates, they were always thanked in writing.

ADMINISTRATION

Early in this decade the Intermediate School was built. It opened on 12 June 1903, much needed as there were so many children to house. The School Block was not large enough to cope with the number of children coming into the workhouse. There was also the question of childhood illness and containment. At the same time the St James' Road Branch Workhouse (converted from a school) came into being. It was hoped to relieve the pressure of Swaffield Road. Both of these premises brought more responsibility for the Guardians and their visiting committees. Children in the Intermediate School were then sent to District Schools for education.

The Intermediate School did not have an external indication of what institution it was. So the Committee authorised the words "Wandsworth Union - Intermediate School" to be carved in stone work over the entrance.

In 1901 the workhouse was certified for 603 adult inmates and there were 733. The Master applied to Mitcham Workhouse to take between 30-40 women. The men would have to go elsewhere, probably to St Giles. However, the inmates did not appreciate this move and many walked back to Swaffield Road!

The Gate Porter also had to "live in". He was paid £30 a year and had board and lodging, washing and uniform. The income would be increased by £1 a year to a maximum of £34. The Gate Porter's job was very responsible. He had to get to know all the visitors, keeping records of traffic and deliveries.

The quarterly "call over" took place in September 1908 and created a Register of the following:-

1. Dates of Admission and Discharges.
2. Trade or Occupation.
3. How employed in Workhouse.
4. Whether families chargeable.

The Guardians wanted to know how many able-bodied inmates so they could try to prevent them settling down in the workhouse, with a view to inducing them to take their discharge and seek work. Quite a task as life was too easy in the workhouse.

Vegetables were grown in the garden at St James' Workhouse. One summer there was a glut of cabbages, the inmates responsible dug them into the ground as they did not know what to do with them. The Matron found out and after angry comments it was decided that any excess vegetables could be sold.

An inmate who lost a leg on board ship requested help to emigrate to Australia to his mother. The £15 fare was granted.

At one time a child was brought in by police. A grandfather who had reported a lost child identified this child and on the back of the admission form, information of the identify was duly written. Later the child was transferred to the Infirmary as unknown. The grandfather complained and received apologies.

It was deemed sensible in 1908 for the Master and Matron to have a safe in their offices. There was a lot more petty cash being used by then and they should have it locked up and kept under control. The safes were supplied by Messrs. Fowle & Sullivan.

That year an inmate lost their temper and threw a chamber pot at a window. He or she ended up in court before the Magistrate and was sent to Wandsworth Prison.

The Master's Office was handling a lot more paperwork. A temporary clerk would help with the workload. The Local Government Board refused to pay and the salary could not be charged to the Metropolitan Common Poor Fund. An application was made to the London County Council, Head Office.

Second rate goods were still being sent to the workhouse. The following is a typical example:

1 gross mens stockings	4 cwt rice
1 gross womens stockings	12 mop heads
14lbs string	3 dozen bass brooms
2lbs sponges	6 dozen mens cord trousers
464lbs vegetables	15lbs Officers Joints (meat).

These poor quality goods were a constant source of aggravation to the Master. The traders knew only too well that second rate goods would be rejected, it was a waste of time and energy issuing them in the first place. Contracts were often lost.

A reward of £5 was offered for the apprehension of the person who abandoned an unknown male child aged about two years old in a garden in Streatham. This offer was almost unheard of at that time. Records do not show if the reward was successful.

A number of rooms in one block were given over to married couples over 60 years of age. They had to produce a marriage certificate; if they were not able to the Master had to apply for one. The married couples only had separate sleeping accommodation. The Master suggested that they take their meals together in a part of the womens dining hall side. The breakfast and supper would be taken at the usual times but the dinner, 15 to 20 minutes earlier. Suitable tables to be provided. The Guardians duly agreed.

Inmates would discharge themselves as and when they felt like it, only to return again soon after. This caused a lot of paperwork, not to mention time, and so after several discharges and returns they were detained for a period of 168 hours under Section 4 of the Poor Law Act 1899. It had the desired effect of making sure there was a good reason for their discharge. The workhouse was only too pleased to give inmates their discharge so long as it would mean they would have a permanent place in the community.

The police brought in a woman that the workhouse said was drunk. The police denied it. So she was admitted and improved the next day. They told the police she should not have been brought to the workhouse and in future they should charge her at the police station and she should go before the magistrate.

At one time the Guardians tried to get the father of a child of a single pregnant woman to pay 5/- towards upkeep. This was a hopeless task as most single women did not know who the father was.

A chimney sweep was appointed. His wages were £14 per annum.

In July 1901 a Bradbury Boot Machine was purchased. It was an All-round AAl repairing machine costing £7. This must have been a good investment as the number of boots to be mended was always on the increase.

The following report by the Master regarding mealtimes in the Old School Block show how seriously supervision was taken:-

I have arranged that when one of the Officers in the Old School Block and 'D' Block is off duty the other is to have her meals sent from the Mess-room, this arrangement will ensure that each of the children's quarters will at no time be left without an Officer in charge and when the Officers are taking their day's leave they are not to go off duty until the morning's work is done (about 9.30) unless under special circumstances sanctioned by the Master or the Matron; and the keys of the bath taps are at all times to be kept in the safe custody of the Officers and at no time are they to be used unless in the presence, or under the supervision of the Officer in charge.

Miss Jackson, Assistant Matron, attended a Committee Meeting regarding her recent sick leave. They suspected she was married. She was granted leave six weeks ago, and the Medical Officer reported that her arm was still very swollen and she was unfit for work at the present time.

Miss Jackson was asked by the Chairman of the Committee whether it was a fact that she was married, but she ridiculed the idea; she was then requested to withdraw and on again entering the room was asked by the Chairman whether she still adhered to the statement that she was unmarried, and she replied she did, but upon a Certificate of Marriage being produced, she admitted that the Certificate in question was correct.

It would appear from the Certificate that Miss Jackman was married on 12th August 1906, at Reading, to Mr F. J. Hicks, the Superintendent of Out-door Labour at the Workhouse, and it also appears that every month since this date she has signed the Monthly Wages Book as "L. Jackman"

Your Committee, after carefully considering the case, suspended Miss Jackman (Mrs Hicks) until the meeting of the Board, and recommended:-

(a) That her appointment as Assistant Matron at the Workhouse do forthwith cease.

(b) That advertisements be issued, inviting applications for the appointment.

18 October 1906

Report of Sub-Committee with reference to the application of the Master of the Workhouse for extra assistance in his Office and Stores.

Present:- Mr. Sullivan (in the Chair); Lieut. E. A. Sanders, R.N.,
*   Messrs Couzens, Palmer, and Rees*

Reporting -

(a) That your Committee considered the question referred to them and, in accordance therewith, the following entry in the Master's Report and Journal, viz.:-

I beg to ask if the Committee will kindly allow me some additional assistance in the office and stores; the work in these departments has so much increased that it is more than the present staff can do with efficiency, and within reasonable hours. During the past month there have been 650 admissions and 597 discharges; this of itself makes a large amount of clerical work, and since the opening of the St. James' Branch, and the Infirm Wards a the Workhouse, the work in the stores department has very much increased. I would suggest that a second clerk be engaged, say at £30 per annum with residential allowances, to assist in the offices. This would relieve the Assistant Master of some of the office work, and he would be able to devote more time to the receipt and issuing of stores.

That the following information was also furnished your Sub-Committee:-

	Year Ended Michaelmas 1900	Year Ended Michaelmas 1906
Average weekly admissions	94	133
Average weekly discharges	93	133
Total Admissions during year	4,879	6,923
Total discharges during year	4,867	6,819
Average number in Workhouse	633	950

That in view of the increase in the number of Inmates in the Workhouse and Branch Workhouse, and the fact that a large number of Infirm Inmates are now accommodated in the Workhouse, your Sub-Committee recommend - That a Second Master's Clerk be appointed, at a salary of £30 per annum, with residential allowances. Report of Sub-Committee with reference to the application of the Master of the Workhouse for extra assistance in his Office and Stores.

Also that year the Committee considered an application by Dr Dodson, Medical Officer:-

That your Committee considered the application of Dr Dodson, Medical Officer of the Workhouse, that he should be supplied with a Deputy.

It would appear that all new admissions have to be examined by the Medical Officer, and classified in writing, for work, diet, &c., between the hours of 9 and 10 o'clock in the morning, and it often happens that on Monday and Tuesday mornings there are sometimes 70 cases to be examined, and as this cannot be done by 10 o'clock, it interferes with the work of the Establishment.

In view of the increase of numbers, and the class of Inmates at Garratt Lane Workhouse, your Committee are of opinion that on certain mornings of the week it is necessary that the Medical Officer should have some assistance to enable him to cope with the work.

If the proposed Deputy is appointed, it will do away with the additional fees at present paid for assistance in Midwifery cases, and with regard to cases in Infirm Wards, &c., will always ensure the prompt attendance of a Medical man in the event of an Inmate being suddenly taken ill, as both the Medical Officer and Deputy will be in communication with the Workhouse per telephone.

Dr R. C. Kirkby, of Earlsfield Road, has acted in a private capacity as Deputy for some time, and understands the duties; and your Committee recommend - That subject to the sanction of the Local Government Board, Dr. R. C. Kirkby be appointed Deputy Medical Officer of the Workhouse, at a remuneration at the rate of £50 per annum, and that he be required to attend the Workhouse at such times as he may be called upon - to administer anaesthetics, and act during the absence of the Medical Officer on leave.

In November 1906 the Guardians were having difficulties with the parents who had children in District Schools. The following report shows the problems:-

That attention had been drawn to the number of children sent to the District Schools who, immediately after admission, have to be brought back to the Intermediate Schools to be discharged to their parents.

Upon the last admission day a child who had been resident in the Intermediate School for over a month, and therefore could hardly be classed as one of the "ins and outs", was sent to Anerley, but before the Officer had left the school, a telephone message was received, stating that the parent was taking her discharge, and the child must be brought back.

It would almost appear, on the face of it, that certain parents, the moment their children are sent to Anerley, decide to take their discharge and then return to the Workhouse the same evening, so that their children shall remain at the Intermediate School.

In view of the expense incurred in taking and bringing back children from the District Schools your Committee are of opinion something should be done to put a stop to this.

At the present time, all the Guardians can do is to require the parents to give 168 hours notice of intention to take their discharge, and as many give notice immediately upon admission, it allows inmates to go out every week.

Your Committee accordingly recommend - That the Local Government Board be asked to advise the Guardians as to what steps can be taken to deal with the cases which are so frequently "in and out".

The parents were obviously frightened they would not see their children again, and perhaps could be "lost in the system" of the Local Government. It can be seen that the problem was not solved as a year later the same scenarios existed:-

The Matron brought to the notice of the Committee that between 23rd November and today, 82 children were sent to Anerley and other schools, and 80 brought back for discharge.

With regard to the foregoing report, under present arrangements, the parents of children (who, perhaps, have been in the Intermediate Schools for weeks and are then sent to the District School) suddenly make up their minds to go out, and the consequence is children have to be brought back to be discharged with them.

Often the parents return to the Workhouse the same evening and the children are again transferred to Intermediate School and after a short stay, may be again sent to the District Schools and perhaps after a few days brought back to be discharged with their parents.

In October 1907 the Medical Officer reported as follows:-

Since my last report, the number of children in "D" Block has increased and this morning there are 20 mothers with children, and 30 children without mothers.

As regards children generally, there are in the workhouse:

Under 3 years	*56*
Between 3 and 8 years	*36*
Between 8 and 1 years	*62*

At Branch Workhouse:

Between 3 and 5 years	*50*

Of School age, there were:

In Intermediate School	*150*
In Workhouse	*98*
	248

In January 1909 the Special Visiting Committee investigated the arrangements for the sale of firewood and the receipt of monies from same, and found that at the Workhouse the Labour Master was allowed to have entire control of the issue of firewood and the receipt of monies.

The Special Committee recommended with a view to greater check:-

(a) *That one "Wood Delivery" Book should be kept in the Master's Office at the Garratt Lane Workhouse and another at the Assistant Master's Office at the Branch Workhouse and that all entries should be made by a member of the Master's Office Staff at the Workhouse and by the Assistant Master at the Branch Workhouse.*

(b) *That two sets of "Wood Delivery "Books be kept at each Establishment for use in alternate weeks, in order that when one book is away from the premises the other book can be used to ensure that a proper delivery ticket is always available for immediate use.*

(c) *That "Wood Stocks Book" be provided for both Establishments, to be balanced up weekly and to be kept in like manner to that recommended in (a).*

(d) *That books be provided for the Labour Master at the Workhouse and the General Officer at the Branch Workhouse, in which shall be entered daily a record of the number of deliveries made to customers. (This book will show at the end of the week the total production and its disposal and the totals will be entered into the Stock Books referred to in (c).*

(e) *That books be provided for each Establishment in which the Gate Porters shall enter full particulars as to all firewood leaving the premises.*

Your Committee adopted the foregoing suggestions and recommend them for adoption by the Board.

In December 1907 the Committee were having to cope with an inmate named Charles Dickens:-

That your Committee considered the letter from the Local Government Board, transmitting copy of a Memorandum made by one of the Board's Officers, after an interview with Chas. Dickens, on 12th November, viz.:-

Charles Dickens complained that, suffering from an affection of the eyes, he was sent by the Medical Officer of the Garratt Lane Workhouse to the Moorfields Hospital, and that on his return to the Workhouse on Saturday night (November 9th), although possessed of a Relieving Officer's Order, he was refused admission by the Gate Porter, acting on the instructions of the Master, and relegated to the Casual Wards. C. Dickens said something about a "call over" being given as the reason for the refusal to admit him. On his leaving the Casual Ward this morning, he came here to report the matter to the Board.

The Medical Officer reported as follows:-

Charles Dickens was first admitted to the Workhouse in 1902. He had some time before, lost the sight of one eye by accident, the other was normal. Being otherwise strong and healthy he was sent to the Test House at Kensington on every admission, until that Institution was closed for able-bodied men.

Since that, now about 4 years ago, Dickens has practically lived in the Workhouse and deterrent work has had no effect upon him.

On several occasions he has told me that if he could only get a glass eye he could get employment, and these, to the number of six, have been supplied by the Guardians, but in spite of this he always returned to the Workhouse within a very short time.

The Statement, that I send him to Moorfields Hospital, is absolutely untrue, the facts being as follows - the Labour Master, as the best authority, tells me that Dickens anticipated that the "Call over" Committee would order him out of the Workhouse, and so on the morning of the 1st inst. He applied to me for spectacles. On questioning him he admitted that he did not require them to do his work with, but said that years ago he had some from a hospital, and he would like another pair. As I did not consider them necessary, I told him he had better go outside and then he could go to any hospital he liked. He has been for some time under the seven days' detention order, and that morning he gave notice and left the house on the morning of the 8th inst. (If I had considered it necessary, or advised him to go to a hospital, I should have asked the Master to discharge him on the 1st inst. As a matter of urgency.)

When he next applied for admission, the Guardians; "order" for Dickens to be sent to the Casual Ward had come into force and he was duly directed there. He stayed there two nights, did his work, and did not complain, or ask to see me. The Superintendent says that at that time Dickens was not wearing spectacles, although he believes he had a pair with him.

Since that he has not been seen, either at the Workhouse or the Casual Ward.

Between 3rd December, 1902 and 8th November, 1907, Dickens was admitted and discharged no less than 74 times.

On 31st October, 1907, Dickens appeared before your Committee upon a re-admission, and was unable to inform them when or where he last had a residence, al

I he could state was he had been "staying anywhere" and as Dickens seemed to regard the Workhouse as a resting place for the remainder of his days, the Committee felt that it was unfair to the Ratepayers of this Union that a man who was to all intents a "wayfarer" and "wanderer! Should be kept in comfort in the Workhouse, and they decided that Dickens should be accommodated in the Casual Wards, which were obviously intended for the reception of destitute wayfarers and wanderers.

In January 1909 the Committee had to deal with the problems in the Inmates Clothing Store:-

The Committee considered the written explanation of the Gate Porter and Portress as to the dirty condition of some of the bags of clothing in the Inmates clothing Store and in which regret was expressed that cause for complaint had arisen.

Mr & Mrs Everdell were called before the Committee and the Chairman impressed on both the necessity of using greater care with regard to the clothing.

That in connection with the foregoing, it was mentioned that the duties of the Gate Porter and Portress had considerably increased and the question of their duties was referred to a Sub-Committee consisting of Mrs Worthy and Messrs. T. W. Palmer and Sullivan, for consideration.

That Your Committee are of opinion that, in future, all Inmates Clothing which has been in Store continuously for two years and upwards should be destroyed and it is recommended accordingly.

Also that month the Master had to deal with a drunken woman:-

Mary Husher, who was charged at the Police Court with breaking a window in the Porter's Lodge, as the Porter refused her admission on account of her drunken condition.

From enquiries, it appears that she was drunk and shouting and if admitted would have disturbed the other inmates and the Porter, by the Master's direction, handed her over to the care of a Police Constable.

As the woman was handed over to the Police there was no likelihood, as described in the press, "of the woman being left to die in the street on a snowy night" and your Committee entirely support the Master's action.

The following three entries in the visitors; book gave the Master and Guardians something to be proud of:-

20th September 1909
I have just visited the Wandsworth Workhouse, conducted by the Master. I specially wish to thank him for his great kindness and to express here my great surprise in finding buildings so clean and so hygienic. I shall carry to France the best impression of an English Workhouse and I shall be very pleased to dissipate the legends which obtain in my country on this subject.
(Signed) PAUL THIBAULT, Professor.
Chateaurox.

9th October 1909
I have much pleasure in saying that I have visited the Workhouse with Mr Rees and in recording my greatest satisfaction with all the arrangements, should think that

everybody can learn from this excellent example. Foreigners like myself, who are interested in poor relief, can take with them a great many valuable and new ideas.

(Signed) Dr FRITZ-SIMON, assessor.

Frankfort-on-Main

1st October 1910

At the invitation of Mr Winfield we have visited the Workhouse and Schools and are pleased to say that we found the comfort of the Inmates well cared for, the place clean and tidy. Great credit is due to the Master and Matron for the manner in which the places are managed.

(Signed) G. WYRER A. WRIGHT

C.E. MASON

Two pieces of Estamine were rejected by the Master. Estamine is an open woven fabric used for making sieves for flour.

Here is a list of the clothing issued to Officers for their work in the Institution:

Female		Male	
OFFICE	WORKHOUSE	OFFICE	WORKHOUSE
Labour Mistress, Laundry Superintendent, Attendants, Portress	2 drill dresses, 1 serge dress, 8 linen aprons, 8 collars, 8 cuffs, 1 pair boots, 1 shawl (issued when requisite)	Indoor Officers such as Labour Master, Gate Porter, Attendant, etc	1 cloth jacket and waistcoat, 2 pairs trousers, 1 light serge jacket, 1 cap (issued every year) 1 overcoat (every two years)
Assistant Matron	As above	Coachmen	1 cloth jacket and waistcoat, 2 pairs trousers, 1 light serge jacket, 1 cap, 2 pairs gloves, 1 overcoat (issued yearly
Laundry Superintendent	As above	Cooks and Assistant Cooks	6 sets overalls, 12 aprons, 6 caps
Washers	4 Aprons	Laundrymen	4 sets overalls

In December 1909 the Master received:-

Received from the Managers of St. John's Schools, Usk Road, 20 School Desks - a few of these I have had cleaned up and they can be used in the old School Block and the remainder with slight alteration can be made into very good garden seats.

1st July, 1909

That your Sub-Committee present the following statistics as the result of their enquiries, viz.:-

MEN

	Between 20 and 30 years of age	Between 31 and 40 years of age	Between 41 and 50 years of age	Between 51 and 59 years of age	Total
Able-bodied	2	8	30	31	70
Not able-bodied	2	5	9	28	44
Feeble Minded	1	0	3	9	13
	4	13	42	68	127

WOMEN

	Under 20 years of of age	Between 21 and 30 years of age	Between 31 and 40 years of age	Between 41 and 50 years of age	Between 51 and 59 years of age	Total
Able-bodied	0	18	27	25	7	77
Not able-bodied	1	10	8	5	14	38
Feeble Minded	0	3	2	3	0	8
	1	31	37	33	21	123

With regard to the able-bodied Men and Women, the following particulars are given:-

MEN			WOMEN		
Single		13	Single		*22
Married	Wife only chargeable in workhouse	4	Married	Husband only chargeable	
Married	Wife and children chargeable	16	Married	Husband and children chargeable	14
Married	Children only chargeable Married wife outside	8	Married	Only self chargeable	4
Married	Wife outside	16	Married	Only Children chargeable	15
Widowers	Self only chargeable	9	Widows	Self only chargeable	2
Widowers	With Children chargeable	4	Widows	With Children chargeable	16
		70			77
				"Only self chargeable	5
				With 1 Child chargeable	5
				With 2 Children chargeable	7
				With 3 Children chargeable	3
				With four Children chargeable	1
				With five Children chargeable	1
					22

With regard to the cases reported as Feeble Minded, the following particulars are given:-

MEN			WOMEN		
Single		6	Single		4
		4	Single	With Children	2
Married	Wife chargeable	0	Married	Husband chargeable	1
Married	With Children chargeable	1			
Married	Wife living outside	3			
Widowers	Self only chargeable	3	Widows	With children	1
		13			8

(e) That your Sub-Committee wish to point out with what aptness many of the Inmates seemed to have (immediately they had the least trouble) adapted themselves to the Workhouse life as a resting place, as the following examples show:-

A.Ashton, aged 59, a bricklayer, Wife maintaining herself outside, been in the Workhouse 12 months, has not been out once to look for a job, in fact could not tell the Committee when he last had a job.

F.Budgett, aged 43, groom, Wife and 2 Children chargeable was granted a fortnight's leave without wife and Children, to seek work, but only remained out two days, evidently preferring the Workhouse to looking for work.

W .Bartlett, aged 47, engineer (Wife left him some time ago), has been in and out of the Workhouse for some time, was in one situation 18 years, the latter portion of which he had a salary of £5 per week, yet, very shortly after losing his situation entirely through his own fault, was obliged to enter the Workhouse.

H. Bradbury, aged 51, labourer, Wife and 2 Children chargeable, been in and out over six years, was allowed out for one month without Wife and family to look for work, but only remained out a day or two, both he and his Wife think that a widowed Sister who has means ought to keep them, and as she refuses, back they came to the Workhouse.

E. Cooper, aged 53, labourer, Widower, no Children, has been in and out of the Workhouse for years, but not once in the last 18 months, notwithstanding he has been on task work the whole period, and, as he has had no home for years, he was informed that he would be recommended to be accommodated in the Casual Ward.

A. Coombes, aged 56, grocer (separated from Wife), has been in Workhouse since December, 1908, and not once been out to look for work; has grown up Children residing at Farnham, and when it was suggested that possibly his Children might be able to find him employment at Farnham, said - he was a Londoner bred and born and did not think the country air would agree with him. Possibly the reason is, if he found work he would have to contribute toward his Wife's support

Charles Louis, aged 46, a cook, married, and Wife have been chargeable about two months. It was suggested that as they had no children, surely either one of *them could get work, but the reply was he couldn't get work as a cook and his Wife had never done any work; but the facts appear to be that they have been living on a relative who died about three months ago; the Wife was told that it was about time she started to do some work.*

Robert Windsor, aged 54, married, tailor, been chargeable since October last, candidly admitted his Wife and Children had left him, and wouldn't have any more to do with him.

(f) *That your Sub-Committee impressed on many the necessity of trying to obtain work, and the following were told they could apply to the Workhouse Committee, with a view of granting them leave without their families for a period, so as to be free to seek employment, as your Sub-Committee know how difficult it is for persons to make a fresh start having children to look after, the first week or two, viz:-*

Christopher Adams, aged 41, One child chargeable.
Frank Budgett, aged 43, Wife and 2 Children chargeable
Robert Hewitt, aged 32, Wife and 3 Children chargeable
Edmund Lock, aged 45, Widower, 3 Children chargeable
James Leach, aged 45, Widower, 5 Children chargeable
Arthur Perrin, aged 44, Wife and 2 children chargeable
Edward Pyne, aged 43, Wife and 2 children chargeable
George Rowland, aged 36, four Children, chargeable.
Thomas Radcliffe, aged 43, Four Children chargeable
John Smith, aged 36, Wife and 5 Children chargeable
Charles Steer, aged 56, Two Children chargeable
John Smith, aged 34, Four Children chargeable
Joseph Skerry, aged 39, Wife and 4 Children chargeable
Walter Simpson, aged 54, Wife chargeable
Eliza Matthews, aged 48, Four Children chargeable
Emma Newman, aged 42, Five Children Chargeable
Kate Stock, aged 31, Three Children chargeable
Eliza Collier, aged 33, Three Children chargeable.
Lucy Morris, aged 34, Six Children chargeable.
Mary A. Bennett, aged 28, Two Children chargeable
Emma Bridge, aged 35, Two Children chargeable

Peter Caffery, aged 33, and disabled, was to be sent to a home for Disabled Soldiers at Portsmouth. He needed an attendant to accompany him and sanction of the Local Government Board was required for the expenditure.

The Visitors' Book was submitted, and contained the following entries:-

17th September 1910

(a) *I have been over the Workhouse today. One reads a lot nearly everywhere in condemnation of the mixed General Workhouse, but when one sees the admirable organisation here, and the obvious happiness of the Inmates, surely it cannot be such a bad place after all. It certainly cannot, if the Master is as kind to all as he has been to me.*

(Signed) W. T. GREIG

(Translation)

8th September 1910

(b) I have been agreeably surprised to see what is done in England for the care of the Poor, and I cordially congratulate the Mater of Wandsworth Workhouse on the care taken for the welfare of the Poor under his supervision.

(signed) E. A. LEBLANE, Professor
Flers, France

BOARDING OUT

The Guardians did all they could to find situations or apprenticeships for teenagers. There was a Boarding-Out Committee who did a lot of good work for their benefit. The following reports show the varied situations and concerns for their future.

(13) That the Master reported as follows:-

John Jacobs, aged 15 and William Trimby, aged 15, were sent to situations at Twewerchy, South Wales, on the 15th October; Alexander Mayhew, aged 16, and James Banks, aged 16, were sent to the same village on 27th October. All the boys that I have sent down into Wales appear to be doing very well indeed, and I have received an application for two more boys, and I hope to have them ready to go during the next week.

And your Committee desire to record their appreciation of the trouble taken by the Master in obtaining situations for Lads.

29 March 1906

(13) That your Committee had before them the case of a lad named John Humphreys, aged 15 years, formerly on the Training-ship "Exmouth", who, six weeks after being placed out, has had to return to the Workhouse.

It would appear that though the lad was on the Training-ship for three years, yet he never was taken on the Tender for sea experience prior to his discharge; consequently, when he was shipped on a small coaster of 65 tons, the lad was sea-sick for a week, and when he was paid off naturally did not want to go for another voyage on such a craft.

Your Committee are of opinion that after three years' training, the ship Authorities ought to have been able to have placed him on a larger craft, and as the Lad still desires to go to sea, it is recommended -

That the Metropolitan Asylums Board be requested to arrange for his re-admission to the ship, with a view to another berth being found for him

(13) That your Committee had under consideration the case of Sidney Elliott, age 15. The Lad some time ago volunteered to go to the Training Ship "Exmouth", but the Father refused to let him join, and the Master of the Workhouse recently obtained a situation for him in Wales but again the Father refused consent.

The father, Arthur Elliott, has been in and out of the Workhouse for some years, and his character is not satisfactory, and his answer to the Committee was "that he should do as he liked with the Boy."

Unless something is done the Lad will be continually in and out of the Workhouse and practically become a loafer.

Having regard to all the circumstances, your Committee are of opinion that Arthur Elliott is not a fit and proper person to have control of the Lad, and accordingly recommend-

(a) That in pursuance of the power vested in the Guardians by the Poor Law Acts (1889 and 1899), Sidney Elliott, aged 15, be placed under the control of the Guardians until he attains the age of 18 years.

(b) That the Lad be sent to a situation, to be found by the Master of the Workhouse.

Reporting -

(1) That Reports as to Apprentices, Children in Schools, &c. were submitted and your Committee gave the necessary instructions and entered same in the Book provided.

(2) That with regard to Apprentices brought before your Committee at the end of the first and second years of their apprenticeships, it is recommended-

That, in the following cases, instalments of premiums be paid, viz.:

Name of Apprentice	Age	Name of Master	Address	Trade	Amount of Instalment	Remarks
Hunter, Robert	16	Ludkin, Robert Hill	33, Wastdale Road, Forest Hill	Boot-maker	2nd instalment £3	Master & Lad attended before Committee
Norris, John Reginald Arthur	15	Eyles, Joseph Richard	26, Aldenham Road, Bushey, Herts	Boot-maker	2nd instalment £3	Master & Lad attended before Committee
Richards, Robert Alfred	15	Roach, Henry	The Saw Mills, Dunt's Hill Road, Earlsfield	Carpenter & Joiner	2nd instalment £3	Master & Lad attended before Committee
Reuss, William	15	Roach, Henry	The Saw Mills, Dunt's Hill Road, Earlsfield	Carpenter & Joiner	2nd instalment £3	Master & Lad attended before Committee
Sale, Frederick	17	Stanton, George Henry	197 Maple Road, Renge	Hairdresser	3rd and final instalment, £4	Master & Lad attended before Committee

Reporting -

(1) That Reports as to Apprentices, Children in Schools, &c. were submitted and your Committee gave the necessary instructions and entered same in the Book provided.

(2) That with regard to Apprentices brought before your Committee at the end of the second year of their apprenticeship, it is recommended-

That, in the following cases, instalments of premiums be paid, viz.:

Name of Apprentice	Age	Name of Master	Address	Trade	Amount of Instalment	Remarks
Batten, Thomas Henry	20	Henslick, Otto W.R.	10 Well Street, Cable Street, E.	Tailor and Breeches Maker	Third and final instalment £5	Lad attended before Committee
Plastow, William	16	Ost, Julian	42 Lordship Lane, East Dulwich	Hairdresser	Third and final instalment £4	Master and Lad attended before Committee

The several paragraphs having been taken seriatim, and carried, it was resolved-

That the acts, proceedings and recommendations of the Boarding-Out Committee, as submitted in the foregoing Report, be approved and adopted.

Reporting -

(1)   That Reports as to Apprentices, Children in Schools, &c., were submitted and your Committee gave the necessary instructions and entered same in the Book provided.

(2)   That a Report was received from the Metropolitan Association for Befriending Young Servants as to girls from this Union dealt with during the past six months, and the same was satisfactory.

(3)   That your Committee had before them an application from James Hudson, apprenticed to Mr F.J. Dean, Grocer, of 1, Alpha Road, Cross Road, Croydon, that his Indentures may be cancelled, to enable him to emigrate to Australia.

A letter was also received from Mr. Roberts, of South Norwood, who is arranging for a party of boys to sail for Australia shortly, stating that the lad was most anxious to go, that his master was willing for the Indentures to be cancelled, and asking the Guardians to agree to the proposal.

A communication was also received by telephone from Mr. Dean, stating that he considered it was the best thing for the boy, as the prospect of going to Australia had, apparently, unsettled him, and if the Guardians agreed to cancel Hudson's indentures, he, Mr Dean, would be willing to take another boy from the Schools, without premium; and, under all the circumstances of the case, it is recommended -

That the necessary steps be taken to cancel the Indentures, with the mutual consent of all parties concerned under the Seal of the Board.

(4)   That, with regard to Apprentices brought before your Committee at the end of the first and second years of their apprenticeship, it is recommended -

That in the following cases instalments of premium be paid, viz.:

Name of Apprentice	Age	Name of Master	Address	Trade	Amount of Instalment	Remarks
Rampton, William	17	Cook, John Henry	24, Hartfield Road, Wimbledon	Boot-maker	2nd instalment (£3)	Master and Boy attended before Committee
Cook, Joseph	16	Wright, Robert	6, High Street, Dulwich Village, S.E	Boot-maker	3rd and final instalment (£4)	Master and Boy attended before Committee

BUILDINGS

April 1900 A Cradle for window cleaning was bought for £2.5/-. Staples for each window cost 5/- each.

In September 1901 a "Calender" was purchased for the laundry. This was a major investment. Two inmates would work at each end of the machine. It had electrical heated rollers with tapes running through them that guided the items from beginning to end. Sheets, draw sheets and pillow cases would be put in one end wet and come out the other end dry, ironed and aired. It revolutionised the laundry drying process.

Early in 1901 a new bakery was built, the old bakery was to be utilised as an Engineers work shop. The cost was around £700.

In October of that year the Committee inspected the rooms at present occupied respectively, by the Matron and the Assistant Master and recommended -

"That the rooms on the ground floor be set apart for the use of the Master, and the suite of rooms on the first floor be set apart for the use of the Matron; that a bathroom be provided for the Master, by converting the present storeroom, adjoining the dining-room, for that purpose. That two bedsteads be provided for the use of the Matron and her daughter; also a carpet and hearthrug."

In January 1902 Hammocks were supplied to inmates when the Casual Wards were full and all the beds were taken.

The Harmonium in the Chapel was almost worn out. A second-hand Organ was to be purchased costing £120.

In 1902 the Guardians authorised the purchase of 100 yards of carpet and 12 hearth rugs as some of the officer's rooms were entirely without carpet and some were quite worn through.

Also in 1902 50 yards of American Cloth were ordered at 1./9d a yard to cover cushions on Wicker Chairs for the inmates.

The Branch Workhouse, St James', needed attention to buildings by 1908. There would have to be a major overhaul of Fire Proofing and Fire Escapes to bring it up to date. They had a wood chopping shed which needed a concrete floor. The Officers' room for relaxation needed papering, they could choose paper up to 9d per piece (roll). St James' had a chapel and the Guardians decided it should have a small organ. An American one was purchased for £12.10/-.

In December 1908 there was a report on central heating equipment giving workload, and staff available to manage it.

Present: Lieut. E.A.Sanders, RN (in the Chair); Messrs, Barns, Chown and Fowle.

Reporting -

(a) *That the Plant to be looked after consists of:-*

3 steam engines (one not working)
2 steam boilers
1 hot water boiler
10 circulating heaters
4 circulating calorifiers
11 domestic service heaters
2 domestic service calorifiers
38 radiators, and 24 others formed of pipes in various rooms, &c.

Kitchen
5 coppers
1 hot plate
1 fish fryer
1 potato steamer
Steam traps, steam valves, and other fittings

Bakehouse machinery
About 36 baths
Flushing cisterns (about 100 w.c's)
The heating apparatus, gas and water services in Blocks "G" and "H"
including 4 baths in Block "H"

The machinery in the Laundry

Fire hydrants

Casual Wards
2 hot water boilers
2 hot water storage cylinder
5 baths

Branch Workhouse
2 steam boilers
2 hot water boilers
1 hot water domestic heater
2 hot water storage cylinders
Heating apparatus
Cooking apparatus
Fire alarms, &c.
Fire hydrants
Electric bells, &c.

(b) *That when the present Engineer was appointed in September 1890, he was provided with an Assistant Engineer and Stoker and the staff is the same today.*

(c) *That since the appointment of the Engineer in 1890, the following additions have been made to his work-*

(1) The new and improved machinery in the Bakehouse.

(2) The boilers, radiators, and pipes throughout the Intermediate Schools.

(3) The boilers and cooking apparatus, radiators and fittings generally, throughout St James' Road Branch Workhouse.

(4) The pipes, radiators, and fittings in the temporary Buildings to accommodate Able-bodied Women at the Workhouse.

(5) The pipes, radiators, hot water boiler, and fittings in the Temporary Iron Buildings for Infirmary Patients at the Workhouse.

(6) The provision of up-to-date machinery (more than double the old), and the provision of Hot Air Drying Rooms at the Workhouse Laundry, also improved hot water services.

(d) That it must be borne in mind that the boilers, and most of the pipes, heaters and fittings throughout the Establishment have been in use for about 25 years, and the repairs and renewals of same get greater each year.

(e) That it has been found necessary to engage a Fitter occasionally to enable the Engineer to cope with the work, as, although he has the assistance of Inmates, still, such help is not very efficient and reliable, and continued assistance from qualified Inmates cannot be relied on.

The Chapel·WANDSWORTH·AND·CLAPHAM·UNION·New Workhouse
T·W·ALDWINCKLE   ARCHITECT.

Photo-Lithographed & Printed by James Akerman, 6, Queen Square, W.C.

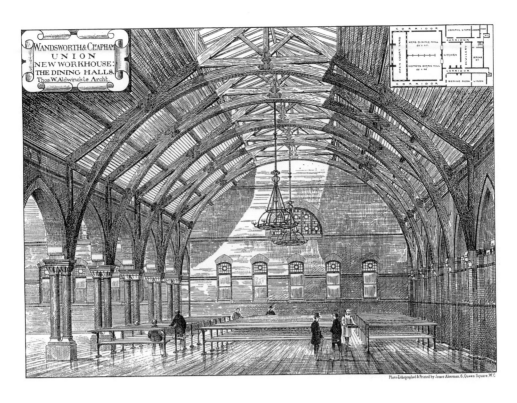

(f) That when the proposed Iron Buildings are erected to accommodate Children from the Intermediate Schools, the work of the Engineer will be still further increased as there will be the boilers and heating apparatus to be looked after and kept in repair.

(g) That the Staffs at the several Institutions consist of:-

    (1) For Workhouse, Branch Workhouse, and Intermediate Schools-
        1Engineer
        1 Assistant Engineer and Stoker.

    (2) For Infirmary-
        1 Engineer
        1 Assistant Engineer and Stoker
        1 Stoker

    (3) For Tooting Home-
        1 Engineer
        1 Assistant Engineer and Stoker

(h) That at present the Assistant Engineer and Stoker is on duty two Sundays out of three, and for this is allowed one-and-half working days a fortnight, which is lost time to the Engineer.

(i) That if another Assistant Engineer is appointed arrangements can be made for the Officers to be on duty only one Sunday out of three, and the time now lost on week days will be utilised in repairs, and, further in the event of the Engineer being absent on annual leave, or from some other cause there will be an Officer capable of carrying out the duties during his absence.

(j)   Your Sub-Committee strongly recommend that a first Assistant Engineer and Fitter be employed at a remuneration of 40s per week.

In March 1910 the following report of the Engineer was submitted with regard to the recent tests of coal:-

That the following report of the Engineer was submitted with regard to the recent tests of coal, viz.:-

Kind	Average Daily Consumption	Percentage of Ashes	Price per Ton	Result
50 tons Derbyshire Bright Screenings	9.3 tons	16.5%	11s 8d average daily cost, £5 8s 6d	Coal totally unsuitable. Very dirty and bituminous, of very uneven quality, indicating an indifferent mixture of various coals. High percentage of ashes, with low calorific value as found by public analyst. Unable to keep steam at proper pressure
10 tons Leicester D.S. Nuts	8.5 tons	11%	15s9d average daily cost £6 13s 10d	Better coal than above, quick burning with a large amount of sulphur, but unsuitable owing to heavy black smoke.
Mapperley Nuts	6.75 tons	12%	16s 3d average daily cost £5 9s 8d	Good coal of even quality, giving plenty of steam but large quantity of smoke, and therefore unsuitable.
14 tons Colliery Slack	7.2 tons	9.2%	14s 9d average daily cost £5 6s 2d	Most suitable of all coals tried. Steam easily kept. Comparative freedom from smoke, very even in quality, with very ordinary percentage of ashes.
House Screenings	6.18 to 7.3 tons	-	13s 3d average daily cost, £4 16s 9d	This coal deteriorated very greatly in quality towards the last, at times causing great difficulty in getting steam. From experience, not to be depended on.

I would suggest that a clause be inserted in the Contract stating the minimum calorific value of the coal to be supplied, say 12,400 B.T.Units, so that some hold could be kept to maintain the proper grade of coal. I also ask for permission to make a further trial of Colliery Slack, should time permit.

And your Committee are of opinion that the request of the Engineer should be complied with, and that in so far as the Contract for the supply of Coal to the Infirmary is concerned, the item "Steam Coal" should be omitted, and fresh Tenders obtained when the full result of the tests being made by the Engineer are known.

That your Committee considered the letter form the Local Government Board, transmitting copy of a Report made by the Assistant Inspector after a visit to the Workhouse Laundry, viz.:-

LOCAL GOVERNMENT BOARD INSPECTOR'S REPORT	REPORT OR RECOMMENDATION OF COMMITTEE
WANDSWORTH UNION (GARRATT LANE) WORKHOUSE LAUNDRY I have inspected this Laundry, accompanied by one of His Majesty's Inspectors of Factories, Miss Tracey. In order that the Laundry may comply with the requirements of the Factories Act, I would suggest the following improvements:-	
(a) Six Hydros. - Provide covers of wire netting or some similar material, such covers to be hinged or otherwise attached to the machines and always kept closed while the hydros are in motion. The spindles should also be fenced where they are not already enclosed in sheaths.	(a) It may be desirable though not absolutely necessary for covers to be provided to the Hydros, &c., and the Master was instructed to get prices for providing the necessary covers, &c.
(b) Collar-machine - Provide more efficient guard. I am advised that the present fixed guard would not avert an accident.	(b) It is not considered that any further protection is necessary.
(c) Stove - The Factory Inspector recommends that either this stove should be removed elsewhere or that a wooden screen, in three removable parts, lined with asbestos, should be provided. She considered this would protect the workers from the heat of the stove, and at the same time still permit of airing being carried on round the stove within the screen.	(c) It is not possible, neither is it desirable, to remove the stove elsewhere as suggested; neither is it considered necessary to provide screens to keep the heat off the Inmate workers.
(Signed) H. K. NISBET 3rd March, 1019	

Report on The Laundry and Boilers that service it:-

The combined report of the Master and Engineer was also considered, viz.:-

PARTICULARS re STEAM BOILERS SUBMITTED TO SUB-COMMITTEE
9TH NOVEMBER 1910

The present plant was laid down when the Institution was opened about the year 1885, and at that time the certified accommodation of the Workhouse was about 600 or just over that number, but during the past 10 or 12 years additions have been made so that the number of Inmates accommodated here at the present time is about 900. Besides this increased number at the Workhouse the Intermediate School has been built, the Branch Workhouse opened and the accommodation at Tooting Home increased.

When the plant was first installed no doubt it was ample for the then requirements of the Institution, as at that time it only had to do the washing and provide hot water and heating for the Workhouse as it was then; now we are doing the laundry work for over 2,200 Inmates and Officers or nearly four times the number than when the place was first opened (and this will be considerably increased when we take the washing from the new Infirmary), and the additions that have been made to the building from time to time has caused a much larger quantity of steam to be required for the heating apparatus and hot water plant.

Up to about eight years ago we were able to manage with one boiler at work and one at rest for cleaning and repairs, and we used to change them about every three months, but the work has gradually increased until up to the present time we are obliged to run both boilers together for about nine months out of the 12, which makes it very difficult to carry out the necessary scaling and repairs, and the boilers having to run for such a long time without a break, they get so badly encrusted with scale that the fires have to be forced to get the sufficient quantity of steam - hence a larger consumption of coal

While this matter of the boilers is being considered, we would suggest that on the grounds of economy as well as utility, the Committee couple with it a water softening plant for steam and laundry purposes.

(Signed) R. OLIVER (Master)

(Signed) THOS. ALDWORTH (Engineer)

From the foregoing it will be seen that the apparent cause of the increased consumption of coal was the boilers being so badly encrusted with scale that the additional fuel had to be used in order to obtain a sufficient supply of steam.

It appears to your Sub-Committee that this wastage of coal will continue unless more boilers are provided, as under the present system it is impossible to have the boilers cleaned out regularly as they should be, and in the opinion of your Sub-Committee the question of providing more steam power should be considered and dealt with as expeditiously as possible, and with this view they submit the following schemes:-

SCHEME A
That the Clerk of Works or an Architect be instructed to prepare a rough sketch plan for the provision and installation of one or more boilers in the present Boiler House of greater capacity than the present ones, also showing what alterations will be necessary to the buildings, so that the same may be submitted to the Board for approval.

SCHEME B
That two new Boilers of a large type be placed in the Stoneyard, so as to relieve the present Boilers of all work other than that of the Laundry.

I have drawn up Rules for the guidance of each Officer, and submit them for the approval of the committee.

For those cases requiring to be frequently moved, three Merlin (wheeled) Chairs are at once necessary - the cost is about £3.5/- each.

On the 25th April cases were transferred from "B" Block Infirm Ward and the same day I notified Dr Neal that we could receive cases in batches of a dozen. Up to now 36 have arrived, making with those from "B" Block a total of 70; tomorrow more are to come from the Infirmary, so that I expect very shortly the whole accommodation will be utilised.

The arrangements appear to be working smoothly and well.

In May 1905 "A" Block opened for the Aged and Infirm and the following is the Medical Officer's report:-

In accordance with the instructions of last committee, "A" Block having been emptied of able-bodied Inmates, has been adapted for aged and infirm cases to relieve the pressure at the Infirmary.

The following plan was adopted as regards accommodation:-

On the top floor, 40 beds	*for those who are able to get about and can go to Ground floor for meals.*
On the middle floor, 30 beds	*for those unable to get up, and whose meals will be served in bed.*
On the ground floor, 25 beds	*for those who get up during the day; the beds here occupy about half the ward, the remainder being used for meals for occupants of this and top floor.*

Total 95 beds

There will probably be a modification of the arrangement of beds to meet the class of cases received.

The staff is as follows:-
1 Charge Attendant
1 Assistant Attendant (on day duty)
2 Assistant Attendants (for night duty)

The Charge Attendant and Assistant for day duty have been engaged, the former at £40 per annum, rising to £45 per annum, and the latter at £32 per annum, with board, lodging, washing and uniform.

The two Assistant Attendants for night duty have been engaged at 28/- per week and uniform but non-resident.

As Charge Attendant, Mr Green, who has had the care of the Infirm men in "B" Block and who has now been transferred to "A" Block, has been selected, as he has proved a thoroughly efficient and reliable Officer.

As Assistant Attendant for Day Duty, W. Draydon, who has just finished his service in the Medical Staff Corps, has been employed.

As Assistant Attendants for night duty I have employed - Thomas Sykes, who has had experience in Asylum and Prison Infirmary and who appears to be a capable Officer; and G. Haddon, late Labour Master.

The uniform required will be the usual serge, and also two white drill jackets for each Officer.

DIETARY

In 1901 a New Dietary was to come into force. The following letter was from the Medical Officer to the Board of Guardians:-

"Re: NEW DIETARY

While the Dietary has been selected in the best manner from the very various formulas allowed, I am of opinion that is dietetic value is not, at least, greater than that of the Dietary which has been on force since 1895.

The Local Government Board regulations do not allow afternoon tea to be given, and no fluid (other than water) is permitted with any lunch that the Guardians may allow.

I am of opinion that as the meals (breakfast, lunch and dinner) come so close together during the winter months (breakfast ends at 8 a.m., lunch at 10, and dinner at 12), the lunch included in the Dietary submitted should only be given during the summer months, or preferably, should be omitted altogether and instead (if sanctioned by the Local Government Board) the present allowance of tea, bread and butter, given at 3 o'clock to all Inmates doing useful work, should be continued all the year round.

The very great latitude as to the composition of the various meals allowed by the Local Government Board order, removes further than ever from the range of probability that which appears to me (after being 15 years the Medical Officer of your workhouse) the great desideratum, to prevent the constant migration of paupers from one workhouse to another, namely, the establishment of a fixed and uniform Dietary for the whole of the Metropolis.

Arthur E. Dodson"

Subsequently the following report from the Master:-

"(a) I beg to report that owing to the increase of work, which the new Dietary will cause, when it comes into operation in March, in the Office, Stores, Dining Hall and Kitchen, it will be necessary to have additional assistance in each of these departments and I would suggest that someone be engaged as "Dining Hall and Stores Attendant". This would relieve the Assistant Master of some of the Stores work, and enable him to give more time in the Office. It would also relieve the Assistant Cook from preparing the Dining Hall tables for meals, so that he would be able to give more help in the Kitchen. And it would further relieve the Wardsman from attending to the cleaning of the Dining Hall and in place of this work he could profitable be employed in assisting and taking the place of the Mechanical Labour Master, when absent, in the manufacture of mineral waters, and in changing of the clothing of the Male inmates, instead of the work being done by the Tailor, who would then be able to give more time to making and repairing.

(b) I would also call attention of the Committee to the inadequacy of the Scullery to cope with the work of the Kitchen and Dining Hall, and as the new Dietary will increase the washing-up by about 2,000 articles per day, I would suggest that a separate scullery be provided for the Dining Hall, in the space between the latter room and front corridor, the work to be carried out by the Inmates.

The breakage of utensils in the Scullery and Dining Hall, during the past six months, has been over 8 dozen articles per week, at a cost of 2/- per dozen and I consider this is largely due to want of better accommodation and supervision in both departments."

Then there was the change in using tinned meat instead of fresh during the summer:-

That your Committee considered the question of the use of American tinned meat at the Workhouse and the Intermediate School, and find-

(a) That the American tinned meat is used during the summer months on Tuesdays instead of Pork at the School, and kept in stock as an alternative diet at both establishments.

(b) That the amount of tinned meat in stock is:-

Workhouse, 826lbs	cost	£20	13	0
Intermediate School, 72 lbs	cost	£ 1	16	0

And recommend -

(c) That the stock of tinned meat be kept for use in emergency, but that when it is exhausted no further supplies be obtained.

(d) That in lieu of the tinned meat issued to the Children at the Intermediate School on Tuesdays, the dinner do consist of:-

YEARS

Children 3 - 8   8ozs dried fruit pudding (baked)

Children 8 - 16   10ozs dried fruit pudding (baked)

And

8ozs of mild pudding each.

(e) That the alternative diet for the Children at the Intermediate School do consist of:-

AGES	CHEESE	BREAD	COFFEE
3 - 8	1oz	4ozs	½ pint (half milk)
8 - 18	2ozs	6ozs	½ pint (half milk)

(f) That the alternative diet for Workhouse Inmates do consist of:-

	COFFEE	BREAD	CHEESE
Men	1 pint	8ozs	3ozs
Women	1 pint	6ozs	2ozs
Children	pint (half milk)	4ozs	2ozs

A meat chopping machine was purchased costing £8.10/-. Children had difficulty in eating the chopped meat, so a mincing machine was purchased for the childrens block.

In 1901 Fish Frying apparatus was purchased costing £52

A Soda Water and Lemonade plant and equipment were to be purchased. It was to supply (apart from the workhouse) the Infirmary and a Tooting Home. The room to house this had to be enlarged, total cost £391.19.8d.

As an experiment for one month, the bread was to be baked with malt extract.

In June 1904 the drinking water was checked.

In October 1906 there were changes to the dietary for able-bodied inmates:-

Breakfast (weekdays)

For women, instead of Coffee on Tuesdays and Cocoa on Mondays, Thursdays and Fridays they be supplied with Porridge each morning.

Dinner on Sundays

Men - 3ozs cheese, 8ozs bread, 1 pint coffee.

Women - 2ozs cheese, 6ozs bread, 1 pint coffee (instead of a Roast Beef Dinner as at present.

Wednesdays

Men and women - Suet Pudding instead of Meat Pudding.

Fridays

Men and Women - Irish Stew instead of Fish

Supper (weekdays)

Women to be supplied with 1 pint Gruel instead of 1 pint Tea. (The object in altering the Sunday diet is to discourage the Inmates, who enter the Workhouse on Saturday night and go out Monday morning, thus receiving relief without doing work in return). That the Dietary Table, in respect of classes other than able-bodied be amended by the substitution of Irish Stew for dinner on Fridays, for Fish.
(This recommendation is made in view of the Fish Dietary not being a popular one).

In 1906 another Gas Oven was purchased in time for Christmas.

The way tea was made was changed at this time. It was to be made in two stages so as not to stew in the coppers. Prices were to be sought for Urns, as they were better for tea and coffee.

In 1908 'Meal' from wheat grinding was to be used in the flour mix for bread. It was selling at a loss as flour.

The workhouse used Canadian oats for porridge. They tried a new supplier (probably cheaper) from Scotland. It had a different flavour and the inmates did not like it. When they next ordered they reverted to Canadian again.

At Easter 1908 one of the Guardians gifted 150 eggs. Hot Cross Buns were always made and in the previous year 6000 were made! This particular year they had one large bun each.

In June the Medical Officer authorised the 760lbs of Fish Delivery to be destroyed. This was the first time the Medical Officer intervened. The contract was cancelled.

The amount of fresh food rejected on delivery rose to enormous proportions in this decade:-

e.g.	495lbs	meat
	1144lbs	fish
	1224lbs	suet
	90lbs	vegetables

Plus a further 17 rejections of various items from October 1909 to June 1910.

ENTERTAINMENT

Concerts were frequent. Many concert parties were only too pleased to come to Swaffield Road and entertain the inmates. In this decade there were 26 concerts.

There were also visits to Theatres. In May 1902 430 inmates visited the Grand Theatre and 420 the Shakespeare Theatre, all behaved well except 4!

In January 1907 270 inmates went to a performance at the Putney Hippodrome by invitation of the Directors - Messrs. Arding & Hobbs, Clapham Junction; Mr Foster, York Road; Messrs. Balls, Brixton; and Mr Trigg, Battersea Rise, kindly lend conveyances to take those inmates who were unable to walk to Putney, and bring them back to the Workhouse.

The Putney Hippodrome opened on 5 November 1906 and had visits like Dickie Henderson of "Tip-toe Through the Tulips" fame (with his soft shoe shuffle) and Marie Lloyd singing there.

The Boxes were priced at £1.1/- and 10/6d. The Family Circle was 9d, the Pit 6d and the Gallery 4d.

It was pulled down in 1971.

In June 1901 20 children go to a Tea Party at Ministering Children's League.

Children also went to Hampton Court by the workhouse bus.

In July and October each year a Mrs Olney would have 100 - 150 inmates for tea. They were often given books or flowers on leaving.

50 girls were entertained to Tea at All Saints School.

Mr Winsford of Broderick Road, Wandworth Common and his friends gave a Musical Entertainment to inmates at the Branch Workhouse.

On Boxing Day 1907 150 children were entertained at St Anne's school and also received toys all round.

On Christmas Day 1908 100 children were invited to a Christmas Tree concert at St Anne's Vicarage.

In November 1910 the children visited a Picture Palace at Earlsfield School. A band came all the way from Weymouth and 40 inmates went to tea at the Branch Workhouse.

The Putney Hippodrome

GIFTS

At Christmas 1902 the magazine "Truth" sent a large box of toys and 95 new sixpences and Tobacco and pipes for the Male Inmates. Every Christmas they gave toys and money to the children.

In November 1903 a large quantity of children's clothing was sent from the Surrey Needlework Guild. This clothing was much appreciated and the Guild continued to send clothing for many years.

In December 1904 toys were given from the Guardians and Officers, also a large box of toys from St Barnabas Church, cards and a football from Mr Leslie Harris, Plants from Mr H., Marchbank.

In October 1905 a large quantity of fruit and flowers were gifted by Rev. Canon. Curtis, Church of Ascension, Balham.

In January 1906 the Reverend A. W. Hooper sent tobacco for the Branch Workhouse male inmates.

The children also had a handsome Scrapbook from the Guardians.

For Christmas 1908 they all had cards and toys, even dolls for the little girls, plus sweets and evergreens for decorations and tobacco for the male inmates.

The visiting committee heard the children singing carols. Great credit was given to the teachers.

A Gramophone and records were received over the Christmas. This must have given enormous pleasure to the inmates.

BRANCH WORKHOUSES

At the Branch Workhouse there were problems with inmates requesting leave:-

That with regard to applications from Inmates to leave the Workhouse without their families, some Inmates renew their application at several successive meetings after their applications have been refused; and, with a view of putting a stop to this, the Master was requested, in the cases where such applications have been refused on account of character, not to bring such cases forward again until one month has expired from the date of the Committee's decision.

In the event of a man producing evidence that he has a likelihood of obtaining employment, the Master will bring such case forward before the expiration of the month.

Coal and coke was difficult to stock-take. The following report seems to have the answer:-

At the present time there does not seem to be any system for taking the coal and coke in stock. It is suggested that the measurements of the cellar be painted up in large figures upon the wall so as to enable me to take an accurate account of the contents and not merely to estimate.

I suggest the following measurements for estimating the coal and coke per ton.

Coal	*46 cubic feet*
Coke	*88 cubic feet*

These measurements are based upon the Army & Navy figures and are used at several institutions.

Your Committee are of the opinion that the foregoing suggestions should be adopted at the several Institutions.

The Branch Workhouse also suffered goods delivered not according to contract. In December 1909 a contractor had to take back 2 tons of coal!

They were also in receipt of Christmas gifts. The children had lots of toys and the adults had cards, letters and an abundance of evergreens for the Wards.

INTERMEDIATE SCHOOLS

At the Intermediate School four Scrubbers were appointed at 2/6d a day with dinner. In July 1903, 50 books were gifted, also monthly magazines for boys, plus a picture.

The Committee recommended that Matron send for patterns of coloured day-jerseys. Also that one evening a week bread and jam be given instead of bread and milk.

In July 1904 a boy aged 12 years was brought in at 7am by police. He was in a very verminous condition. Dinner was given him at 12.30 after which he climbed out of the top-most window in the building which had insufficient window fastenings.

The school also had to buy a mincing machine for the benefit of the very young children's meat.

The school became overcrowded very quickly. There were 180 children when they were licensed for 150. The floors seemed damp, they were to be treated and stained as 30 children were sleeping on the floor. Thirteen bedsteads had to be purchased, the remaining 17 children under school age, were sent back to the Workhouse.

It soon became obvious that further staff would be needed for the young children as more supervision was necessary.

At Christmas 1904 the school had their first Christmas Tree. Also the Matron reported the following gifts:-

144 toys and 85 sixpences from "Truth"
Toys and 42 lbs of sweets, from Messrs. Auburn and Heaviside
Toys and about 40 handsome books, from "Uncle Toby" of the Newcastle Chronicle.
80 threepenny pieces from Mr Beveridge (so that with the pieces received from "Truth" each child received a silver coin)
That Mr Murrin entertained the Children on Christmas Day with the Gramophone and Mr & Mrs Knight gave the children a Lantern entertainment on Boxing night.
That 50 children were entertained by the Girls' Friendly Society yesterday at Putney Bridge Road and each child received a beautiful toy.

Also on Boxing Day many of the children went to an entertainment at St Anne's Church and came home laden with toys.

In 1905 they had four more entertainments and from one of them came home with oranges and sweets.

The Reverend Norman Campbell of St Anne's took 40 younger children to Wimbledon Common in the summer of 1905.

By now the school was overcrowded once again and 40 children had to be taken to Anerley School.

A piano was bought for the school from Messrs. Munt Brothers for £25.

At Easter in 1906 all the children had an Easter Egg.

They were also gifted a Rocking Hose and a quantity of toys from a Mrs Wright of Earlsfield

Beautiful flowers were given by the Earlsfield Congregational Church and Sunday School, also fruit and flowers from Reverend Norman Campbell at St Anne's Church.

In August 30 children (infants) were taken to St Anne's school treat.

The School received 100 jackets for the children in mixed sizes from a Mrs Grove. They would have cost 4/5d each.

In January 1907 a box of dolls was sent from the Woking Girls Home, South Street.

At the same time 60 older boys and girls were invited to a Sunday School Concert by Reverend Norman Campbell.

A visit to the Shakespeare Theatre to see Aladdin was arranged for 130 children.

At Easter all the children had an Easter Egg from Mrs Beveridge, a Guardian, she also sent a dolls house and toys. More toys and some picture books were gifted from a Mrs Harris of Clapham.

The Caius College Bank gave an entertainment.

One of the boys absconded nine times, the Committee recommended he be sent to an Industrial School.

In June the children were taught how to use the fire escapes.

In July 130 children went to Bushey Park with the children from St Anne's Sunday School.

In December of that year a boy from the school was to attend a school for the blind at Bolingbroke Grove - he was given 2d a day for his lunch.

Also in December a fire alarm practice was held, every one was out of the buildings in two and a half minutes.

At Easter 1908 Mrs Beveridge, a Guardian, once again gave all the children an Easter Egg. They also had a Giant Egg, which was full of sweets for Easter Monday from a Mrs Knight of The Grove, Wandsworth.

In June 1908 a 3-year-old child died after developing Measles.

Four Officers took 100 children to Astead Woods which was a treat from St Anne's Church.

The Matron ordered 100 Counterpanes; when they were delivered she wanted to reject them. However, the manufacturer wrote to her and after further inspection they were accepted. Records do not show what the manufacturer put in his letter to change the Matrons mind.

In December 1909 they received 16/6d and 230 toys from the "Truth" magazine. They also had cards, toys, a Union Jack flag and three Gramophone "plates" from one of the Guardians.

A Christmas Tree Party was held for 100 children at the St Anne's Vicarage Room.

At Easter in 1910 every child had an egg for breakfast.

In June 200 children were invited to a treat at St Anne' Church.

The boys at the School were issued with Cricket Shirts.

The Matron made arrangements for the children to attend the Premier Picture Palace, but the Sub-Committee of the Education Committee of the London County Council objected to the school being closed for the purpose of the children going to the Picture Palace.

The clerk reported that upon hearing from the Matron of the refusal (this morning), he had sent to the London County Council Offices and tried to get the decision of the London County Council modified, but without result.

The decision of the London County Council has caused inconvenience, inasmuch as the Manager of the Theatre proposed to give the children, if they had been sent at one time, a special show of pictures and provide them with tea, toys, etc.

Arrangements have been made now for the children to be taken in two batches to the ordinary performances.

In February 1910 the Matron reported:-

That Mr & Mrs Bennett invited 200 children to the Pantomime at the Shakespeare Theatre on 10th instant. During the interval Mrs Bennett sent down to every child a glass of hot milk, a bun and an orange and I need scarcely say that the children spent a very enjoyable afternoon.

I beg to call attention to the need of the appointment of a Relief Officer.

The Staff of Attendants at present consists of a Head Attendant, Needle-woman Attendant and five Attendants, a total of seven.

Leave of absence is granted to each officer two evenings a week, one whole day a month and half-day each Sunday, and the need of a Relief Officer is felt, as on certain occasions three officers have to be absent at the same time and the buildings being separate, makes it very difficult, it being impossible to spare more than one officer to look after 100 odd boys in the new building.

I would respectfully suggest that an Assistant Attendant be appointed as the Relief Officer, say at a salary of £18.00, rising £1.00 annually to £20.00 per annum with resident allowances.

In October 1910 the Committee had to consider the following letter from Reverend O. Craig:-

St Anne's Vicarage
Wandsworth

To the Wandsworth Guardians,

Gentlemen

You will be aware that I have been arranging for the Religious Teaching of the children at the Intermediate Schools during the last three years. The numbers have, however, of late, so greatly increased and the difference in age is so wide that both in the interest of the children and for the discipline of our School Children, some modification is necessary.

I would suggest that the best provision for the Intermediate School Children would be that they had Sunday School Teaching in their own Schools on Sunday morning in three groups and that the elder boys and girls should come up to the service for children at St Anne's, while a Service was held for the juniors in their Schools - or in the Chapel of the Union. If the Guardians were minded to make some such arrangement as this, I should be willing to undertake the duties with our staff, if a proportionate increase were made in the grant. I would be responsible for the services and for finding really good teachers for the children and would supervise the management with my brother Clergy.

I shall be very glad if the Guardians will consider this proposal; and if they have any other suggestions to make I shall be glad to meet them in any way for the sake of the children; at present we cannot do justice to them, and they are interfering with the good order of the Sunday Services.

I am Gentlemen,
Yours faithfully,
OSWALD CRAIG.

It was recommended that the Rev. O. Craig be asked to carry out the arrangements suggested above and that an honorarium of £25.00 per annum be granted to him for so doing. The Committee would be glad if he would arrange for the younger children attending Church also.

In December 1910 tooth brushes were to be purchased for the children.

Also in December the children were given an orange and a Fairy Play. There were new decorations for Christmas and a performance of Beauty and the Beast. 240 children went to see the Pantomime "Sinbad".

These are the first reports on "surprise stocktaking". It is recommended that such reports be referred to the Finance Committee:-

Stocktaker's List	Figures in Books	Remarks
Bacon 76 lbs	87 lbs	11 lb Ham not weighed by Stocktaker
Cocoa 22 lbs	134 lbs	Master states 1134 lbs were in stock
Coffee 58 lbs	78 lbs	Master states 78 lbs were in stock
Linen Sheeting 1,297.¾ yds	1,297.¾ yds	Ticket marked 86 read upside down is 98
Intermediate Schools		
Bread 162 lbs	163 lbs	
Chocolate 31 lbs	32½ lbs	
Coffee 2 ¹⁴⁄₁₆ lbs	3 lbs	
Flour 64½ lbs	61 lbs	
Loaf sugar 7 lbs	6¼ lbs	
Demerara sugar 39¾ lbs	38 lbs	
Tapioca 19½ lbs	19 lbs	
Tea 116½ lbs	116¼ lbs	
Soda 137 lbs	140 lbs	
Coloured Tabling (nil)	7 yds	Issued out, but not booked up at time of stocktaking
Calico 7¼ yards	8½ yards	
Linen 5¾ yards	5½ yards	

Report of Sub-Committee of Workhouse Committee, appointed to consider the complaints made with regard to certain Officers, by the Matron of the Intermediate Schools, together with matters generally arising therefrom.

Present: Mr Sullivan (in the Chair); Mrs Blackmore, Rev. T.E. Grout, Messrs. Hare, Palmer, and Parrott.

Reporting:

(a) That your Sub-Committee interviewed the following Officers:-

Dr. Donson, Medical Officer.

Miss Gavin, Matron

Miss Veall, Assistant Matron

Attendants Bushell, Cullen, Tottman, Vaughan, Hancock, and Langdon

Housemaid Green

Scrubber Gornell and

House Porter, Ames.

(b) That with regard to the complaints made by the Matron (excepting that referring to Attendant Langdon), there was no corroborative evidence, and what the Matron reported appeared to have been found out, not by herself, but chiefly from hearsay.

(c) That there appears to be very much discontent existing amongst the Officers, and consequently a good tone does not prevail, owing, it appears to your Sub-Committee, to the ungovernable temper of the Matron, who seems to lack the tact necessary for one in authority. As more than one Officer expressed it, "she says things in a temper for which she is sorry after," and, in fact, in no instance had any Officer a good word for the Matron, which must be obvious to anyone, cannot altogether be the fault of the Officers.

(d) That several Officers mentioned that the children were given "bread and water" punishment far more in this Institution than in others where they had previously been; but on reference to the punishment book this was not borne out, and on two cases being mentioned, no entry of any such punishment was found in the book. If this book is not a correct record of punishments, it shows great laxity, and is liable to lead to unkindness to the children, besides which, any punishment should not be inflicted without the consent of the Medical Officer.

(e) That your Committee finds that the Matron is not altogether particular as to what she says to the children, or to Officers in front of the children, or even in front of the Guardians. This is not conducive to happy relationship between the Matron and Officers or between the Officers and children, and may possibly account for the number of the latter absconding.

(f) That the Matron has not made use of the "leave book" when leaving and entering the Establishment, neither has she seen that the officers have entered the times of their return to the Establishment, consequently your Sub-Committee were unable to accurately ascertain whether the officers returned punctually from their leave, or what time the Matron was away from the Institution, and it seems to your Sub-Committee that with three Senior Officers it ought not to be difficult to arrange for one of them to remain on duty till ten o-clock, and see that the Officers do return punctually at that hour.

(g) That though the act of gross unkindness to a child (for which Attendant Langdon was dismissed by the Board) was witnessed by three other officers, Attendant Cullen, Scrubber Gornell and House Porter Ames, yet it does not appear to have been thought necessary by anyone to report the fact to the head of the Establishment at the time. It was about a fortnight later reported by House Porter Ames, and his reason for then reporting it can only be attributed to the fact that the two Attendants in that particular block had, to put it broadly, "Fallen out". It appears to your Sub-Committee incredible that such an act of unkindness could have occurred in a well regulated Institution without the head of that Institution becoming immediately aware of it.

(h) That your Sub-Committee are not altogether satisfied with the action of the Matron in locking a lad named Taylor (who returned after absconding) in the Isolation Room (at the top of the building) from Good Friday morning until Monday evening, and it appears to be doubtful if he would then have been let out if the room had not been required to isolate a suspected case of infection disease.

(i) That during the course of enquiries as to whether officers were allowed to chastise the children, the Matron remarked that the Porters Hookway and Ames did sometimes "cuff" the boys, but she had not reported the matter to the Guardians, and it seem to your Sub-Committee that the only person who ought to be allowed to correct a child, is the head of the Establishment, and that any deviation from the rule should be reported to the Guardians at their next meeting.

(j) That it has not been the practice for the Attendants, nor do they seem to have received any instructions from the Matron, to report to her any cases of children who did not appear to have control of the calls of nature, and it appears to your Sub-Committee a serious matter, as it stands to reason that when this occurs two or three times a day with a child, such child is greatly in need of medical attention, and ought to be seen by the Medical Officer who attends daily at the School.

(k) That your Sub-Committee are of opinion that Miss Gavin does not appear to sufficiently realise that she, as the head of the Establishment, is responsible for all details for the good working of the Institution, as the following instance will show:-
In reply to a question as to the lavatories, and the provision of toilet paper, she seemed quite uncertain as to whether any was provided or not, and when pressed for a definite answer, said she supposed that if the Attendants had wanted any they would have asked for it, which answer can hardly be considered a satisfactory one. In fact, one Attendant who has charge of the younger children remarked she had only been given two rolls of toilet paper in four years, and then only because some of the children were unwell.

(l) That from the evidence of the Attendants, it seems that for years bad feeling had existed between them and the Matron, that they were afraid to ask the Matron for anything, and, as one officer put it, " if we make application for anything we get snubbed."

(m) That some of the Officers complained that on several occasions sufficient rations had not been provided for their meals. In the Dietary Table sufficient is provided, and it can only be surmised that the note on the Officers' Dietary Table, viz.: "That this scale represents the maximum consumption authorised, but does not entitle the Matron to issue, nor any Officer to demand, the quantities set forth, unless required for actual consumption," - has been too literally read by the Matron. It is only fair to say that the shortage has not occurred just recently.

(n) *That in the opinion of your Sub-Committee a person who is unable to control her temper can hardly be expected to satisfactorily control a large Establishment to the comfort of the officers and Children, and your Sub-Committee with regret have to report that Miss Gavin, the Matron, is so situated.*

(o) *That having regard to all the circumstances, and to the necessity of the good working of the Establishment, your Sub-Committee are of opinion that the following should be called upon to send in their resignations:-*

(1) Miss Gavin, Matron.

(2) Miss Veall, Assistant Matron.

(3) Attendant Cullen.

(4) Scrubber Gornell.

(5) House Porter Ames.

And your Committee have considered the foregoing Report and recommend the adoption by the board -

(a) That Miss Gavin and Attendant Cullen be called upon to resign.

(b) That Scrubber Gornell and House Porter Ames be called before the

Board and severely censured by the Chairman.

The Matron reported the following:-

That with regard to the letter from the Local Government Board, transmitting copy of a letter received from Walter Silbey, relative to his children, Lilian and Edith, aged 11 and 9 years, your Committee find that the reason the Children were sent to Anerley Schools on Friday, 14th October ult., and brought back on 15th inst., was owing to the Matron of the Intermediate Schools having overlooked the fact that the father had given notice of his discharge.

With regard to the complaint as to the "Girls hair being cut close to their heads", enquiry was made of the Managers of the Schools and the reply was that it was left to the discretion of the Medical Officer to have the hair of children under 12 years cut, on admission to the Schools, but in this case the hair would not have been cut had the School Authorities been aware of the fact that the children had been sent down on that day to be removed on the next

Your Committee regret that the Medical Officer of the Schools considered it necessary to order the hair of the child aged 11 to be cut, having regard to the fact that she had been in the Intermediate School from 3rd October until she went to the Schools on 14th October and the hair could not have been dirty.

MEDICAL

On 23rd October 1902 the Guardians received the following report from the Medical Officer:-

SCHOOL BLOCK -

This morning there are 51 Girls, 64 Boys, and 4 Adults - Total 123, in this Block, being 87 in excess of the certified number.

On Thursday, 16th instant, a case of chicken-pox occurred, and as far as possible immediate disinfection was carried out, and no further cases have, up to now, occurred. This case, however, prevents us sending to Anerley this week; but I would ask that they be requested to receive next week instead, and that, in the meantime, the Relieving Officers be instructed to send in as few Children as possible.

I beg, again, to point out how dangerous this continued over-crowding is to the health of the Children, especially as many of them are very young.

For some reason or other the Anerley authorities have requested us, on the last four admission days, not to send any Children under seven years of age, with the result that this class now constitutes almost half the total number in the Block

And the Clerk was instructed to request the Relieving Officers to refrain from sending children to the Workhouse, as far as possible, and for the School authorities to be asked to receive Children on Friday, the 31 instant.

(Letter submitted from North Surrey School District, stating that 27 Children can be received on the 31st instant.)

(8)   That your Committee again considered the Report of the Master, which was referred back from the Board, viz.:-

The Workhouse is now getting into a very over-crowded state, the numbers having increased from 594, a fortnight ago, to 675 today, an increase of 81 in a fortnight; and I would respectfully suggest that the Guardians consider the advisability of converting the present married couples' quarters into a dormitory for aged men.

The married quarters consist of 16 separate rooms, and, at the present time, these are occupied by only four couples, and if provision for these four couples could be made elsewhere, and the partitions removed, it would make accommodation for 58 beds.

As it is desirable that accommodation should be retained at the Workhouse for married couples, there being six couples now chargeable, your Committee recommend-

That, as a temporary measure, a partition be erected down the centre of the Ward in question; by this means accommodation will be provided for about 19 additional beds, and for eight married couples

In 1903 attention was called to the number of married women admitted to the workhouse for the Lying-In Ward, whilst the husband remained outside; and it is recommended that, in future when an application is received for the admission of a married woman, the Relieving Officer be instructed, if the case is not urgent, to bring the matter before the Combined Relief Committee prior to using the order; but if the case be an urgent one then to issue the order, and bring the husband before the next meeting of the Committee.

In May 1909 a letter in The Times prompts the Medical Officer to make the following report:-

The Guardians will be interested no doubt to know that the 3000th birth since the opening of the Lying-in Ward—- took place on the 28th November last—-there have been 17 deaths; 12 directly to childbirth (only two during the last 10 years), and it must be remembered with regard to these deaths that a number of cases are sent here as a last resource after attempts at delivery have been unsuccessfully made outside.

The Committee considered a letter from the Local Government Board upon the advisability of training Probationer Midwives at the Workhouse, and received a report from the Medical Officer thereon as:-

Re: TRAINING PROBATIONER MIDWIVES

With reference to the question of using the cases in the Lying-in Ward for training of Probationer Midwives, where the Lying-in Ward is in close proximity to an Infirmary or other training school, it is quite feasible that good use might be made of the cases occurring. In this Workhouse there is at present no possible living accommodation for any Probationer while taking her cases. It is not desirable that any such Probationer should live in any lodging except under the strictest sanitary conditions. Each pupil has to attend the routine work of her cases in the Lying-in Ward under the personal supervision of a qualified officer at least four months. The total number of confinements in our Lying-in Ward yearly is about 180 and not more than five or at the most, six pupils could be trained here if proper accommodation is provided.

A.E. DODSON.

Having regard to the above report they do not recommend any action being taken upon the Local Government Board's letter at the present, but the matter should be further considered in three months' time.

After a few months there was a further report from the Medical Officer:-

I beg to draw attention to the state of the Lying-in Ward. Since 1st September last we have had 73 cases, of which no less than 47 have taken place in the night time. Last month we have had 22 cases and as these are mostly first cases and the mothers inexperienced, the work by day and night has been very great.

On Saturday last every bed was full and three cases had to be temporarily accommodated in "D" Block. I considered it necessary to engage extra assistance, and Mrs Carlisle, who on previous occasions has similar work, is now taking charge of the Ward at night time.

There are more than 30 pregnant Women in the House, and as about 50 per cent are admitted in labour, in generally a dirty state, I think the time has arrived when a permanent Night Assistant should be appointed, in accordance with the opinion frequently expressed by the Local Government Board Inspectors.

The Committee recommended that subject to the sanction of the Local Government board, an Assistant Midwife for night work be appointed at a salary of £30 per annum, rising £1 annually to £32 per annum, with rations and indoor uniform, and an allowance of 6/- weekly in lieu of lodging.

The Committee approved the engagement of Mrs Carlisle, as temporary Assistant Midwife for night duty.

(13) That your Committee received the following report from Dr Dodson, Medical Officer of the Workhouse:-

To the Workhouse Committee of the Wandsworth Union.

In the "Times" and other daily papers of the 26th April last, a letter from "Mrs Sidney Webb" appeared with the title,

WHAT HAPPENS TO THE WORKHOUSE BABIES?

It refers first to the Lying-in Wards and then to the Workhouse Nurseries. Comparisons are drawn between various institutions, and five London Unions are mentioned by name ("to take only some of the good cases") to show that in these the infantile death rates are satisfactory as compared with "the best Maternity Hospitals."

As Wandsworth Union is not mentioned, I am led to presume that it is not to be classed as among "the good cases," and under the circumstances, I think it right to place before you the following facts:-

First, as regards the Lying-in Ward. Mrs Sidney Webb states that the average infant mortality for the first week in a London Workhouse Lying-in Ward is 42.4 per 1,000. I have abstracted from my records, particulars from the 1st January, 1892 to 31st December, 1908, relating to the Lying-in Ward of this Workhouse, and I find that during that period 2,414 births have taken place, of which 615 were of legitimate and 1,799 of illegitimate children. The deaths have been as follows:

Under 1 day old, 29	*Under 5 days old, 3*
Under 2 days old, 12	*Under 6 days old, 2*
Under 3 days old, 9	*Under 7 days old, 3*
Under 4 days old, 2	

Total, 60; or an average of, say, 24 per 1,000. Of these 60 deaths, nearly all of illegitimate children, no less than 39 were due to "premature births" and the others to conditions due to what Mrs Sidney Webb appears to ridicule as being of little importance, namely, "pre-natal and maternal conditions." From my 24 years experience as Medical Officer I assert that these conditions must be taken into account before a true verdict can be given or a fair conclusion drawn.

The mothers of these illegitimate children, at least as regard this Workhouse, come chiefly from the factory hand, hawkers, and domestic servant classes.

What are "pre-natal and maternal condition?" It must first be conceded that for healthy offspring it is necessary that the mothers, while carrying, shall be healthy, well-fed, and, most important of all, in my opinion, free from worry and anxiety; but what do we find in our Workhouse cases?-

1st - That almost invariably, directly a girl finds out her condition, she doses or is dosed with noxious drugs, patent pills, &c., and an already generally feeble constitution is still further enfeebled.

2nd - Their position in life prevents the having of anything like appropriate food, &c., for a prospective mother.

3rd - As regards mental worry, the months of anxious waiting and dread, the prospect of being a social outcast with the burden of a "fatherless" child, must and does have a tremendous effect upon both mother and offspring.

To compare statistics of Workhouse cases with those of the "best Maternity Hospitals" or of the general population, is manifestly unjust and unfair. We deal with an entirely different class, and with experience of all three classes I claim that we have nothing to be ashamed of in a rate of mortality of 24 per 1,000 in infants during the first week. Bred and born under the conditions I have enumerated, children must lack "backbone and stamina" and a power of resistance practically all through their lives.

Many of our lying-in-cases are admitted in labour in a filthy condition, half-starved, from insanitary homes, and often after fruitless attempts at delivery have been made by doctors and midwives outside. Our "operative" cases are much above the average of those among the general population, and yet our results are at least as satisfactory as under better conditions outside.

The second part of Mrs Sidney Webb's letter deals with Workhouse Nurseries, and the following "facts" are quoted, confirmation being asked of any "mother." This restriction may handicap my opinion, not being a mother myself, but as Medical Officer I must claim to criticise the "facts" as regards this Workhouse.

Statement No 1 - "In some Workhouse Nurseries the babies never get into the open air from the time they are born until they die or leave at 3 or 4 or 5." (Whether months or years are not stated.) "This facts seems incredible," &c.

In this Workhouse the infants are from a few days old taken into the open air. After a month they are sent out in perambulators on to the Common with their mothers and in charge of a nurse, for several hours daily when the weather is fine. At other times they are kept by day in well ventilated and light day-rooms or covered sheds. By night, care is taken that the dormitories are kept wholesome and well ventilated.

Statement No 2 - "Whilst the nursing staff is slowly improving in most nurseries of general mixed Workhouses, the babies are still handled in the main by 'pauper' women, many feeble-minded and imbecile."

In this Workhouse no imbecile or feeble-minded inmate is ever allowed to "handle" or look after the children. (In fact, imbeciles are not kept in the Workhouse). If "pauper" women means the mothers of the children, I am not cognisant of any one more suitable in most cases; and to class them as unfit to "handle" their own children is to cast an unjust slur upon them as a class. My experience is that their children, even if illegitimate, are still dear to them, and their motherly instincts are quite as acute as amongst the general population outside.

Statement No 3 - "In some Workhouse Nurseries there is not even a trained nurse in charge," &c.

In this Workhouse, by day, a Charge Nurse with two capable assistants, and, by night, a properly qualified nurse, are always on duty to look after both mothers and children.

Statement No 4 - "There is no 'quarantine' of new comers; a perpetual stream of infants, from nought to four, pours in from the worst home conditions, without a probation ward, straight into the nursery," &c.

This statement is the most difficult to answer of all. First, as regards a child of "nought" one wonders how an obviously non-existent child can pour into a Workhouse. As regards young children generally, to provide "proper quarantine" accommodation, each unit should be kept quite separate for at least two or three weeks. We admit here, to the Workhouse, very often 40, 50, or even more young children a week, and to talk of providing "proper" quarantine accommodation for such a number is obviously impossible and verging on the ridiculous. We place them under clean and sanitary conditions as far as possible in the Receiving Wards before they are sent to the Nurseries, and, in spite of Mrs Sidney Webb's concluding statement, "No wonder that measles and whooping cough are troublesome," I must say that my experience does not coincide with her opinion.

In conclusion, I believe that both in the Lying-in Ward and in our Nurseries the mothers and the children are thoroughly well looked after, better fed, better clothes, and better cared for in every way than among the poorer classes outside, and that considering the "pre-natal and maternal condition," the Guardians of this Union have every reason to be satisfied with "What happens to the Workhouse Babies."

(Signed)ARTHUR E DODSON.
Medical Officer
May 13th,1909

In 1907 the subject of Venereal Disease reared its ugly head. The following report comes from a recent "Call-over".

(a) *Your Committee interviewed a number of young men who had been admitted suffering from itch and syphilis, and it is suggested that the Board should seriously take into consideration the question of whether it would not be possible to allocate a small Ward for these cases at the Workhouse, so that the men who have become chargeable simply through their own fault, should not reap the benefits and comforts of an Infirmary for nothing, but should be put to work and do something towards repaying the cost of their keep.*

(b) *That your Committee also saw several cases of gout, and are of opinion that these might very well be accommodated in an Infirm Ward at the Workhouse, as they could be seen every day by the Medical Officer, and directions for treatment carried out by Attendants.*

With regard to (a), the Medical Officer reported that the total number of adult cases suffering from itch, transferred to the Infirmary from the Workhouse during the past 12 months, was 11; that all cases under 16 years are treated in the old School Block, and that there was no Ward available at the Workhouse for the treatment of either itch or syphilis - the number of the latter treated in the Workhouse during the past year being 127.

With regard to (b) the Medical Officer reported; "Ever since the Infirm Wards have been opened, dozens of cases of short ailments, such as diarrhoea, sore throats and asthma, have been treated here, when only a few days' rest and medicine are necessary. We have at present no less than 58 cases of gout and rheumatism in the Infirm Wards, and it is the rule for two or three cases beyond the certified accommodation to be under treatment, rather than send them to the Infirmary.

The fact that taking the Male Infirm Wards only, the accommodation is 100 beds, last year we passed 274 cases through - only 26 were taken to Tooting and of the remaining 248 a very large number were of the nature specified above and the Infirmary was relieved to a corresponding extent.

It would appear from the foregoing, that cases of gout etc., could be treated at the Workhouse, but the want of accommodation is again brought to notice. Under the circumstances, your Committee can only recommend - that all itch cases in the Infirmary be kept in a separate Ward, and the Medical Superintendent be asked, if possible, to give such particular Inmates a similar diet to that which they would receive were they Inmates of the Workhouse.

In November 1909 the Medical Officer gave a report on the health of the inmates:-

The general health of the adult Inmates is satisfactory. On the 6th inst. Three children were passed here from Hammersmith Parish, and one of them was found to be suffering from chicken-pox and was transferred at once to the Infirmary, the other two were isolated as far as possible in the Old School Block.

What to do with the children is the question now. In "D" Block, for mothers with infants and infants without mothers, there are today 54 children; 14 are over 3 years of age and should be at St James'.

At St James' we have 39 children, of whom 15 are over 5 years of age, and should be at the Intermediate Schools.

In the old School Block there are 61 children (25 girls and 36 boys) of whom 45 are of school age. In this Block many of the children are and have been for some time cured of the complaints for which they are admitted; but want of room at the Intermediate Schools has prevented them being moved.

In the Receiving Wards at the Workhouse, on the female side, there are 33 girls, and on the male side, 32 boys - total 65 - and of these 62 are of school age.

To summarise, we have 219 children (not reckoning 6 newly born in the Lying-in Ward) in the Workhouse, including:-

At St James'	*15 of school age*
At old School Block	*45 of school age*
At Receiving Wards	*62 of school age*

122

The Intermediate School has its full number, 150, and this brings the total to 272. With the exception of one case of doubtful chicken-pox in "D" Block we are free from any infectious disease.

The Clerk was directed to try and arrange for the admission of some of the children to the District School and the Strand Union Schools as soon as possible, so as to relieve the pressure.

By this time there had been 3000 births in the Lying-in Ward.

An Assistant Midwife was newly appointed to cope with the workload.

TRANSPORT

A new Tilted Van was given by a Mr Witmee, it cost £445.10/-. A Tilted Van has a canvas covering.

By this time the old bread van was unfit for deliveries and could be used for general purposes. A new bread van was to be purchased.

The Master decided that Lunatics were to be taken to the Asylum by train instead of using Guardian conveyance.

CHAPTER 3: *The First World War and the Trade Inions - 1920*

ADMINISTRATION

An advertisement for a Wardsman at the Branch Workhouse resulted in 69 applications.
In February 1911 the Medical officer reported the following:-

THE OLD SCHOOL BLOCK

On Monday last the remainder of the Patients from this Block were transferred to the Infirmary. It will interest the Guardians to know that since the building was first opened in 1904, no less than 2,989 cases of skin disease and other ailments of children, have been treated there - 1781 were boys and this side has been all the time under the charge of Miss Gibson, who has now been transferred to the New Infirmary. 1208 were Girls, under the care of Miss Roberts until 1906 and since that of Mrs Hearnden. I know of no more troublesome or worrying cases that those of skin disease in children and I am pleased to be able to bear testimony to the most excellent work done by these nurses, which have led to results I consider entirely satisfactory. There is one point in connection with this detached building and that is in its relation to the Intermediate School. It has been my rule to remove to the School Block from the latter, any case of even suspected illness and no doubt much spreading of disease has thereby been prevented. To send all such cases to the Infirmary will not only entail the sending of many of apparently trivial nature, but also gives liability to catch other diseases when there. Now that we have so many children to deal with here, I consider it essential that we should have some proper accommodation here in charge of a properly qualified nurse.

With regard to the present use of the Old School Block, I would suggest that as soon as possible, this should be taken as a temporary lying-in-ward during the cleaning of "E" Block. It is two years since anything was done here and the Wards, Labour Rooms, Kitchen, &c., and Corridor require painting."

In April the Master pointed out the wintertime admissions and discharges:-

	ADMISSIONS				DISCHARGES			
	Men	*Women*	*Child*	*Total*	*Men*	*Women*	*Child*	*Total*
Jan 2nd	17	7	7	**31**	8	3	13	**24**
Jan 6th	10	20	6	**36**	17	6	7	**30**
Jan 30th	8	11	12	**31**	7	2	24	**33**
Feb 6th	7	6	10	**23**	6	4	6	**16**
Feb 16th	12	1	11	**24**	5	2	6	**13**
Feb 21st	10	6	10	**26**	8	5	1	**14**
Mar 6th	5	8	25	**38**	15	14	3	**32**
Mar 7th	29	6	10	**45**	10	6	9	**25**

And as children have to remain in the Wards for some days until they can be admitted to the Intermediate Schools, it shows that more accommodation is absolutely necessary, and your Sub-Committee are of the opinion that this can best be provided by putting another storey on the present Wards - it is therefore recommended that the Workhouse Committee do approve of the proposal and that the matter be referred to the Works Committee to get out the necessary particulars for submission to the Local Government Board.

The Medical Officer reported:-

At the last meeting of Committee I reported that the last of the sick cases had been removed to the old Information from "H" Block and the Master reported that the vacated accommodation was being filled up by transferring the Aged and Infirm Inmates from the body of the House to make room for the boarded-out people at Mitcham and St. Giles'. On Friday last those from Mitcham (98 in number) had all arrived. On examining them I found nearly half suffering from chronic complaints eligible for St. John's Infirmary. I therefore telephoned to the acting Medical Officer, who replied that he was unable to take any more cases there and he understood they had received all the people we had to send. Up to then, only one-half of the Aged and Infirm cases had been removed down to "H" Block, filling one ward and the chronic cases from Mitcham were therefore, accommodated in the other two Wards. Yesterday 34 people, including 19 women, were brought back from St. Giles' and of these 6 were sent to "H" Block, where the number this morning is 98.

If all the Wards (120 beds) are to be occupied by this class of case - and apparently, it will be a very short time before they are full up - it will be necessary to have both Day and Night Attendants and there should certainly be a properly qualified nurse in charge.

And the matter was adjourned for a fortnight to see how many cases could be accommodated at the St. John's Hill Infirmary.

In July the Master reported as follows:-

The Coronation festivities, which were kept at the Workhouse on the 26th and at the Branch Workhouse on the 29th - instead of the 22nd June - passed off very nicely. The special dietary so kindly sanctioned by the Guardians, was much appreciated by the Inmates and Officers and the amusements provided by the Bank, Punch and Judy and the Pierrots throughout the afternoon and evening was thoroughly enjoyed by all. At dinner time a congratulatory telegram was sent to the King, who replied tendering his thanks for the good wishes expressed. On Thursday, the 29th June, 28 of the Inmates, by special invitation of H.M. the King were taken in brakes to attend at Stafford House to witness the procession of St. Paul's and the Guildhall. Throughout the festive season several of the men and women were allowed special leave and the behaviour of all classes of Inmates was very satisfactory.

An Officer had been found to be a driver:-

That with regard to Ambulance Driver Flight, it appears this Officer is suitable for the appointment of Motor Ambulance Driver if he is given about a week's tuition in driving, as he has not done motor driving for sometime since he obtained his certificates; and in order to make him proficient, leave of absence was granted and it was left in the hands of the Chairman of the Committee to arrange for Flight to have the necessary tuition. Subsequently:-

That the Resolution of the Guardians of 9th February 1911, to the effect that advertisements be issued for Motor Ambulance Driver - be rescinded and:-

That W.H., Flight at present Ambulance Driver, be appointed Motor Ambulance Driver at a remuneration of 42/- weekly and uniform.

That the Master reported as follows:

21st September 1911

The bread, during the past month, has not been up to the usual standard of good quality. The very hot weather which we have experienced has made matters very difficult for the Bakers to keep the yeast in a satisfactory condition; but the fault is in some measure due to the flour which we are getting under the present Contracts. It being rather dark in colour and it is very weak, consequently the yield of bread per sack of flour is not up to the standard. From my long experience in this matter I am convinced that it is not always sound economy to have the lowest priced flour, for this reason - the flour may be of fairly good quality, but faulty in other respects, either in colour or strength or sometimes both, hence the quantity of bread produced is from two to three-quarters per sack short of the proper standard, as well as being sometimes unsatisfactory in quality."

That your Committee received the following report from the Master of the Workhouse:-

10th May 1911
LADIES AND GENTLEMEN,
In accordance with the Resolution of the Board, I now beg to submit my report on the Workhouse for the Year ended Lady-day 1911.

The Garratt Lane and Branch Workhouses are certified for 1,168 Inmates, viz.:- 898 at the Workhouse, Garratt Lane, and 270 at the Branch Workhouse, St James' Road, and the highest number maintained at these Institutions during the year was 1,248, and the lowest 1,012.

The number of Inmates at the commencement of the Mid-summer Quarter, 1910		*1,169*
Number of Admissions during the year	6,092	
Number of Births during the year	166	*7,427*
Number of Discharges during the year	6,271	
Number of Deaths during the year	31	*6,302*
Number of Inmates remaining at the end of Lady-day Quarter 1911		*1,125*

At no time during the year did the numbers at the Branch Workhouse exceed the certificate; but, for a short time, at Garratt Lane, the number of Inmates was in excess of the certified accommodation. The principal period of overcrowding was from the 6th to the 12th weeks in the Christmas Quarter, when the highest number maintained above the certificate was 80. The overcrowding was mainly due to the number of children maintained in the Workhouse owing to outbreaks of infectious disease at the Schools and the inability of these Institutions to relieve the Workhouse of this class of Inmate. It is satisfactory to note that the number of Male Inmates, classed as able-bodied (viz, from 16 to 60 years of age), has been below the average almost throughout the year

The Male Inmates have been employed as far as possible at their several trades, viz, Fitters, Smiths, Bricklayers, Carpenters, Plumbers' work and Painting, Tailoring, Shoemaking, Mat-making, and Baking, and those of unskilled labour have been utilised as labourers to the several trades, and in Wood Chopping, Fibre Picking, and Cleaning.

The Females have been employed in Needlework, Cleaning, and Laundrywork.

At the present time, about 87 Male Inmates are sent out to work at other Institutions under the Board, and to act as Messengers at the Clerks' Office and for the Relieving Officers, viz.:-

Tooting Home (principally in the garden)	*19*
St John's Hill Infirmary	*30*
St James' Infirmary	*15*
Messengers at the Clerks' Office, Relieving Officer, &c.	*23*
	—-
Total	*87*
	==

During the year I have found situations for 13 boys at Treorchy, in South Wales, making a total of 26 sent to that District. Of this number, two only have been returned as unsatisfactory, and 24 are still there. All these boys are in regular work and earning good wages and appear to be very contented. In May last, while taking a week-end holiday, I made a special unofficial and unexpected visit to Treorchy in order to satisfy myself that they were properly treated and looked after. I saw most of the boys and went to several of their homes. They all expressed themselves as being very comfortable and liked their work. The people with whom they lived spoke very well of their conduct generally, and the boys looked happy and well cared for.

BAKING DEPARTMENT - During the year 2,220 sacks of flour have been made into bread and cakes for the several Establishments - the bread averaging 92¾ - 94 lb loaves to the sack.

SHOEMAKING - 68 new pairs of boots have been made and 4,416 pairs repaired.

TAILORING - 57 new garments have been made and 3,412 repaired.

ENGINEER'S DEPARTMENT - Executing all general repairs and upkeep of the engines, boilers, gas and water plants and the laundry machinery at the Workhouse and Branch Workhouse, and the engineering repairs at the Intermediate Schools, and most of the old gas pendants, brackets, and Wenham burners in the Dining Hall, Corridors, Day Rooms, Dormitories and Workshops at the Workhouse have been removed and replaced with Rego lamps and Bray's inverted burners. Guards have been fixed to all the machinery and hydros in the Laundry by the Engineer's staff.

The following articles have been made in the Carpenter's shop for the several Institutions, and Offices, and general repairs carried out under the supervision of the Superintendent of Mechanical Labour:-

1 Cabinet with 24 drawers, for Clerk's Office

    1 Cabinet with 9 drawers]

    1 Cabinet with 10 drawers]   *For the*

    1 Combination counter-top cupboard]   *Finance*

    2 Tables]   *Office*

    2 Large Cabinets, 12 drawers each]

    1 Large Cabinet, 15 drawers]   *For the*

    1 Cabinet, 6 drawers]   *Record*

    1 Large Cupboard]   *Office*

    3 Tables]

    1 Combination Cupboard with 9 drawers, for Clerk's Office]

St James' Infirmary

    1 Combination Cabinet and Desk, with 20 drawers, for Medical Superintendent's Office

    1 Stand for safe

    1 Platform, with steps, for Kitchen

    1 False bottom for tank

    1 Key board

    2 Letter boxes

    1 Large carving board

    12 Small carving board

    12 Bread boards

    18 Large boards for cleaning waterproof sheets

Superintendent Registrar's Office

    1 Cabinet

    1 Glass case with brass rack for notices

    1 Set shelves

    1 Wooden case with 10 pigeon holes

    1 Letter box

    1 Pair steps

Out-Relief Offices

1 Cabinet, with 6 drawers	Mr Brocking
1 Table	Mr Eastoe
1 Table	Mr Driscoll
1 Table	Mr Mantle

Intermediate Schools

    3 Large cupboards

Workhouse

6 Sleeve boards	5 Tables
10 Servants' boxes	1 Door
6 Stools	4 Sash frames
13 Notice boards	10 Trays, for Kitchen
4 pairs steps	6 Trestles for laundry
6 Hammock rests for children	3 Skirt boards for laundry
2 Cupboards	18 Wheelbarrows

and a number of small articles such as soap boxes, towel rollers, washing boards, &c.

All general repairs for the Workhouse, Branch Workhouse, and the Intermediate Schools have been done by Inmate labour.

3,990 yards of tar paving; old yards picked up; tar paving broken, mixed and re-laid with new topping; 5,277 yards tar paving redressed with tar and sand.

PAINTERS' WORK - 44 rooms; ceiling and walls washed down, ceilings distempered, walls painted 3 coats, and doors and woodwork varnished, 20 rooms; Stores, Larders, &c., ceilings and walls washed off and distempered, all woodwork cleaned and varnished. 9 Officers' rooms; ceilings washed off and distempered, walls washed down, and all woodwork cleaned and varnished. 6 Day Rooms; ceilings washed off and distempered, walls washed down and iron girders painted 1 coat; 8 rooms disinfected, distempered and painted. 3 Annexes ("H" Block); ceilings and walls thoroughly washed off, ceilings distempered, walls painted 2 coats, and all woodwork cleaned and varnished. 870 yards guttering cleaned out and painted 2 coats, inside and out. 512 yards rain-water pipe painted 2 coats. 272 yards iron railings, Intermediate Schools painted 4 coats. 107 iron sashes washed and painted 3 coats. 14 double doors painted, grained and varnished. 13 doors painted and varnished, 98 sashes and frames re-stopped, painted, &c.

BRICKLAYERS' AND PLUMBERS' WORKS - All general repairs at the Workhouse, Branch Workhouse, and Intermediate Schools have been done by Inmate labour

FIREWOOD - Firewood to the value of £1,455 has been produced and sold during the year.

MATRON'S DEPARTMENT - In addition to the good work done by the Girls' Aid Committee, the Matron has found situations for and placed into suitable service 18 women who were not of the class to be helped by the Committee; this is often a very difficult class of Inmate to deal with or place out as not only do some of them enter the Workhouse with the second or third child, but in many cases have otherwise lost their characters, but notwithstanding these difficulties it is pleasing to note that the majority of the women are now doing fairly well and going on satisfactorily.

NEEDLEROOM - 10,483 articles of bed linen, male and female body linen and female clothing have been cut out in the Matron's Stores and made in the Needleroom, and 118,463 articles have been repaired.

LAUNDRY - 1,601,017 articles have been washed during the year, averaging 30,749 per week and at the present time (now that we have the St James' Infirmary Laundry work to do), about 36,000 articles are passing through the Laundry each week.

There are many other items one might mention to show the usefulness of the work done by the Inmates, but this would make the report long and tedious. That economy in administration has been studied and practised is evidenced by the fact that according to the latest Local Government Board return, this Workhouse is one of the lowest in the cost per head in the Metropolitan area.

I am, Ladies and Gentlemen,

Your obedient servant

(Signed) R. OLIVER

Master

That the following report was received from the Medical Officer in respect of Year ending 31st March, 1911

ADULT INMATES - The health of this class of Inmate of both the Main and the Branch Workhouse has been satisfactory.

CHILDREN

(a) OF SCHOOL AGE - The inadequacy of the accommodation for this class in the Intermediate Schools has been proved by the fact that for a considerable portion of the year a number of Children have had to be accommodated in the Receiving Wards of the Workhouse, a most unsatisfactory arrangement which can only be remedied either by more frequent admission to Anerley Schools or the provision of more accommodation here.

(b) THREE TO FIVE YEAR OF AGE - This class has, as far as possible, been accommodated at the Branch Workhouse, where 40 beds are provided, and the health has been excellent on the whole, and the improvement in the weakly ones marked. We have of course, with no probationary accommodation, had outbreaks of infectious disease, but immediate isolation and disinfection have kept them within very moderate limits.

(c) UNDER THREE YEARS OF AGE - This class occupied the "D" Block at the Workhouse and is a continual source of anxiety on account of outbreaks of infectious disease. These Children are of the most susceptible age and the continual running in and out of the mothers for a few hours or a few days is a fertile source of infection.

LYING-IN WARD - In this Block 178 Mothers have been delivered of 179 Children (96 boys, 83 girls); 75 of the children were legitimate, 104 illegitimate. With regard to the mothers of illegitimate children, 62 were delivered of 1st child, 25 were delivered of 2nd child, 16 were delivered of 3rd or more. Twenty-three of the mothers in this class were under 20 years of age. Ninety cases were admitted in labour and in only one of these was the head free from nits or pediculi. Twenty-eight cases were of complicated labour requiring instrumental or surgical assistance. There has been no maternal death.

SKIN DISEASES BLOCK - The old School Block in which these cases had for nearly seven years been treated, was closed in January by transfer of the Children to the old Infirmary. The fact that practically 3,000 (2,989) Patients passed through and were cured in this Block proves the value of fresh air and plain food in dealing with this class of ailment

TEMPORARY ACCOMMODATION FOR INFIRMARY PATIENTS - On the 13th March these Wards with 120 beds were theoretically closed after being in use for three years, during which time 578 women, many suffering from acute illness, were treated to their own satisfaction (I am not aware of a single case of complaint) and to the benefit of the ratepayers.

RECEIVING WARDS - My reports for a long time past have drawn attention to the inadequacy of the accommodation of the Wards considering the number of admissions now compared with the first years of the opening of the Workhouse. The enlargement which is now under the consideration of the Guardians will, I hope, adequately meet the requirements and enable the admissions to be fairly and properly dealt with, which was impossible when very frequently 60 to 70 had to be crowded into sleeping accommodation for 24.

With regard to the female admissions, I would supplement my remarks as to the state of heads of the women admitted in labour by saying that in spite of the improved conditions under which the poor can, if they like, live, and in spite of improved and free education more and more dirty heads are admitted and women do not appear to appreciate their responsibility, either as regards themselves or their children, and evidently consider that the first duty of the officers of the Workhouse is to remedy a condition which could easily be prevented by the use of such cheap commodities as soap and water outside.

In conclusion, I wish to gratefully acknowledge the excellent work of the Assistant Medical Officer, of the Nurses in the Lying-in Ward, the Sick Wards, the Infirm and other Wards, and the assistance I have received from every officer in both Workhouses, and which has materially contributed to making the year's medical report, in my opinion and I hope in the opinion of the Guardians, a satisfactory one.

(Signed) ARTHUR E. DODSON,
Medical Officer
May 11th, 1911

In July 1911 the Workhouse had a visitor from Japan:

This is, I believe, one of the most important organisations which have been established by human kind to occupy for conditions of social life.

(Signed) T. KAKIHARA
Chief Justice of District Committee, Osaka, Japan

An inmate, H.C. Burroughs was sent to a farm in Cornwall.

A new Committee room was refurbished by inmate labour. The Committee recorded their appreciation.

Among some rejections, was 8 pieces of "Nainsook". This was a muslin like "Jaconet", a cotton fabric.

In 1911 a water meter was fitted to the Casual Wards by the Metropolitan Water Board and two meters were fitted in the Workhouse laundry.

Also in 1911 another horse was purchased and a further coachman appointed.

In January 1912 the Master, Mr Oliver, became ill and died. Arthur J Morgan was subsequently appointed Master.

On 18th April 1912 the Guardians recommended the purchase of "Tell Tale Clocks". These were a kind of automatic registering device, as a time clock.

Further reward offered for information on a female child abandoned on 30th May 1912. The child was accepted into the Workhouse and named.

That the Master reported as follows:-

I beg to suggest that an extra Officer be appointed who could be called 'Needle-Mistress' and who could take charge of the old women (numbering from 100 to 120) and who are now without proper supervision and do most of the needlework.

I need scarcely point out that the amount of needlework to be done in this Establishment is very considerable, and if this Officer be appointed, she could not only *do a considerable amount herself, but could also supervise the work of the old people.*

And your Committee recommend - That, subject to the sanction of the Local Government Board, a "Needle Mistress" be appointed, at a salary at the rate of £30 per annum, rising £1 annually to £35 per annum.

1st January 1914

I have been privileged to visit the whole of the Institution and should like to congratulate the Chairman and Committee and Master and Matron on the wonderful improvement I observe in every department.

(Signed) HUBERT CURTIS
Chairman of the Board

In March 1914 a servant was appointed for the Master and Matron) (a husband and wife team), the salary was £18 per annum rising by £1 a year to £20 with uniform.

The Guardians needed to know the breakdown of the able-bodied/not able-bodied in the Workhouse. It must have taken a considerable time interviewing 861 inmates to gather the following information:-

(b) *That 500 men and 361 women (861), were interviewed, and the circumstances attending their admission to the Workhouse were carefully enquired into, and the reason for remaining, and it would appear that the greater number are there through some disability either physical or mental.*

(c) *That the following statistics are submitted as the result of enquiries:-*

MEN	Between 20 and 30 years of age	Between 31 and 40 years of age	Between 41 and 50 years of age	Between 51 and 60 years of age	Between 61 and 70 years of age	Between 71 and 80 years of age	Between 81 and 90 years of age	Total
Able-bodies	2	6	16	14	-	-	-	38
Not able-bodied	6	8	14	56	266	102	10	462
TOTALS	8	14	30	70	266	102	10	500
WOMEN								
Able-bodied	13	22	10	14	-	-	-	59
Not able-	18	14	27	47	109	76	11	361
bodied								
	31	36	37	61	109	76	11	361

With regard to the able-bodied Men and Women, the following particulars are given:-

MEN

Single or Widowers	*10*
Married (Wife chargeable)	*2*
Married (with Children chargeable; Wife living outside)	*8*
Married (Wife and Children chargeable)	*11*

Married (Wife and Children outside)	*5*
Widowers with Children	*2*
	38

WOMEN

Single or Widows	*13*
Married (Husband chargeable)	*5*
Married (Husband allowed out)	*3*
Married (deserted; no Children chargeable)	*2*
Married (deserted, or otherwise apart from Husband; with Children chargeable)	*9*
Married (in for confinement)	*1*
Widows (with Children chargeable)	*11*
Single (with Children chargeable)	*8*
Single or Widows (in for confinement)	*7*
	59

Includes 4 Women who are under 20 years of age
Feeble-minded persons are counted among the not able-bodied.

(d) *With regard to the men it will be observed that only 38 can be classified as able-bodied, many of them are of poor physique and could not compete with the really able-bodied in the Labour Market - in fact those who ought to be at work outside, and who, in your Sub-Committee's opinion could obtain situations, number less than a dozen, and most of these are married with families, and it is not considered desirable that they should be allowed out without their families - several having on various occasions been granted leave, for say period of a month to look for work, but the result has been that in many cases owing to loss of character, or lack of energy, they had to return.*

With regard to men between 50 and 60 several explained the reason of their inability to obtain work was the fact that being over 50 was a great draw-back.

In their endeavours to get work they sometimes get taken on by old foremen who have known them for years, but when the heads of the firms come round and see them at work, the foremen are instructed to discharge them, and they are thus unable to get continuous work and finally drift into the Workhouse, thus showing that the effect of the Workmen's Compensation Act has not improved the condition of the middle aged and elderly men.

A goodly number of the Inmates do their utmost to find employment even to walking as far as Wales when it was rumoured work was to be found there, but were unable to obtain it and had to retrace their steps, as they found employers declined to engage them on account of age.

Firms changing hands, or going into bankruptcy, or reduction of staff, was frequently given as the cause of having to seek the assistance of the Poor law and a word of sympathy and encouragement was accorded to these cases.

Some of the younger men were instructed to go out at once and try for employment, whilst in others they were informed their cases would be brought up again.

Others with families dependent were advised to make application to the Workhouse Committee for leave.

(e) *That your Sub-Committee was much struck with the number of married men, especially over 60, whose wives had left them, or were remaining outside and earning their livelihood.*

Many had not seen their wives for years.

In many cases the wife was living with either a son or daughter but accommodation could not be provided for the father.

In some cases the cause was the inability of the father to get on with his relatives.

(f) *That regarding the women, although the number of able-bodied may on the face of it appear large, it must be borne in mind that 14 are over 50 years of age, that some are chargeable owing to their husbands having deserted them or being in prison (their homes having been disposed of), that some are single women with one or more children.*

It may safely be taken for granted that no woman need remain in the Workhouse, if in possession of a good character, as the Matron is always ready and does obtain situations for them, whilst with regard to single women with first child, the "Girls' Aid Committee" assists them to obtain situations and also with monetary help to support the child for a time.

The Master was directed to bring several cases to the notice of the Girls' Aid Committee, and in other cases it was impressed upon the mothers the necessity of obtaining maintenance orders against the fathers of their children.

(g) *That there is no doubt drink was the cause of some of the cases coming into the House, but this did not show particularly prominent in the course of enquiry.*

(h) *That it will be observed that there are in the Workhouse nearly 200 Inmates who are eligible for old-age pensions, and in response to enquiries as to the reason the Old-age Pension had not been taken advantage of, the reply invariably was either:*

(1) They had no friends to go to and the amount was insufficient to live on without assistance, or

(2) They could not get on with relatives.

In fact several cases came under notice where the Pension had been taken up but the recipients had to return to the Workhouse, owing to their inability, as one or two put it "to exist outside" whilst one old man (about 80) said he liked the Workhouse best as he could do some work (chopping wood).

Inmates approaching 70 years of age were instructed how to obtain the Old-Age Pension, and recommended to take it up if they had any relatives or friends who could provide them with a bed free of charge, but in these cases where there did not appear to be any likelihood of help forthcoming, the Sub-Committee did not urge them to leave the establishment, as without assistance the Pension is not sufficient to maintain them in London.

(i)   That careful and searching enquiries were made as to whether Inmates had sons able to assist their parents; and a number of cases were referred to the Collectors, and the Clerk as instructed to communicate with children in certain cases.

(j)   That in a few cases enquiries were directed to be made relative to the husbands of deserted women, and also as to settlement.

That your Committee received the following Report on the Sub-Committee, viz.:-

(A)   That your Sub-Committee considered the arrangements for dealing with the washing from Tooting Home and St. James' Infirmary, and in connection therewith the following Report form the Acting Master of the Workhouse, viz.-

With reference to the Laundry work, I have gone into the matter with the Engineer and Head Laundress, and we cannot get the whole of the washing home to each Institution we wash for at the end of each week. We can wash everything, but the trouble comes in drying. For the past three months we have been unable to scarcely dry anything in the Drying Ground owing to the wet weather - and the Laundress informs me this trouble always occurs this time of the year - and we have had to rely solely upon our Horses and Drying Rooms, which, for the whole of the work, are inadequate. The Engineer suggest that the old Box Mangle - which is practically worn out - be done away with in the Laundry and another Calender put in its place. This would help us greatly, but this would not prove sufficient - in fact, to sum the matter up, we are of opinion that under the existing circumstances, so far as the sorting, drying, ironing, and finishing off work is concerned, we cannot meet the demands placed upon us.

(B)   That the following Officers were interviewed, viz.:- Miss Todd, Matron St James' Infirmary; Mr Hickmott, Master Tooting Home; Mr Hartley, Acting Master; Mrs Rogers, Matron; Miss Lock, Laundry Superintendent; and Mr Aldworth, Engineer at the Workhouse.

(C)   That the trouble appears to be the inability of the Laundry Staff to clear up one week's washing before another consignment is sent in, and the arrears have been gradually accumulating, as the following shows, viz:- On a Saturday in December, 1911, the number of articles remaining in the Laundry belonging to the Tooting Home was 1, 642, but on Saturday, 16th March, 1912, this number was 3,431.

(D)   That Mr Hickmott stated that prior to the opening of the St. James; Infirmary, difficulty was experienced in getting the Tooting Home washing done at the Workhouse, but since the Infirmary washing was partly done at the Workhouse, the difficulties had been greater and it is not possible to properly check all the articles as the delivery was not made at Tooting until about 3.30 on Saturday afternoons.

(E)   That it is necessary that the arrears of work should be cleared off as quickly as possible as it is neither conducive to the good working of the Establishments nor the life of the material for goods to be lying at the Laundry for weeks, and in view of the fact that the Officers have to furnish during the course of next month reports to the Guardians as to the stocks agreeing with the Inventories.

Your Sub-Committee accordingly recommend -

> (1) That the washing at St James' Infirmary and Tooting Home be, for a period of four weeks, done at outside Laundries so as to enable the Workhouse Laundry Staff to clear up the goods now lying there.

(2) That the Workhouse Committee do take into consideration the question of the provision of the following:-

(A) Another Calender.

(B) A Waterleap Flannel Washer or similar machine.

Recommending -

(1) That the necessary steps be taken to provide a "Summerscales" Calender.

(2) That it be an instruction to the Laundry Officials at the Workhouse to arrange that the articles, when taken out of the Hydros, be unfolded before being taken to the Drying Rooms. At the present time the articles are simply taken in the trolleys to the Drying Rooms as they come out of the Hydros, and full advantage is not taken of the rooms owing to the delay in opening out the articles to place them on the rods.

(3) That an additional Laundrywoman be engaged to supervise the Drying Horses and Drying Rooms.

(4) That with a view to clearing up arrears, the whole of the washing from Tooting Homes, for a period of four weeks, be done at outside laundries.

(5) That the question of the provision of a "Waterleap" Flannel Washer or similar machine, be deferred until the new Master and Matron have taken up their duties and are in a position to report as to the necessity or otherwise of increasing the machinery.

Reporting:-

(a) That your Sub-Committee visited three Laundries and inspected the "Wardle" continuous Drying Machine; and, from their own observations and enquiries made elsewhere, are of opinion that the machine is an excellent one, and suitable for what is required at the Workhouse Laundry.

(b) That Messrs. Wardle & Co., have been asked to give an estimate for providing and fitting up one of their No. 6 Drying Machines.

(c) That the amount of such estimate is £258. 12s .6d., which your Sub-Committee consider a reasonable one, and it is recommended - That, subject to the sanction of the Local Government Board, a Contract be entered into with Messrs. W. W. Wardle & Co., for supplying, fixing, and leaving in thorough working order.

November, 1913.

That your Committee considered the Report of the Departmental Committee of the Local Government Board, together with the Draft of suggested Poor Law Institutions Orders, and beg to submit recommendations to the Board thereon, viz.-

Suggested provision in Draft Order	Observations and Recommendations of Special Committee
PREAMBLE Provided always that nothing contained in this Order shall (1) apply to an institution which is carried on under separate administration in pursuance of a special Order relating to that institution and is provided for the reception and maintenance of: (a)Children, or (b) persons suffering from disease of body or mind; or (2) affect the operation of a special Order relating to an institution such as is referred to in paragraph (1) of this proviso; or (3) alter or otherwise affect the existing regulations with regard to the relief of destitute wayfarers and wanderers.	That the Institutions Order do not apply to Cottage and Scattered Homes for Children, Intermediate Schools, or receiving Homes for Children not under Special Orders.
ARTICLE 6 - In every case in which an inmate is admitted without an order of the Guardians, the Guardians shall, at their next ordinary meeting, decide, subject to the Regulations for the time being in force with respect to relief, and to any statutory provision affecting the case, whether relief shall be continued, and, if so, in what form, and shall make an order accordingly.	That it should not only be the Guardians who are to decide whether relief shall be continued to an inmate admitted without an order of the Guardians as provided by the Draft Order, but that the Guardians should have the power to delegate such duty to the House or some other Committee.
ARTICLE 7 - An inmate shall immediately on his admission be placed in a receiving ward, and shall be searched in accordance with Regulations made by the Guardians in pursuance of Article 47. Any articles found upon the inmate which are prohibited by Act of Parliament, by Order of the Board, or by regulations made by the Guardians, shall be taken from him and disposed of as the Guardians direct.	That this Article be so amended that only "prohibited" articles taken from an inmate may be disposed of as the Guardians direct.
ARTICLE 11 - That dietary of the inmates, other than the inmates of sick wards and lunatic wards and the infants, shall be in accordance with Dietary Tables in the Form 1 (in Schedule B) made in the manner prescribed by the Regulations contained in Schedule A.	Under present arrangements Dietary Tables are weekly and this is proposed in Draft Order, but it is recommended - That the Dietary be formulated for a fortnight, so as to enable a greater variety of meals to be prescribed.
ARTICLE 18 - The Matron, or in the case of an inmate of a lunatic ward or an infant, such officer as the Guardians appoint shall (1) Where a bed-card is in use, cause correct copies of the entries relating to the diet of the patient made by the Medical Officer or Assistant Medical Officer upon the Record-paper to be immediately entered on the bed-card; and (2) Subject to the provisions of Article 17, make suitable arrangements for the custody of the Record-papers in use.	That this Article be amended so as to provide that in addition to the "Matron", as now provided by the Draft Order, "the Nurse or other officer in charge of the ward, or such other officer as the Guardians direct" shall have the duties therein provided, i.e., of causing entries relating to diet to be entered on the bed-cards and to make suitable arrangements for the custody of the record papers.

Suggested provision in Draft Order	Observations and Recommendations of Special Committee
ARTICLE 19 - (1) An inmate of the sick wards or of the lunatic wards shall, subject to the provisions contained in sub-division (4) of this Article, receive, as the Medical Officer or Assistant Medical Officer may direct, either the Dietary for Infirm Inmates or the Special Dietary for those inmates mentioned in Schedule A, or one of such dietaries as the Medical Officer may with a due regard to the Regulations contained in Schedule A have prescribed in the Form 9, together with such extras as the Medical Officer or Assistant Medical Officer may in any case direct. (2) The Medical Officer shall in like manner prescribe in the said Form dietaries for the infants above the age of eighteen months, and the Medical Officer or an Assistant Medical Officer shall also prescribe such extras as may in the case of a particular infant be necessary. (3) Notwithstanding anything contained in the preceding paragraphs the Medical officer or Assistant Medical Officer may if he thinks fit prescribe in writing a special diet for the individual inmate of the said wards or any infant. (4) An infant in arms whose mother is in the institution shall, so far as may be practicable and proper, be suckled by the mother, and such an infant shall not be weaned except on a written direction of the Medical Officer or Assistant Medical Officer. The Medical Officer or Assistant Medical Officer shall enter on the Record-paper all necessary directions in regard to the feeding of each infant under the age of eighteen months.	That a special Dietary should be prescribed for expectant mothers.
ARTICLE 25 - The Guardians shall take such steps as may be necessary to ensure that any child in the institution shall receive religious and other instruction suited to his age and capacity.	That the paragraph be so amended as to ensure Religious teaching being in accordance with the entry in the Creed Register.
ARTICLE 29 - (1) Subject to the provisions of any enactment in that behalf, an Inmate may discharge himself from the Institution upon giving reasonable notice to the Master of his wish to do so. (2) Unless the Guardians (subject to the requirements of the Relief Regulation Order 19(1) otherwise direct, all the family of the Inmate shall be discharged with him. Provided that where a member of the family of the Inmate requires relief on account of sickness, accident, or bodily or mental infirmity, the Master may, subject to any directions given by the Guardians permit that member to remain in the Institution after the discharge of the head of the	That the following be added to Article 29. That in the case of a married woman of satisfactory character residing in the Workhouse, and her husband being also an Inmate, the consent of her husband be not required to enable her to take her discharge.

Suggested provision in Draft Order	Observations and Recommendations of Special Committee
family, and shall in that case report his action to the Guardians at their next meeting. (3) Where an Inmate who is under the care of the Medical Officer gives notice of his intention to discharge himself, the Master shall forthwith cause the Medical Officer to be informed.	
ARTICLE 31 - The inmates shall, subject to any directions given on grounds of health or physical or mental capacity by the Medical Officer, be kept employed according to their capacity and ability, and, except so far as is otherwise provided in this Order, shall not receive any allowance or other compensation in respect of their labour: Provided that (1) only necessary work shall be performed by the inmates on Sunday, Good Friday and Christmas Day; (2) an inmate who is advanced in pregnancy, or recently confined, or suckling an infant shall only be employed at work which has been approved by the Medical Officer as being suitable for her and for such hours as the Medical Officer advises; and, (3) an inmate shall not, unless approved for the particular employment by the Medical Officer and acting under the immediate supervision of a paid officer, be employed in any capacity in the sick wards, lunatic wards, or nurseries, and shall not in any circumstances be employed in nursing a sick inmate.	That paragraph (2) read - "an inmate who is an expectant mother, or recently confined,..."
ARTICLE 35 - The Guardians may, by a special direction to be entered on their Minutes, order a refractory inmate to be punished by confinement in a separate room, with or without an alteration of diet similar in kind and duration to that permitted by Article 34 for a disorderly inmate; but an inmate shall not be so confined for a longer period than twenty-four hours, or, if it be deemed right that the inmate shall be taken before a Justice of the Peace, for such longer period as may be necessary for that purpose.	That the House Committee as well as the Guardians be able to order the punishment of a refractory inmate by confinement.
ARTICLE 41 - An inmate who (a) is over 60 or under 12 years of age, or who is infirm, sick, or of unsound mind, or is advanced in pregnancy, recently confined, or suckling an infant; or (b) has within seven days been under the care of the Medical Officer; shall not be punished by alteration of diet, or by confinement, unless the Medical Officer shall	That the words in (a) "or is advanced in pregnancy" be eliminated, and instead, insert, "or is an expectant mother".

Suggested provision in Draft Order	Observations and Recommendations of Special Committee
have previously certified in writing that injury to the health of the inmate is not reasonably to be apprehended from the proposed punishment; and any modification diminishing the punishment which the Medical Officer may suggest shall be adopted by the Master.	
ARTICLE 42 - Corporal punishment shall not be inflicted except (a) on a male child who is disorderly or refractory; (b) by the master or an officer specially authorised by him for the particular occasion; (c) in the presence of at least two officers, of whom the Master shall be one; (d) with a rod or other instrument, such as shall have been approved by the Guardians or the House Committee; and (e) after the expiration of two hours from the commission of the offence for which the punishment is inflicted.	That in the first line (a) insert after "child" the words "under 14 years of age."
ARTICLE 44 - (1) The Guardians shall, at their first meeting after the Fifteenth day of April in each year, or at the meeting immediately succeeding that meeting, appoint from their own body a Committee (in this Order referred to as "the House Committee") to be the Visiting Committee and to discharge the duties hereinafter prescribed. (2) The members of the House Committee shall be not less than five and not more than twenty-four in number	(2) That no limit be fixed as to the number of members of the "House" Committee.

Reporting:-

That your Sub-Committee considered in detail the Poor Law Institutions Order, and the Poor Law Institutions (Nursing) Order, 1913, and the Circular letter therewith, as affecting the Workhouse and Branch Workhouse, and report as follows:-

ART. NO.	SUB-SEC	ORDER	REPORT OF SUB COMMITTEE
1		Sets out definitions of "child" as between the ages of 3 and 16 years, and "infant" under the age of 3 years. "The Sick Wards" as provided for the reception of sick inmates and including maternity Wards.	With regard to children a number are accommodated at present in a separate house at the Branch Workhouse, and before 31st March, 1915 (see circular letter and Art. 4), it will be necessary to make some other arrangement for their accommodation and as the Guardians have to report to the Local Government Board before September, 1914, it is recommended - That the Workhouse Committee do take the matter into consideration in three months time. With regard to "Sick Wards" the only Wards affected will be the Maternity Wards as no sick cases are retained at the Workhouse but drafted to the Infirmaries.
2 & 3		Management of the Institution. It is necessary to define the class or classes of inmate to be accommodated in the respective Institutions.	It is recommended:- (a) That the Branch Workhouse do accommodate healthy able-bodied male inmates and male inmates who although not able-bodied are healthy, (b) That the Workhouse do accommodate:- (1) Able-bodied males and females. (2) Inmates who although not able-bodied are healthy. (3) Infirm inmates. (4) Cases in Lying-in Ward. (5) Infants. Children will be admitted as at present with their parents to the receiving Wards but immediately transferred to the Intermediate Schools. The Master reported - "Every effort is made to classify inmates in the Workhouse in accordance with their character. Separate bedrooms are reserved for the decent old people. In the event of an old man being very undesirable he is transferred to another class and consequently receives less privileges than he otherwise would do. The Infirm Ward is sometimes used for decent old men." (See Art. 1)

ART. NO.	SUB-SEC	ORDER	REPORT OF SUB COMMITTEE
4 5		Refers to Children. Relates to admissions.	Is practically the same as at present except orders are to be available for six days from date of order.
6		Deals with admissions "without Orders."	It will be necessary for the Workhouse Committee to report on these cases to the Guardians.
7		Relates to admissions being placed in the Receiving wards and being examined by the Medical Officer.	This is as at present.
8		Relates to Inmates found upon admission to be ill being transferred to Sick Wards or other Institutions suitable for the treatment of the cases, etc.	This is as at present.
9		Relates to searching, bathing, and storage of clothing of Inmates upon admission.	Proposed regulations are submitted under Art. 47.
10		Relates to classification of Inmates,	Under Art, 2 reference is made to this question, but it is recommended that the Workhouse Committee be empowered to give directions as to transfer of Inmates from one class to another as occasion may arise. Art. 10 (2a), see also Art. 3.
	2(b)	The Medical Officer is also to re-examine the Inmates at such times as may be necessary, or of any Inmate at his special request and a record is to be kept of such examinations.	This is a new provision and will be carried out.
	3(a)	The Guardians may direct that special classes of Inmates may be grouped together for Divine service, meals, or special purposes.	This is done at present, and it is recommended to be continued.
	3(b)	The Master may employ an Inmate of one class in premises set apart for another class.	This is as at present.
	3(c)	The parents of an infant or child in the same Institution are to be allowed daily access to the infant or child unless the Medical Officer otherwise directs.	This is a new provision and will apply only to infants, as children are not retained in Workhouse.

ART. NO.	SUB-SEC	ORDER	REPORT OF SUB COMMITTEE
	3(d)	Inmates are to be allowed to see, at reasonable intervals, any members of family in another Institution provided by the Guardians.	Rules submitted under Art. 47.
	4	Provision is to be made for married couples over 60 years of age to live together, or in cases where one of them is infirm, sick or disabled.	The present rules provide for married coupled with good characters and 4 years' residence, to be provided for at Tooting Home but it is recommended that the Workhouse Committee be empowered to deal with cases not coming under the foregoing rules.
11		Provides as to Dietary Tables being in accordance with Dietary Tables attached to the Order.	It will be necessary to amend the present Dietary Tables so as to provide for Tea being given to able-bodied Men, and it is recommended that the Medical Officer and Master prepare revised Dietary Tables, if possible, for fourteen days instead of seven so as to provide greater variety.
	(1)	Authorises the Medical Officer to certify a departure from the Dietary Tables, and the Guardians may approve such departure for a period not exceeding one calendar month, but the matter must be reported to the Local Government Board.	This is a new provision.
	(2)	The Medical Officer is empowered to vary the diet for particular Inmates until the next meeting of the Workhouse Committee, who can continue, if desired, up to one calendar month.	This is a new provision.
	(3)	Authorises the Master, if an Inmate is unable to eat, on any day, a particular ration, to substitute another ration.	This is a new provision.
12		Fermented or spirituous liquors not to be allowed to Inmates (other than in Sick Wards) except by order of the Guardians upon special recommendation of Medical Officer.	No fermented or spirituous liquors have been allowed for a number of years.
13		On 'Xmas Day, or some other day near thereto, and selected in lieu of 'Xmas Day, ordinary Dietary Tables may be suspended and Special Fare given.	This is as at present with regard to 'Xmas Day.

ART. NO.	SUB-SEC	ORDER	REPORT OF SUB COMMITTEE
14		Gives directions as to weighing rations if desired by Inmate.	This is as at present.
15		Prescribes that until new Dietary Tables are submitted and approved, present ones remain in force.	See Article 11.
16&17		Provides for a Record Paper being kept in respect of each sick case, and the filling up of same, and if necessary bed cards being provided.	This will only refer to the Lying-in Wards - certain forms are already provided and will be amended to meet the requirements of order.
18		Provides for Matron or other Officer to make entries as to diet on bed cards from "Record Paper," and for arrangements to be made for custody of Record Papers.	This is a new regulation, and it is recommended that Matron be the Officer responsible.
19	1	Prescribes that the Inmates of Sick Wards are to receive the diet assigned to them by the Medical Officer.	This is as at present.
	2	The Medical Officer is to frame Dietaries for infants above 18 months.	Recommended - That Medical Officer submit Dietary Tables.
	3	Medical Officer can prescribe special diet for Inmate of Sick Ward.	This is as at present.
	4	No infant in arms to be weaned except upon written directions of Medical Officer, and the Medical Officer is to enter on Record Paper all necessary directions as to feeding of each infant under 18 months.	This is a new regulation and will be carried into effect.
	5	An entry on Record Paper by Medical officer as to Diet or Extras shall stand good for a period not exceeding one month. Order for fermented or spirituous liquors only stands for period not exceeding 8 days.	This is a new regulation and will be carried into effect.
20	1	A statement signed by Nurse or Officer in charge of Sick Ward showing Diets or Extras to be furnished to Master daily.	This is a new regulation and will be carried into effect.

ART. NO.	SUB-SEC	ORDER	REPORT OF SUB COMMITTEE
21		Where provisions or fermented or spirituous liquors are required urgently for Sick Ward cases the officer in charge of Ward is to requisition and get the Medical Officer to initial counterfoil of requisition after.	This is a new regulation and will be carried into effect.
22		Medical Officer to draw up code of instructions with regard to bathing of Inmates of Sick Wards and Infants, and to make such entries as may be necessary in any particular case on record paper.	This is a new regulation and will be carried into effect.
	4	Provision is to be made for married couples over 60 years of age to live together, or in cases where one of them is infirm, sick or disabled.	The present rules provide for married coupled with good characters and 4 years' residence, to be provided for at Tooting Home but it is recommended that the Workhouse Committee be empowered to deal with cases not coming under the foregoing rules.
11		Provides as to Dietary Tables being in accordance with Dietary Tables attached to the Order.	It will be necessary to amend the present Dietary Tables so as to provide for Tea being given to able-bodied Men, and it is recommended that the Medical Officer and Master prepare revised Dietary Tables, if possible, for fourteen days instead of seven so as to provide greater variety.
	(1)	Authorises the Medical Officer to certify a departure from the Dietary Tables, and the Guardians may approve such departure for a period not exceeding one calendar month, but the matter must be reported to the Local Government Board.	This is a new provision.
	(2)	The Medical Officer is empowered to vary the diet for particular Inmates until the next meeting of the Workhouse Committee, who can continue, if desired, up to one calendar month.	This is a new provision.
	(3)	Authorises the Master, if an Inmate is unable to eat, on any day, a particular ration, to substitute another ration.	This is a new provision.

ART. NO.	SUB-SEC	ORDER	REPORT OF SUB COMMITTEE
12		Fermented or spirituous liquors not to be allowed to Inmates (other than in Sick Wards) except by order of the Guardians upon special recommendation of Medical Officer.	No fermented or spirituous liquors have been allowed for a number of years.
13		On 'Xmas Day, or some other day near thereto, and selected in lieu of 'Xmas Day, ordinary Dietary Tables may be suspended and Special Fare given.	This is as at present with regard to 'Xmas Day.
14		Gives directions as to weighing rations if desired by Inmate.	This is as at present.
15		Prescribes that until new Dietary Tables are submitted and approved, present ones remain in force.	See Article 11.
23		Refers to Lunatics.	Does not affect Workhouse.
24		Directs that every infant under 18 months shall be examined by Medical Officer or Assistant Medical Officer not less than once a fortnight.	This is a new regulation and will be carried into effect.
25		The Guardians are to take such steps as may ensure that any child shall receive religious and other instruction suitable to age and capacity.	This is a new regulation and will be carried into effect.
26		Provides that any Minister entering Institution to impart religious instruction, etc., is to do so, but to avoid interfering with discipline of Institution, etc.	This is as at present.
27		Provides that prayers are to be read morning and evening and as to divine service.	This is as at present.
28		Provides for new form of Creed Register.	New Creed Register will be provided.
29		Provides as to the discharge or leave of absence of Inmates.	This is as at present.
30		Authorises Master to grant temporary leave.	See Art. 47

ART. NO.	SUB-SEC	ORDER	REPORT OF SUB COMMITTEE
31		Refers to discipline and work and provides that Inmates shall be kept employed "according to capacity and ability," and are not to receive allowance or other compensation for labour except as provided in Art. 49 whereby Guardians can give Tobacco or Snuff and extra allowance of dry tea and sugar or prepared tea, except to able-bodied men.	Before being put to work Inmates are always examined by Medical Officer, and he decides what labour a particular inmate is to be put to. (See Art. 49).
		This Article provides that no Inmate is to be employed in Sick Wards or nurseries except under immediate supervision of paid officer and is prohibited from being employed to nurse sick cases.	-----
32		Provides as to dealing with disorderly Inmates.	-----
33		Provides as to dealing with refractory Inmates.	-----
34		Provides for punishment of disorderly Inmates and authorises bread and water diet being given by Master pending direction of Guardians.	See Art. 47
35, 36 37, 38 39 & 40		Authorises Guardians to order refractory Inmates to be confined in special room for 24 hours.	This method of dealing with refractory Inmates has not been in use for many years and is considered unnecessary.
41		Prescribes that certain Inmates are not to be punished without the certificate of the Medical Officer, in writing.	It is now the practice to obtain opinion of Medical Officer in such cases.
42		Corporal Punishment.	Does not refer to Workhouse.
43		Punishment Book.	This Book has been amended, and in addition to being presented to Workhouse Committee will have to be submitted to the Guardians.
44		Provides for the constitution of Workhouse Committee - (a) That Guardians shall, after April 15th in each year, appoint a House Committee to also act as Visiting Committee.	

ART. NO.	SUB-SEC	ORDER	REPORT OF SUB COMMITTEE
		(b) That the number of such Committee shall not be less than five, and the quorum three, or such greater number as the Guardians direct. (c) The House Committee to elect a Chairman, and if desired, a Vice-Chairman. (d) A member of House Committee to hold office for a year, and if any vacancies occur the Guardians to fill such vacancies.	It will be necessary for Guardians to fix quorum.
44	(2)	House Committee may be empowered to deal with more than one Institution. The House Committee are to keep a record of proceedings and make reports to Guardians, as set out in Art. 45.	Recommended that the House Committee also supervise Branch Workhouse, as at present.
45		House Committee shall - (a) Meet at such intervals as Guardians or Committee think fit. (b) Cause the Institution and Stores to be inspected once in every fortnight for two or more members, some inspections to be made without previous notice.	(a) The Workhouse Committee now meets (except during summer months) fortnightly and, in addition, surprise visits are made by Committees of three members. (b) Ditto
		(c) Consider at each meeting reports made by officers, entries made in Punishment Book, Alcohol Book, and any other Books as they think fit. (d) Afford Inmates opportunity of making complaints or applications and report to Guardians thereon. (e) Interview at each meeting Inmates admitted to Institution since last meeting, examine Orders of admission and make recommendations to Guardians with regard to the relief in each case admitted otherwise than by Order of Guardians. (f) Report to Guardians after each meeting or inspection, transmitting, also, reports made by Officers (Articles 58 to 61), and to make recommendations in regard to management as Committee think fit.	With exception of Alcohol Book, which is never used, this is done at present. This is the same as at present, but in future it will be necessary to report on cases to Guardians. At present time all new admissions excepting maternity cases are seen by House Committee, but it will be necessary in future to report certain cases to Guardians. The arrangements whereby relief is renewed to Inmates by a Sub-Committee of House Committee would appear to be still practicable. In addition to method of present reporting, the reports of Officers will have to be incorporated.

ART. NO.	SUB-SEC	ORDER	REPORT OF SUB COMMITTEE
		(g)Once in every half-year furnish a full report as to condition of establishment, and transmit half yearly reports of Master, Medical Officer, and Chaplain.	This is a new regulation.
		(h) Consider and report upon matters referred to them by Guardians. In the circular letter which accompanied this Order it is pointed out that the Committee will not be an executive body but will act under the directions of the Guardians, and will be subordinate to them. It will not be the duty of Committee to administer Institution, but to report to Guardians.	This is practically as at present.
		(i) Committee will have to keep a Special Report Book, and enter therein proceedings at their meetings and copies of every report made to them for submission to Guardians.	This is a new regulation.
46		Women's Committee - This provides for constitution of a Committee (if considered desirable) of persons other than Members of the Board of Guardians, and the Guardians can draw up regulations for such Committee.	In this Union there are a number of Lady Guardians and it is recommended that they be appointed a special section of the House Committee to visit the Lying-in Wards and Nurseries and interview Maternity Cases so as to avoid such cases appearing before the House Committee.
47		Provides for general control by Guardians of Institutions, and directs that they are to draw up regulations as to:- (a) Searching of Inmates and prohibition and disposal of articles not proper to be brought in.	The existing Order is as follows:- Duties of Porter - Each person shall, upon his admission into the Workhouse, be searched by or under the inspection of the proper Officer, and all articles prohibited by any "Act of Parliament," or by this Order, which may be found upon his person shall be taken from him, and, as far as may be proper, restored to him on his departure from the Workhouse. To search any male person entering or leaving the Workhouse whom he may suspect of having possession of any spirit or other prohibited article, and to require any other person entering the Workhouse whom he may suspect of having possession of any such spirit or

ART. NO.	SUB-SEC	ORDER	REPORT OF SUB COMMITTEE
			prohibition articles, to satisfy him to the contrary before he permit such person to be admitted. To examine all parcels taken by any person out of the Workhouse and to prevent the undue removal of any article from the premises. Similar duties appertain to the Portress - It is recommended - That in the event of any article other than those set out below (f) such articles be considered as coming under the heading of "prohibited" and be taken from such Inmate by the Porter or Portress and handed to the Master or Matron for disposal. That fermented or spirituous liquors be at once destroyed.
		(b) That hours of rising, going to bed, meals, &c.	Regulation submitted herewith.
		(c) The bathing and cleansing of children and adults other than sick cases.	Ditto
		(d) As to authorising Master to grant temporary leave to Inmates. (Art. 30).	Recommended - That Master be so authorised.
		(e) As to authorising Master to punish disorderly Inmate by withholding privileges or substituting bread and water diet between meetings of Committee, (Art. 34.)	Ditto
		(f) As to gifts to Inmates in addition to provisions, tobacco, &c., allowed by regulations. (Art. 50.)	Recommended - That the following be the list of articles which may be brought to the Workhouse for Inmates: - Grapes, oranges, plain biscuits, sponge, cakes, uncoloured acid drops, tea and sugar. Recommended-
		(h) As to Inmates visiting members of family in another Institution provided by the Guardians (Art. 10 (3).)	That parents be allowed to visit their children in the Intermediate Schools once each month, in the Anerley Schools once in three months. In the event of any parent wishing to visit a child which may be in any other Institution, application to be dealt with by the House Committee. This will not affect visiting cases at Infirmary or sick notices.

ART. NO.	SUB-SEC	ORDER	REPORT OF SUB COMMITTEE
		(i) As to husbands and wives and children who may be in Workhouse being allowed to visit one another. The Clerk is within 14 days after the making of such regulations to forward copies of the foregoing to the Local Government Board who have the power within one month to amend same.	*Recommended-* *That visiting take place in Dining Hall on Saturdays from 4 to 4.30pm.*
47	(2)	*A Guardian may visit at reasonable hours.*	-----
48		*Provides that two Inmates above 7 years of age (except married coupled) not to occupy one bed.*	*This is as at present.*
49		*The Guardians can direct that a specified allowance of tobacco or snuff be given to infirm inmates or those engaged upon exceptional or specially disagreeable work.*	*Recommended that an allowance of 1 oz. of tobacco be given to all male Inmates over 60 years of age and to those under 60 engaged in "exceptional work" such as:- Cleaning drains, cleaning boilers, working in stoke hold, working in bakehouse.*
		The Guardians can also direct that a specified allowance of prepared tea or dry tea with sugar and milk be given to Inmates except able-bodied males (class 1) apart from the ordinary diet.	*Recommended that all Inmates except class 1 (able-bodies men) be allowed 1/2 pint prepared tea in addition to the ordinary diet.*
50		*Provides for gifts to Inmates.*	*See Art. 47.*
51		*Provides as to times for visiting of Inmates.*	*See Art. 47.*
52		*Provides that the names of every officer, inmate, or person entering or leaving Institution to be entered in book.*	*This is as at present.*
53		*The Master is to keep certain books.*	*This will be carried out.*
54		*Where Master engages temporary Nurse the Guardians are to pay reasonable remuneration.*	*This is as at present.*
55		*A book is to be kept showing when Inmates, other than in sick wards, apply for treatment, and particulars as to nature of complaint, etc., is to be entered.*	*A book is already kept but will be amended to conform to regulations.*

ART. NO.	SUB-SEC	ORDER	REPORT OF SUB COMMITTEE
56		Provides for copies to be exhibited of:- (a) Dietary tables in rooms where meals are served. (b) Regulations as to disorderly or refractory persons, punishments, etc., in dining hall (Arts. 32-36), also rules made under Sec. 47 - in the dining hall. (c) Bathing regulations in the bath rooms.	Many of these are already exhibited in the respective rooms, but further copies will be exhibited to conform to the regulations.
57		Deals generally with duties of officers and carrying out all lawful orders and directions.	-----
58	1 & 2	Prescribes duties of Master, gives directions as to management and admission.	This is as at present.
	3	Prescribes delivery notes or invoices to be submitted to a Committee.	Recommended that invoices be submitted to the House Committee.
	4	Master is to notify married couples upon reaching 60 years of age that they have the right to live together.	This is a new regulation.
	5	Is to inform Medical Officer when prompt examination of case admitted is necessary and in other cases of urgency also to take care that all sick and infants are duly visited by Medical Officer.	This is as at present.
	6	To engage temporary Nurse upon report from Medical Officer.	Ditto
	7	To report to Medical Officer any case of Lunacy.	Does not refer to Workhouse.
		He is also to examine every infant under 18 months at least once a fortnight. (Art. 24).	By this Regulation Medical Officer is to make the examination.
	3	To examine every infant or child within 24 hours of transfer to another Institution.	This is done at present.
	4	Relates to Lunatics.	Does not affect Workhouse.
	5	Is to give directions to officers in charge of sick wards as to treatment and nursing.	This is done at present.

ART. NO.	SUB-SEC	ORDER	REPORT OF SUB COMMITTEE
		Is to report to Local Government Board within 24 hours any sudden death occurring amongst Inmates.	This is as at present.
	7	To report to Master any case of serious or dangerous illness, also refers to lunatics.	This is as at present, but lunacy cases are not dealt with at Workhouse.
	8	Refers to Lunatics.	Lunacy cases not dealt with at Workhouse.
	9	To furnish Medical Officer of Health with information as may be directed by Local Government Board.	This is a new regulation.
	10	To give to the House Committee or Guardians, when required by them, information as to particular Inmates also to certify in writing on the request of any Inmate, the sickness or cause of his attendance upon him.	This is as at present. This is as at present.
	11	To submit at each meeting of House Committee a report dealing generally with Institution.	This is a new regulation.
	12	To submit half-yearly a full report as to condition of Institution and on other matters which Guardians may desire.	Ditto
	13	Where making entries in books to employ the terms set out in a book entitled "The Nomenclature of Diseases"	Ditto
60	1 to 6	Prescribes duties of Matron:- To exercise supervision and assist Master in general management and take charge of linen, etc.	This is as at present.
	7	Is to keep a report book to be submitted by Master and report on any matters she considers necessary.	This is a new regulation and report book will be provided.
61 & 62		Refers to duties of Superintendent Nurse and Head Nurse.	See Nursing Order below.
63		Refers to duties of Midwife.	This is already carried out.
64	1 to 3	Prescribes duties of Chaplain, and sets out duties.	At present time, the Chaplain, Nonconformist Minister, and R.C. Priest (cont. on page 124)

(cont. on page 124)

ART. NO.	SUB-SEC	ORDER	REPORT OF SUB COMMITTEE
	4	Provides for a report book being kept.	each submit report of visits, but it is recommended although "Chaplain" is only mentioned, that all three Officers should submit report books to House Committee and half-yearly reports.
	5	Provides for half-yearly report being made by Chaplain to House Committee for transmission to Guardians.	
65		Prescribes that Guardians are to provide the necessary books, forms, &c.	-----
66		Prescribes that when anything done under Order before 31st March, 1914, is to be deemed to have been done pursuant to Order.	-----
67		Provides that Order is to come into force on 31st March, 1914.	-----
68		Provides that Order is to be cited as the Poor Law Institutions Order, 1913.	-----

POOR LAW INSTITUTIONS NURSING ORDER

ART. NO.	SUB-SEC	ORDER	REPORT OF SUB COMMITTEE
1		Sets out the meanings of expressions used in the Order.	-----
2		Directs that where there are 100 beds for sick cases a Superintendent Nurse is to be appointed.	These paragraphs (2 & 3) do not refer to Workhouse as the only Sick Wards will be the Lying-in Wards (12 beds), and the only Nurse in the Establishment is the officer in charge of the Infants Block.
3		Directs that in Institutions where three or more Nurses are employed and the number of beds for sick cases is under 100, a head Nurse is to be appointed.	
4		Directs that when neither a Superintendent Nurse nor Head Nurse is required to be employed and the Establishment does not contain a fully qualified Nurse, the Guardians shall after obtaining advice of Medical Officer appoint a Nurse or submit to the Board proposals whereby such skilled nursing (including provision for cases of emergency) as may be likely to be required for the Inmates of the Institution will be available.	All cases of sickness arising are promptly transferred to the Infirmaries, but it might happen that a case may arise where removal is not possible, and it is recommended that an "emergency nurse" be appointed.

(cont. on page 125)

ART. NO.	SUB-SEC	ORDER	REPORT OF SUB COMMITTEE
5	3	Directs that no person is to perform nursing duties unless she has been trained.	The present Day Gate Portress, Mrs Robinson, is a certified Nurse, and it is suggested that her appointment be in future "Day Gate Portress and Emergency Nurse" and that in consideration her salary be fixed at £25 rising £2. 10s annually to £35 per annum.
	2	Defines the qualifications of Midwives.	The Medical Officer reported that the present Midwife conformed to the requirements.

Recommending:-

(15) That the necessary books and forms be provided and that the Officers be directed to carry the Regulations into effect.

That your Committee considered a letter from the Local Government Board Inspector relative to the Staff of Officers at the Lying-in Wards, and in which it was suggested that having regard to the fact that pupils are trained at the Wards, the Guardians should consider whether it is not possible to dispense with one of the Assistant Midwives, and received a Report from the Medical Officer upon the proposal, which was as follows:-

With reference to the extract from the report of the Local Government Board Inspector in which it is suggested that it might be possible to reduce the Staff of the Lying-in Ward by discontinuing the services of the Assistant Midwife for night duty, I beg to report that it is admitted that there has been a decrease in the number of confinements here, the total for the year ending 31st December last being 142 compared with 164 during the previous year - for the reason for their decrease I would refer to my Report to the Committee on the 7th November last, when I said:-

"In the Lying-in Ward recently the number of births has been considerably below the average due no doubt to the fact that pregnant women are now kept at the Infirmary for delivery. When the Lying-in Ward was originally opened it was on the ground that Infirmaries were not proper places for such cases - according to yesterday's weekly return, 2 births have taken place at St. James' and one at St. John's Hill Infirmary. Hitherto, it has been the rule to transfer all labour cases possible to the Lying-in Ward on the first onset of symptoms."

During the year specified above, no less than 30 cases have occurred at St. James' and 5 at St. John's Hill Infirmary.

I hope now that the Lying-in Ward or rather its responsible officer has been approved by the Central Midwives Board, for the training of pupil Midwives, that this valuable teaching material may find its way here, for 35 cases means that I should be able to sign up at least one, in fact, nearly two more pupils yearly. I may say that for 25 years practically every case complicated and uncomplicated came under my care with, I think, perfectly satisfactory results, judging by statistics I have submitted from time to time, and which I hope to add to shortly when our records reach 4,000 cases.

Our present Staff is:-

One Charge Midwife.
One Assistant Midwife for Day Duty.
One Assistant Midwife for Night Duty.

Their hours:-

For those on Day Duty, from 7.30am to 8pm, and 7.30am to 6pm on alternate days, with three days leave per month.

The Night Midwife is on duty from 8pm to 7.30am every night with the exception of one night per week, when she commences duty at 10pm, and two whole nights per month when her place is taken by the Assistant for Day Duty.

The addition of pupil Midwives does not really affect the question, for as the Local Government Board probably know, the Central Midwives Board insist that the care of each case of childbirth not only at the actual birth, but for at least 10 days after, must be certified as being performed under the supervision of a qualified Midwife, a statement that cannot truthfully be certified if the pupil is to be left in charge of the Ward without the supervision of a qualified Midwife.

Another point which must be considered is the fact of the irregular supply of cases, we frequently get three or four cases in 24 hours and then may go as many days without one at all. I am unable to suggest any remedy for this.

My reasons for not agreeing with Miss Sansfeld's suggestion may be summarised as follows:-

(1) That if all the cases which should be sent here are sent here (and if this was possible in the days when we had only one ambulance, and a cab had frequently to be requisitioned, it is surely much easer now with three horse ambulances and a motor ambulance), there will be no decrease in the numbers annually.

Indoor stone breaking cells

(2) That is not fair or reasonable to expect an Officer after being on duty for 12 hours by day to get up and do night duty as well, especially considering that a majority of cases take place during the night. And here I may mention that this very argument was used by Miss Stansfeld herself when supporting my application for an Assistant Midwife for night duty some five years ago.

(3) That it is not fair either to the Patients or to the pupil Midwife that the latter should be in responsible charge for 12 hours.

(4) That unless there is an Assistant Midwife for night duty, it is a physical impossibility for a pupil alone to attend to all the duties to the Patients and Infants, not to mention actual cases of child-birth, and that Inmate help would have to be employed which in my opinion would be a most undesirable thing.

(Signed)ARTHUR E. DODSON, M.D.,
Medical Officer
26thMarch, 1914.

Indoor stone breaking cells and the sleeping quarters shown above

On August 4th, 1914, the First World War broke out.

LOCAL GOVERNMENT BOARD,
WHITEHALL, S.W.,
11th March, 1915.

ORGANISATION OF LABOUR

SIR,

I am directed by the Local Government Board to state that they have received a communication from the Committee of Imperial Defence, who have had under consideration the necessity of securing the best organisation of the labour force of the country in existing circumstances. In view of the needs of recruiting and of the demand for labour for the manufacture of war materials and for the production and transport of the necessary supplied for the population, the Committee of Imperial Defence emphasise the importance of releasing male labour of high physical quality, so far as possible, from other occupations, and of substituting, where necessary, men of more advanced years, or, where the conditions allow, women workers.

The Board are aware that local authorities generally have done much to facilitate the enlistment of those of their employees who are eligible for military service, and who can be spared, and they are far from suggesting that the normal staffs should be depleted to such a degree that the services for which the local authorities are responsible could no longer be carried on with efficiency. But at a time when the vital interests of the country imperatively require that as many fit men as possible should be added to the Army, when the manufacture of munitions of war is hampered by lack of labour, and when the same cause gives rise to difficulties in the supply and transport of food, fuel and other necessaries - difficulties which have largely contributed to the recent increase in prices - the Government are compelled to remind the local authorities of the importance of making adequate arrangements for utilising to the best advantage the available supply of labour. They would urge that only men who are indispensable for the work of the local authority should be refused permission to enlist; that artisans who belong to trades needed in the arsenals, dockyards, and armament factories should, wherever possible, be released and encouraged to find employment there; and that where there is a demand for labourers on the railways, in the docks, and on farms, &c., the local authorities should facilitate the transfer to those employments of any men who can be spared and who can there find suitable occupation and remuneration. In pursuance of this policy it will be necessary to economise labour to the greatest extent possible, and where substitutes are needed, to engage only men who are not eligible for the Army and not suited for the occupations to which labour should be transferred. There are some posts in which the employment temporarily of women in place of men may be practicable.

At the outset of the War there was reason to fear that unemployment might be widespread. The Government Committee on the Prevention and Relief of Distress suggested to local authorities that they should have in readiness schemes for new works and buildings which could be put into operation in case serious unemployment should arise. Local Authorities have in general responded to this suggestion, and in most cases such schemes are ready or in an advantaged stage of preparation. Happily, however, after the first few weeks, the trade of the country recovered from its dislocation, and the enlistment of large numbers of men and the execution of war contracts have in most districts converted the problem to be faced from one of unemployment to one of shortage of labour. In these circumstances an opposite policy is indicated, and it becomes necessary to avoid the inception of all new works except such as are of pressing necessity either for reason of public health or on account of war requirements.

Moreover, it is essential to see that capital as well as labour is made available in the directions in which it can best further the national interests during the war, and, as you are no doubt aware, the Lords Commissioners of His Majesty's Treasury have decided to restrict capital issues by local authorities as well as by public companies, within the narrowest limits.

After the termination of the war, when the men return from the Army and when the war contracts cease, it is possible that the question of unemployment may again become acute. The schemes for now works and buildings, which have been or are being prepared, would then be of the greatest value, and undertakings, which are now reluctantly postponed owing to the need of economising both capital and labour, could then be carried into effect with double advantage.

The Board direct me to enclose a copy of the Memorandum entitled "Officers of Local Authorities on Naval or Military Service," which they issued on the 21st August, last.

In that Memorandum the Board indicated their view that Local Authorities might properly keep open the places of officers in their employ who joined His Majesty's Forces with their permission, and the Board think that a similar view might, if the Local Authority were willing, apply to those persons in their employ who, in the present emergency, enter other employments, as suggested in this circular.

The Board are aware that the policy which, in accordance with the conclusions of the Committee of Imperial Defence, they recommend in this circular may involve the employment by Local Authorities of less efficient labour, the postponement of many desirable work and some public inconvenience. But they have no doubt that that difficulties will be faced and the inconvenience cheerfully borne in view of the needs of the time and the gravity of the issues at stake.

I am, Sir,
Your obedient Servant,
(Signed) H. C.MUNRO,
Secretary

THE CLERK TO THE LOCAL AUTHORITY

OFFICERS OF LOCAL AUTHORITIES ON NAVAL OR MILITARY SERVICE

The Local Government Board have prepared the following memorandum for the information and guidance of Local Authorities (including Poor Law Authorities).

On the 6th instant the President stated, in reply to a question in the House of Commons, as follows:-

"I am advised that it is competent to any local authority to grant leave of absence to persons in their employment who have been called out for active service as members of the Army Reserve or Territorial Forces, and to make reasonable payment in respect of their wages or salaries to persons authorised by them to receive the money."

The Board think that Local Authorities may properly grant leave of absence to officers in their employ who are already in His Majesty's Forces, or who join them with their permission, and may properly make such allowances in respect of salary as they think reasonable in the particular circumstances.

The Board further consider that Local Authorities may properly pay temporary substitutes for officers who are summoned or volunteer with their permission for Naval or Military Service.

The Treasury Regulations and Instructions of the 11th and 20th August, 1914, dealing with the case of Civil Servants on Naval or Military Service, provide for the payment to them or to their representatives during their absence from Civil duty of their full Civil Pay less a deduction on account of Navy or Army pay and allowances. For all ranks below Commissioned Officer this deduction will be at the rate of seven shillings a *week, together with the actual amount of any Army separation allowance paid to the family of a married man.*

As regards a Commissioned Officer the deduction will be equal to his active service pay (allowances being neglected).

The Civil Posts of those officers and men will not be permanently filled during their absence on Naval or Military Service, and that service will count for Civil Pension and for increments of Civil Salary.

LOCAL GOVERNMENT BOARD.

21ST August, 1914
LOCAL GOVERNMENT BOARD,
WHITEHALL, S.W.,
10th September, 1914

MILITARY OCCUPATION OF POOR LAW PREMISES

Sir,

I am directed by the Local Government Board to advert to their letter dated the 31st March last, with reference to the compensation to be paid in respect of the military occupation of premises belonging to Poor Law Authorities.

In paragraph 7 of that letter it was suggested that claims for compensation might be held back until the Guardians had re-occupied their premises. Their further experience in this matter, however, leads the Board to the view that it is desirable that in every case interim claims should be submitted, and I am accordingly to request that on the expiration of the current half-year such claims in relation both to initial expenditure at the commencement of the military occupation and to current expenditure up to the 30th September may be submitted at the earliest practicable date. The claims should, if possible, be forwarded in the course of the month of October, and should not be delayed for the audit of the accounts of the half-year.

Each claim should be submitted in triplicate, and may conveniently be arranged in a form similar to that appended. It should be accompanied by a statement (which need not be duplicated) showing precisely how the amount of each item entered in Tables I and II has been reached. The Board will be willing to consider a draft claim, accompanied by this statement, if it should be thought convenient to forward a draft before the formal claim is submitted.

It will be observed that the headings entered in Table I corresponded to those scheduled to the printed letter of 31st March last. Where a saving has been effected under any heading in table I the gross amount of any additional expenditure under that heading should be entered in that table and a similar heading should be inserted in Table II with an entry showing the gross amount of the saving. Such savings may be expected to arise in connection with, e.g., the ordinary expenditure on repairs, the ordinary cost of relief to casual paupers (if the casual wards of the Union are closed during the military occupation), or even in some cases as a result of the cost of the displaced Inmates being less than would have been the case if they had remained in their own quarters. In any case in which expenditure has been incurred on the instructions of the Military Authorities, a reference sufficient to identify the requisition should be forwarded with the claim.

In their letter of the 31st March the Board explained that the general basis of the arrangements for compensation would be such as, while avoiding extra expense to poor rates, would prevent any profit being made for those rates out of the military occupation. They find that in some quarters the expression used has been somewhat narrowly interpreted, and it has been understood that the arrangements permit of a saving (as distinguished from a profit) being made by the Guardians. This is not so; the contrary is clearly implied in the statement that the Army Council will only make good the additional expenditure falling upon the poor rates as a result of the military occupation.

The amount to be claimed, therefore, is the difference between the amount which has actually been expended by the Guardians during the period covered by the claim (including all expenses borne by the Common Fund of the Union on behalf of the Military Authorities) and the amount which would have been expended by them if the military occupation had not taken place. It will usually be found that the latter amount can most readily be estimated from the ascertained figures for a corresponding period of the previous year, due allowance being made for variation of price, and of the number of Inmates.

Attention is specially directed to paragraph 5 of the letter of 31st March. In some instances the approval of the Board has not been obtained for arrangements made for the maintenance of displaced Inmates. Where this is so, the necessary steps should at once be taken, in view of the possible difficulties in regard to the payment of compensation which are referred to in the paragraph.

I am, Sir.

Your obedient Servant.

(Signed) A. V. SYMONDS

Assistant Secretary

That your Committee received and adopted the following Report on the sub-Committee of the Workhouse Committee with reference to the Receiving Ward accommodation at the Garratt Lane Workhouse, viz.:-

21st March 1911

That your Sub-Committee considered the question referred to them.

The present Receiving Wards provide accommodation for 19 men and 19 women, including children and were erected in 1885 when the certified accommodation of the Workhouse was for 645 inmates - since that time additions have been made and at present the wards have to accommodate cases admitted for -

The Workhouse	certified for	898
Branch Workhouse	certified for	275
Intermediate Schools	certified for	202
		1377

The Board recently decided that the Old School Block should be utilised as a Receiving Ward for children and this will provide accommodation for 36 children apart from the adults; but even with this, the accommodation will be far from sufficient or satisfactory.

All discharges and Admissions pass through these Wards and it is desirable -

(a) That those going out should be kept separate from those awaiting admission.

(b) That suitable rooms should be provided in which the Medical Officer can examine the cases admitted.

(c) That the accommodation should be so arranged that those inmates admitted at a reasonable hour are not disturbed by those coming in at all hours of the night.

(d) That Day Room accommodation should be provided.

On Christmas Day 1913 the Guardians reported that they found the Institution thoroughly clean and well decorated. Children well cared for and enjoying the roast beef and Christmas Pudding.

In December 1914 the Committee recorded their appreciation of the labours of the Officers in entertaining the inmates on Christmas Day.

A Register was kept of inmates wishing to see the Committee. When seen the decision on each case was recorded in the book which was submitted to the Board for information.

During 1915 instructions were given for a reward to be issued to enable the prosecution and conviction of the person or persons abandoning a child. The child was eventually identified. Records do not show if anyone was prosecuted.

In June 1916 the committee considered a letter signed by 41 inmates of "A" Block relative to the conduct of an inmate. The inmate concerned was sent to Belmont Workhouse.

In May 1917 the visiting Committee found children in the garden having tea. They were suitably impressed.

The temporary closing of the Branch Workhouse found all the inmates transferred to Swaffield Road by 30th June. The service of the following had to be dispensed with; the Acting Assistant Master, the Matron and a Cook.

LOCAL GOVERNMENT BOARD
WHITEHALL, S.W.,
30th November, 1914

OFFICERS ON WAR SERVICE - METROPOLITAN COMMON POOR FUND

Sir,

I am directed by the Local Government Board to advert to their memorandum of the 21st August, relative to the allowances to be made in respect of salary in cases where Officers of Local Authorities (including Poor Law Authorities) have been summoned or have volunteered with permission for Naval or Military Service. As intimated in that memorandum, the Board consider that Boards of Guardians may properly make reasonable allowances to such officers in respect of salary and pay temporary substitutes.

The Board have had occasion to consider, in connection with representations which have been made to them, what charges may properly be allowed in such circumstances in the case of Officers of Metropolitan Poor Law Authorities whose remuneration is wholly or partly a charge on the Metropolitan Common Poor Fund. They have decided that, as regards the absent Officer, the charge on the Fund may be such an amount actually paid as does not exceed the difference between the charge made on the Fund for salary and allowances, when the Officer was in receipt of his ordinary remuneration, and his Navy or Army pay plus separation allowance. With regard to any necessary substitute, they will be willing to sanction a temporary appointment with a view to his salary and emoluments being repaid out of the Fund.

I am, Sir.

Your obedient servant,

A. V. SYMONDS,

Assistant Secretary.

The Clerk to the Guardians.

The Committee received an application from Mr C.W. Francis, Assistant Cook, for permission to join His Majesty's Forces, and recommend - That his application be granted and that he be paid such weekly amount as, when added to his pay and allowances, will bring his remuneration up to the amount he is in receipt of as an Assistant Cook.

The Committee received an application from Mr F. Dart, Assistant Attendant, asking for permission to join His Majesty's Forces and from Mr T. Sear, Second Assistant Engineer, asking for similar permission to work in Government factories in the manufacture of munitions of war, and recommend - that their applications be granted, and that they be paid such weekly amounts as when added to their pay and allowances, will bring their remuneration up to the amount they are at present in receipt of from the Guardians.

That it may be of interest to the Board generally to know that one of the Intermediate School lads has been to see the Matron and since he joined the sea service -

"Was under fire of Submarine on Transport off Fastnet and wounded - transferred to another which sunk by Submarine off Cardiff - then transferred to Collier, which was also sunk in the Mediterranean - afterwards transferred to another vessel which took part in the Battle of Jutland and was sunk - now serving on a Mine Sweeper."

The Clerk was directed to convey the Committee's good wishes to the youth.

That your Committee considered a petition from a number of the inmates asking that on leave days the hour for return might be 7.45pm.

The Master, in view of the very dark nights and the fact that the majority of the inmates are very aged, gave instructions that they must return by 6 o'clock. The inmates can leave as early as 8am. Your Committee consider that 6pm is quite late enough, under present circumstances and the Master's action was approved.

In May 1914 the Master reported:-

I beg to report that I have given an extra allowance of 1 oz tobacco weekly to certain Inmates over 60 years of age who were engaged upon disagreeable work.

The Resolution of the Board of the 19th February, 1914, only refers to Inmates under 60 years of age engaged in exceptional work but as most of the drain cleaning, etc., is carried out by men over 60 years of age who are called upon to do work other than in the ordinary working hours, or of an exceptional nature such as cleaning drains, working in bakehouse, etc., I be authorised to issue an extra 1 oz tobacco weekly to each man.

With regard to the men sent to work on the grounds of Tooting Home from the

With regard to the men sent to work on the grounds of Tooting Home from the Branch Workhouse, all of them are over 60 years of age and I beg to suggest that their work should be regarded as exceptional and that the additional allowance of ½ oz of tobacco weekly which was given them prior to the Poor Law Institutions Order coming into force, be again granted.

It should be borne in mind that the men in question go to Tooting Home all weathers whereas the ordinary Workhouse Inmate is not so affected.

And your Committee recommend- That tobacco be issued as above suggested by the Master.

In 1915 the Workhouse was re-designated as an "Institution". It was still generally referred to as the "Workhouse" and run in the same way.

That your Committee received and adopted the following report of the Sub-Committee and recommend the same for adoption by the Board:-

Sub-Committee of "House" Committee
8th July 1914.

Reporting:-

(a) *That your Sub-Committee considered the question of the removal of the Children from the Branch Workhouse in accordance with the Regulations of the Poor Law Institutions Order, 1913, and in connection therewith a suggestion made by the Medical Officer of the Workhouse in his Annual Report, that, in the interest of the Children's health it would be a good thing if it could be arranged that the whole of the Children now in the Intermediate Schools could be accommodated in the St. James' Road Buildings, and the present Schools utilised as a Branch Workhouse.*

(b) *That whilst your Sub-Committee consider the St. James' Road site preferable to the Swaffield Road site for Children, they regret that it is not practicable to carry out the suggestion, for the following reasons:-*

  (1) *The close proximity to the Infirmary, and the noise of Children disturbing the Sick Patients.*

  (2) *The unsuitability of the Branch Workhouse for Children, the building being very old and would require to be reconstructed.*

  (3) *That the Intermediate Schools are not large enough to accommodate the Adult Inmates who would be displaced in the event of the Branch Workhouse being used for Children;*

and it is therefore Recommended:-

  (1) *That the Children be in due course removed from the Children's House in the Branch Workhouse, and accommodated in the Intermediate Schools.*

  (2) *That as the services of the two Attendants at the Children's House will not be required after the removal of the Children therefrom, that one Attendant be transferred to the Intermediate Schools for Night Duty, and that the other be found employment in one of the other Institutions.*

  (3) *That the piece of land adjoining the Casual Wards be utilised as a playground for the small Children, and that the Master obtain prices for the necessary turf, and that trees be planted on the side facing Swaffield Road.*

(c) That your Sub-Committee had under consideration the question of accommodation being provided for "married couples" ineligible for transfer to the Cottage Homes at Tooting, and report that when the detached Block at the Branch Workhouse is vacated by the Children, that accommodation can easily be provided there for such married couples at very little expense, and it is recommended accordingly.

The several paragraphs having been taken seriatim and carried, it was Resolved - That the acts, proceedings and recommendations of the "House" Committee for the Swaffield Road and St. James' Road Institutions, as submitted in the foregoing Report, be approved and adopted.

16th March 1915

1. The Board received and opened Tenders for the supply of Provisions, Necessaries, Clothing, &c., and it was Resolved - That the Tenders of the persons named in the following Schedule be accepted, and the Common Seal of the Guardians affixed to the necessary Contracts:-

WORKHOUSE, ST. JOHN'S HILL INFIRMARY, ST JAMES' INFIRMARY, TOOTING HOME AND INTERMEDIATE SCHOOL

ARTICLES	NAME & ADDRESS OF CONTRACTORS	PERIOD OF CONTRACT
POTATOES	Messrs. Higgs & Co Orpington	1st April 1915 to 30th June 1915
VEGETABLES (Sec. A)	Messrs. A. H & A. E. Sullivan 8 The Parade, Tooting, S.W.	ditto
PAINT, OILS, &c	Messrs. Middleton Bros., St George's Street, E.	1st April 1915 to 30th April 1915
VARNISHES (Mander's, or Nobles & Hoare's)	Mr. H. E. Olby 311 High Street, Lewisham	1st April 1915 to 30th June 1915
Ditto (Smee & Dodwell)	Messrs. Norman Smee & Dodwell, Miles Lane, Mitcham	ditto
GLASS	Mr. H.E. Olby 311 High Street, Lewisham	ditto
MEAT	Messrs. G.S. Miller and Sons 2 Belle Vue Road, Upper Tooting, S.W.	ditto
CHEESEMONGERY	Messrs. Webb, Sons & Clarke, 124 & 124a Kings Road, Chelsea, S.W.	ditto
BACON (Item 117a)	Messrs. Bowles, Nicholls & Co., 18 King Street, Snow Hill, E.C.	ditto

ARTICLES	NAME & ADDRESS OF	PERIOD OF CONTRACT CONTRACTORS
BUTTER (Item 118)	ditto	ditto
Ditto (Items 120 & 121)	Messrs. Webb, Sons & Clarke 124 & 124a Kings Road, Chelsea, S.W.	ditto
YEAST & MALT EXTRACT	Messrs. Waterer & Co., 94 New North Road, N.	1st April 1915 to 30th June 1915
GROCERY	Messrs. G. T. Cox & Sons 31 King William Street, E.C.	1st April 1915 to 30th April 1915
COFFEE	Messrs. D. R. Evans & Co., 68 Farringdon Street, E. C.	ditto
COCOA	Messrs. G. T. Cox & Sons, 31 King William Street, E.C.	ditto
JAMS & MARMALADE (Item 184)	ditto	ditto
Ditto	Messrs. D. R. Evans & Co., 68 Farringdon Street, E.C.	ditto
TINNED & BOTTLED FRUITS	ditto	ditto
MEAT EXTRACT (Item 189)	Messrs. Bovril Ltd., Old Street, E.C.	ditto
Ditto (Item 190)	Messrs. Oxo Ltd., Thames House, Queen Street Place, E. C.	ditto
FISH	Messrs. J. Everett & Co., Fish Docks, Grimsby	ditto
MARGARINE	Messrs. Dowdall, O'Mahoney & Co., 6 Union Quay, Cork.	ditto
POULTRY	Messrs. Miller & Sons 2 Belle Vue Road, Upper Tooting, S.W.	ditto
CORNCHANDLERY	Messrs. G. T. Cox & Sons, 9 & 10 St. Mary-at Hill, E.C.	ditto
TOBACCO	Messrs. Redgwell & Co., 193 York Road, Battersea.	1st April 1915 to 30th September 1915
MANURE	Messrs. Miller & Sons, 2 Belle Vue Road, Upper Tooting, S.W.	ditto

ARTICLES	NAME & ADDRESS OF CONTRACTORS	PERIOD OF CONTRACT
HOUSE COAL	Messrs. Thorpe, Head & Co., Wharf Road, St. Pancras, N.W.	1st April 1915 to 30th April 1915
STEAM COAL (Item 216)	Messrs. Charrington, Sells, Dale & Co., Pier Wharf, Wandsworth, S.W.	ditto
COAL (other)	ditto	ditto
COKE	ditto	ditto
MILK	The Salisbury, Semley & Gillingham Dairies, Fisherton, Salisbury, Wilts	1st April 1915 to 30th September 1915
SOAP	Messrs. John Knight, Ltd., Silveretown, E	1st April 1915 to 30th April 1915
SOFT SOAP	Messrs. Cook & Co., Bow, E	ditto
SOAP (CARBOLIC)	Messrs. Middleton Bros., St George's Street, E	ditto
OILMAN'S GOODS	ditto	ditto
DISINFECTANTS	ditto	1st April 1915 to 30th June 1915
MACHINE & OTHER OILS	ditto	1st April 1915 to 30th April 1915
FLOOR POLISHES	Messrs. Pryke & Palmer 40 & 41 Upper Thames Street, E.C.	1st April 1915 to 30th April 1915
HARDWARE	Messrs. H & C Davis & Co., 1 The Pavement, Clapham	ditto
ENAMELLED HARDWARE	ditto	ditto
ENGINEER'S FITTINGS & SUNDRIES	ditto	ditto
STEAM PIPE & FITTINGS	ditto	ditto
BUILDER'S IRONMONGERY	ditto	ditto
CUTLERY	ditto	ditto
NAILS & SCREWS	ditto	ditto

ARTICLES	NAME & ADDRESS OF	PERIOD OF CONTRACT CONTRACTORS
SCREWS (Nettlefold's)	Messrs. Bownson, Drew & Clydesdale 225 Upper Thames Street, E.C	ditto
TOOLS	Messrs. Pryke & Palmer, 40 & 41, Upper Thames Street, E.C.	ditto
INCANDESCENT GAS FITTINGS, ETC.	Messrs. H & C Davis & Co., 1 The Pavement, Clapham	ditto
ELECTRICAL FITTINGS	ditto	ditto
MEN'S & BOYS' CLOTHING	Messrs Milns, Cartwright & Co., 69-72, Hatfield Street, S.E.	1st April 1915 to 30th September 1915
HATS & CAPS	Messrs. S. W. Hart & Co., 81 Cannon Street, E.C.	ditto
DRAPERY (Cotton Goods)	Messrs. Milns, Cartwright & Co., 69-72 Hatfield Street, Blackfriars, S.E.	1st April 1915 to 30th September 1915
LINOLEUM	ditto	ditto
WOOLLEN GOODS	ditto	ditto
HABERDASHERY	Mr. W. S. Simons 79 Chatsworth Road, Clapham	ditto ditto
MALE OFFICERS' UNIFORMS	Messrs. Carter & Sons, 24 Old Kent Road, S.E.	ditto
MATERIALS FOR FEMALE OFFICERS' UNIFORMS (Section A) (Section B)	Messrs. Milns, Cartwright & Co., 69-72 Hatfield Street, S. E. Messrs. S. W. Hart & Co., 81 Cannon Street, E.C.	ditto
HOSIERY	Messrs. T. Wallis & Co., Holborn Circus, E.C.	ditto
LEATHER, GRINDERY, &c.	Messrs. J. Pangbourne & Co., 15-17 Liverpool Road, N	1st April 1915 to 30th June 1915
BOOTS AND SHOES	ditto	ditto
EARTHENWARE	Messrs. Green & Nephew 5 Upper Thames Street, E.C.	ditto
GLASSWARE	ditto	ditto

ARTICLES	NAME & ADDRESS OF CONTRACTORS	PERIOD OF CONTRACT
INDIAN-RUBBER GOODS	Messrs. G. MacLellan & Co., Glasgow Rubber Works, Maryhill, Glasgow	ditto
CHIMNEY SWEEPING Workhouse Branch Workhouse St John's Hill Infirmary St James' Infirmary Tooting Home Intermediate Schools	Mr R. T. Evans 39 Cambourne Road, Southfields.	1st April 1915 to 31st March 1916
CONVEYANCE OF PATIENTS TO ASYLUMS	Mr George Sutton "Spread Eagle" Yard, Wandsworth	1st April 1915 to 30th September 1915
SUPPLY OF HORSES ON HIRE	Messrs. Balls, Ltd., 308 Brixton Hill, S.W.	ditto
TUNING PIANOS, &c.	Messrs. Creswell, Ball & Co., 60 High Street, Wandsworth	1st April 1915 to 31st March 1918
ADJUSTING SCALES	Messrs. Vandome, Titford & Co., 5 & 7 St. Mary Axe, E.C.	ditto
CLOCK WINDING	Mr C. J. Quinn 64, Balham High Road	ditto

CLERK'S ESTIMATE OF EXPENDITURE FOR THE RELIEF OF THE POOR, &c.
For the HALF YEAR ending 30th SEPTEMBER, 1915
STATEMENT
OF
Estimated Liabilities and Assets to 31st March, 1915

Liabilities	£	Assets	£
Relieving Officers	510	Net Balance of Treasurer's Account on	6,053
Steward of the St John's Hill Infirmary	250	1st March 1915	
Stewart of the St. James' Infirmary	160		
Master of the Workhouse	120	Contributions to be received from	
Master of the Tooting Home	100	Parishes, due 5th March, 1915:	
Matron of the Intermediate Schools	20		
Clerk to the Guardians (Monthly Salaries	520	Battersea　　　　　　7,870	
and Petty Cash)		Wandsworth Borough　　16,689	
Quarterly Salaries and Superannuations	1,950		24,559
Invoice Account - Workhouse (including	15,000		
Branch Workhouse), Infirmaries, Tooting		Collectors, Masters and Stewards, and	1,400
Home, and Intermediate Schools		other Receipts	
Maintenance of Patients at Belmont	200	London County Council - One Quarter's	2,465
Workhouse	130	Grant for Indoor Poor, at 4d. per head	
Relief of Non-resident Poor		per day, to 31st March, 1915.	
Maintenance of Lunatics in Asylums, &c.	12,750	London County Council - Grant in aid	11,600
Extra Medical Fees	30	Of Maintenance of Lunatics	
Printing, Stationery, Advertisements, &c.	400		
Contribution to the Metropolitan Common	1,794		
Poor Fund	900		
Maintenance in Certified Schools and			
other Institutions	250		
Registration Expenses			
Vaccination Expenses	250		
Relief Offices and Dispensaries, including	250		
Cost of Medicines and Medical	50		
Appliances			
Funeral Expenses of Out-door Poor			
Out-relief Tradesmen	250		
Incidental Expenses	250		
Instalment and Interest on Loans	1,153		
Poor Rate Collector's Superannuation	50		
Paving Church Lane	231		
	37,568		
Estimated balance on 31st March, 1915,			
after payment of all Liabilities in respect of			
the Half-year, and required to provide for			
Out-relief payments, &c., during the period			
necessarily elapsing between the end of			
the Half-year ending 31st March, 1915,			46,077
and the payment of the first instalments			
by the Parishes.	4,278	Deduct Loan Accounts	4,231
TOTAL	41,846	TOTAL	41,846

Reporting:-

(1) That the Clerk submitted his Estimate of the probably expenditure for the Half-year ending 30th September, 1915, and your Committee having gone carefully into the matter, approved the same, with slight amendment; and accordingly recommend - That the figures as now submitted be adopted by the Board, and that Contribution Orders be served upon the Borough Councils accordingly, viz.:-

18th March, 1915
STATEMENT

Showing the EXPENDITURE during the Half-year ended 30th September, 1914, and also the particulars of the ESTIMATE of RECEIPTS and EXPENDITURE for the Half-year ending 30th September 1915.

Receipts	£	Expenditure	Actual Expenditure, Half-year ended 30th Sept., 1914	Clerk's Estimated Expenditure, Half-year ending 30th Sept., 1915	Amount recommended by Finance Committee
Estimated balance on 31st March, 1915 after payment of all Liabilities in respect of that Half-year, and required to provide for Out-relief payments, &c., during the period necessarily elapsing between the end of the Half-year, and the payment of the first Instalments by the Parishes.	4,278	In-maintenance, (Workhouse, Branch Workhouse, Infirmaries, Tooting Home, Intermediate School, and Belmont Workhouse)	19,771	22,000	22,000
		Out-relief	6,201	7,000	7,000
		Relief to Non-resident Poor	231	250	250
		Medical Expenses	1,565	1,800	1,800
		Maintenance of Lunatics in Asylums	23,359	25,750	25,750
One Quarter's grant for Indoor Poor, at 4d per head per day to 30th June, 1915 2,463		Salaries of Officers	17,435	18,000	18,000
		Rations of Officers	4,722	5,200	5,200
		Uniforms for Officers	499	550	550
		Superannuation Allowances	1,430	1,500	1,500
		Extra Medical Fees	72	75	75
Ditto, to 30th Sept, 1915 2,490	4,953	Furniture and Property	1,235	1,600	1,600
London County Council - Medical Officers' Salaries and Cost of Drugs	4,500	Ordinary Repairs and Alterations to Buildings	1,150	1,000	1,000
		Painting Works at St. John's Hill Infirmary	227	300	100
London County Council - Poor Law Teachers' Salaries	1,200	Painting works at Intermediate Schools	79	200	300
		Painting Works at St. James' Infirmary	---	1,500	500
London County Council - Registrars' Fees	27	Provision of Linen Room and Scrubbers' Room at Tooting Home	75	---	---
		Painting Works at Board Room	37	---	---
London County Council - Balance of Grant in aid of Maintenance of Lunatics	4,000	Alterations to Medical Superintendent's & Steward's Houses at St James' Infirmary	25	---	---
Sundry Amounts received by Collectors, Stewards, Masters and Clerk	3,700	Provision of Water Softening Plant at Workhouse	66	---	---
		Repairs to Boilers at Workhouse	75	---	---
		Extension of Boiler House at Workhouse	47	---	---
Sale of Firewood	350	Provision of Double Doors and Windows at St James' Infirmary	44	---	---

Receipts	£	Expenditure	Actual Expenditure, Half-year ended 30th Sept., 1914	Clerk's Estimated Expenditure, Half-year ending 30th Sept., 1915	Amount recommended by Finance Committee
	149	Electric Motor at St John's Hill			
Amounts to be received from Grant Under Section 2 of the Agricultural Rates Act, 1896, as follows:		Infirmary (balance)	60	---	---
		Printing, Stationery and Advertising	1,202	1,200	1,200
		Postage, Telegrams, &c.	160	160	160
(a) To be applied to Common		Horse-hire and Ambulance			
Fund Expenses		Expenses	499	500	500
(b) To be applied to expenses		Purchase of Wood for chopping	26	600	600
separately charged to the		Rates, Taxes and Insurance	3.480	3,550	3,550
Parishes: £ s d.		Relief Offices and Dispensaries	429	500	500
Battersea 0 0 8					
Wandsworth	5				
Borough 5 3 8					
Carried forward	23,162		84,201	94.035	92.835
Brought forward	23,162	Brought forward	84,201	94,035	92,835
Amount to be provided for by the Contribution Orders, as follows:-		Contribution to Metropolitan Common Poor Fund	2,017	2,500	2,500
In respect of -		Contribution to North Surrey School District	11,367	11,765	11,765
Common Fund Charges including Instalments and		Contribution to Metropolitan Asylum District	40,113	47,115	47,115
Interest on Loans 150,098		Maintenance in Certified Schools And other Institutions	1,874	1,875	1,875
		Registration Expenses	525	550	550
In respect of		Vaccination Expenses	760	800	800
Separate Charges 100	150,198	Subscriptions to Hospitals	146	150	150
		Legal Expenses	1,469	50	50
		Union Assessment Committee Expenses	276	450	450
		Instalments & Interest on Loans	11,496	9,820	9,820
		Insurance Stamps	285	300	300
		Miscellaneous Expenses, viz.:-			
		Emigration 94			
		Apprentice Fees 39			
		Audit Stamp 50			
		Maintenance of Inmates Under Orders of Removal 158			
		Cost of Removing Inmates to their Settlements 58			
		Travelling Expenses of Children to and from Schools, and of Visiting Committees, &c. 117	516	550	550
			155,045	169,960	168,760

Receipts	£	Expenditure	Actual Expenditure, Half-year ended 30th Sept., 1914	Clerk's Estimated Expenditure, Half-year ending 30th Sept., 1915	Amount recommended by Finance Committee
		Separate Charges - Poor Rate Collector's Superannuation	100	100	100
			155,145	170,060	168,860
		Margin to meet contingencies, and to provide for Expenses, during the period necessarily elapsing between the end of the Half-year ending 30th September, 1915, and the payment of the first instalments by the Parishes		5,000	5,000
TOTAL	173,360	TOTAL		175,060	173,360

Forwarding the following Circular Letters:-

(1)

LOCAL GOVERNMENT BOARD,
WHITEHALL, S.W.
4th August, 1915

ECONOMY IN EXPENDITURE

Sir,

In their Circular letters of the 11th and 25th March last, the Local Government Board drew the attention of local authorities to the need for the organisation of labour and the restriction of borrowing, with the consequent postponement of many desirable works.

Mr Long fully recognises the useful action which has been taken by local authorities to give effect to the suggestions of these Circulars, but, in view of the gravity of the present situation, he feels it his duty to impress upon all local authorities the urgent need for strict economy in every branch of expenditure whether capital or revenue.

The Prime Minister in a speech in the City of London, on 29th June, emphasised the vital necessity of husbanding resources and avoiding all unnecessary expenditure. He said:-

"If the money that is spent in these days on superfluous comfort, or luxuries, whether in the shape of goods or in the shape of services means the diversion of energy which could be better employed in the national interest, either in supplying the needs of our fighting forces in the field or in making commodities for export, which will go to reduce our indebtedness abroad. On the other hand, every saving we make by the curtailment and limitation of unproductive expenditure increases the resources which

could be put by our people at the disposal of the State for the triumphant vindication of our cause."

It is evident also from the tenour (sic) of recent debates that Parliament is impressed with the view that there is room for further restriction in the expenditure which ordinarily falls upon the rates.

The need for increasing Imperial taxation renders the question of local rates one of very pressing importance, and emphasises the necessity for local authorities adopting a different attitude towards their expenditure. To assist the individual to meet the increased calls in respect of Imperial taxation, it is extremely important that every effort should be made to reduce the local rates. Items of expenditure which would probably be regarded as necessities in ordinary times, must now be carefully scrutinised with a view to ascertaining to what extent they can be avoided or postponed. The fact that reduction of expenditure may cause some inconvenience to the public can no longer be regarded as a reason for continuing that expenditure at its former level. Expenditure on such objects as parks, recreation grounds, libraries, street lighting and watering, and the running expenses of all institutions require careful investigation with a view to possible economies. In some cases considerable economies should be possible, but even small economies are valuable, particularly where they involve the freeing of labour for other more immediately important functions.

For similar reasons Mr Long would suggest that, whilst not unduly relaxing the standing of public health administration in their area, local authorities should, as far as possible, refrain from requiring the execution of work, the cost of which has to be borne by private individuals, unless the work is urgently necessary for the removal of nuisances or for the protection of health. For example, the issue of notices for the making up of private streets, ought, in Mr Long's view, to be postponed for the present unless the circumstances are very exceptional. Even in cases where some works are essential, it will, he thinks, usually be found practicable to arrange for repairs of a temporary character to be carried out by the owners or frontagers.

A Committee has been appointed by the Government to inquire and report what savings in public expenditure, in view of the necessities created by the war, can be effected in the Civil Departments without detriment to the interests of the State, and Mr Long suggests that every local authority which has not already done so should appoint a committee with similar functions as regards expenditure out of the local rates. Such a Committee could also do valuable work in connection with the consideration of the estimates for the rates.

The Board would be glad to receive reports from time to time of the nature and extent of any savings which local authorities may have been able to effect.

By studying economy on the lines suggested above - even in details - local authorities will be rendering most valuable assistance in what is the paramount duty of the country at the present time - the successful prosecution of the war; and Mr Long feels that he can rely upon the willingness of the authorities to co-operate to the fullest in this National effort.

I am, Sir,
Your obedient servant,
(Signed) H. C. MONRO
Secretary
(4th August 1915 No. 180.)

THE ELECTION AND REGISTRATION ACT, 1915

LOCAL GOVERNMENT BOARD,
WHITEHALL, S.W.
4th August, 1915

Sir,

I am directed by the Local Government Board to forward for the information of the Guardians the accompanying Memorandum setting out certain provisions of the Elections and Registration Act, 1915, relating to the postponement of local elections.

I am, Sir,
Your obedient servant,
(Signed) H. C. MONRO
Secretary
(10h August 1915 No. 181.)

The Clerk to the Guardians

ELECTIONS AND REGISTRATION ACT, 1915
POSTPONEMENT OF LOCAL ELECTIONS

The Elections and Registration Act, 1915, which received the Royal Assent on the 29th July last, makes provision, amongst other matters, for the postponement for a period of a year of the elections of local authorities and other bodies, for the filling of casual vacancies, and for purposes incidental thereto. The effect of the provisions of the Act on this subject are as follows:-

The next statutory elections of county and borough councillors, district councillors, guardians, and parish councillors, are postponed for a year, and the term of office of the existing councillors and guardians is accordingly extended by one year. But this provision is to apply only where the next statutory election would take place before the first day of July, nineteen hundred and sixteen. (Section 1(1)).

Until a new register comes into force any casual vacancy, requiring to be filled by election, amongst the members of any county council, any borough council, any district council, any board of guardians, or any parish council, instead of being filled by an election, is to be filled by means of the choice by the council or board of a person to fill the vacancy and a councillor or guardian so chosen is to hold office in the same manner in all respects as if he had been elected to fill the vacancy (Section 1(2)).

The provisions of the section may be applied, if necessary, to the election, appointment or co-option of the chairman, vice-chairman, elective auditors, or members of any kind of local or other body or committee thereof by order of the Local Government Board as respects local bodies and by order of the appropriate Government Department as respects any other bodies, and may be so applied with the necessary modifications and either generally as regards all bodies of any particular kind, or specially as regards any particular body or bodies. In the year nineteen hundred and sixteen the day of election of a chairman of a county council in England and Wales, other than the London County Council, is to be the day of the first ordinary quarterly meeting of that council after the eighth day of March in that year, and nothing in any Act of Parliament is to require the council to hold a meeting for the election of the chairman or of aldermen apart from other county business. (Section 1(3)).

Any provisions of any Act or Order or regulations relating to any such councillors or guardians, or to any such chairman, vice-chairman (or members of a local or other body, are to be construed as if they were modified in such a manner as to give effect to the provisions of this section and the Local Government Board as respects councillors, guardians, or local bodies, and the appropriate Government Department as respects any other bodies, if any question arises, are empowered to specify by Order the actual modification which is to be made in pursuance of this section. (Section 1 (4)).

If any question arises as to the appropriate Government Department by which an Order should be made under this section, that question is to be determined by the Treasury, and their decision on the matter is to be conclusive for all purposes. (Section 1(5))

For the purposes of the foregoing provisions the expression "councillor", includes "alderman", the expression "borough" includes "metropolitan borough," the expression "statutory election" means an election to fill the place of councillors and guardians retiring on the expiration of their term of office, and the expression "existing councillors and guardians" means councillors and guardians who are in office at the time when the next retirement of councillors or guardians after the passing of the Act would, but for the Act, have taken place. (Section 1(6)).

Local Government Board
10 August 1915.

A letter from the Guardians of the Parish of Lambeth:-

"Dear Sir,
I am directed by the Guardians of this Parish to inform you that they have had under consideration the effects of Section V of the Army Regulations, dated the 16th September, 1915, with reference to the issue of separation allowances to dependents of soldiers.

Cases have been brought to their notice in which such dependents whilst inmates of the Infirmary have been informed that under the Regulations the amount of their separation allowances will cease, and despite the advice from the Medical Officer, having regard to their physical condition, inmates have taken their discharge from the Infirmary rather than suffer the loss, for the time being, of their separation allowance.

Cases have also occurred in which, in consequence of the fear of losing their allowance, persons suffering infection diseases have refused treatment in the Infirmary and as a result the disease has infected other members of the family.

In the second place the Guardians find that the Regulations create a distinction between Poor Law Infirmaries and public general hospitals, by continuing the allowance while soldiers dependents are inmates of the latter and continuing it whilst they are inmates of the former institution. At the present time the hospital accommodation of London is taken to such a large extent for the treatment of wounded soldiers, that a considerable number of people who, in normal time, would resort to the hospitals, now have to seek admission to Poor Law Infirmaries. The distinction which the Regulations endeavour to create, which has not been a real one for many years past, having regard to the scope and efficiency of the large Metropolitan Infirmaries, is at the present time entirely unjust and illogical.

In the third place the stoppage of the allowance of dependents of soldiers chargeable to the Guardians and the retention of the same by the War Office is unfair to the ratepayers, as it throws upon the rates the charges for the maintenance which should be borne by the former.

In the opinion of the Guardians the separation allowance of dependents of soldiers should continue during chargeability and it should be open for the Guardians to deal with these cases identically the same manner as they do with cases of civilians chargeable and by taking into account all the means of the dependants and their liable relatives, assess the amount of the contribution required from them in respect of maintenance, etc.

The Guardians are aware of the powers possessed by the War Pensions Committees, but with their experience of the work of these Committees they are convinced that they have neither the knowledge nor the staff, nor are their offices open sufficiently frequently to enable them adequately to deal with the serious position which the Regulations first mentioned create. One instance which will suffice to indicate the serious deficiency in this respect is that of the wife of the soldier who, having applied to the Relieving Officer of this Parish for Medical attention, under circumstances which admitted of the War Pensions Committee providing her with the necessary assistance she as referred to the Local War Committee, who stated that her case would be considered on the following evening. In the meantime, as no action was taken by the War Pension Committee, the Guardians found it necessary to admit her to the Infirmary, where she underwent an operation some hours before the War Pensions Committee were making their preliminary enquiries into the case.

I am therefore, to state that the Guardians, in view of these circumstances and others which have come to their notice, regard the effect of the War Office Regulations as a grave scandal, and in order that they should be no party to a continuance of this scandal, they have decided to discontinue informing the War Office of cases of dependents of soldiers becoming chargeable to them. They have also directed that the Metropolitan Boards of Guardians be informed of their decision, in the hope that they will support the action of this Board, either by adopting a similar course or by bringing pressure in other ways upon the War Office to amend the Regulations objected to.

Yours faithfully,
JAMES L. GOLDSPINK
Clerk to the Guardians

The Clerk to the Guardians
Wandsworth Union."

Each Christmas the Guardians authorised expenditure for decoration and extras. One Christmas they authorised £5.0s.0d. for records for the Gramophone and games for the men in "A" Block. £2.0s.0d. for coloured paper, etc., and £2.10s.0d for toys for the children and £2.0s.0d for Christmas decorations. A few decorations were purchased each year which built up to make a large collection for all the wards including the Dining Hall.

Inmates were given uniform clothes to wear and their own clothes were stored. This created a huge problem. The clothing store was checked and as found to have 1550 bags of clothes. 1068 were clean, 264 soled and 218 moth eaten. This resulted in the

Committee's decision that all clothing held continuously for two years should be destroyed.

A lot of clothing was rejected from suppliers:-
72 Army coats.
9 pieces house flannel.
56lbs leather.
24 overcoats.
114 tweed suits.
13 pairs Officers boots.
44 dungaree jackets.
200 lbs butt leather.
12 dozen boys stockings.
267 yards Forfar.

Furniture had been stored for 44 cases. Owners had either left the Institution, died or now in Asylums and no likelihood of being discharged. The Master put an advert in the Wandsworth Borough News of the complete list, in case anyone wished to claim any items, otherwise they would be sold.

When men over 60 went on leave in the winter, they were given overcoats to wear.
The firewood that the inmates had sawn was quite a lucrative occupation, but the sale of the firewood needed supervision at the Branch Workhouse.
A report shows the problem:-

That your Sub-Committee considered the question of the arrangements made for supervising the sale of firewood and also other matters relating to the Branch Workhouse.

That Mr Sullivan mentioned that on Friday morning the 12th January instant he had visited the Branch Workhouse at nine o'clock and on proceeding to the wood sheds, found one truck loaded up with firewood and two others partly loaded by the Inmates without any supervision, - after waiting 20 minutes, during which time the men completed the loading, the General Officer appeared and in response to an inquiry said he was responsible for the firewood being counted.

Mr Sullivan then saw the Assistant Master, Mr Musto, and informed him of the loading taking place without supervision and he stated that it was possible to check the numbers after the trucks were loaded, but upon Mr Sullivan having the bundles counted, it was found that in one truck there was an excess of 36, in the second 27 and the third 6, or a total excess of 69.

That your Sub-Committee interviewed Mr Musto, Assistant Master, General Officer Bell and Inmate Wagorn, and were not at all satisfied with the explanations given as regards (a) firewood, (b) the Officers' messes and (c) reading of prayers at breakfast time and can only arrive at the conclusion that the fault lies in want of supervision and in your Sub-Committee's opinion, Mr Musto, Assistant Master, has failed to realise that he, as the chief resident officer of the establishment (to the Master of the Garratt Lane Workhouse) for the good order and supervision of all matters in the Institution.

Report from the Visiting Committee dated 29th December 1913:-

We the undersigned, have this day visited this workhouse, inspecting the various departments. There were no complaints. This section of the workhouse Committee having on previous occasions noticed the great age of the men sawing wood, the Master submitted a return showing that the ages ranged - Between 30 to 40, 3; 41 to 50, 1; 51 to 60, 11; 61 to 70, 124; 71 to 80, 38; 81 to 90, 1; averaging 71 years.

From this number are supplied the labour for Gardens at Tooting Home Branch Workhouse, also Messengers and it is recommended - That in lieu of hand sawing an Electric Motor be introduced - Estimated cost £40 to £45, apart from the cable.

(Signed),   E.A. SANDERS. G. B. MUTTER.
T. W. PALMER.

(The consideration of the foregoing proposal was adjourned).

The Committee considered an offer from Messr. Shepherd & Co., to supply between 60 and 80 fathoms of firewood @ £7. 12s. 6d per fathom. In view of the difficulty of obtaining firewood, the Committee recommended that the offer be accepted upon condition that delivery was made at either Institution within a period of three months, and that the timber proposed to be supplied be of good quality. (The Master and Chairman of the Committee were asked to visit the Wharf and inspect the sample of the timber in question). The Clerk reported that this had been done and the sample quite satisfactory.

The Clerk reported that with regard to the Tender accepted for firewood at the meeting of the Combined Relief and General Purposes Committee, that the Contractors wished to supply half in "deal batten and scantling ends" (a measured size) and as a matter or urgency it was decided that the Tender of Messrs. Priddy and Hale for supply of 90 fathoms "deal batten and scantling ends" @ £6.14s.6d per fathom, be accepted.

That the Clerk reported as to the Firewood Account, it would appear to be necessary, in view of the increased price of Timber, to revise the present charges and it is recommended - That the prices to be charged for Firewood be as follows:-

To Shopkeepers 4s.3d per 100 bundles

To Shopkeepers 4s. per 100 if ordered in lots of 500

To Private Consumers 4s. 9d. per 100 bundles

Chips 1s. 6d per sack (The present prices are 3s.3d., 3s.2d., 3s.6d respectively.)

An Inmate was sent to Belmont Workhouse which trained Farm Workers. As he was fit enough to tramp the country, it was thought he could walk to Belmont! There was also a Farm Training Colony at Wallingford, near Didcot, Reading, the poor man was lucky not to have been sent there.

The Report of the Committee appointed to Revise Forms for Contract:-

It was Moved by Mr.Rees, and Seconded by Mr. Mutter - That the Report be received and adopted.

The Report was as follows:-

11th February, 1916.

Present:-   Mr Rees (in the Chair); Messrs. Fowle, Mutter and Norman

Reporting:-

That your Committee went through the Forms of Tender, and recommend -

(a) *That advertisements be issued inviting Tenders for the undermentioned periods -*

THREE MONTHS

Potatoes	*Vegetables*

SIX MONTHS

Paints and Oils	*Oilman's Goods*
Meat	*Disinfectants*
Cheesemongery	*Machine and Other Oils, Motor Ambulance Oils*
Bacon	*Floor Polishes*
Butter	*Hardware*
Margarine	*Enamelled Hardware*
Yeast and Malt Extract	*Cutlery*
Grocery	*Clothing - Men's and Boys'*
Coffee	*Hats and Caps*
Cocoa	*Drapery - Linen Goods*
Jams and Marmalade	*Ditto - Cotton Goods*
Tinned and Bottled Fruits (Section A)	*Ditto - Miscellaneous*
Meat Extract (Section B)	*Ditto - Miscellaneous*
Tea	*Woollen Goods*
Fish	*Haberdashery*
Poultry	*Male Officers' Uniforms*
Cornchandlery	*Female Officers' Uniforms*
Tobacco	*Hosiery*
Coal and Coke	*Leather, Grindery, etc.*
Milk and Cream	*Boots and Shoes*
Primrose and Mottled Soap	*Earthenware*
Soft Soap & Carbolic Soft Soap	*Glassware*
Carbolic Soap	*Surgical Dressings*

TWELVE MONTHS

Varnishes	*Dripping, Fat, Bones, etc.*
Chimney Sweeping	*Hogwash*
Funerals	*Conveyance*
Horse-hire	

(b) *That no Tenders be invited for set periods in respect of the following, but that officers be instructed to obtain quotations for supplies as required, viz.:-*

Glass	*Bonnets*
Engineers' Fittings & Sundries	*Linoleum*
Steam Pipes and Fittings	*Blankets*
Builders' Ironmongery	*Counterpanes*
Nails and Screws	*Female Officers' Uniforms (Section A)*

Screws (Nettlefolds)	India Rubber Goods
Tools	Medicine Bottles
Incandescent Gas Fittings	Clothing - Piece Goods
Electrical Fittings, etc.	Brushes

Reporting:-

(1) That your Committee went through the Forms of Contract, and where necessary revised them, and recommend - That advertisements be issued inviting tenders for the supply of the following-

(a) FOR THE RPERIOD OF THREE MONTHS-

Potatoes	Coffee
Vegetables	Cocoa
Eggs	Jams
Yeast	Marmalade
Grocery	

(b) FOR PERIOD OF SIX MONTHS -

Tinned and Bottled Fruits	Drapery - Miscellaneous, Sec. B
Meat Extracts	Haberdashery
Tobacco	Materials for Officers' Uniforms
Cornchandlery	Hosiery
Milk and Cream	Leather, Grindery, &c.
Oilmen's Goods	Boots and Shoes
Disinfectants	Earthenware
Floor Polishes	Glassware
Cutlery	Chimney Sweeping
Drapery - Miscellaneous, Sec A	Surgical Dressings

(c) For a period of Three Years -
Tuning Pianos, &c.
Adjusting and Repairing Scales
Clock Winding

(d) For a period of Twelve Months -
(a) Funerals
(b) Purchase of Fat, Bones, Rags and Hogwash
(c) Scaling Boilers
(d) Dispensing for Out-door Poor

(2) That no Forms of Tender have been prepared in respect of the following, and the Officers are to obtain quotations as goods are required, viz.:-

Paints, Oils, &c.	Brushes
Varnishes	Clothing (Piece Goods)
Glass	Men's and Boys' Clothing
Manure	Hats and Caps
Soaps	Drapery (Linen Goods)
Machine and other Oils	Drapery (Cotton Goods)
Hardware	Blankets
Enamelled Ware	Bonnets
Engineer's Fittings	Linoleum

Steam Pipes and Fittings	Counterpanes
Builder's Ironmongery	Woollen Goods
Nails and Screws	Male Officers; Uniforms
Tools	Female Officers' Uniforms
Incandescent Gas Fittings	India Rubber Goods
Electrical Fittings	

(3) That with regard to the undermentioned articles, these are now Controlled and the following have been registered to supply -

Meat - Messrs. G.S. Miller & Sons
Cheese and Bacon - Messrs. Reeves & Fussell
Condensed Milk - Messrs. G. T. Cox & Sons.
Margarine - Margarine Clearing House

(4) That the Clerk was requested to communicate with the Food Controller relative to the supply of Tea.

On the 11th November 1918 the First World War ended.

On the 14th July 1919 the Trade Unions brought in the 48 hour Scheme which meant that all the Attendants and Officers had changes to their working hours which caused considerable havoc to the Masters and Matrons of the different establishments, as their off duty hours had to be covered.

That with regard to the question of the 48 hour Scheme as it affects the Lying-in Ward, the Master at the last meeting reported as follows:-

In order that the 48 hour Scheme may work satisfactorily, it will be necessary to secure the services of an additional Assistant Midwife. It would be a great convenience to the Institution if she could be made entirely non-resident, as night officers under the scheme commence duty at 10pm and it is impossible to retain the Cooks on duty until that hour. I should be glad if you could come to some decision as to the salary to be paid to this official.

And the matter was then adjourned in order that he might consult the Medical Officer on the question. The Master reported:-

I have spoken to the Medical Officer and he is of the opinion that an extra Assistant Midwife is required. The present Staff consists of a Midwife, two Assistant Midwives and two Pupil Midwives and in the last twenty-two weeks the number of births occurring in the ward was 33. Having regard to the present Staff and the small number of births, your Committee disagree with the opinion of the Medical Officer and are of opinion that it is possible with the present Staff to arrange for them to work only 48 hours weekly and recommend that no additional staff be provided.

Demands followed, as could be expected:-

From the National Union of Corporation Workers, as follows:-

Dear Sir,

A Conference of Poor Law employees, representative of all grades in the Poor Law Service in the Metropolitan area, was held on March 20th, at which resolutions were adopted, asking for increased wages, reduction of working hours, &c., and amendments to the Poor Law Officers' Superannuation Act 1896. The Conference requested the Executive Committee of the National Union of Corporation Workers to forward the requests to the Boards of Guardians in the Metropolitan area and to the Local Government Board; and further, to conduct negotiations in connection therewith on behalf of the employees.

My Executive Committee have directed me to forward the enclosed applications to the Boards of Guardians in London, and I shall be pleased if you will place same before the next meeting of your Board, trusting they will accede to the request in respect of their employees.

With reference to enclosure 1 (Wages, &c.,), in the event of your Board not agreeing to the request, we ask that they agree to submit the matter to the Ministry of Labour for arbitration.

With reference to enclose 2 (Superannuation), this is a matter which, in our opinion could be best dealt with by a joint Conference of representatives of the Board of Guardians, their employees, and the Union. We respectfully suggest that the Boards of Guardians convene such a Conference at an early date in order to consider the proposed amendments and arrive at a definite arrangement in the matter.

Yours faithfully,

(Signed) T. McGRATH

Assistant Secretary

ENCLOSURE 1

WAGES - An advance of 50 per cent, on pre-war rate of wages or salary, in addition to, and irrespective of bonus.

HOURS - A 48 hours working week, consisting of 8 hours a day for 6 days a week, and one clear day's rest in seven, without reduction in pay.

After the stipulated 8 hours duty each day, all employees, both indoor and outdoor staff to be free from duty, this to apply also in the case of resident officers in outdoor staff.

OVERTIME - Wherever possible such to be dispensed with, but in case of necessary extra duty, such duty to be paid for at the rate of time and a half.

Each day to stand by itself for the purpose of calculating overtime. Time worked in excess of 8 hours each day to be classed and paid for as overtime.

HOLIDAYS - fifteen days' annual leave with pay, without prejudice to employees who are at present in receipt of more than 15 days.

Boarded staff to be paid ration money when on annual leave.

RESTRICTIONS - Special restrictions or employees, such as requiring resident officers in outdoor staff to live in the immediate locality of their work, to be withdrawn.

The above wages and conditions of employment to take effect as and from April 1st, 1919.

ENCLOSURE 2 - SUPERANNUATION

(a) An officer or servant who shall become incapable of discharging the duties of his office by reason of permanent infirmity of mind or body, or who shall have attained the age of 55 years, or who shall have completed an aggregate service of 30 years, shall have the right to claim and be entitled to receive a pension, after ten years' service, of ten-fortieths of full salary or wages and emoluments at the time of retirement, with an addition of one-fourtieth for each additional completed year of service up to a maximum of thirty-fortieths.

(b) In the event of retirement through loss of office, an officer or servant shall be entitled to pension according to above-mentioned scale.

(c) In the case of death of an officer or servant who has completed ten years' service, or was in receipt of a pension at time of death, the widow of such officer or servant shall be entitled to receive a pension equal to half the amount he would have been entitled to, or was in receipt of at time of death.

(d) In the case of death of an officer or servant and there being no widow to claim, there shall be paid to the next-of-kin dependent (in the case of such officer or servant not having received a pension), a gratuity, consisting of one year's salary or wages and emoluments after 10 years' and up to 15 years' service; one and a half years' salary, &c., after 15 years' and up to 20 years' service, two years' salary, &c., after 20 years' and up to 25 years' service; and two and a half years' salary, &c., after 25 years' and up to 30 years' service. In the case of an officer or servant dying and having been in receipt of a pension at time of death, and having received less than 2½ years' pension, there shall be paid to the dependent the balance of the 2½ years' pension.

(e) That the provisions of the Superannuation Act be extended so that an officer or servant having served under Boards of Guardians or Councils in Scotland or Ireland, shall be entitled to have such service counted for the purpose of superannuation.

(f) That provision be made to include in the amended Act all offices or servants who contracted out of, or who do not participate in the provisions of the "Poor Law Officers' Superannuation Act, 1896.

The above are the proposed amendments to the "Poor Law Officers' Superannuation Act, 1896", as passed by the Conference of Poor Law Officers, held on March 20th, 1919.

(Signed) T. McGRATH
assistant Secretary,
National Union of Corporation Workers

Referred to Special Committee appointed this day   (26th March. No 610)
(Minute No. 43)

From the Poor Law Workers' Trade Union of England and Wales, as follows:-

Sir,

I am directed by the Central Executive Committee to state that at a Conference of Poor Law Officials (members of the above Union), it was decided to petition His Majesty's Government to forthwith make it obligatory for Boards of Guardians to adopt for its employees a working day not exceeding eight hours, with one clear day's rest in seven, and one afternoon off duty per week equivalent to Saturday afternoon.

I was, however, instructed to appeal to your Board to favourably consider the proposal with a view to its immediate adoption. You are doubtless aware of the great unrest and dissatisfaction in the Poor Law Service, and one of the chief grievances is the excessive long hours of duty, often amounting on an average from 70 to 80 hours per week and even in some cases as much as 90 hours per week. This dissatisfaction can be readily understood when you realise that the Poor Law Worker cannot but fail to observe that the whole of the working community is making rapid progress towards tolerable conditions, both in wages and hours of labour, whilst he is, and has been for many years past, quite at a standstill. The remedy is entirely in your hands and justice can be given without any recourse to pressure from other authorities. May I appeal therefore for your favourable consideration of this proposal, and I shall be glad to hear of its adoption.

Although you may not possibly agree to this proposal, but yet consider that something should be done to obtain a uniform betterment of the conditions of the Poor Law Officer throughout the Country, may I ask your Board to adopt the following resolution and forward a copy of the same to the Local Government Board and to your local Members of Parliament.

"That this Board of Guardians views with considerable apprehension the great unrest and dissatisfaction that is prevalent in the Poor Law Service owing to the Service conditions generally applicable to Poor Law Officers, and appeals to His Majesty's Government to support the Petition of the Poor Law Officers demanding a reduction of the hours of duty, and asking for a commission to be appointed to enquire into the grievances of the Service, with a view to the rectification of the same, and a uniform action throughout the country being taken by all Boards of Guardians."

I shall be obliged if you will kindly inform me what action your Board has taken on this question.

I am, Sir,
Your obedient Servant
(Signed) G. VINCENT EVANS,
General Secretary

(Referred to Special Committee appointed this day)   (31st March. No 670)
(See Minute No. 43.)

November 1919

FROM THE POOR LAW WORKERS' TRADE UNION, as follows:-

Dear Sir,

REPORT OF THE DEPARTMENTAL COMMITTEE ON THE SUPERANNUATION OF PERSONS EMPLOYED BY LOCAL AUTHORITIES IN ENGLAND AND WALES

I am directed to call your attention to the following resolution adopted at a mass meeting of Poor Law employees held at the Memorial Hall, Farringdon Street, London, on Saturday, the 11th October, 1919, on the above mentioned report:-

That this mass meeting of Corporation and Poor Law Workers, without prejudice to any claim we may have to Superannuation without deduction from wages, hereby enter an emphatic protest at the recommendations of the Departmental Committee re Superannuation for persons employed by Local Authorities and direct the officers of the Unions to take energetic steps to secure satisfactory amendments to the same. Further we appeal to all employees concerned to have nothing to do with the Scheme until so altered.

I am to point out that the proposals of such Committee, if adopted by Parliament, will be compulsory on all persons (temporary employees excluded) employed by County Councils, Borough Councils, Urban District Councils, Poor Law Servants, etc., and the Guardians are doubtless well aware that there has been for many years past, considerable feeling in the Service that the present Poor Law Officers; Superannuation Act of 1896, (which it is proposed to repeal) requires many amendments to make it satisfactory for the good of the Service Generally.

For comparative purpose I am to direct your attention to the proposals under the Departmental Committee's report, as compared with the existing Superannuation Act and the amendments to be asked by the employees:-

	Departmental Committee's Amendments Report	Poor Law Officers' Super- Annuation Act 1896	Suggested
Contributions	5 per cent	2 per cent	2½ per cent
Benefits	1/60th	1/60th	1/40th
(for each year's service)			
Retirement age	65 years	60 years	55 years
Service	40 years	40 years	30 years

Other amendments are considered necessary, but the foregoing are of primary importance for the present.

I am to point out that the Departmental Committee in taking evidence, did not hear the workers' suggestions on the matter, but dealt more or less, with the higher graded officials who are better able to meet the requirements of the suggested scheme.

I am to ask your Board to kindly consider the whole question with a view to passing the following resolution and forwarding a copy of the same to the Prime Minister, the Minister of Health and the local Members of Parliament:-

That we have considered the representations of the Poor Law Workers in regard to the operation of the suggestion of the Superannuation proposals contained in the Report of the Departmental Committee on the Superannuation of persons employed by Local Authorities in England and Wales and would urge His Majesties Government to consider the question of re-opening the deliberations of such Committee with a view to the workers' suggestions being placed before them, or to amend the suggested proposals of such Committee in the following manner:-

Contributions	2½ per cent instead of 5 per cent
Benefits	1/40th for each completed year's service instead of 1/60th
Retirement	At the age of 55 years or after 30 completed years' Service Instead of 65 years or 40 completed years service.

I shall be obliged if you will kindly notify me the decision of your Board on this matter.
I am, Dear sir,
Yours faithfully,
G. VINCENT EVANS
General Secretary.

The Clerk to the Guardians   24th October, 1919
(Referred to Finance Committee)

The following entries were made in the Visitors' Book, viz.:-

(a)   From the Members visiting the Institution, 21st July 1919.

We have visited the Dining Hall and several of the Blocks,. The menu was very well chosen and excellently cooked and served. All the arrangements for the Peace celebrations were admirable. The dinner was followed by an alfresco concert in the afternoon and an evening concert by the Staff in the large hall.
(Signed) E. HILL H.B. ROGERS
A.A. PECKSEN
21st July 1919

That the Master reported that the Peace celebrations took place in the Institution on 21st July 1919, that the dietary provided was in accordance with that approved by the Board: that in the afternoon a concert party provided an entertainment, also the Band from the Anerley Schools; that in the evening a concert was given to the Inmates by the Staff. The proceedings during the day were much appreciated by the Inmates and they desired to express to the Guardians their sincere thanks.

In connection with the foregoing, your Committee desired the Clerk to convey to the officers the Committee's appreciation of their labours in entertaining the Inmates.

That instructions were given for No 5 Ward to be used as a Recreation Room for the Officers, the piano being transferred there from the Day-room and prices being obtained for Wicker Chairs. This is necessitated by the 48 hour working week, the Officers having more time off duty than formerly, when they either left the building or remained in their respective rooms.

That at the request of the Combined Relief and General Purposes Committee, our Committee investigated the circumstances under which the furniture belonging to Fanny Bolton, now deceased, was sold and find that the usual procedure was adopted.

At the Committee on the 21st August last the Master reported that there was a considerable accumulation of Inmates furniture in the Stores and he asked that some of it might be disposed of to make room for any further lots of furniture arriving. The Master duly submitted to the Clerk a list of 32 lots of furniture in store and the Clerk having made enquiries, it was decided that 22 lots should be sold and prices were obtained from a number of dealers. The furniture belonging to the late Fanny Bolton realised the sum of £4.10/- which was paid to the Treasurer in respect of her maintenance. The woman was admitted to the Infirmary on 6th January 1919, transferred to Tooting Bec Asylum on 23rd January 1919, afterwards transferred to Banstead Asylum on 10th October, died on 1st December 1919 and was buried by the Guardians.

As is usual in such cases the Clerk communicated with the Medical Superintendent of Tooting Bec Asylum on 25th August 1919, as to whether there was any likelihood of the Patient being discharged in the near future and the reply was that she was worse mentally and there was practically no prospect of her being discharged as recovered.

The furniture was with others sold in September last.

In 1919 there was a comparison of the amount of Insurance that Swaffield Road paid.

INSTITUTION	INSURANCE COMPANY	BUILDING			CONTENTS		
		1914	PRESENT TIME	AMOUNT RECOMMENDED	1914 TIME	PRESENT RECOMMENDED	AMOUNT
SWAFFIELD ROADINSTITUTION							
Main building	Alliance Assurance Co.	73,950	110,925	150,000	9,050	13,575	20,000
Iron Building	Ditto	800	1,200	1,400	250	375	500
New Infirm Wards	Ditto	2,100	3,150	4,000	500	750	1,000

Special Committee, re Conciliation Committee:-

30th June 1920

Present - Mr Winfield (in the Chair); Miss Brown, Lieut. E. A. Sanders, R.N., Messrs. Line and Mason

Reporting -

That in connection with the decision of the Board of the 20th May, 1920 (Vol. 29, p. 90), that the Guardians agree to the general principle of the formation of a joint Conciliation Committee, with the object of setting up machinery to adjust any differences which may arise from time to time in the hours of duty, salaries, wages, and general conditions of the offices and servants employed by the Board, also (Vol. 29, p. 103), that a joint meeting be held in the first instance of six Guardians and six Officers, with the proviso that this number may be increased in order that all sections of the Staff should be represented, your Committee considered that question of the regulations necessary to form such Conciliation Committee, and recommend - That the following be adopted, viz.:-

(1) That the Committee be established for the purpose of dealing with matters of disagreement which may arise in reference to (A) hours of duty; (B) salaries, wages and emoluments; (C) general conditions of employment.

(2) That the Committee consist of twelve members, six to be elected by the Guardians and two from each of the following bodies: the Poor Law Workers' Trade Union (Wandsworth Branch), the Municipal Employees' Association (Wandsworth Branch), and the National Poor Law Officers' Association.

(3) The Clerk to the Guardians or his deputy, and representatives of the Officers' Associations as set out in paragraph (2) selected by themselves shall be entitled to attend all meetings of the Committee in an advisory capacity with power to enter into debate but not to vote.

(4) The Chairman of the Committee shall be a member of the Guardians' section, and the Vice-Chairman a member of the Staff section, or vice versa. The presiding Chairman shall retain his vote as a member of the Committee, but shall have no casting vote.

(5) The Officers' side of the Committee shall appoint one of its members to act as Secretary, and the Guardians' side likewise.

(6) The quorum shall be four members on each side of the Committee.

(7) The ordinary meetings of the Committee shall be held (at times to be determined hereafter) at the Guardians' offices, Wandsworth, as often as may be necessary, and shall be summoned by the Secretaries acting jointly, after consultation with the Chairman and Vice-Chairman.

The first meeting shall beheld within fourteen days after the adoption of this scheme and the election of the representatives of the party concerned. An agenda, containing the business to be considered, shall be circulated at least four clear days prior to the meeting.

(8) Business not on the Agenda shall be taken only by permission of the meeting.

(9) It shall be competent for any applicant in connection with business to be dealt with, to interview the Committee, on request being submitted from the representatives of the employees.

(10) The Committee shall be elected not later than the 1st day of May in each year (excepting the year of inception) for the ensuing twelve months. The first representatives to be elected under this Constitution shall hold office until the 30th April, 1921.

(11) Casual vacancies shall be filled by the parties concerned. The members elected shall serve for the remainder of the term of office of the representative creating the vacancy.

(12) The Guardians will deal with all applications for increase of salary and other matters affecting officers, as at present: but in the event of any officer or officers being dissatisfied with the Guardians' decision, he or they shall forthwith notify the Clerk to the Guardians who will at once notify the respective Secretaries of the receipt of such notification, and such Secretaries shall forthwith do what is necessary to bring the matter in question before the Conciliation Committee in accordance with paragraph (7).

(13) Meetings of the Committee shall be held when convenient, and it shall be a provision that when a meeting is held at a time when any member of the Staff section would ordinarily be on duty, arrangements shall be made whereby his attendance at the Committee will be assured.

(14) No motion shall be considered to have been carried at the Committee unless two-thirds of the members present on each side are in favour thereof.

(15) The decisions of the Committee shall be signed by the Chairman and the Secretaries, shall be reported forthwith to the Board of Guardians and become operative, subject to the sanction of the Board and Departmental approvals. PROVIDED that if an agreement is not arrived at within a period of six weeks from the date of the decision of the Committee (the month of August not being included in the said period of six weeks), the question at issue shall be referred to Arbitration under the provisions of the Conciliation Act, 1896, or to some Arbitrator approved by the Committee. PROVIDED ALSO that the said period of six weeks may be extended by agreement. In case no decision is reached, after a vote has been taken on the question, the matter at issue shall be adjourned to a further meeting which shall be agreed upon at the moment. If no decision is arrived at after

discussion at such second meeting, the matter at issue shall be referred to the decision of the Arbitrator as provided above.

The decision of the Arbitrator shall be binding upon the principal parties thereto, subject to sanctions of the Poor Law Statutes, Orders, Regulations, or any other Statutes affecting the matter at issue.

(16) The Annual Meeting for the election of Chairman, Vice-Chairman, and officers of the Committee shall be held in the month of May in each year, and shall be the first meeting after the ordinary election of representative of the parties concerned.

(17) The Constitution of the Committee shall only be amended at a special meeting of the Committee convened for the purpose. Notice of the proposed amendment must be given to the members at least fourteen days before the meeting, and to the General Secretaries of the Poor Law Workers' Trade Union and the Municipal Employees' Association for the approval of the Central Executive Committee of such Unions, and to the National Poor Law Officers' Association.

From the London Guardians' Association as follows:-

Dear Sir,

Re: *JOINT DISTRICT CONCILIATION COUNCIL FOR THE POOR LAW SERVICE FOR LONDON AND GREATER LONDON*

I beg to inform you that the London Guardians' Association have for some time past had under consideration the question of the formation of the above Council. In conjunction with the following Officers' Association, viz.:-

National Poor Law Officers' Association (London and District Branch),

Poor Law Workers' Trade Union,

National Union of Corporation Workers, and the

Municipal Employees Association,

A Sub-Committee has drafted a Provisional Form of Constitution and Rules which will submitted for approve to an adjourned conference of the London Guardians' Association and the Officers' Associations, to be held at those offices on Thursday next, the 11th December instant, at 7 o'clock p.m. I have received a notification from Mr Arthur Chapman (Chairman of the Conference and President of the London Guardians' Association), that at the adjourned Conference, he will move that a meeting of two representatives of each Board of Guardians in London and Greater London be called to appoint eight members to represent Boards of Guardians on the proposed Conciliation Council, the other eight members being, of course, appointed by the Officers' Associations. Each Board of Guardians will be invited to send the name of one member to be voted upon for this purpose. After the adjourned Conference Meeting, I will send you a copy of the Provisional Form of Constitution and Rules for the Joint District Conciliation Council and a notification of the date when the proposed meeting referred to above, will be held.

Yours faithfully,

(Signed) H. GRANGER HOLDER

Hon. Sec

(See Minute No.59)

(9th December. No. 2,611).

The ramifications of the Mental Deficiency Act 1913, were taken very seriously as the following correspondence shows:-

The following correspondence has taken place -

WANDSWORTH UNION
Board Room and Offices,
St John's Hill, Wandsworth, S.W.18
14th January 1918

Dear Sir,

MENTAL DEFICIENCY ACT, 1913
MARY SIMPSON, 63, Hydethorpe Road, Balham

The father of the above has applied for the girl's admission to an Institution. He states that he has endeavoured to get her into a Home, but has failed, and as his eldest daughter is shortly leaving home, there is no one to look after the girl, he being a widower.

I find that on the 2nd instant you notified Mr Simpson that the Council had decided to place the case under supervision, and it appears to the Guardians, therefore, to be a case for the Council to deal with.

I shall be glad to hear from you as to what can be done in the matter, to avoid the girl being admitted to the Guardians' Institution.

Yours faithfully,
(Signed) F. J. CURTIS
Clerk

The Asylums Officer
London County Council
(Asylums and Mental Deficiency Committee)
13 Arundel Street, Strand, W.C.2

LONDON COUNTY COUNCIL
Asylums and Mental Deficiency Committee
13, Arundel Street, Strand, W.C.2
15th January, 1918

Dear Sir,

MENTAL DEFICIENCY ACT, 1913
MARY SIMPSON

I am obliged to you for your letter of the 14th instant. It is a fact, as you say, that this girl has been placed under supervision for the purpose of the Mental Deficiency Act, 1913, it is felt, however, that as the child is paralysed, supervision at home does not really make adequate provision for her care. The fact of the girl's physical helplessness however, makes it impossible for the Council to secure her admission to any of the limited Institution accommodation which is available at the present time, and it is no doubt this circumstance which has led the father to make application for the case to be dealt with by the Guardians.

Yours faithfully,
(Signed) H. F. KEENE
Asylums Officer

The Clerk to the Guardians,
Wandsworth Union.

WANDSWORTH UNION
Board Room and Offices,
St John's Hill, Wandsworth, S.W.18
17th January 1918

Dear Sir,

MENTAL DEFICIENCY ACT, 1913
MARY SIMPSON

I am in receipt of yours of 15th instant. In view of the fact that the girl has been placed under supervision for the purposes of the Act, do I understand that, as the Council are responsible for the safety of the child, they will pay for her maintenance in the event of her being admitted to one of the Guardians Institutions.

It was mentioned to me some time ago that the Council had arranged for the Managers of the Metropolitan Asylum District to provide accommodation for cases such as this, and if this is so, could not the girl be sent there by your Committee under the arrangement?

Yours faithfully,
(Signed) F. J. CURTIS
Clerk

The Asylums Officer
London County Council
(Asylums and Mental Deficiency Committee)
13 Arundel Street, Strand, W.C.2

LONDON COUNTY COUNCIL
Asylums and Mental Deficiency Committee
13, Arundel Street, Strand, W.C.2
18th January, 1918

Dear Sir,

MENTAL DEFICIENCY ACT, 1913
MARY SIMPSON

Thank you for your letter of the 17th instant. If the Guardians agree to deal with this girl's case on the application of her father, it would not be possible for the Council to bear the expenses of maintenance. The arrangement with the Metropolitan Asylums Board to which you refer has not yet been made, although I am in negotiation with the Clerk to the Board as to the terms on which an agreement might possibly be entered into for the use of some accommodation provided by the Board for the reception of cases of mental defect at the charge of the Council. I do not know, however, that even if such an arrangement were in force the Board would agree to receive this child, and in the meantime I am given to understand the need for her to receive institution care, which the local authority cannot at present provide, is urgent.

Yours faithfully,
(Signed) H. F. KEENE
Asylums Officer

The Clerk to the Guardians,
Wandsworth Union.

31st January, 1918

Having regard to the foregoing, your Committee recommend -

(A) That a copy of the particulars be transmitted to the Boards of Guardians of the several Metropolitan Unions and Parishes.

(B) That Messrs. Young, Son & Ward, Solicitors, do obtain Counsel's opinion as to the best means to be adopted to enforce the carrying out of the provision of the Mental Deficiency Act, 1913, by the "Local Authority" responsible for London.

The Chairman of the Board submitted his Triennial Statement as follows:-

It has been my custom, during my long tenure of the Chair, at the end of the Board to give a resumé of what has happened in the past three years. Today I have to refer to what has happened during the past six years, and that may be summed up in the significant phrase - "carrying on."

Not long after the new Board came into existence in 1913, War was declared, and we had to endure all the hardships and anxieties of the same. This is not the place to speak of the War, except in so far as it affects the Board of Guardians, and this report will not admit of the various items to which I alluded six years ago.

At the commencement of hostilities, 89 men joined His Majesty's Forces; 8 Nurses offered their services, and 4 went on munition work. Of those, 9 have been killed in action or have died of wounds, 2 have been reported missing, and 1 was killed during an air raid' 4 have died of pneumonia since leaving the Army. We tenderly think of those who have laid down their lives for the cause of righteousness and freedom, and commit to the God of all comfort those who are mourning their loss.

Amongst those who have survived are our Second Assistant Clerk and the Matron of the St. James' Infirmary. Each of these has gained distinctions - Lieutenant Harlow has won the Military Cross and Bar, and Miss Todd has been decorated with the Royal Red Cross (first class) and was mentioned in Sir Douglas Haig's dispatches, in 1916, and in 1918 received the Military Medal and was made an Honorary Associate of the Order of St. John of Jerusalem.

The absence of the Second Assistant Clerk made it extremely difficult for the work to be carried on in the office, and we had to substitute monthly meetings of the Board and Institutional Committees for the usual fortnightly ones. From the day, however, in which matters have been carried on under the able conduct of our Clerk, I do not think that the work has in any way suffered, and I doubt whether there are many of the Board today who deem it necessary to revert to the former plan.

TOOTING HOME - Owing to the fearful carnage of modern warfare and the countless number of wounded which were being daily sent from the battle-field, we felt it our duty to offer one of our Institutions as a hospital to the Stage, and on the 1st May, 1915, we handed over Tooting Home. It took some time to house the old people who in their declining years used to enjoy the peace and beauty of their surroundings, and still longer to adopt the Home as a Military Hospital, and it was not until the beginning of August that the first patients arrived.

Since that time the total number who have been treated has reached the large sum of 121,944. The Home is still occupied and has become a hospital more particularly for Neurasthenic patients, and from the alterations already made and the additions contemplated, I am afraid it will be some years before we have it again at our disposal.

It may be asked where the old people have gone to, and my answer is - "I cannot tell". Only a comparatively few are domiciled at the Workhouse, but the friends of the majority, not liking the sound of the Workhouse, have taken them under their care.

The War has taught us many things, and in this instance it has taught us this fact that many of those old people might have been kept by their relatives and never have come under the care of the Guardians.

In addition to giving up Tooting Home as a hospital, we have placed three of the Wards at St. James' Infirmary for the use of the wounded, and during the last four years 1,485 have been treated. I am glad to know that under the skilful care of the Medical Superintendent, only 4 deaths have occurred, and the majority have been rapidly restored to health.

In speaking of St. James' Infirmary it may be of interest to report that during the year ended March, 1918, 5,003 patients have been under treatment, and we owe a debt of gratitude to our Medical Staff, and especially to our Nurses, who have often had to do the work of two, that the Institution has kept up its reputation for the skill and care bestowed upon the patients.

We have missed the presence of Miss Todd, and we are glad to know she is returning shortly, but Miss Barnard has nobly risen to the call of duty and has done her best under very difficult circumstances.

THE WORKHOUSE, now called the "Swaffield Road Institution," suffered a year or two ago, a great loss in the death of Mrs Morgan. Few Matrons of a Workhouse ever excelled her, and few had such inspiring influence for good. She combined in her person qualifications so seldom found together - a sense of discipline and a real love of the inmates. It must be some consolation to her husband to know that her bright nature and affectionate care will long remain a cherished memory.

The numbers in the Workhouse are much less than they used to be, for while in March, 1913, they amounted to 969, in 1919 they were 595.

While on the subject of Institutional relief, it may be of interest to recall that in 1913 those chargeable in our Institutions numbered 2,964, and in Institutions outside the Union, 3,333, making a total of 6,297. In 1918 the numbers in our Institutions were 1,873; and in other Institutions, 2,494, making a total of 4,367.

Those in receipt of Out-door Relief in 1913 numbered 1,518; in 1918, 1,240, making a reduction on the whole of 2,208. Possibly, when normal conditions return, these numbers will go up again; and it is a little surprising to one who remembers the state of unemployment after the South African War, to notice that while at the present time more than a million a day is spent on relief for unemployment and no conditions of work imposed, we were not allowed to relieve the able-bodied without resort to the degradation of the Stone-yard and similar conditions of enforced labour.

It may be thought that at this juncture I should touch upon the proposed changes in the Poor Law and the threatened demise of the Guardians. I will content myself with saying very little. No one who has had the experience of many years of the innermost working of the Poor Law but must feel, I suppose, that there is much room for improvement, and that many things might be altered for the better. I feel, myself, that our Infirmaries would be better placed under a Ministry of Health and brought up to the status of State Hospitals; that children in our Poor Law Schools would have a better chance in life if they were taken at once from the stigma of the Poor Law and placed on a footing with the children in the State Schools of the country' that it should be our aim to do away, as far as possible, with Institutional relief and make provision for the aged to end their days in their own homes; but it does not seem to me that you will alter things for the better by the mere change of names, or by handing over the duties of the Guardians to other bodies already overburdened with work. To do this is merely to leave the poor to the tender mercies of officialdom, and to take away that human touch which often goes a long way to the mitigation of suffering and trouble.

We stand at the parting of the ways, and he would be a bold man who would prophesy as to the future. Let us pray that whatever happens it may tend to the uplifting of the downcast and the bringing about of happier conditions for the generations yet unborn.

My work lies in the past and not in the future; and as I look back upon the years I have occupied this Chair, my thoughts revert to many who shared with me the labours of the Board, and who have passed beyond the bourne - especially those who were with us at the opening of the present Board. I think of John Chown with his vehement nature, his interest in every detail, and kindly heart; of William Penfold, who for many years represented the Board on the Metropolitan Asylums Board; of Father Kelly, whose cheery face and genial nature ever made for happiness; of John Norman, whose fearless character and deep commonsense was recognised even by those who differed from him; of Edward Couzens who, in spite of failing years, set an example of devotion to duty of William Phillips, whose kindly personality won the affection of all; and last, but not least, of that courteous old gentleman, Frederick Scott Tanner, who was ever ready to pour oil on the troubled waters and bring together those who were estranged. These have been called hence, and left the work in which they played no inconsiderable part, to be carried on by others. Let those who in a few weeks will resume the labours of the Board, strive, whether that Board be the last or not, to sink party differences and personal recriminations, and uphold the best traditions of public life in spending themselves for the good of the community.

And now I must close. There is always a note of sadness in the phrase - "The last time." Today I have signed the Minutes for the last time, and in a short while this room will know me no more, and one would be less than human if one did not feel a momentary pang at relinquishing a work in which I have been engaged so long; but as most of you know, I have for some time wished to retire, and have only kept on because of the War, and though I was over-persuaded to allow myself to be nominated for election, I have definitely withdrawn from the contest.

For nearly twenty years I have presided over the Board; and in so long a time it cannot be but that I must have made mistakes, misunderstood others, judged harshly, spoken unadvisedly; but my colleagues have been good enough to overlook my failings and at each triennial election to renew their confidence in me. Few men, I imagine, have passed through a long course of public life with less friction, few have met with kinder friends or more generous appreciation of their efforts; and now the time has come for us to part, and as we do so let me say "Good-bye," but let me say it in no *formal manner, but in its fullest and deepest sense, that God may be with you, collectively and individually, guiding your work and enriching your lives.*

(Signed) HUBERT CURTIS

The following is an internal inquest into the death of a child.

The Committee had under consideration the circumstances attending the decease of Albert Perry upon whom an inquest was held, the verdict being that "death was due to bronchitis and scalds about the chin, and further that it was accidental." The mother of the child was interviewed, also Dr. Dodson, the Medical Officer and Attendants Godden, Wright, Summers and Martin. It would appear that the young children were having tea in the garden on Sunday, sitting at the small table provided; that the cups of hot milk were placed in the centre of the table to cool and that while the Attendant was seeing to another child, Albert Perry reached one of the cups and attempted to drink the milk. Being hot he did not do so, but scalded his lip and chin and spilt most of the milk on the table. Attendant Wright evidently did not think much of it, but wiped his mouth and later on put some ointment on his chin. The matter does not appear to have been reported to the Doctor until Tuesday morning, when the child did not seem very well. He was seen again by the Doctor on Wednesday afternoon, but on Thursday morning he became suddenly ill, was removed to the Infirmary and died soon after. The Medical Officer does not connect the Bronchitis with the slight scald on the chin, but more with teething for which the child had been under treatment and the post-mortem examination showed that no scalding had taken place inside the lips. Your Committee find that nothing was reported either to the Doctor or the Matron, both of whom visit the Block at least once daily, by any of the Attendants and accordingly recommend - That Attendant Godden be censured and Assistant Attendant Summers and temporary attendant right be severely censured for dereliction of duty in not entering the occurrence in the Report Book.

Two families were allowed to reside in the Receiving Wards as a family unit, instead of being accommodated separately. However, all did not go smoothly and records prove the concession to the families was not repeated.

That with regard to the case of Frederick William Reekie, your Committee decided that he and his family should continue to be lodged in the Swaffield Road Institution and that he should pay the sum of 17s. 6d per week for accommodation.

That with regard to the case of Ernest Albert Topps who, with his wife and family had to be admitted to the Institution owing to their being evicted from their lodgings, your Committee arranged for this man and his family to be lodged in the Receiving Ward for the present, he to contribute the sum of£3. 10s. 0d per week in respect of lodging and food for himself and children.

That your Committee had under consideration the cases of the families Reekie and Topps, who are being housed in the Receiving Ward. Since the last meeting Doris Topps has come into residence. Friction appears to have risen between the two families and they were both informed that if they could not agree they would have to look for accommodation elsewhere. Mrs Topps was also informed that the two eldest girls, who are over 16, ought to be able to be accommodated elsewhere nearer their work and the charge in respect of the Topps family was also increased to £4. 4s. 0d per week.

That your Committee further considered the case of the Topps family, who are housed in the Receiving Wards. At the last meeting it was decided to charge £4. 4s. 0d per week for board and residence of the man and his family and the two eldest daughters. Since this time one of the daughters has left. Mrs Topps was interviewed and appeared far from satisfied with the arrangements and it was decided that such arrangements should cease and the family be provided with the use of the furnished rooms, gas, warming and lighting, at a charge of 30/- per week, they providing their own food. Mrs Topps was also informed that if any further complaint arose as to their conduct the Guardians would refuse to allow them the use of the Receiving Wards any longer.

That your Committee had under consideration the case of the Topps family, who are housed in the Receiving Wards. At the Board meeting on the 26th February last, it was decided that Mr Topps should pay a rental of 30/- per week for the use of the furnished rooms, gas, warming, lighting and washing of bedding. Mr Topps asks that the rent should be reduced, as he finds it impossible to clothe his children properly.

At the present time the income of the family (which consists of three adults and five children) amounts to £5. 13s. 0d per week, out of which he assists an older daughter to the extent of 3s. 6d weekly. Having regard to all the circumstances, it is recommended - That the rent in question be reduced to 20/- weekly.

Records do not show how long they all stayed!

In 1920 the Master informed the Committee of his intention of getting married and applied for permission for his intended wife to reside with him on the premises. He was willing to pay a fair charge for her board and lodging.

Instructions were given for a "Reward Bill" to be issued offering to find the parents of an unknown child at the Institution.

A Subscription of £1. 1/- per annum was to be paid to the National Lending Library for the Blind, so that talking books may be sent in for the blind inmates.

In June 1920 an inmate was sentenced to one months hard labour for insulting one of the female Officers.

The Clerk drew the attention of the Board to the new War Bonus granted to the Civil Service, the details of which are as follows:-

On the first £91. 5s. 0d	*(i.e., 35s per week), 130 per cent*
On the next £108. 15s. 0d	*(i.e., 35s per week), 60 per cent*
On the next £200. 0s. 0d.	*(i.e.,,35s per week), 45 per cent*

Although salaries above £500 are not specifically referred to, it is understood that the new bonus will apply to salaries up to £1,000.

The scheme is to date from 1st March, 1920, and the bonus is to be varied according to fluctuations in the cost of living. For the first year a revision is to take place at the end of each four months from 1st March, 1920; after the first twelve months revisions will take place every six months.

The increase in the pre-war cost of commodities arrived at by the Board of Trade is 130 per cent, and at each revision, for every rise or fall of 5 points in the official cost of living figures, the total initial bonus will be increased or reduced by 5/130ths, i.e., 1/26th.

The scheme applies to all classes irrespective of age or sex, but only to salaries and emoluments based on pre-war conditions, i.e., any increase must have been given for merit and not owing to the increase in the cost of commodities.

Resolved - That, subject to the sanction of the Ministry of Health -

(1)   The new Civil Service War Bonus be adopted for whole time Outdoor and Indoor Officers and half-day Scrubbers and Cleaners (permanent and temporary_, so far as cash payments, based on pre-war scale, are concerned (i.e., any increase must have been given for merit and not owing to the increase in the cost of commodities), and that the method of arriving at the bonus to be paid Officers with emoluments in kind be that suggested by the Clerk's Memorandum.

(2)   That gratuities based upon the above bonus in accordance with the suggestions of the letter from the Ministry of Health, dated 14th May, 1920 (Circular 91), be paid to Registrars of Births and Deaths.

(3)   That the War Bonus for other part time Officers remain as at present, viz.- one-third of their salary.

(4)   That the above date from 1st March 1920.

MEMORANDUM OF THE CLERK, above referred to (copy of which was sent to each Guardian):-

In the event of the Guardians deciding to adopt the new War Bonus granted to the Civil Service, it appears necessary, in order to place Officers without emoluments on an equality with those with emoluments that the bonus should be on all cash payments to both Indoor and Outdoor Officers, provided such payments are on a pre-war basis and any increases are in consequence of merit and not owing to the increased prices of commodities.

Regard must be had, however, to the fact that Officers receiving emoluments in kind (board, lodging, washing or uniform), suffer no loss so far as such emoluments are concerned and hence receive the full War Bonus on the pre-war value of same, and this must be taken into account when arriving at the bonus to be paid to Officers whose salary, plus the pre-war value of their emoluments, exceeds £91 5s. 0d per annum.

Thus, the bonus of an Outdoor Officer receiving £115 per annum salary, whose emoluments (pre-war) were valued at £15 per annum, should be arrived at as follows:-

Pre-war value of emoluments	*15	0	0	
130 per cent. On above (extra cost incurred by Guardians)	19	10	0	*£91. 5s. 0d
	*76	5	0	Salary
	99	2	6	Bonus (*130 per cent.) payable to Officer.
	38	15	0	Salary
	23	5	0	Bonus (60 per cent.) payable to Officer.
Total	£271	17	6	

February 1920

Reporting:-

That our Committee had under consideration the question of the expenditure of the Guardians in connection with Printing, Stationery, Books and Advertising, and, with a view to materially reducing the same, recommend -

(1) *That a new system of printing the Agenda and Minutes be adopted whereby the reports of Committees will not have to be printed twice, as at present, and the number of copies ordered each Meeting reduced to 80 Agendas and 70 Minutes.*

This will mean -

    (A) *That no copies of Agendas will be placed on the Board Room tables, and it will be necessary for the Members to bring to the Meeting the copies sent them for perusal.*

    (B) *That the reports of Committees will be printed separately from the ordinary Agenda, and when adopted by the Board will not be re-printed in the Minutes, as at present, but only a reference made thereto as to adoption and any amendment thereon. This will save the double printing of the reports, as when the Minutes are printed, a copy of the reports can be attached thereto to make the same complete.*

(2) *That the Abstract of Tenders, at present in use by the Guardians when accepting tenders, be abolished and a typewritten list of the names of the tenders substituted.*

(3) *That the present elaborate sheets submitted by the Settlement Officer be reduced to a foolscap form showing the result only of that Officer's work.*

(4) *That the Weekly Statement be abolished, and a Statement for the last week in each month substituted - the number ordered being reduced to 60 copies. (See Minute No. 69)*

(5) *That 300 Annual Reports be ordered in future instead of 375, as at present, and that in addition to the information furnished in the last Annual report, the number of each class of Officer employed be shown in each Institution, but it is not suggested that the dietary tables be inserted therein.*

(6) *That advertisements -*

    (A) *For Probationers and Nursing Staff generally be placed in the "Nursing Mirror" only.*

    (B) *For Domestics be placed in the "Daily Chronicle" and the "Daily Herald" only.*

    (C) *For Officers with knowledge of Poor Law be placed in the "Poor Law Officers' Journal" only.*

    (D) *For Contracts in the "Local Government Chronicle," "Local Government Journal," "Contract Journal" and "Daily Telegraph."*

(7) *That the whole question of advertising be reconsidered in six months' time.*

Further reporting:-

That with regard to books, the Clerk has for some time been ordering less expensive bindings and generally endeavouring to reduce the expenditure under this heading by standardising them, and he will continue to do so.

That the Clerk submitted a list of Officers who had been on annual leave during the Quarter ended 30th September, 1919, to whom it is necessary that a temporary increase of salary should be given in order to give effect to the Guardians' proposal to give them a money allowance in lieu of rations, and it is recommended - That the salaries of the undermentioned Officers be increased by the amount set out against their respective names, viz.:-

NAME	OFFICE	NO. OF DAYS	AMOUNT TO BE PAID EACH OFFICER
Morgan, A J	Master	18	6 7 2
Talbot, F	Acting Matron	20	2 19 9
Southgate, A.G.	Assistant Master	17	2 15 5
Gilbart, E	Master's Clerk	14	11 5
Middleton, A	Storekeeper	14	15 2
Bass, T.W.	Attendant	14	1 6 7
Sherwood, F	Attendant	14	1 10 5
Robinson, J.C.	Porter	14	1 18 0
Robinson, A	Portress	14	1 10 5
Dean, R	Attendant	14	1 10 5
Godden, L	Children's Nurse	14	1 10 5
Lance, A	Attendant	14	1 10 5
Thain, H	Attendant	14	1 10 5
Fry, A	Attendant	14	1 10 5
Bird, E	Attendant	14	1 10 5
Lashmar, M	Assistant Laundress	14	1 2 10
Knight, M	Attendant	14	1 10 5
Summers, D	Nursery Attendant	14	1 2 10
Hamper, W	Attendant	14	1 10 5
Robinson, M	Labour Mistress	14	1 10 5
Danby, M. C.	Midwife	14	1 10 5
Cowen, N	Laundry Superintendent	14	1 10 5
Tucker, E. A.	Babies' Attendant	7	11 5
Wilson, E	Second Assistant Laundress	7	11 5
Jones, M	Master's Maid	14	1 2 10

26th February 1920

That your Committee considered the question of Officer's Uniforms, and recommend -

(A)   That the following be the scale in future:-

OFFICE	SWAFFIELD ROAD	ST JAMES' AND ST JOHN'S INSTITUTION	INTERMEDIATE SCHOOLS INFIRMARIES
Indoor Officers, such as Labour Master, Gate Porter, Attendants, Storekeeper	3 suits with 2 pairs trousers, in 2 years; 1 overcoat issued every 3 years, caps as required.		
Non-resident Gate Porters, Hall Porters, Mortuary Attendants, Receiving Wardsmen and Attendants		2 suits with 2 pairs trousers, in 2 years; 1 overcoat every 3 years; caps as required.	
Male Attendants and Male Nurses (St. John's Hill Infirmary).		2 suits with 2 pairs trousers, 8 drill jackets in 2 years, 1 overcoat every 3 years, also 6 aprons per annum.	
Male Cooks	4 suits overalls, 6 aprons, 6 caps		
Kitchenmen and Scullerymen		4 suits overalls and aprons	
Storekeepers, Store Porters and Barber	4 White jackets, 6 aprons	4 white jackets, 6 aprons	
Stewards		3 drill jackets 1st year, 2 drill jackets after	
Dispensers		6 drill jackets 1st year, 2 drill jackets after	
Medical Officers		2 drill jackets	
Engineers, Assistant Engineers, Stokers, Carpenters, Drainmen, House Porters, Coal Trimmers, Laundrymen	4 suits overalls	4 suits overalls	3 suits overalls
Mattress Maker		6 aprons 1st year, 3 aprons after	
Dispensary Porters		4 coats and 6 aprons 1st year, 2 coats and 3 aprons after	
Ambulance Drivers and Attendants		1 motor cloth suit (lined) every 3 years, 1 serge suit (both with knickers) every 2 years, 1 overcoat in 3 years, caps and leggings as required.	
Laundrywomen	4 overalls	4 overalls	
Scrubbers	2 overalls and 4 aprons	2 overalls and 4 aprons	
Matron's Storekeeper		1 serge dress, 1 alpaca dress, 3 belts, 8 aprons, 4 caps, 8 collars, 8 pairs cuffs	

OFFICE	SWAFFIELD ROAD	ST JAMES' AND ST JOHN'S INSTITUTION	INTERMEDIATE SCHOOLS INFIRMARIES
Laundry Superintendent, Linen Checker, Attendants, Portress	3 drill dresses, 8 aprons, 8 collars, 8 pairs cuffs	3 drill dresses, 8 aprons, 8 collars, 8 pairs cuffs	3 dresses, 8 aprons, 8 pairs cuffs, 8 collars, 4 caps
Matron			3 dresses, 6 caps
Assistant Matron	3 drill dresses, 8 aprons, 8 collars, 8 pairs cuffs	1 alpaca dress, 3 cotton dresses, 10 aprons, 4 caps, 6 pairs cuffs, 8 collars, 3 belts (1st year); subsequent years only 2 cotton dresses, 8 aprons	3 dresses, 8 aprons, 8 collars, 8 pairs cuffs
Home Sisters		1 alpaca dress, 3 cotton dresses, 10 aprons, 4 caps, 8 pairs cuffs, 8 collars, 3 belts (1st year); subsequent years only 2 cotton dresses, 8 aprons	
Sisters and Charge Nurses	4 overalls	3 cotton dresses, 10 aprons, 4 caps, 8 pairs cuffs, 8 collars, 3 belts (1st year); subsequent years only 2 cotton dresses and 8 aprons	
Probationer Nurses and Assistant Nurses		3 cotton dresses, 10 aprons, 4 caps, 8 pairs cuffs, 8 collars, 3 belts (1st year); subsequent years only 2 cotton dresses and 8 aprons	
Staff Nurses		10 aprons 1st year; otherwise same as Probationer Nurses	
Cooks and Assistant Cooks		3 dresses, 12 aprons, 4 caps, 8 collars (1st year); other years, 8 aprons, 8 pairs cuffs	3 dresses, 12 aprons, 4 caps, 8 collars (1st year); other years 8 aprons, 8 pairs cuffs
Messroom-maids, Housemaids, Kitchenmaids, &c.		3 dresses, 12 aprons, 4 caps, 8 collars (1st year); subsequent years, 2 dresses, 8 aprons	3 dresses, 12 aprons, 4 caps, 8 collars, (1st year); subsequent years, 2 dresses, 8 aprons

Note: Where necessary Female Officers to be supplied with capes.

(B) That in the event of the above issue being insufficient owing to uniform being damaged through the nature of the work, the Officers be authorised to issue extra garments to replace the damages ones.

(C) That uniforms be issued half-yearly.

(D) That the officers be allowed to retain the old garments in future, with the exception of the last issue prior to an officer leaving the service of the Guardians, which must be returned to Store.

(E) That with regard to those officers who have to provide for the making of their own uniforms, the sum of 6/6d per dress be allowed.

(5) That your Committee approved of the list of clothing Probationers are required to provide during their three months on trial.

That the value of Poor Law Officers emoluments should be increased to at least 100 per cent above the value assigned to them on or before 31st July 1914 and that where the pre-war stated value of each emolument was obviously below their true value on the 31st July, 1914, that fact should be taken into account.

Also calling attention to the fact that the Ministry of Health will now sanction the payment of money allowances in lieu of rations to officers while on annual leave of absence.

From the Association of Poor Law Unions and Parishes of London and Greater London (the London Guardians' Association), as follows:-

Dear Sir,

I am directed by the Association of Poor Law Unions and Parishes of London and Greater London (the London Guardians' Association) to inform you that at a General Meeting of the Association held on Friday 16th July inst., they received, approved and adopted the following report of their Executive Council, viz.:-

Principal Officers   £200 per annum
Subordinate Officers   £100 per annum

Such amounts are arrived at as follows, viz.:-
Principal Officers - Board £52, lodging £76, washing £12, attendance £60=£200
Subordinate Officers - Board £39, lodging £39, washing £9, uniform £13=£100

I am further directed to ask that with a view to uniformity in the Metropolis and Greater London, the values suggested by the London Guardians' Association be adopted by your Board of Guardians.

Yours faithfully,
(signed) CHAS.J. CROSS, Hon. Sec
24th July 1920

BOARDING OUT

In view of the general rise of prices, the direction given in No. 14, of the second paragraph of the circular letter of the 17th December, 1915, may be read as authorising without further reference to the board, the increase of the payments made in respect of the maintenance of Boarded-out children up to a maximum not exceeding seven shillings and sixpence a week.

Report from the Boarding-Out Committee:-

(1) That Reports as to Apprentices, Children in Schools, etc., were submitted and your committee gave the necessary instructions and entered same in the Book provided.

(2) That a report was received from the Metropolitan Association for Befriending Young Servants, as to girls from this Union dealt with during the last six months, and the same was considered, on the whole, to be satisfactory.

(3) That a letter was received from Messrs. Young, Son & Ward, Solicitors with reference to the lad, William Reuss, apprenticed to Mr Roach of Earlsfield who had an injury to his thumb, and it is recommended - That the necessary proceedings be taken to set a Declaration of Liability at the County Court to enable Reuss to obtain half wages at any time should he be incapacitated from work through his injury.

(4) That a letter was received from Mr H. Roach, Joiner, etc., of Earlsfield, reporting that one of his apprentices, James Conquer, had met with an accident whilst working a morticing machine whereby he had lost two fingers and it is recommended - That the matter, as to registering relative to compensation, be referred to Messrs. Young, Son & Ward, Solicitors.

Further Reporting:-

That the third and final instalment of apprenticeship premium (£4) be paid to Mr Albert Ratcliffe, Bootmaker, of 7 King Edward's Parade, East Finchley, in respect of John Begg, aged 16 years. The Master and the Boy attended before the Committee.

A lot of work was done to find situations or apprenticeships for the teenagers. The following list is an example of some of the situations found:-

2 girls for situation in the Scilly Isles.
Boy sent to a baker.
24 boys sent to the Metropolitan Association for Befriending young Servants.
2 boys sent to Treorchy.
Boy sent to the Scilly Isles.
Boy sent to a FarmTraining Colony.
2 boys aged 16 to a bootmakers.
3 boys sent to a Paino Manufacturer.
3boys sent to a Farm Training Colony in Australia. Cost £12. 0s. 0d., each.
£20 per year maintenance for Joseph Slinn formerly Anerley School, gained a scholarship for two years.
£30 per year for Dorothy Coombs of Anerley School also gained a scholarship for 2 years.
Girl sent to a Hairdresser.
Boy sent to a Grocer cost £4 per year.
Boy sent to an Industrial School.
2 boys sent to a Wood Carvery and Joinery Centre, aged 15 years.

That with regard to Apprentices brought before your Committee at the end of the first and second years of their apprenticeship it is recommended - That in the following cases instalments of premiums be paid, viz.:-

174

Name of Apprentice	Age	Name of Master	Address	Trade	Amount of Instalment	Remarks
Boulton, George R.	17	Mr D. W. Grover	Woodchester Mills, Stroud, Gloucestershire	Pianoforte Maker	Third Instalment £4	The Master reports satisfactorily. Also satisfactory report received from the Supt. Of Anerley School.
Rabbetts, William Atherton	17	Mr A. G. Jones (of Arthur's Press, Ltd.)	Vale Mills, Woodchester, Stroud, Gloucestershire	Letterpress Printer (Machine Manager) Letterpress Printer (Compositor)	ditto	ditto
Wheeler, Herbert Frederick	17	ditto	ditto	ditto	ditto	ditto

The Clerk reported that in the under-mentioned cases the time had expired in which lads had been sent to trial with a view to apprenticeship, and as enquiries had proved satisfactory, it is recommended - that upon the Indentures being signed by the parties concerned the Seal of the Board be affixed to such Indentures, and in the first two cases the first instalment of the agreed premium be paid:-

Name of Apprentice	Age	Name of Master	Address	Trade	Amount of Instalment	Remarks
Eagle, Thomas	14	Messrs. A. Robinson	4 Bennett's Yard, Marsham Street, Westminster	Joiner	£3	Boy attended before Committee.
Weatherley, Albert E.	14	ditto	ditto	Wood Carver	£3	Ditto
Burns, John	14	Sheraton Glass Manufacturing Co.	Hayes, Middlesex	Glass Blower	No Premium	Boys will reside at Hostel, and earn sufficient to provide for maintenance, &c. Clerk to interview lads, and obtain their signatures to forms of Indenture.
Cook, Fred	14	ditto	ditto	ditto		
Fox, Albert	14	ditto	ditto	ditto		
Reid, William	15	ditto	ditto	ditto		
Smithers, William	15	ditto	ditto	ditto		
Spooner, Joseph	15	ditto	ditto	ditto		

DIETARY

The Master reported as follows:-

"With regard to the introduction of Rabbits as a change in the Dietary, I beg to report that the change has been a very agreeable one to the inmates, but that it is not a source of economy. This is due, first to the fact that the present cost of Mutton is 2¼d per lb less than the previous Quarter; and secondly that English rabbits, costing 8d per lb, are used instead of Australian, costing 6d per lb, which were suggested."

Your Committee recommend - that the issue of English rabbits be continued.

The following Report was submitted:-

A short time ago we prepared and you approved a War Dietary for the inmates, based on the Official suggestion that the main saving must be on the Meat ration. Accordingly, while this was reduced considerably below the limit laid down by the Food Controller, the Bread and Flour ration was exceeded to the extent of about a pound per head weekly. Now things have altered considerably, and the great urgency of at once reducing the Bread and Flour ration within the prescribed limit becomes apparent. We beg to suggest the following alterations:-

Instead of the Bread and Cheese dinner on Mondays, we suggest that the whole of the inmates shall have Boiled Beef, Rice and Vegetables and also that Ox Hearts and Vegetables be provided on Wednesdays in lieu of Meat Pudding, which involves the use of a considerable quantity of Flour. We further suggest that porridge be served for breakfast on Sundays in lieu of Bread and Margarine. On Tuesdays we suggest that Suet Pudding be abolished and the portions of Rabbit increased.

(Signed)ARTHUR E. DODSON, M.D., Medical Officer

ARTHUR J. MORGAN, Master

On the 12th December, 1917, a circular letter read as follows:-

Sir,

I am directed by the President of the Local Government Board to refer to the circular letters issued by the Department upon the 17th December 1915 and the 8th December 1916, on the subject of the reduction of the work normally falling upon Poor Law Authorities and this Department and to the circular letter issued on the 25th February last on the subject of the dietaries in use in Poor Law Institutions.

DIETARIES

The Guardians are aware that a revised scale of rations for the general public has been issued by the Ministry of Food. References in the Board's circular letter of the 28th February last to the Food Controller's scale should from the present date be read as being references to the scale now issued, or to any future scale that may from time to time replace it and where necessary, the dietaries in force should, without delay, be altered to bring them within the new scale.

In the event of the allowance of bread, flour and other cereals under the Food Controller's scale in force being less than that provided for by the Dietary Tables, an additional ration of potatoes or other vegetables may be given at any meal in lieu of the excess cereals. For the adjustment of individual needs, and for the prevention of waste, the guardians may direct that all rations of potatoes and other vegetables may be served in accordance with the Rule 7(b), relating to the service of bread, in Schedule

A of the Poor Law Institutions Order 1913. A sufficiency of fat may be allowed for variety in cooking such rations.

I am, Sir.

Your obedient Servant.

H. C. MONRO, Secretary

The Clerk to the Guardians.

The Medical Officer submitted the following report to Dietaries, viz.:-

At the beginning of last year the Food Controller issued instructions as to rations, based on a great shortage of potatoes and a good stock of cereal foods. Our dietary was altered accordingly. Now a new situation has arisen, new instructions have been published by the Controller, and the Local Government Board have issued orders for Workhouse Dietaries to be brought into line with the new scale, necessitated by the large available supply of potatoes and the great shortage of cereal foods.

The rationed articles now are bread, other cereals, meat, fats and sugar.

BREAD - The allowance is divided, as all the other rationed articles are, into six classes, according to the conditions of labour, the average being 5 lbs per head per week. Under our present dietary the average is 4 lbs, so that there is a considerable saving under this head.

OTHER CEREALS - The only article consumed to a large extent under this head is OATMEAL used for the breakfast porridge (this is now made with only 2½ ozs of crushed oats, to the pint instead of 4 ozs allowed by the Local Government Board ingredient table). The gross amount used per week exceeds the "ration" allowance by about 400 lbs, and I am unable to suggest any alteration or substitution without decreasing the food value of the meal or overstepping the allowance of other rationed articles such as bread, margarine, &c. It must be borne in mind, too that the scale of rations is for guidance of the general public and they are able to have fish or other food as part of their breakfast.

RICE - Another cereal, will now be replaced almost entirely by potatoes and other vegetables for the mid-day meal, an allowance of 16 ozs for men and 12 ozs for women being provided. The issue will be regulated, as the bread is, according to individual requirements to save waste.

MEAT - The consumption according to present dietary is under 2 lbs per head per week now allowed and no alteration is required.

FATS (including butter, margarine, dripping and other fats) - Butter has not been used her for a long time, and the margarine and other fats are well within the rational allowance; in fact, there is a surplus of at least 2 ozs per head.

SUGAR - The consumption of this also is below 8 ozs per week allowed by the new Regulations.

The only alteration needed, therefore, is practically the substitution of potatoes for rice, and this I think, can be done without any deterioration of the food value of the Dietary.

The sick and children will not be affected, as their individual wants are as before, left to the discretion of the Medical Officer.

The suggested alterations for the Inmates generally contained in this report have already been put in force and the result is satisfactory.

(Signed)A. E. DODSON, M.D.
Medical Officer
10th January, 1918.

The Master suggested a change in the dietary, sausages instead of Salt Beef one day each week. A contractor supplied the sausages @ 7½d a pound which saved £27. 0s.0d a month. The inmates enjoyed the change.

Another change in the dietary was tried but it did not "go down very well" with the inmates. Ox hearts were substituted for Topside of Beef! Not surprisingly, the inmates complained so the Beef was reinstated.

The inmates had Bacon on Mondays. The Master decided to change it to Mutton. There were no complaints with this change.

The Poplar Union was having meat supplied by a system whereby meat was drawn from cold storage direct under an arrangement with the Board of Trade. A report was made to the Committee in the hope that they would sanction the system to avoid all the meat rejections. Between August 1910 and October 1914, 666 lbs of meat was rejected. Other food rejections were:-

Fish	1978 lbs
Potatoes	950 lbs
Greens	168 lbs
Coffee	56 lbs
Fruit	36 lbs
Milk	40 Quarts
Flour	25 Sacks

ENTERTAINMENT

Concerts were an eagerly awaited regular feature and given on the stage at one end of the Dining Hall. In three years they had 24 concerts. Other entertainments featured outings of various kinds. The following are some examples:-

The Mother's Union entertained 12 old women to tea at St. Mary's Branch, Battersea. Mrs Olney entertained160 inmates to tea twice a year. 50 old men from the Branch Workhouse were taken to Wimbledon and provided with tea.

The children were not forgotten. One outing for them was a Tea and Punch and Judy Show for the children of the Branch Workhouse. Gifts for them included a Dolls Cot, Toys, Scrapbooks, Books, Magazines and even plants and fruit.

GIFTS

Evergreens were gifted each Christmas, to most of the wards and many churches sent cards. Oranges were often sent to the Institution at Christmas.

Further gifts included:-
Books and periodicals from Mr Bolus.
Books and toys from Mrs Wormill, from Balham.

Over 400 books from Putney Library.

Papers and periodicals.

100 books from Wandsworth Library.

Illustrated papers from Mr Sullivan.

Plants from Rev. Canon Curtis

Half an ounce of tobacco for the men from the Chaplin.

Wooden balls for the children.

A quantity of toys and sweets for the children at the Branch Institution.

25 x 1oz tobacco for the male inmates of the Branch Institution.

Cakes and sweets for the children at the Branch Institution.

A Mrs Blackmore presented a book of Nursery Rhymes set to music for the children at the Branch Institution.

The Darien Photographic Co.   SHAKESPEARE THEATRE, LAVENDER HILL.

BUILDINGS

There was a small fire in the Oakum Picking Shed in the Casual Wards, damaging the floor.

Concern was expressed by the Committee that young childrens beds in the Workhouse did not have sides.

It was decided that an American Organ or Harmonium should be purchased for the Chapel. Cost £10. 0s. 0d.

Laundry starch had become difficult to obtain so the Committee gave instructions for soft collars and cuffs to be supplied to female staff.

The boilers in the laundry needed descaling, cost £23. 0s. 0d. Additional machinery was needed, a 108 inch Calendar and 1 inch "Water-leap" flannel washer - £69. 5s. 0d. Also a steam ironer, cost £170. 0s. 0d. There were less women Inmates in the laundry in 1914 so additional paid women had to be employed. The Master suggested with regard to the use of washing powder in the laundry in lieu of soap and soda, and the Committee authorised washing powder be used for a period of three months. An assessment was to be made at the end of the experiment. The Master submitted a comparative statement as to the cost of Soap and Soda consumed in the Laundry and Nivalbo Washing Powder during a similar period and it would appear that a considerable saving is effected by the use of the Washing Powder referred to, instructions were given to the use of the same to be continued.

Some beds were taken out onto the balconies in the summer. In April 1912 the Medical Superintendent reported:-

I feel I ought to draw attention to the excessive heat and glare, in the summer months, on the top uncovered balconies. The discomfort is so great that the beds have to be brought in for many hours of the day, which is a great pity and unquestionably ought not to be. And it is recommended:-

(a) That the top balconies be covered in.

(b) That the matter be referred to the Works Committee.

The Master submitted a list of articles required in connection with the provision of accommodation for aged Married Couples. There were married couples in St. James's. Cost of refit £570. 0s. 0d.

The Boiler House needed an extension and a fitter was appointed. Coal was delivered 10 tons at a time.

The Dining Hall needed distemper and the Roof woodwork Varnishing. Cost £39.18s. 0d. The heating also needed attention, the Committee waited for the Engineers report.

The Committee considered that the heating in Blocks "H1" and "H2" was insufficient and gave instructions for four "Tortoise" Stoves to be purchased.

1917

(17) That your Committee considered the following reference from the Board, viz.- "That it be an instruction to the 'House' Committee of the Swaffield Road Institution to obtain and report monthly to the Board detailed reports from the under mentioned Officers relative to the working of the water softening apparatus at that Institution:-

(A) The Master, as to its value economically, with regard to the washing of articles of clothing, &c.

(B) The Engineer, as to whether any evil effect had been caused to new boilers - whether the life of the old boilers has been extended in consequence of the use of soft water, whereby it has been unnecessary to scale - the percentage, as near as possible, of soft water used in boilers in addition to that condensed from the exhaust."

But having regard to the fact that the water softening apparatus has been used during the same period as a soap powder, which has a softening effect, adjourned consideration of (A) for the present. With regard to (B), instructions were given for the Engineer to report thereon in a month's time.

(19) That with regard to the following reference from the Board, viz.- "As to whether any evil effect had been caused to new boilers - whether the life of the old boilers had been extended in consequence of the use of soft water, whereby it has been unnecessary to scale - the percentage as near as possible, of soft water used in boilers in addition to that condensed from the exhaust" - the following report of the Engineer is submitted:-

LADIES AND GENTLEMEN,

In accordance with instructions, I herein beg to report upon the condition of the steam boilers in connection with the water softening apparatus.

The system I have adopted in the management of the boilers is as follows:-

All the condense water from the steam used in the Laundry is gathered up from the various machines and apparatus, and returned to a large tank situated in the boiler house. This water is quite free from any carbonate or other scale-forming properties. The make up water is taken from the water-softening apparatus, and run into the same tank in the Boiler-house and is pumped therefrom into the boilers by the boiler feed-pumps. The temperature of this feed water at times reaches as high as from 160o to 170 o Fah, which in itself means a considerable saving of fuel.

CONDITION OF THE BOILERS

Nos. 1 and 2 are the old boilers, and were put in at the time the Institution was built, which was about 1885, and have therefore been in use a matter of 31 years; the greater part of this time they have been working night and day. During last summer, 1916, the brickwork of those boilers was entirely removed down to the foundation for the purpose of renewal, and I took the opportunity of thoroughly inspecting the boilers both inside and out, and the only defects I could find as a slight erosion or a small space on the outside of No. 1 boiler, which was not more than 1/32in. deep in any place, and a slight wastage of a few rivet heads on the bottom of the front end plate where the hot damp ashes strike when cleaning out the furnace fires.

On No. 2 boiler there was no outside deterioration whatever, with the exception of a few rivet heads in the same position as on No. 1. Upon examining the inside of these boilers, which I did thoroughly, I could practically find no visible defects, either pitting or other deterioration, and there is no doubt the boilers are in a better condition now than they were previous to the introduction of the condense and softened feed water, as considerably less scale is formed and some of the old scale has been removed.

I may mention that these boilers were inspected inside and out by two Inspectors of the Vulcan Boiler Insurance Co., as well as myself, with the same result.

With reference to Nos. 3 and 4 boilers - these are the new boilers, and were placed in position and started to work in October, 1913, and are giving very satisfactory results. There is a slight amount of incrustation on the inside, but no pitting or other deterioration whatever, either inside or out, so far as possible ascertainable. This slight scaling is owing to the shortage of labour and consequent difficulty in attending properly to the water-softening apparatus.

The average evaporation of treated water for four days
was, per 24 hours   8,920 galls
The average evaporation of condense water for four days
was, per 24 hours   3,875 galls
                                                 ―――――――

Total evaporation per 24 hours   12,795 galls

The consumption of treated water is nearly 2½ times the amount of condense water

I am, Ladies and Gentlemen,
Yours obediently,
(Signed) THOS. ALDWORTH, Engineer

Jan, 11th, 1917"

That your Committee considered the letter from the Local Government Board with reference to the consumption of Coal in Poor Law Institutions, and requesting that the Guardians will, without delay, obtain a report upon the requisitions submitted on their behalf to the Coal Controller, and the annual consumption indicated by these requisitions. The reports should in every instance in which the annual rate of consumption (in fueltons, i.e., including gas, electricity, &c., at the values consigned to them by the Coal Controller) is in excess of the rate of 1¾ fuel tons per head per annum, state the facts which are regarded by the Institutional offers as justifying the excess. The Board have little doubt that, on careful consideration of such reports, the Guardians will, as a rule, be able to issue directions which will at least increase the economy which is no doubt already practised in the Institutions in comparison with the pre-war rates of consumption. Also stating that arrangements have been made by the Coal Controller to supply to the Board copies of reports which he is obtaining upon the plant and consumption of Coal in Poor Law Institutions, and that it is proposed to supply copies of these reports for the instruction of the Poor Law Authorities concerned.

The Master submitted the following statement:-

The amount of Fuel allowed according to this letter represents 1¾ tons per head per year. The basis of our calculation must be on our certified accommodation, for whether the Institution is full or contains a considerable number of vacancies, it has to be kept warmed throughout, and the people fed.

On this basis therefore, the certified accommodation is   910
The average number of Resident Officers is   45
                                                     ―――――

Giving a total of	955 persons
	===

This number worked out at 1¾ tons per head represents	1,670 tons
The amount of Fuel allowed by the Coal Controller	
(including Coke) represents	1978 tons
The amount of Gas allowed reduced to tons of Fuel is	200
	———
Making a total of	2,178
	===

A difference, therefore, of 508 tons or, roughly speaking, 10 tons per week.
The total consumption for 3 years has been:-

1916	1917	1918
2,596 tons	2,561 tons	2,492 tons = 2½ tons per head for 1918.

I find the weekly amount of Washing in the Laundry

For the year ended 30th September, 1918, is	23,000 articles
Washing for this Institution	10,000
Washing for St. James' Infirmary	10,500
Washing from the Intermediate Schools	2,500

In other words, 13,000 articles are washed every week for Institutions other than our own.

It should be noted that some departments of the Institution are built of corrugated iron, which are some distance away from the main Institution.

It must be borne in mind that in addition to the resident Staff, meals have to be provided for a number of non-resident Staff.

Your Committee are of opinion that every endeavour has been made to keep the consumption down to the minimum, and it is impossible to bring it within the scale mentioned in the letter of the Local Government Board of 1¾ tons per head per annum.

INTERMEDIATE SCHOOLS

The Matron of the Intermediate Schools reported:-

(a) The receipt of the following:-
    100 sixpenny-pieces and toys from "Truth" (magazine)
    Sweets from Mrs Blackmore, Guardian.
    Flowers, cards, books and sweets from Mrs Knight
    Books and cards from Mrs Harrison.
    Books and cards from Mrs Sparkes.
    Books and cards from Miss Thomas.
    Books and cards from Miss Cheshire.
    Books from Rev. T. Haines.

(b) That 200 Children had been entertained at St Anne's Vicarage on 26th December and given toys and 40 Children were entertained by the Ministering Children's League, Putney, on 3rd January.

(c) That Dr and Mrs Miller, Miss Jameson and Mr West gave an entertainment to the Children upon the occasion of the Christmas Tree.

Reports from the Matron and Medical Officer of the Intermediate Schools:-

Annual Report.
During the year,

1629 children have been admitted to the Schools.
242 children have been transferred to the Infirmaries.
327 children have been transferred to Anerley Schools.
20 children have been transferred to Strand Schools.
81 children have been transferred to Roman Catholic Schools.
3 children have been sent to Service.
4 children have been sent to Training Ship "Exmouth".
3 children have been sent to Working Boy's Homes.
171 children have been brought back from Anerley Schools.
19 children have been brought back from Strand Schools.
82 children have been brought back from Roman Catholic Schools.

Considering the number of "ins and Outs" and the fact that there is no probationary accommodation, the general health has been excellent, and only three cases of infectious disease have occurred, viz.:-

Diptheria, 2
Scarlet Fever, 1

In every case, immediate removal and disinfection of the infected room and clothing, have prevented spreading of the disease and I have to gratefully acknowledge the great assistance rendered by the Staff in this respect and also the promptitude of the Borough council in disinfecting when required.
(Signed)E. WARREN, Matron
A. E. DODSON, Medical Officer   May 1912

That year the Schools held the May Festival on 25th May.

A Racquet and 12 balls were gifted along with plants, flowers, a box of Bon-bons and toys from the Guardians.

The Workhouse was not the only establishment to suffer rejects. The Schools had their fair share. Here are some examples.

1 dozen Hair Brushes
76 yards Maroon Flannel
69 lbs Fish
214 yards Flannel
4 pairs of Lace Curtains
56 lbs Vegetables
3 pieces of Loom Sheeting
12 dozen pairs Gloves
18 lbs Fresh Butter
2 pieces "Linsey" (cloth made of Linen and Wool)
6 dozen tins Condensed Milk
24 dozen pairs Stockings
200 yards Flannel
6 dozen pairs of Knickers

"... AS IT WAS IN THE BEGINNING."

There were four concerts given by different groups. The Christmas Tree celebrations were held each year generally in the first few days of January. It was followed sometimes by a concert. The young children loved Punch & Judy shows. One year 192 children went to a Pantomime at the Shakespeare Theatre, given by a Mr Dudley Bennett.

The Shakespeare Theatre was situated in Battersea and was opened in 1896 for Dramatic productions. It was converted for cinema performances in 1923. In 1940 sadly it was seriously damaged by bombs and demolished in 1957.

Mrs Olney, who entertained the inmates at the Workhouse, also gave her time to the children at the Schools with help from her friends. One day she entertained all the children and each had a toy.

The older children were taken by St. Anne's Sunday School to Oxshott. The younger children were entertained in the School.

St Anne's Church was known as a Pepper Pot Church because of the shape of the Bell Tower. The Church cost £14,510.14s.9d to build. The building of the Church started in 1822 and was completed in 1824. It was consecrated on 1st May 1824. Enclosure of the site had wrought iron railings on the north and east sides and oak fencing on the south and west sides. The Bishop disapproved of the fencing and refused to consecrate the grounds for burials.

Two coaches took 49 children to Bognor and 40 children to Hampton Court.

The youngest children were taken with the St Anne's Sunday School children to Mill House where they played and were entertained in a field. It was the St. Anne's Sunday School Annual Treat.

Mrs Worthy, of Battersea Congregational Church brought the Sunday School children to entertain the Schools children on the night of the Christmas Tree Entertainment which had been fixed for the 1st January 1914.

Miss Wood of Nightingale Lane and Miss Cobb of Surrey Lane South both gave an entertainment later in the same month. The children also had toys and books from Millicent, Duchess of Sutherland, Mr Blackmore and Mr Sullivan.

A Mr Morgan gave the children a Gramophone entertainment.

In December 1915 they had a Lantern Entertainment.

In February 1916 The Band of Hope gave the children another Lantern Entertainment.

In July the children were again included in the St Anne's Sunday School Summer Treat.

In 1917 the Manager of the Lyric Play House, Wandsworth, offered to let the children see the pictures free of cost.

In the summer all the children went to Wandsworth Common for an outing.

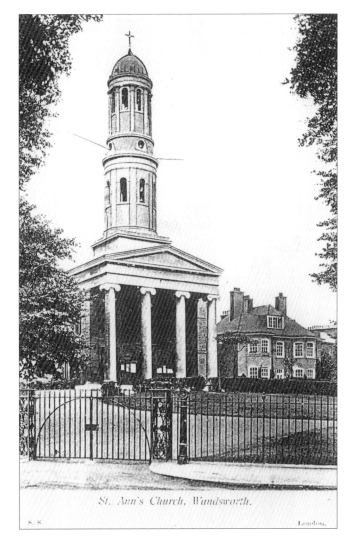

St. Ann's Church, Wandsworth.

In 1919 the Boxing Day entertainment was given by the Chaplain of St. Anne's Church at the Vicarage. They had gifts of toys and books. The "Truth" magazine donated 50 sixpences as well.

A cheque for £3. 1/- from the Wandsworth Peace Celebrations, this and the sixpences from the "Truth" magazine paid for a visit to the Pantomime.

In 1920 the older children went for a drive and tea to Virginia Water.

A Mr Roff, a member of the Bank of Hope, gave the children a Lantern Entertainment.

Some of the male inmates were sent to stoke the boilers at night in the winter to keep the classrooms warm for the children in the bitter cold weather.

The Matron authorised surprise stocktaking in the schools.

The Matron requested prices for light weight jackets for the boys in the summer months.

There was a change of Matron in the Schools. When advertised there were 89 applications for the new Matron!

A water tap and cup was supplied for the children's playground.

A little cripple girl was sent to a cripples nursery at Regents Park, the entrance fee was £1.0s.0d.

The Schools Committee approved of £5.0s.0d to be spent on Christmas toys and games, and 10/- on decorations.

Boys aged between 10 and 13 years "volunteered" for the training ship "Exmouth".

Fruit, sweets, cards, toys and a scrapbook were all gifted by a Mrs Hill of Wakefield Road, Mrs Worthy, Mrs Polsue of St James Road, and Mrs Rudge of Trinity Road. A Mrs Hellier of St Anne's Park Road gifted a swing.

The Schools had difficulty in employing attendants as the present rate of remuneration was so low. Reference to the Finance Committee was suggested.

A decision was made to give the children cocoa at tea time instead of tea to drink.

There was a number of young children's beds close by the boys dormitories, adjoining the school rooms. The boys were to be moved to accommodation it the main building. This would be a saving of lighting and dispense with one attendant, one relief attendant and a ward maid. (It was hoped to find these surplus staff other positions).

At tea-time the children were to have fruit cake instead of bread and dripping.

The Committee considered a letter from the London County Council Education Department, suggesting that the playground should be divided so as to separate the boys from the girls; and having gone thoroughly into the matter, were of the opinion that the proposal was quite unnecessary and as this view was supported by the Local Managers of the Schools, it was recommended that the London County Council be informed accordingly.

That your Committee further considered a letter from the Ministry of Health, transmitting extracts from a report of Miss L.W.Wamsley, one of their women Inspectors, after a visit to the Schools:-

(a) *DENTAL. There are still no arrangements for dental treatment. Eleven girls, very few of whom were "ins and outs" were pointed out as needing extractions or conservative treatment. The doctor's medical report for the year was very satisfactory.*

(b) *The Matron was not in. The Assistant Matron accompanied me around the Home, which was in very satisfactory domestic order: and the children looked well nourished. They were also clean and tidy in their personal appearance. The babies leave School at 12 and return at 1.40pm during which time they and the other children have to be washed, dressed and fed. If arrangements with the Education Authorities could be made for a rather longer interval in the middle of the day the children between 3 and 4 would certainly benefit by a sleep in their cots after dinner. I saw two children asleep in school with no support for their backs, and I was informed that they often fall asleep at the table after dinner and have to be roused to go back to school.*

Having heard the report of the Medical Officer, who was in attendance, upon the subject, we beg to report -

(a) *That your Committee adhere to their former recommendation, viz.:- That children requiring dental treatment be sent to the London County Council School Clinic. (The Committee understand that children between 3 and 5 years of age are attended to here as well as the other children).*

(b) *That no action appears necessary at present upon the subject raised.*

However, there had been further thoughts on the subject of the sleep for the young ones:-

That with regard to the question of allowing the children between 3 and 5 years of age to have a sleep after their mid-day meal, there are at the present time only about 12 children affected and instructions were given for such children to attend school in the mornings only, to be put to sleep after the mid-day meal and then taken out for a walk, if possible.

The Medical Officer reported:-

With regard to the new Dietary Order, the children here have always been fed according to appetite and discretion. There is only one alteration I think might be made and that is instead of the dinner of boiled or baked fruit pudding, followed by bread and margarine, meat stew followed by milk pudding should be substituted. The young children (3 to 5 years of age) have a milk pudding every day. With regard to nutritive value of the present-day margarine, this has been recognised here for some time and dripping has been used as far as possible as a substitution.

And the Committee recommended that the proposed alteration be adopted.

An observation by the Visiting Committee:-

That the sanitary arrangements in the Babies' yard and playground will require alteration to make them suitable for the children that are being transferred from the St. James' Road Branch Institution, and it will be necessary to connect the Assistant Matron's bedroom with the night telephone. Your Committee recommend - That the matter be referred to the Works Committee.

LYING-IN WARD

(See Minute No. 35.)

The Lying-in Ward was training pupils in Midwifery. In 1916, five more pupils had passed the exam of the Central Midwifery Board.

The reputation of the Lying-in Ward of the Institution had travelled, as one of the Visiting Committee members found out:-

I, the undersigned, today interviewed the expectant mothers and entered particulars in the book kept for the purpose. It should be noted that most of the young women were natives of the provinces and not settled in this Union.
(Signed)E. CASSIDY

One summer's day the Visiting Committee found three tiny babies in the garden in their prams and made the comment that it was greatly to their benefit.

The first Assistant Midwife had been allowed to reside off the premises. She was asked to become a resident officer again and when she refused she was asked to resign.

MEDICAL

The Medical Officer recommended that the aged inmates be given dentures. The Committee disagreed on account of expense.

CHAPTER 4: *The Conciliation Service, and the Unemployed - 1930*

ADMINISTRATION

A member of the community found a bank book and took it to the Police Station. The following explains what happened: -

That your Committee had under consideration the case of Margaret Cooper and the application of Mrs Hall for some compensation for finding a bank book and some Consol Bonds.

Margaret Cooper was admitted to the Institute on 6th April 1920. Search was made at her lodgings for a bank book, but it could not be traced. Her goods were afterwards removed to the Swaffield Road Institution and sold and it would appear that the bank book and the bonds were in a small bag mixed up with Christmas cards and consequently were not noticed. Mrs Hall bought the cards for a shilling and when turning them out to give to her children she found the bank book etc., and forthwith took them to the Police Station. Your Committee are of opinion that Mrs Hall's action in taking the property to the Police Station is deserving of consideration and they accordingly recommend - That, subject to the sanction of the Ministry of Health, she be granted a gratuity of £5. 0s. 0d.

The Committee gave instructions that in future in engaging the scrubbing and laundry staff, preference is to be given to unmarried women, widows or women with sick husbands dependent upon them and when a married woman is engaged a special report of the conditions necessitating this to be made to your committee.

From the National Poor Law Officer's Association (Incorporated), London and District Branch, as follows: -

Sir,

Conforming with the request of the Ministry of Health, your Board will no doubt have under early review the remuneration paid to their Officers, with a view to the completion of the statement for general sanction.

I am directed by the members of the above Branch of the National Poor Law Officers' Association (Incorporated) respectfully to ask that the Guardians may give favourable consideration to their suggestion that the prevailing system of remuneration by Basic Salary plus a fluctuating bonus, should now be abandoned and that the Basic Salary be augmented by the equivalent of a sum not less than 10/13ths of the present bonus and form a fixed Salary for each Officer.

It is felt that the suggestion is reasonable and will assist in the efforts now being made to stabilise conditions. Perhaps you will be good enough to inform me of any action taken by your Board.

I am Sir,

Your obedient Servant,

(Signed) R. ISSELL PARTRIDGE

Hon. Secretary

Special Committee re-Conciliation Committee

7th February, 1921.

Present: Mr Winfield (in the Chair); Miss Brown, Lieut. E.A. Sanders, R.N., Messrs. Line, Mason and Pecksen.

There was also present:

Councillor Deighton, representing the Municipal Employees' Association'; Mr Crook, representing the Poor Law Workers' Trade Union; and the following officers - Mr Evans, Stewart; Mr Harlow, 2nd Assistant Clerk; Mr Harvey, Storekeeper', Sister Parker', Mr Wilcox, Assistant Relieving Officer' Mr Doe, Stoker, and Mrs Hall, Scrubber.

Reporting -

That your Committee conferred with the representative of the Unions and the officers relative to the scheme approved by the Board on the 15th July, 1920 (Vol.29, p.190). The scheme, as adopted by the Guardians, provided that a Joint Conciliation Committee should be set up "to adjust any differences which may arise from time to time in the hours of duty, salaries, wages and general conditions of the officers and servants employed by the Board," (this was in accordance with the original application of the Poor Law Workers' Trade Union) but did not altogether comply with the scheme submitted by the Trade Unions which provided for setting up a Joint Committee for the purpose of dealing with all questions which might arise with reference to hours of duty, salaries, wages, emoluments, &c., and the general conditions of employment. This meant that all applications for increases of salary and wages would have to be submitted to the Joint Committee instead of being considered by the Finance Committee in accordance with the present arrangement.

Your Committee, with a view to meeting the Unions in the matter, recommend -

(1) That the regulations framed on the 15th July, 1920, be amended so as to provide that the Joint Committee shall deal with all questions which may arise with reference to hours of duty and general conditions of employment.

(2) That if the foregoing be carried, the regulations for such Conciliation Committee be as follows:-

Scheme as decided on by the board on the 15th July, 1920	*Scheme as now recommended*
(1) That the Committee be established for the purpose of dealing with matters of disagreement which may arise in reference to (A) hours of duty' (B) salaries, wages and emoluments'; (c) general conditions of employment.	*(1) That the Committee be established for the purpose of dealing with matters of disagreement which may arise in reference to (A) hours of duty' (B) salaries, wages and emoluments'; (c) general conditions of employment.*
(2) That the Committee consist of 12 members, 6 to be elected by the Guardians and 2 from each of the following bodies: the Poor Law Workers' Trade Union (Wandsworth Branch), the Municipal Employees' Association (Wandsworth Branch), and the National Poor Law Officers' Association.	*(2) That the Committee consist of 12 members, 6 to be elected by the Guardians and 2 from each of the following bodies: the Poor Law Workers' Trade Union (Wandsworth Branch), the Municipal Employees' Association (Wandsworth Branch), and the National Poor Law Officers' Association.*

Scheme as decided on by the board on the 15th July, 1920	Scheme as now recommended
(3) The Clerk to the Guardians, or his deputy, and representatives of the Officers' Associations, as set out in paragraph (2), selected by themselves, shall be entitled to attend all meetings of the Committee in an advisory capacity with power to enter into a debate, but not to vote.	(3) The Clerk to the Guardians, or his deputy, and representatives of the Officers' Associations, as set out in paragraph (2), selected by themselves, shall be entitled to attend all meetings of the Committee in an advisory capacity with power to enter into a debate, but not to vote.
(4) The Chairman of the Committee shall be a member of the Guardians' section, and the Vice-Chairman a member of the Staff section, or vice versa. The presiding Chairman shall retain his vote as a member of the Committee, but shall have no casting vote.	(4) The Chairman of the Committee shall be a member of the Guardians' section, and the Vice-Chairman a member of the Staff section, or vice versa. The presiding Chairman shall retain his vote as a member of the Committee, but shall have no casting vote.
(5) The Officers' side of the Committee shall appoint one of its members to act as Secretary, and the Guardians' side likewise.	(5) The Officers' side of the Committee shall appoint one of its members to act as Secretary, and the Guardians' side likewise.
(6) The quorum shall be four members on each side of the Committee.	(6) The quorum shall be four members on each side of the Committee.
(7) The ordinary meetings of the Committee shall be held (at times to be determined hereafter) at the Guardians' Offices' Wandsworth, as often as may be necessary, and shall be summoned by the Secretaries acting jointly, after consultation with the Chairman and Vice-Chairman. The first meeting shall be held within fourteen days after the adoption of this scheme and the election of the representatives of the party concerned. An agenda containing the business to be considered shall be circulated at least four least days prior to the meeting.	(7) The ordinary meetings of the Committee shall be (held at times to be determined hereafter) at the Guardians' Offices' Wandsworth, as often as may be necessary, and shall be summoned by the Secretaries acting jointly, after consultation with the Chairman and Vice-Chairman. The first meeting shall be held within fourteen days after the adoption of this scheme and the election of the representatives of the party concerned. An agenda containing the business to be considered shall be circulated at least four least days prior to the meeting.
(8) Business not on the agenda shall be taken only by permission of the meeting.	(8) Business not on the agenda shall be taken only by permission of the meeting.
(9) It shall be competent for any applicant in connection with the business to be dealt with, to interview the Committee, on request being submitted from the representative of the employees.	(9) It shall be competent for any applicant in connection with the business to be dealt with, to interview the Committee, on request being submitted from the representative of the employees.
(10) The Committee shall be elected not later than the 1st day of May in each year (excepting the year of inception) for the ensuing twelve months. The first representatives to be elected under this Constitution shall hold office until the 30th April, 1921.	(10) The Committee shall be elected not later than the 1st day of May in each year (excepting the year of inception) for the ensuing twelve months. The first representatives to be elected under this Constitution shall hold office until the 30th April, 1921.

Scheme as decided on by the board on the 15th July, 1920	Scheme as now recommended
(11) Casual vacancies shall be filled by the parties concerned. The members elected shall serve for the remainder of the term of office of the representative creating the vacancy.	(11) Casual vacancies shall be filled by the parties concerned. The members elected shall serve for the remainder of the term of office of the representative creating the vacancy.
(12) The guardians will deal with all applications for increases of salary and other matters affecting officers, as at present' but in the event of any officer or officers being dissatisfied with the Guardians' decision, he or they shall forthwith notify the Clerk to the Guardians, who will at once notify the respective Secretaries of the receipt of such notification, and such Secretaries shall forthwith do what is necessary to bring the matter in question before the Conciliation Committee in accordance with paragraph (7).	(12) The guardians will deal with all applications for increases of salary and other matters affecting officers, as at present' but in the event of any officer or officers being dissatisfied with the Guardians' decision, he or they shall forthwith notify the Clerk to the Guardians, who will at once notify the respective Secretaries of the receipt of such notification, and such Secretaries shall forthwith do what is necessary to bring the matter in question before the Conciliation Committee in accordance with paragraph (7).
(13) Meetings of the Committee shall be held when convenient, and it shall be a provision that when a meeting is held at a time when any member of the staff section would be ordinarily on duty, arrangements shall be made whereby his attendance at the Committee will be assured.	(13) Meetings of the Committee shall be held when convenient, and it shall be a provision that when a meeting is held at a time when any member of the staff section would be ordinarily on duty, arrangements shall be made whereby his attendance at the Committee will be assured.
(14) No Motion shall be considered to have been carried at the Committee unless two-thirds of the members present on each side are in favour thereof.	(14) No Motion shall be considered to have been carried at the Committee unless two-thirds of the members present on each side are in favour thereof.
(15) The decisions of the Committee shall be signed by the Chairman and the Secretaries, shall be reported forthwith to the Board of Guardians and become operative, subject to the sanction of the Board and Departmental approvals. PROVIDED that if an agreement is not arrived at within a period of six weeks from the date of the decision of the Committee (the month of August not being included in the said period of six weeks), the question at issue shall be referred to Arbitration under the provisions of the Conciliation Act, 1896, or to some Arbitrator approved by the Committee. PROVIDED ALSO that the said period of six weeks may be extended by agreement. In case no decision is reached, after a vote has been taken on the question, the matter at issue shall be adjourned to a further meeting which shall be agreed upon at the moment. If no decision is arrived at after discussion at such second meeting, the matter at issue shall be referred to the decision of the	(15) The decisions of the Committee shall be signed by the Chairman and the Secretaries, shall be reported forthwith to the Board of Guardians and become operative, subject to the sanction of the Board and Departmental approvals. PROVIDED that if an agreement is not arrived at within a period of six weeks from the date of the decision of the Committee (the month of August not being included in the said period of six weeks), the question at issue shall be referred to Arbitration under the provisions of the Conciliation Act, 1896, or to some Arbitrator approved by the Committee. PROVIDED ALSO that the said period of six weeks may be extended by agreement. In case no decision is reached, after a vote has been taken on the question, the matter at issue shall be adjourned to a further meeting which shall be agreed upon at the moment. If no decision is arrived at

Scheme as decided on by the board on the 15th July, 1920	Scheme as now recommended
Arbitrator as provided above. The decision of the Arbitrator shall be binding upon the principal parties thereto, subject to sanctions of the Poor Law Statutes, Orders, Regulations, or any other Statutes affecting the matter at issue.	after discussion at such second meeting, the matter at issue shall be referred to the decision of the Arbitrator as provided above. The decision of the Arbitrator shall be binding upon the principal parties thereto, subject to sanctions of the Poor Law Statutes, Orders, Regulations, or any other Statutes affecting the matter at issue.
(16) The Annual Meeting for the election of Chairman, Vice-Chairman and officers of the Committee shall be held in the month of May in each year, and shall be the first meeting after the ordinary election of representatives of the parties concerned.	(16) The Annual Meeting for the election of Chairman, Vice-Chairman and officers of the Committee shall be held in the month of May in each year, and shall be the first meeting after the ordinary election of representatives of the parties concerned.
(17) The constitution of the Committee shall only be amended at a Special Meeting of the Committee convened for the purpose. Notice of the proposed amendment must be given to the members at least fourteen days before the meeting, and to the General Secretaries of the Poor Law Workers' Trade Union and the Municipal Employees' Association for the approval of the Central Executive Committee of such Unions, and to the National Poor Law Officers' Association.	(17) The constitution of the Committee shall only be amended at a Special Meeting of the Committee convened for the purpose. Notice of the proposed amendment must be given to the members at least fourteen days before the meeting, and to the General Secretaries of the Poor Law Workers' Trade Union and the Municipal Employees' Association for the approval of the Central Executive Committees of such Unions.

Further Recommending -

That employees of the Guardians appointed as members of the Conciliation Committee be granted the necessary leave of absence to enable them to attend the meetings of the Committee. The Unions will inform the Clerk to the Guardians of the appointment of such officers, who will communicate with the heads of the respective Institutions so that the officers, upon production of the notice convening the meeting, will obtain the necessary leave.

THE UNEMPLOYED
8th September 1921

Reporting: -

(1) *That in accordance with the instructions of the Board your Committee had under consideration the letters from the Battersea Unemployed and the Workers' Committee, the Battersea Trades' Council and Labour Party, and the Battersea Labour League, relative to complaints made as to the treatment of the unemployed and their families during their period of sojourn in the Institution, from 21st July to 27th July, 1921.*

(2) *That at the meeting on the 18th August a deputation from the Battersea Unemployed and Workers' Committee, consisting of Mrs. Lewry, Mrs. Nutley, Mrs. Reilly, Messrs. Andrews, Holmes and Waller, were received, and having submitted their complaints in writing were interviewed.*

The Master, Matron, Medical Officer and a number of the female staff were also interviewed.

At the meeting on the 25th August the deputation received consisted of Mrs. Lewry, Mrs. Nutley, Mrs. Probert, Mrs. Reilly, Messrs. Andrews and Holmes.

(3) That the Committee sat for two afternoons (2.30 pm till about 7pm), carefully considered the complaints brought forward in the statement presented by the unemployed, and listened to witnesses selected by the unemployed from amongst themselves.

(4) That a meeting of your Committee was held on 21st July, at 2.30pm (the same day as the first arrivals in the evening), and it would appear that at 2.30pm 151 "House Orders" had been issued by several Relieving Officers. It is regretted that this information was not officially conveyed to the Committee, as had this been carried out it is possible that something might have been done to mitigate some of the complaints that were afterwards made, but they wish to point out that many of the complaints would also have been avoided if such "House Orders" had been used as they were issued instead of being retained until late at night.

In consequence of the applicants arriving all together it was not possible to ascertain who had Orders and who had not, but the Master reported that the approximate number of unemployed in the Institution was as follows: -

Thursday, 21st July	150	52	102	304
Friday, 22nd July	105	50	102	257
Saturday, 23rd July	98	46	103	247
Sunday, 24th July	96	46	103	245
Monday, 25th July	95	45	102	242
Tuesday, 26th July	-	-	-	241
Wednesday, 27th July	-	-	-	240

(5) That the principal complaints made and the Committee's observations thereon are set out below: -

Complaint	Report of Committee
(a) That on the first night only 6 diapers were issued for about 45 children.	That the Matron reports that 4 dozen diapers were issued the first night.
(b) That no milk was available for the babies.	That it appears one night feed was given in accordance with the rules of the Institution.
(c) That no water was available in the building formerly used as a Lying-in Ward until the attention of the Master had been drawn to the fact on Saturday evening by some of the Guardians.	This was due to the fact that the building having been closed for some time the usual precaution was taken of turning the water off, and it is to be greatly regretted that in the unprecedented circumstances the Master had overlooked this, but it is noted that he immediately remedied this when complaint was made by the Guardians visiting; it is considered that the staff visiting the wards during Friday and Saturday should have been aware of the deficiency and have immediately reported the same to the Master.

Complaint	Report of Committee
(d) That the rice pudding served to some of the Inmates had no sugar or milk with it and smelled of paraffin.	The Committee after careful investigation cannot find any reason for the use of paraffin in the Kitchen, as the only paraffin on the Establishment is stored in the Engineer's Shop. The rice pudding was prepared in the ordinary manner according to the Dietary table, the milk and sugar being mixed in bulk.
(e) That the bread supplied was sour.	The Committee would point out that there is only one Bakery from which all the Establishments are supplied and no complaints were received of the bread supplied at this time from either Officers or Inmates in any other Institution. It should be noted that the same quality of bread is issued for both Inmates and Officers, including the Medical Staffs at the Hospitals.
(f) That a dirty feeding bottle was issued for Mrs. Lewry's baby.	No complaint was apparently made at the time to any Officer, and your Committee are of opinion that the complaint is not substantiated.
(g) That the "Glaxo" supplied on the Friday morning was very poor.	It was admitted by the Nurse in charge of Children's Block that she was short of "Glaxo" on that morning about 8 o'clock, and it had to be diluted to make it go round. It is to be regretted that the Officer in charge did not apply for more "Glaxo" from the Stores, but it must be borne in mind that the Officer had, owing to the exceptional circumstances, been on continuous duty up to 4am (16 hours).
(h) That no soap was available on Saturday morning, and this state of things continued until the arrival of some of the Guardians in the evening.	Doctor reported that when he took round some soap in the morning he found some already there.
(i) That Nurse pulled the bandages off Mrs. Lewry's scalded fingers roughly and she was not properly attended to.	Nurse denied this and Mrs. Lewry admitted that in future dressings the Nurse did them nicely.
(j) That Doctor told Mrs. Reilly he was only attending them "as a favour," and on occasions the unemployed were unable to see the Medical Officer at the Receiving Ward, although a time had been fixed for them to do so.	The Doctor denies this. By the Regulations it is the duty of the Medical Officer to examine each person on admission, but on the occasion in question it was not possible to adhere to such Regulations, and the only course open was to attend those who wished to see him, and

Complaint	Report of Committee
	there is no evidence that the Doctor refused to see any case.
	There is, however, a conflict of statements as to the times the unemployed were told they could see the Medical Officer, as also the times they left the Dining Hall. (It was alleged that the Inmates were unable to see the Medical Officer at the time appointed by him as they were in the Dining Hall.)
	It appears that on Tuesday, 26th July, when the unemployed did attend at the Doctor's Room, he was in the Building, and it is difficult to understand why his attention was not drawn, before leaving the building, to the fact that Inmates were wishing to see him.
	A similar occurrence took place on Wednesday, 27th July, and your Committee are of opinion that there was laxity on the part of the Gate Staff in this respect and regret if there was any inconvenience caused thereby.

To the Clerk to the Guardians of the Wandsworth Union. Requisition for Extraordinary Meetings of Guardians.

We, the undersigned, being seven of the Guardians of the Poor of the Wandsworth Union, do hereby require an Extraordinary Meeting of the Guardians of the said Union to be summoned, to be held at the Guardians' Office on Tuesday, the 11th day of October, 1921, at 10.30 o'clock in the forenoon, to take into consideration the circular on Relief to Unemployed, from the Ministry of Health, also any alteration in the scale of relief that may be deemed advisable.

    J.R. ARCHER
    C.M. CHALMERS
    M. ROBINSON
    A.G. PRICHARD   *Guardians*
    A.A. PECKSEN
    HARRY B. ROGERS
    B. COLEMAN

The Board proceeded to receive deputations from -
    The Battersea Unemployed and Workers Committee (three representatives)
    The Wandsworth Unemployed and Workers Committee (three representatives)
    The Tooting unemployed Committee (three representatives)
    Whose principal demands were - That the scale of relief for the Unemployed should be increased to a weekly sum of -
    £1 for man
    £1 for wife
    10s for each child
    Rent, and such coal as may be necessary

Single persons over 18 years of age to receive 30s per week and such coal as may be necessary.

Single persons under 18 years of age to receive 15s per week and such coal as may be necessary.

That the District Medical Officer be empowered to order clothes, food and nourishment without consulting the Relieving Officer of the District.

Sons and daughters earning up to 35/- per week not to be taken into account and deducted when arriving at the "Income" in regard to Scale Relief.

"Wanderers" tickets to be issued to men who are travelling through the country in search of work.

Grants for redeeming tools and other articles in pledge.

Recognition of the "Unemployed" as a Union and two members of the Committee of such Union to be allowed to sit with the Relief Committees when "Scale" Relief is being administered.

The Board proceeded to consider a circular letter from the Ministry of Health, as follows:-

POOR LAW RELIEF AND UNEMPLOYMENT

Ministry of Health
Whitehall, S.W.!.
8th September, 1921.

Sir,

In view of the distress arising from the continuance of exceptional unemployment and large numbers who in various parts of the country are dependent upon Poor Law relief at the present time, the Minister of Health deems it desirable to draw the attention of the Guardians to some of the more important rules which should guide them in the administration of relief. The Minister has had the advantage of consulting the Association of Poor Law Unions in England and Wales, and he is assured that they are in entire agreement with him in attaching importance to the observance of these rules.

It has been long recognised, both by the Central Department and by Boards of Guardians generally, that relief given under the Poor Law should be sufficient for the purpose of relieving distress, but that the amount of the relief so given should of necessity be calculated on a lower scale than the earnings of the independent workman who is maintaining himself by his labour. This is a fundamental principle, any departure from which must in the end prove disastrous to the recipient of relief as well as to the community at large, and, although the Minister has no desire unduly to fetter the discretion of the Guardians as to the manner or method in which they afford relief, he will feel bound to exercise the powers which he possesses and to disapprove a departure from the Relief Regulation Order authorised by Article XII, thereof in any case in which the relief given is contrary to this principle. The Minister thinks it necessary for this purpose to require that, when reporting departures under Article XII of the Relief Regulation Order, the Clerk to the Guardians should give sufficient particulars as to the amount of relief granted, either generally or in particular cases, to enable the Minister to satisfy himself that the amount given is not in excess of what is necessary in accordance with the above-mentioned rule.

The next board principle to be observed is that relief should not be given without full investigation of the circumstances of each applicant for relief. The giving of indiscriminate relief without proper investigation is demoralising to the recipients, and is an injustice to the ratepayers. The Minister suggests, for the consideration of the Guardians, that they should require each applicant to sign a form containing a complete statement as to the income of his household from all sources. Orders for relief should be given for short periods only, and further investigation should precede the renewal of the orders. In no case should relief be given in money until the case has been before the Guardians and reported on by the relieving officer. In some unions it may be necessary for the Guardians to employ additional staff for the purposes of investigation, and the Minister hereby sanctions the employment of such additional staff as may be reasonably necessary for this purpose.

The greater proportion of the relief granted to the cases now in question should be given in kind, and where the Guardians do not supply relief in kind from their own out-relief distribution stores, the orders on tradesmen should specify in detail the particular articles to be supplied. Prices at which the articles are to be supplied should be arranged beforehand with the tradespeople supplying them. It will generally be found desirable that the payments to tradespeople should be made direct from the Clerk's office and not by the relieving officers.

As there appears to be some misapprehension in regard to the power of the Guardians to give sufficient relief to pay rent, the Minister wishes to point out that while the regulations prohibit the Guardians or their officers from paying rent directly to the landlord, they do not prevent the Guardians, in considering the amount of relief to be afforded to any particular person, from taking account of the expense being incurred by such person in providing lodging. It is desirable, of course, that the Guardians should satisfy themselves that any part of the relief which they have given for the purpose of paying rent is in fact devoted to this purpose and they should therefore require the production by the recipient of relief of his rent-book or other evidence that the rent is being duly paid.

The Guardians are reminded that any relief which may be given to, or on account of, any person above the age of 21, or to his wife, or any members of his family under the age of 16 in accordance with the regulations may, if the Guardians think fit be given by way of loan. The Minister considers it desirable that the Guardians, wherever practicable should adopt this course, and all reports notifying departures under Article XII of the regulations should include a statement as to the extent to which this policy has been adopted. It is suggested that the form of declaration which, as recommended above, should be signed by each applicant should include an undertaking to repay the relief that may be granted.

The Minister fully appreciates the difficulties with which the Guardians have to contend at the present time. He is confident that they will recognise their grave responsibility both to those who apply to them in distress and to the public whose funds they administer, and he has no doubt that on the present occasion, as in the past, he can rely on their discharging their arduous duties with both courage and sympathy.

I am, Sir,
Your obedient servant,
A. V. SYMONDS,
Secretary

Discussion ensued:-

It was MOVED by the Rev. A.G. Pritchard and Seconded y Mr. Archer -

That this Board expressed its extreme dissatisfaction at the fact that the circular letter from the Ministry of Health on Poor Law Relief and Unemployment, assumes that unemployment is a local rather than a national responsibility and that distress arising therefrom is a problem for the local Guardians to deal with at the expense of the already overburdened ratepayers, presumably without any assistance from the Government except in the form of unsought advice and instructions upon matters of detail connected with the administration of relief to the unemployed.

Having regard to the fact that the Government evidently intends the local ratepayers shall bear the whole of the burden of relief given because of unemployment, this Board, being representative of the local ratepayers, resents the interference of the Ministry of Health in the matter and declines to accept their suggestions as to the greater proportion of the relief being given in kind, including an undertaking, by the recipients, to repay to the Guardians any relief that may be granted.

Upon the MOTION being put to the Vote there appeared -

For the Motion (13 Votes) - Mrs. Ashby, Mrs Chalmers, Mrs Coleman, Mrs Dawson,
Mrs Massey, Mrs Robinson, Rev F.J. Flanagan, D.D., Rev. A.G. Pritchard,
Messrs. Archer, Eland, Mason, Pecksen and Rogers.

Against the Motion (9 Votes) - Miss Brown, Miss Hill, Rev. M. Williams, Messrs.
Grundy, Harding, Hill, King, Palmer and Sullivan.

Declined to Vote (3) - The Chairman, Lady Dawnay and Mr Line.

Whereupon the Chairman declared the MOTION to be carried, and it was RESOLVED and ORDERED accordingly.

It was MOVED by Mrs Ashby, Seconded by Mr Grundy and RESOLVED -

(a) That the present investigators be kept entirely on investigations and clerical assistance to be given to the Relieving Officers.

(b) That payments to Out-Relief tradespeople be made direct from the Clerk's Office and not by the Relieving Officers.

It was MOVED by Mr Archer, Seconded by Rev. A. G. Pritchard and RESOLVED - That it be an instruction from the Board, that when applicants for "scale" relief appear before the Sectional Committees they be informed the number of weeks such relief has been put on.

It was MOVED by Miss Hill and Seconded by Mr Harding - That the Board adhere to their present scale of relief to the unemployed.

CONCILIATION SERVICE

The Master reported:

A large number of unemployed were admitted to the Institution on the 21st ultimo and remained here until the 27th ultimo. During that time a great amount of extra time had to be worked by the staff in excess of the 48 hours and I shall be glad if payment for extra time could receive your favourable consideration.

THE UNEMPLOYED

Further recommending:-

That the Ministry of Health be asked to extend the time for repayment from the Fund on a flat rate basis up to the end of February (instead of the 4th February as already provided), having regard to the large amount of work involved in getting the proposed scheme into working order.

The following is the scale referred to in recommendation of the foregoing report:-

SCHEDULE

1. *Outdoor relief shall not in any case be charged upon the Fund in excess of a sum which will raise the weekly income of the applicant or of the household of which he is the head or a member:*

(a) *Beyond the sum shown in the scale as appropriate for him for that household, or*

(b) *beyond a sum less by ten shillings a week than the standard rate of wages for the time being recommended for work people of Grade A under the agreement of the London Industrial Council for non-trading services (manual labour). Whichever sum be the less, not exceeding*

	s.	d.	
For man and wife or two adults living together	25	0	*a week*
For children under 16			
For a first child	6	0	*a week*
For second or third child	5	0	*a week*
For a fourth or any subsequent child	4	0	*a week*
For an adult living with parents or relatives	10	0	*a week*
For an adult not so living " "	15	0	*a week*

Fuel up to 1 cwt, a week in winter, November 1st to March 31st, or ½ cwt in summer April 1st to October 31st, or its equivalent in money (not exceeding 3s in winter and 1s 6d in summer) may be granted in addition to the above amounts.

Reporting i.e., Relief to Unemployed:-

That your Committee considered, upon reference from the Board, the question of relief to the unemployed (having special regard to the single able-bodied men and women in receipt of out-relief at present), and with a view to the more efficient administration of this class of relief, recommend -

(a) *SINGLE WOMEN UNDER 30 YEARS OF AGE. That a Special Committee consisting of all the lady members of the Board be appointed to deal with these cases, and authorised to send girls to Mabys Training Homes, or give relief, as may be thought desirable.*

(b)* *SINGLE MEN. That this Committee be authorised to deal with these cases, and, where suitable, make arrangements for their being sent to the Hollesley Bay Training Colony, which is administered by the Central (Unemployed) Body for London.*

(c)* *LADS of 16 TO 18 YEARS OF AGE. That this Committee be authorised to deal with these cases and endeavour to have suitable lads admitted to the Hollesley Bay Training Colony, or where they express a desire to emigrate, apply to the Ministry of Health for their sanction to expend such sum as may be necessary for that purpose.*

(d)* *That the present scale be considered the maximum, a less amount being granted should the Relief Committees think desirable.*

(e)* *That as a general rule the scale be altered to half money and half kind, but that this be varied where thought necessary by the Relief Committees by increasing the amount in kind and decreasing the amount in money.*

(f)* *That where relief is given in excess of the scale to an expectant mother a medical certificate be obtained by the Relieving Officer.*

(g) *That hawkers, costers, rag and bone sellers, flower sellers, street musicians, &c., be not put on scale relief but left to the Relieving Officers to deal with.*

(h)* *That in cases of single men residing at home, the Relieving Officers be instructed to ascertain, before reporting to the Committee, the total income of the household.*

(See Minute No. 10(f), page 165).

(i) *That the resolution of the Board prohibiting Relieving Officers from writing to the employers of relatives of applicants, unless instructed by the Guardians, be rescinded.*

IT WAS MOVED by Mr Archer, Seconded and Resolved - That in the case of single parents residing in lodgings - (a) The words "apart from relatives", be understood to mean "not living with parents"; (b) That where a person resides regularly in a common lodging house this be considered as coming under the heading "lodgings".

The weekly scale of relief for Unemployed will in consequence be as follows:-

(a) *10/- per man.*
   10/- per woman
   7/- for first child
   6/- for second child
   5/- for each subsequent child
   Plus rent up to 15/- weekly
   Account to be taken of any income rent, rent book to be produced weekly. Labour Exchange ticket also to be seen.

(b) *That such allowance be issued in the proportion of two-thirds money and one-third kind.*

(c) *That in the case of single persons having relatives entirely dependent upon them, or residing in lodgings, apart from parents (including regular residence in a common lodging house) the weekly relief be as follows - 2/6 money, 7/6 kind and rent allowance, not exceeding 7/6 weekly.*

(d) *That with regard to single persons residing with parents the weekly relief (10/-) be given as follows - 2/6 money, 7/6 kind.*

(e) *That the Tickets issued on Out-Relief Tradesmen be available on any Tradesman within the Union.*

(f) That with regard to the "earnings" of gown-up children, no account be taken of such earnings when under 30/- each weekly when arriving at the "Income" in regard to the scale relief.

(g) That in regard to children in receipt of war pensions, where such pension is in excess of the relief sale, it be an instruction to the Relieving Officers that in computing the weekly allowance such children are to be excluded in making the necessary calculation.

(h) That with regard to reserve pay where such reserve pay is received quarterly the amount is to be spread over the quarter and a proportionate weekly sum reckoned as income in arriving at the sum to be paid as scale relief, it being understood that the Relieving Officers will ignore the fact of the men receiving the total sum at the end of each quarter, as having averaged it over the quarter it would be unfair to the recipient to decide that having received a lump sum he was not entitled to the scale.

(i) That when ascertaining what a man's rent is, it is also to be ascertained how much be received from sub-letting; also each applicant should be required to produce his rent book weekly, and the registration card from the Labour Exchange.

The meeting terminated at 1.48pm.

UNEMPLOYMENT: CO-OPERATION BETWEEN BOARDS OF GUARDIANS AND OTHER LOCAL AUTHORITIES

Sir,

I am directed by the Minister of Health to state that he has, in conjunction with the other Ministers concerned, been giving consideration to the question of extending the arrangements for co-operation between the Poor Law Authorities and the other public authorities concerned with measures for the relief of unemployment.

1. The Minister of Labour has agreed that arrangements shall be made for the appointment of representatives of Boards of Guardians upon the Local Employment Committees and has issued to the Committees an invitation to make a temporary addition to their membership for this purpose and to co-opt representatives of Boards of Guardians and of public bodies engaged in providing relief works in the area. The Minister of Health is sure that Boards of Guardians will gladly avail themselves of this opportunity in any case in which members of the Board are not in fact already members of the Local Employment Committees.

2. Section 6 of the Unemployed Workers' Dependants (Temporary Provision) Act, 1921, provides that in determining whether out-door relief shall or shall not be granted to a person in receipt of, or entitled to, a grant under the Act, the Authority having the power to grant relief shall take into account the amount of the grant; and further that, during the operation of the Act, the operation of Section 27 of the Unemployment Insurance Act, 1920, is to be suspended. The effect of this provision is that the whole of any amount received by way of unemployment benefit, or of grants under the new Act, is to be taken into account as weekly income by the Guardians considering the application. It is desired that the arrangements to be made to give effect to the enactment should be such as to

obviate any unnecessary clerical work or any reference to the local office of the Ministry of Labour in cases in which it is highly improbable that the Local Office would be in a position to correct the statement made by the applicant.

An applicant for relief by reason of want of employment will, in the ordinary course, be asked the amount, if any, which he is receiving by way of unemployment benefit or dependants' grant. If his statement does not agree with the amount which, by his age, usual occupation, domestic circumstances, &c., he would appear qualified to receive and the Guardians are not otherwise satisfied as to the accuracy of his statement, the actual facts should be ascertained from the local office of the Ministry of Labour. In such cases, it is suggested that the form, of which a copy is appended, should be handed to the applicant and he should be requested to present it at the Local Office for completion.

3. The Minister of Pensions has directed that particulars of the amount of any pension, allowance or grant which is, or has been, in payment by the Ministry or Local War Pensions Committee may be given confidentiality to public bodies, including Boards of Guardians. It is, however, hoped that the Guardians will be able to avoid numerous applications for these particulars by requiring the production of a pensioner's identity certificate (ring paper) which discloses the actual amount of pensions. Should there be cases in which an applicant for relief is believed to be in receipt of some pension which is not admitted by the applicant, or should the applicant while admitting the receipt of a pension be unable to produce his identity certificate, the local War Pensions Committee will be prepared to complete a form of inquiry on this matter. The form should be generally similar to that suggested in this circular for use in making applications to the local office of the Ministry of Labour, containing in the first part the name and address of the applicant for relief and the statements made by the applicant as to the non-receipt of a pension or the amount of pension received. In the second part provision should be made for the confirmation or correction of the applicant's statement by the Local War Pensions Committee.

4. A similar procedure should so far as applicable be adopted in obtaining information from local authorities and committees as regards the supply of meals or of milk, either gratis or at a reduced price, under the Education Act, 1921, or the Maternity and Child Welfare Act, 1920. The Guardians should ascertain from the authorities acting within their area the general lines on which assistance is given by them in each of these directions, and, if an applicant who appears likely to be receiving such assistance under the local scheme, does not admit the receipt of assistance under it, he should be given a note showing - as in the other cases mentioned in this letter - the statement made by him, and requested to take the statement to the appropriate officer for confirmation or correction.

5. In a number of cases, it will be possible to make arrangements on similar lines with other public and voluntary bodies concerned in the administration of assistance, and wherever practicable this course should be taken.

6. In a certain number of areas there are already in existence schemes for the Mutual registration of assistance. The Minister endorses the principle of such registration, and will be prepared, so far as he may have power, to further the operations of

such schemes. The initiation of a scheme at the present time, however, would involve both expense and delay, and the Minister therefore considers it generally preferable that action should now be taken on the lines laid down in the earlier paragraphs of this letter.

7. *It will be obvious to the Guardians that it is incumbent on them to be prepared to provide, on the request of other public and other authorities who are parties to a scheme of co-ordination on the lines indicated in this letter, such information as may be reasonably required by those authorities and may be in the possession of the Guardians. The Minister believes that such information is already in the majority of Unions made available when sufficient grounds are shown for the request.*

I am, Sir
Your obedient Servant,
H.W.S. FRANCIS
Assistant Secretary
23rd November 1921

The Clerk to the Guardians.

In this decade the rejections continued, causing the same inconvenience.

112lbs Harricot Beans
10 Gallons Engine Oil
400 lbs Inmates Fish
25lbs Officers Fish
20lbs Dried Haddock
1 ton of Soap
38 yards of coloured Tabling (hemmed sail cloth)
½ doz 4½v Batteries, Messrs H C Davis & Co
½ doz 3½v Bulbs
14lbs Celery, Mr H Bolton
2 Reams of Brown Paper, Messrs Wrightman & Co
1 Uniform Suit and Overcoat, Messrs Milns, Cartwright & Reynolds & Co.
1 Jacket, 1 Vest
3 doz bottles of Salad Cream, Messrs. E Laws & Co.
1-4 gallon Tea Urn, Messrs H C Davis & Co.
1-7 gallon Tea Urn, Messrs H C Davis & Co.
1 doz Enamel Bowl, Mr L Richmond
53lbs Bacon, Mr J F Percival Ltd.
180 Eggs, Mr J F Percival Ltd
12 yards Flannel, Mr G Miller
52½ Yards Calender Felt
1 Uniform Cap, Messrs. Milns, Cartwright, Reynolds & Co.

The Institution loaned 200 blankets to the unemployed marchers at Latchmere Baths, none were returned!

Recorded in the Visitors Book:-

My wife and myself have just visited the many departments and have been deeply impressed by the high state of splendid efficiency and spirit of happiness and content shown and mentioned by the patients and inmates. This is a great tribute to the Chairman (Mr Fowle) and his public spirited colleagues and to the Matron and Master.
Henry Jackson,
Mayor of Wandsworth

From the National Poor Law Officers' Association (Incorporated) as follows:-

Dear Sir,

BONUS AND SUPERANNUATION

The attention of the Council of this Association has been called to a resolution on the above subject passed by the Newmarket Board of Guardians, copy of which has been forwarded by that Board to the Minister of Health, the Association of Poor Law Unions, every Board of Guardians in England and Wales and certain other local authorities.

The Council desire to point out to your Board:-

(1) *That the latest scale of Bonuses (commonly known as Award No. 102) is quite fair both to the Guardians and the officers, providing as it does, for an automatic decrease as the cost of living goes down. Under this scale the bonuses have already been reduced by no less than 12/26ths - approximately 50 per cent - since 1st September, 1921; and there will be a further substantial reduction of bonus under the scale on 1st September, next.*

(2) *The Poor Law Officers' Superannuation Act 1896, is not at all comparable with the Schemes of Pension for Civil Servants, the former being on a contribution basis and the superannuation allowance being based on the average annual salary and emoluments of the Officer for the last five years of service, whereas Civil Servants' pensions are based on their actual remuneration at the date of retirement. Civil Servants also receive on retirement in addition to their annual pension a lump sum not exceeding one and a half times the amount of their salary and emoluments.*

It will therefore be seen that in the case of those Poor Law Officers who have recently retired, their superannuation allowance based on the average remuneration (including bonus) for the last five years' service will amount to a smaller sum than in the case of Civil Servants whose pensions are based on the salary and 75 per cent of the bonus.

In the case of Poor Law Officers still in the Service their five years' average will gradually decrease as time goes on, although they will have contributed to the Superannuation Fund a larger amount during the period when the bonuses were highest.

My Council also desire to remind your Board that, compared with the total number of Poor Law Officers only a very small number of members of the Service have been or will be superannuated on bonus as well as salary and emoluments.

It therefore follows that the vast majority of Poor Law Officers, who have been paying and are still paying contributions, are unlikely to be superannuated on remuneration which will include any bonus at all. Consequently, if legislation is passed - in accordance with the suggestion of the Newmarket Guardians - to provide that no bonus at all or only a proportion of the bonus shall be reckoned for the purpose of assessing the superannuating allowance of Poor Law Officers, it naturally follows that those officers, who have for the last few years been paying superannuation contributions on bonus which is not to be reckoned as part of the average remuneration for the purpose of reckoning superannuation, should be repaid the amount of such contributions.

That would mean repayment by Boards of Guardians of thousands of pounds and it is therefore submitted that even from a financial point of view it will be to the advantage of Boards of Guardians generally to preserve the existing position.

I am directed by my Council to ask that you will lay these facts before your Board and to express the hope that the Board will decide not to support the above-mentioned resolution of the Newmarket Guardians.

Yours faithfully,
JOHN SIMONDS
Secretary
14th June 1922

The Clerk to the Guardians

The Visitors' Book contained the following entry, viz:-

We the undersigned members of the Board, had the pleasure of visiting this Institution this Christmas Day and wish to express our hearty appreciation of everything which has been done by the Master, Matron and Staff to ensure the happiness of every inmate of this Institution. The whole of the Wards are beautifully decorated and great praise is due to all concerned. We waited to see dinner served and everything was exceptionally good. The inmates very much appreciated the beer kindly given them by Messrs. Young & Co.

Signed

S BAKER	G HILL
D GRUNDY	P C KIPPAX
F M GLANVILL	T HARDING
C VARLEY	T W PALMER
A E JOHNSTON	H B ROGERS

That your Committee desire to express their thanks to all the officers of the Institution for the services rendered by them in entertaining the inmates at Christmas time and subsequently.

METROPOLITAN COMMON POOR FUND

II am directed by the Minister of Health to say that he would be glad to have the views of the Metropolitan Borough Councils and Boards of Guardians in regard to the continuance of Section 1 of the Local Authorities (Emergency Provisions) Act 1923, provides for the temporary extension of charges on the Metropolitan Common Poor Fund until the 1st April next.

In view of the continued prevalence of unemployment it appears to the Minister that there must be some provision, on the general lines of the existing legislation, for equalising poor law expenditure throughout London, and he is sure that the richer authorities will once again agree to share part of the burden of the poorer parts of the Metropolis.

The Minister accordingly suggests for consideration:-

(a) That, subject to any modification that may seem desirable, the extension of charges on the Fund in respect of both in-door and out-door relief should be continued for a further temporary period of say, two years;

(b) That the charge in respect of in-door relief should be, as now at the rate of one shilling and three pence per day;

(c) That the expenses in respect of out-door relief should continue to be calculated by reference to a flat rate; and

(d) That this flat rate should remain at 9d per day.

The Minister would at the same time be prepared to consider any suggestions that may be made to him with a view to preventing any unfair inflation of the number of out-relief cases in respect of which claims may be made on the Fund.

I am, Sir,

Your Obedient Servant

17th December, 1923

(Suggestions agreed to)

ADMINISTRATION OF VACCINATION ACTS

Sir,

I am delighted by the Minister of Health to state that he has had under consideration the question of the administration of the Vaccination Acts and he is not satisfied that the Acts are being properly administered in districts. Cases have been brought to his notice in which statutory declarations of conscientious objection to vaccination have been accepted by Vaccination Officers although they have been made by some person other than the legal guardian of the child, and various other irregularities have occurred which he is advised render the statutory declaration of no effect; while in some districts the prosecution of defaulters has entirely ceased.

The present prevalence of smallpox in certain parts of the country emphasises the importance of securing that the Vaccination Acts are strictly administered, and that exemption from penalty for neglecting to cause a child to be vaccinated is only obtained in conformity with the law; and the Minister thinks it desirable that he should state what the law provides in regard to the vaccination of children.

The obligation to cause a child to be vaccinated is imposed by the Vaccination Acts upon the parent or person having the custody of the child, and under section 29 and 31 of the Vaccination Act of 1867 penalties are imposed on the parent or person having the custody of a child who neglects to cause the child to be vaccinated, or after vaccination to be inspected, unless he renders a reasonable excuse for his neglect. In ordinary circumstances the father is the person having the custody of a legitimate child, and the obligation therefore rests upon him unless, by reason of his death, illness, absence or inability, or for any other cause, the mother or some other person has the custody of the child. The Vaccination Act of 1907 provides that no parent or other person shall be liable to any penalty under section 29 or section 31 of the Vaccination

Act of 1867 if within four months of the birth of the child he makes a statutory declaration that he conscientiously believes that vaccination would be prejudicial to the health of the child, and within seven days thereafter delivers or sends by post the declaration to the Vaccination Officer of the district. It is clear, therefore, that if the father has the legal custody of a child and neglects to cause the child to be vaccinated, he is not exempt from penalty unless he himself makes a declaration of conscientious objection.

The Minister considers it important that Vaccination Officers should be accurately informed as to the law on this point, and that they should make it clear to parents and guardians that the person having the legal custody of the child is responsible for causing the child to be vaccinated and is liable to prosecution if he neglects this duty and fails to make a declaration of conscientious objection to vaccination in the manner and within the period provided by the statute.

It is also necessary that a Vaccination Officer should scrutinise every statutory declaration which he receives with a view to satisfying himself that the declaration has been made by the person who would otherwise be liable to penalties under the Vaccination Acts and is in all respects in order, e.g., he should verify that the person before whom the declaration is made is an officer authorised to receive such declarations and that the declaration has been made, as the law provides, in his presence. It may be assumed (in the absence of evidence to the contrary) that this has been done where the date inserted by the declarant is the same as that inserted by the officer before whom the declaration was made; but where the two dates differ, the declaration should not be accepted without further inquiry.

The duty of taking proceedings for enforcing the provisions of the Vaccination Acts is imposed upon Vaccination Officers without any directions from this Department or the Guardians, but the Guardians are required to ascertain from time to time whether those officers are performing the duties imposed upon them under the Acts and the Vaccination Orders made by the Local Government Board, and to report to the Minister any case of continued neglect on the part of a Vaccination Officer. In present circumstances the Minister considers it essential that proceedings should be taken in every case of default.

I am at the same time to forward herewith copies of an Order which has been made under the Vaccination Acts prescribing a new Form of notice of the requirement of vaccination, in substitution for Form A contained in the First Schedule to the Vaccination Order (No. 11), 1907. The effect of the Order is to eliminate from Form A the form of statutory declaration and to provide that forms for this purpose may be obtained from the Vaccination Officers. The Order will come into operation on the 1st September next and copies of the new Form A will be forwarded in due course to the Registrars of Births and Deaths.

I am to request that a copy of this Circular and of the Order may be handed at once to each Vaccination Officer in the Union. Forms for the purpose of statutory declarations will be forwarded to the Guardians as soon as possible for distribution to the Vaccination Officers.

I am, Sir, your obedient Servant,
A K MACLACHLAN
23rd July 1923

It was decided in January 1924 that "Wandsworth Union, Swaffield Road Institution" should be painted on the large main gates.

In January 1925 the Mayor of Battersea visited the Institution and recorded:-

I have visited this Institution and am pleased to report that I am delighted with all the arrangements made for the happiness and welfare of the inmates. This reflects great credit on all the officials of the Institution.

Signed   C E MASON
Mayor of Battersea

That your Committee considered the question raised at the Board Meeting relative to aged Inmates being allowed to lie on the beds in the afternoon and report that no objection has ever been raised to them lying in bed should they so desire, but lying on the beds is not conducive to cleanliness. Also one is prevented from going to bed at any time he or she may wish, your Committee see no reason to make any alteration in the present arrangements.

3rd September 1925

That at the request of the No 3 Relief Committee, your Committee interviewed John Thomas Leeder with regard to how he was employed during the short intervals when he discharged himself. They find that he goes on tramp for short distances, but as he is 55 years of age, in poor health and has been constantly in and out of the Institution for 37 years, it does not appear possible to do anything for him.

The Visitors Book contained the following entry:-

On behalf of the Women's Section of North Battersea Labour Party I thank the Master of the Swaffield Road Institution for his courtesy and information given on our visit. We were greatly impressed by the cleanliness and arrangements. We were exceedingly pleased to find very old people quite happy and contented and wish to appreciate the married couples' quarters.

Signed   M VARRAN, J.P.   Secretary
*   E PAYNE,   Asst Secretary*

That your Committee considered a memorandum of the Clerk relative to the complaint of some of the Female Officers at this Institution as to the inefficiency of rations, from which it appeared that there was very little difference in the consumption per head at this Institution as compared with that at St. John's Hospital, that the Clerk had consulted the Master with regard to the dietary being varied and it now appeared to be satisfactory. In connection therewith your Committee approved of the following suggestion of the Clerk:-

(a) There are two Messes, but from what I can gather, it is no one's business to supervise them, and I would suggest:-

1) That the Assistant Matron do supervise one Mess; and

2) That the General Officer do supervise the other.

The Matron occasionally to visit to see that things are in order.

(b) With regard to the supply of coal for officers' rooms, this appears to me to be unnecessary, as a Recreation Room with piano has been provided as in other Institutions and I suggest:-

1) That no fires be provided in officers' bedrooms except in cases of illness.

2) That the female officers be informed that the Guardians expect them to use the Recreation Room provided.

That in connection with the concerts given at this Institution, it would appear that refreshments provided for artists and visitors have been charged up under "Officers' Rations". The Clerk pointed out that this was unfair to the officers as it increased the cost of their rations and it was not a legal charge. He therefore suggested that application be made to the Ministry of Health to sanction light refreshments being given to those artistes who give their services and your Committee recommended - that this be done.

June 1926

Permission was given for a party of students from Battersea Polytechnic, training in Public Health to visit the Institution. These visits became a regular feature.

In July the Committee accepted with thanks the offer from the Chaplain of a wireless Crystal Set for the Officers' Recreation Room.

In September 1927 the Committee approved the suggestion of the Master that "D" Block (Nursery) should be used for nursing mothers and their children and for isolating new admissions, the remainder of the children being accommodated in "E" Block, which could be adapted for the purpose of installing a large verandah on one side of the building and removing two partition walls to enable a playroom and a dining room to be provided. This matter is receiving the attention of the Works Committee.

The Christmas expenditure for 1927 was as follows:-

£4 for toys, £8 for decorations (this was a very high amount, records do not show what was actually purchased) and £2 for gramophone records.

An entry in the Visitors Book for Christmas Day 1927:-

We have visited the Wandsworth Union this day and it is the firm opinion of us all that as far as possible every provision has been made for the inmates. Our thanks is due to the Master for the information conveyed to us during our tour of the wards.

Signed	C HUGHES	W H MORRISON
	P HADDANY	T MORAN
	W H BATCHELOR	E B SKINNER
	W SUTTIE	J KILLICK

Delegation from the Wandsworth Branch of the National Union of General and Municipal Workers.

In April 1928 a carpet was purchased for the Master and Matron from Messrs. Maple & Co. Ltd., cost £15.10/-.

The Tennis Court in the grounds of the Institution which was for the staff to use was to be "Topped" (resurfaced) and be made fit to play on.

The Mineral Water plant had broken down in May and the estimate from Messrs. Barnet & Foster was £13 to put it in first class order.

That the Nursery was to be placed in charge of a nurse thoroughly qualified and trained in Children's Nursing and Maternity Work and that advertisements be issued for such an officer, to be known as "Infants Charge Attendant".

In June 1928 the Committee accepted the quotation of Messrs. H. Tiffin & Son for the destruction of beetles, and cockroaches (in the kitchens) for one year at the rate of £28.

In November 1928, instructions were given for a call-over of inmates, if they are able-bodied, how long they have been there and what work they were doing. Decisions would be made then as to what action to take. Life had become very comfortable for the inmates, and they did not make any effort to find employment outside the Institution.

In December of that year, the Committee accepted the quotation of Messrs. West Bros. Lombard Wharf, Lombard Road, for the purchase of 900 old flour sacks for £17.16.3d. Messrs. West Bros., eventually found that 72 of the sacks were quite useless and asked the Guardians to accept payment for 828 sacks only. The Committee acceded to their request.

The Committee authorised the hire of a piano for a fortnight over the Christmas period.

In January 1929 the Committee had a difficult situation to attend to. They had under consideration an allegation that an officer had cashed a cheque for an inmate and retained the greater part of the money. They adjourned the matter for further enquiries and instructed the Master to see all of the officers were acquainted with the regulations as to money found in possession of inmates.

A further allegation of an officer cashing a cheque and retaining the greater part of the money was found to be the work of a temporary officer, who had left the Institution.

Also in January the Committee approved of the residential and non-residential male and female officers holding a social evening in the Recreation Room from 7.30 - 11.30pm once a month during the next three months.

In February a letter was submitted from the Society of the Battersea Committee Charity Organisation, asking permission for a party of four students to visit the Institution on the afternoon of 12th and 14th February and the Committee acceded to their request.

It was proposed that an Installation of an Internal System of Telephones, would enable the Laundry, Bakehouse and Mattress Shop be utilised further for work from other institutions.

Local Government Act 1929

Primary object of proposals is the revision of the basis of rating of agricultural, industrial and transport properties with the view of placing the rating of these properties on a more rational basis and assisting in the revival of agriculture and the basic industries. The proposals involve not only important changes in the machinery of Local Government but also fundamental alteration in the financial relations between Imperial Exchequer and local authorities and it is stated that rating relief and the change in Local Government are connected parts of one single policy.

There had to be improvements and extensions to Poor Law Institutions as a matter of urgency. The following survey complies with this order.

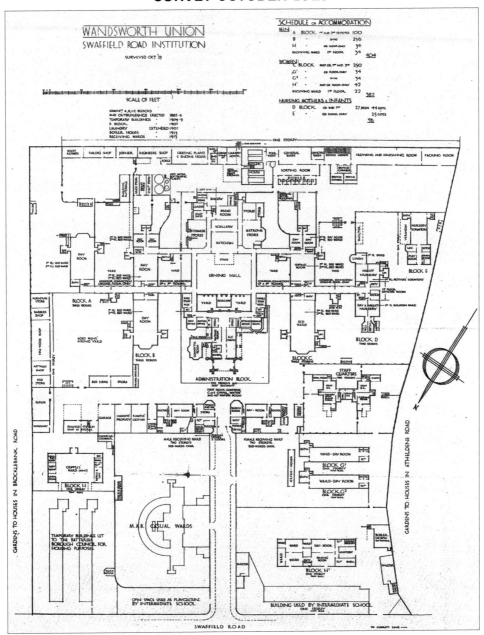

WANDSWORTH - SWAFFIELD ROAD INSTITUTION

General Description. This Institution consists of a symmetrically arranged group of buildings on a rectangular-shaped site of about 7½ acres, with a centrally planned approach from Swaffield Road. The site is bounded on the east, west and south by the gardens of residential properties, and on the north by M.A.B. casual wards and an annexe to the institution where 3 blocks, of a temporary kind, are used for supplementary institutional purposes, and some temporary buildings let to the Battersea Borough Council for housing purposes.

The receiving ward blocks are suitably placed adjacent to the main entrance to the institution. Beyond these, but in a central position, is the administration block, with dining hall and kitchen in the rear of the usual communication corridors connecting with four day room and ward blocks (two of which are double) on the ground floor and with the dormitories to two ward blocks on the first floor. The male pavilions (A and B) are on the eastern side, and those for females (C and D) towards the west, with a further block (E), comprising the nursery section, detached from the southwards of block D.

Along the southern boundary are various workshops, the boiler house and the institution laundry. Other workshops and stores occur on the eastern and northern sides; and a two-storey staff block to the north-west of blocks C and D. The main part of the institution buildings date from 1885, and are of brick construction in apparently sound condition.

The certified number, in respect of accommodation, is 901, but an application in respect of a reduction of this figure to 882 is understood to be before the Ministry of Health. The 'peak' period appears to be reached in April and May, the number recorded in May 1927 being 732, falling at Christmas in that year to 640. Provision is made for 464 aged and infirm, 96 infants up to 3 years of age, and 266 able-bodied inmates - while provision is also made in the receiving wards to the extent of 56 (both sexes), making a total of 882. Sick persons are not dealt with at this institution; the inmates appear to be regarded as '"sick" after being confined to bed for about three days, when they are then transferred to St. James's Hospital. No provision is made for maternity cases, but some exists for nursing mothers, and spare beds are reserved for children, as a relief for the intermediate (residential) school nearby.

The three main day room and dormitory blocks (A, B and C) are of three storeys and of a width that enables them to take four lines of beds, separated by longitudinal dwarf partitions. The wall facing is of brickwork, or with a thin finish of "dinging" lined with artificial jointing and painted. In some cases, as for instance the day and night nursery (Block D) the walls are already plastered on the ground floor to a considerable extent, but not on the upper storey where, in a portion, staff are accommodated. The internal wall faces of block E (one-storey), also used as a children's section, are entirely plastered. These two latter blocks (D and E) are, in the charter of their treatment, distinctly above the standard of the remainder, and are appropriately sub-divided, as to planning, to meet the special purposes which they serve. The method of heating at present is by open fires. It may be added that blocks B and C are reasonably well provided with smaller rooms for day room, dormitory and service purposes. The floors generally - except in respect of Block E, where they are of oak - are becoming much worn and before long will need renewal.

In addition to the accommodation of a permanent character two long-shaped buildings of somewhat temporary construction, north-west of the main institution, and of one-storey, are used for the accommodation of aged and infirm women, and except for some defects in respect of sanitation and a lack of suitable service rooms, these blocks appear not unsuited to this purpose. The same may be said of a wider block (H1) further to the north of the latter, which, however, is partitioned off down the centre - the day rooms, dormitories, etc., consequently somewhat lacking in effective lighting and cross-ventilation. A further block (H) generally similar in character, and particularly defective in respect of natural lighting, occurs adjacent to the northern angle of the main institution site, and is used as a male cripples' ward, is of two storeys, but provides only 6 sleeping rooms for nurse attendants and sitting, day and recreation rooms.

The lavatory accommodation is of an obsolete type, and, calls for some reconsideration. The provision in respect of baths and other sanitary accommodation is inadequate in many cases, for example, in block B, there are only 2 baths for 336 men. Some of the internal WCs against external walls are not provided with separate windows.

Administration. The administration block is conveniently arranged with offices of the usual kind in the front portion; centrally placed dining hall, adjacent to the main corridor with direct service to the kitchen. The latter, however, is lacking in adequate natural lighting and means of ventilation. The Chapel is on the upper floor of the front portion of the administration block, and is understood to afford seating accommodation much in excess of normal requirements.

The various store rooms of the kitchen section and their means of access are satisfactory; and the bakery appears to meet requirements in respect of the supply of bread for the institution.

The boiler house beyond this point is well arranged, and of its four Lancashire Boilers only two appear to be necessary for the work required, even in the winter. A new scheme for central heating and hot-water system is now in hand, and as a consequence of this and the alterations in piping, radiators, etc., generally throughout the building, it is anticipated that a good deal of internal redecoration will become necessary.

The laundry (adjacent to the boiler house) is on spacious lines, but at present undergoing a process of remodelling and re-equipment. It may be noted that the laundry work of St. James's Hospital, Wandsworth, is carried out at this institution (about 40,000 articles per week). The adjacent old and disused cells for refractory persons are to be adapted as a mess room for the laundry staff.

Observations and proposals. The conditions generally at this institution enable it to be regarded as serving its purpose suitably, though, as already pointed out, there are certain directions in which remodelling and reconditioning works are desirable to meet some of the more obvious deficiencies and defects. From this point of view the following recommendations, in respect of such outstanding points, are submitted:-

(a) A general re-organisation and re-equipment as may be necessary, of the sanitary annexes to the portions of buildings used by inmates; and the provision of a more satisfactory floor and wall finish to meet more appropriately the circumstances. In the latter connection the use of light colours of paintwork is desirable to obtain the maximum lighting value from the windows, which are, in many cases, restricted in area.

(b) Some special attention to improve the natural lighting and ventilation of the kitchen and ancillary rooms. The provision of a white tile dado in the kitchen on the liens of the adjacent scullery would, in itself, effect considerable improvement.

(c) Some remodelling and decoration works are called for to the female staff quarters block, and the possibility of adapting the main committee room in the front portion of the administration centre as a day room for nurses is suggested for consideration if and when it ceases to be required.

(d) Consideration of the improvement or reconstruction of block H for crippled male inmates.

(e) Some reconditioning of the yard paving near block H1 in the north-western angle of the site.

All London Poor Law authorities were abolished as from 1st April 1930. The functions of the Poor Law authorities (with minor exceptions) and their Staffs (subject to provision for compensation where necessary) together with their assets and liabilities, will be transferred to the Council. The Council will therefore become responsible for the consideration of applications for relief and the administration of Home assistance (including domiciliary medical relief) the provision of Institutional treatment; Poor Law children of school age and Poor Law children generally.

The Guardians control of the Institution had come to an end. They had performed their task with integrity, fairness, care and concern for 44 years at Swaffield Road. In their place a Committee was founded directed by the London County Council with sub-committees for different areas of administration.

In December 1930 a letter was received from the daughter of a late inmate expressing gratitude for the treatment received by her late father.

An unknown baby was admitted to the Institution. The child was named and records amended.

An entry in the Visitors Book by the Committee:-

We have this day visited the New Ward and Nursery and found everything in good order. We found some of the old people did not eat their meat pudding and we think they should have a milk pudding afterwards. The Committee instructed the Medical Officer to make slight alteration in the diet cases where the old people were unable to eat meat pudding.

The Committee had under consideration the suggestion of a member that the inmates attending concerts should each be provided with a scone and a cup of coffee. It was for the Master to report thereon. Adjourned for three months.

The matron reported that owing to the number of vacant beds in the female Infirm Wards, she proposed to close one of the wards using the staff for holiday duty, and the Committee approved of this suggestion. They also instructed the Clerk to notify other Metropolitan Unions and Parishes of the available accommodation.

The question of providing suitable accommodation near the laundry for the staff to change their clothes be referred to the Works Committee.

The Master reported that laundry staff bring food in to cook for their lunch and having discussed the matter the Committee recommended:-

(a) *That the hours of the laundry staff be amended as follows:-*
Mon-Fri 8am - 12noon, 1pm - 6pm with a break at 3 - 3.15pm
Sat 8am - 12.15pm.

(b) *That there shall be no break during the morning and a small meal be provided during the break in the afternoon in place of the lunch.*

(c) *That no food be brought in by those members of the laundry staff for whom lunch and dinner are provided.*

A request of male and female officers to bathe at the Institution and have their towels washed in the laundry was refused.

In 1930 there were 26 Institutions with 22,011 beds, made up of healthy aged, healthy cripples, healthy able-bodied permanent, healthy able-bodied temporary, and cases to be sorted out. Under the Relief Regulation Order 1930.

An 18-year-old boy had been awarded a senior county (teacher's) Scholarship at Reading University. The Education Committee asked that the Public Assistance Committee afford financial assistance of £5 for books and £1 a week to enable him to take up the Scholarship. This was agreed.

In August 1930 there was a review of classification of the inmates, aged, infirm and semi-sick to be transferred. It was proposed that Swaffield Road was to be utilised solely for able-bodied inmates.

It was agreed that boys aged 9 and over could play in the parks accompanied by an officer.

BUILDINGS

In April 1921, the Bakehouse needed overhauling, it was necessary to purchase bread for several Institutions that were supplied, from Contractors.

The Committee considered the price of a Cold Chamber for storage, they found one for £32, supplier would be Messrs. W. Douglas & Sons Ltd., Putney. The Master was to inspect it and if satisfactory to purchase one.

The Master submitted the following Report as to the weekly cost of working the Laundry:-

	£	s	d
Necessaries	9	19	9
*Coal	22	6	3
Coke		17	6
Wages and emoluments	45	1	9
Water	4	1	9
Gas		7	6
Boiler cleaning	1	8	6
Oils		16	0
	85	1	7

This statement has reference to the summer months and does not include gas or heat for warming the Laundry.

*Best Welsh Coal has been used.

(Number of articles washed, week ending 15th July - 37, 223).

Reporting -

(A) That your Sub-Committee considered a statement made at the Combined Relief and other Purposes Committee with reference to washing done in the laundry, and in connection with an interview of the Laundry Superintendent, two Assistant

Laundresses and nine officers. The Laundry Superintendent, one of the Assistant Laundresses and one Ironer, said that they had brought in a few articles of personal washing to be done, but the others denied that they had ever brought in any laundry work or seen anyone else do so.

(B) *That it seemed to be the opinion of the Laundry Superintendent (who had previously worked in commercial laundries) and also the second Assistant Laundress that, as heads of department, they were entitled to bring in their personal belongings to be washed.*

(C) *That no evidence was produced to show that washing of personal belongings was done to an appreciable extent, but with a view to preventing any washing being brought in by anyone, it is recommended -*

   (1) *That it be an instruction that all bags, baskets and attaché cases brought in by officers are to be left at the Gate Porter's Lodge.*

   (2) *That the Master do draw up fresh regulations for the laundry work, ensuring therein that no washing is to be done for officers other than that allowed by the Guardians and according to terms of employment.*

(3) *That such draft regulations be submitted to the Swaffield Road Institution Committee for approval.*

26 September, 1926

That the Clerk reported relative to the furniture stored at this Institution, and the recommendations of your Committee are set out below:-

CP No	Name	Institution	Date of First Admission	Report of Clerk	Recommendation of Committee
13479	Beeby, Martha	Swaffield Road Institution	2/1/25	Suggest furniture should be sold	To be sold
13269	Creagh, Jeanetta	Swaffield Road Institution	29/12/24	Ditto	Ditto
50903	Holloway, Fredk. W	Swaffield Road Institution	23/5/21	Ditto	Ditto
76705	Kellett, Mary	Swaffield Road Institution	12/1/26	Desires furniture retained	Not to be sold
58571	Michell, Maggie	Swaffield Road Institution	25/9/25	Suggest furniture should be retained	Ditto
68252	Miller, Louisa	Swaffield Road Institution	4/5/25	Ditto	Ditto
75955	Newton, Ellen L.	Swaffield Road Institution	4/11//25	Suggest furniture should be sold	To be sold
69478	Reid, Sarah A	Swaffield Road Institution	17/2/26	Suggest furniture should be retained	Not to be sold
33975	Ribbens, Mary	Swaffield Road Institution	6/3/26	Ditto	Ditto
2110	Rowe, Elizabeth	Swaffield Road Institution	2/2/24	Desires furniture retained	To be sold
575	Stacey, Harriet	Swaffield Road Institution	5/7/26	Suggest furniture should be retained	Not to be sold
72292	Symes, Elizabeth	Swaffield Road Institution	2/8/23	Suggest furniture should be sold	To be sold
53164	Wilkins, George	Swaffield Road Institution	22/11/24	Desires furniture retained	Ditto
26334	Robinson, Gertrude	Swaffield Road Institution	17/6/24	Suggest furniture should be sold	Ditto
65730	Robinson, Eleanor	St John's Hospital	26/2/24	Ditto	Ditto
78007	Blanch, Eleanor	St John's Hospital	23/4/26	No prospect of patient being discharged	Ditto
7374	Boncey, Emma	St John's Hospital	21/11/25	Ditto	Ditto
2028	Gearing, Sarah	St John's Hospital	13/1/26	Ditto	Ditto
76535	Golding, William	St John's Hospital	4/1/26	Ditto	Ditto
60689	Lomas, Annie	St John's Hospital	7/7/24	Ditto	Ditto

CP No	Name	Institution	Date of First Admission	Report of Clerk	Recommendation of Committee
28886	Plested, Joseph	St John's Hospital	15/7/26	Suggest furniture should be retained	Not to be sold
28598	Green, Prudence	St John's Hospital	16/3/26	Ditto	Ditto
63968	Hobbs, Henry	Long Grove Mental Hosp	10/4/26	Ditto	Ditto
5546	Holloway, Emma	Long Grove Mental Hosp	26/1/26	No prospect of patient being discharged	To be sold
75260	Jackson, Daniel	Long Grove Mental Hosp	24/8/25	Suggest furniture should be retained	Not to be sold
31472	Judd, Dorothea	Long Grove Mental Hosp	22/1/26	Ditto	Ditto
256	Morgan, Amy E	Long Grove Mental Hosp	14/10/25	No prospect of patient being discharged	To be sold
72207	Bond, Emma	West Park Mental Hosp	12/12/24	Ditto	Ditto
4839	Butterfield, Alice	West Park Mental Hosp	11/12/24	Ditto	To stand over
42643	Ellis, Mabel F	West Park Mental Hosp	19/2/25	Ditto	To be sold
80467	Sisley, Caroline	West Park Mental Hosp	18/6/26	Suggest furniture should be retained	Not to be sold
38454	Blake, Elizabeth	Horton Mental Hospital	28/8/25	Ditto	Ditto
57937	Kelf, Gertrude M	Horton Mental Hospital	29/11/23	No prospect of patient being discharged	To be sold
				Ditto	Ditto
54917	Cook, David A	Hanwell Mental Hospital	6/2/26	Suggest furniture should be retained	Not to be sold
18574	Fisher, Georgina A	Tooting Bec Mental Hosp	19/3/26	Ditto	Ditto
77578	Hancock Mary M	Banstead Mental Hosp	5/4/26	Ditto	Ditto
76127	Latham, Clara A	Banstead Mental Hosp	2/12/25	One child chargeable at Anerley Schools. Letter sent asking woman to remove furniture	To remove
60268	Hawkins, Nellie				
4948	Talmadge, Ernest			Man discharged from, Swaffield Road Institution 29/3/26. Letter sent asking him to remove furniture	Ditto
80605	Argent, Elizabeth			Deceased - buried by Guardians	Not to be sold
21054	Bray, Emma			Ditto	To be sold
64557	Fisher, Mary A			Ditto	Ditto
3329	Hanney, William			Ditto	Ditto
151	Pearce, Jane			Deceased - furniture can be sold	Ditto
16441	Schroll, Sophie K M			Deceased - buried by Guardians	Ditto
27795	Walker, Marion			Ditto	Ditto

Report of the "House" Committee for the Swaffield Road Institution, 2nd March 1927:

That as a matter of urgency instructions were given for the following work to be carried out under the direction of the Clerk of Works in Wards G1 and G2 by the Institutional staff-

(a) *Baths to be shifted and an extra range of 4 basins to be fixed in each bathroom.*

(b) *An additional WC to be provided for each Ward.*

(c) *The present ranges of basins to be replaced by stronger ones*

(d) *The present WCs to be renewed and the flooring removed and re-laid with concrete.*

And the Clerk will report the matter to the Works Committee.

In October 1927 the Master reported that the ovens in the Bakery appeared to have outgrown their period of usefulness and the dough machine required overhauling and it is recommended that the matter be referred to the Works Committee. The last time the Bakehouse needed attention was in 1921.

In June 1928 the Clerk was instructed to bring to the notice of the Works Committee the question of connecting all the lavatory basins with the hot water system when the new Engineering Scheme was installed and of replacing the taps presently in use with others of a more suitable design.

In July the Matron reported the considerable difficulty in satisfactorily pressing the patients own clothing received from St James' Hospital owing to the machine in use not being suitable for this particular kind of work, she requested the purchase of a Hoffmann Garment Presser.

In August the Sub-Committee reported that they had selected carpets for the Master's Office and Assistant Master's sitting room from Messrs. Arding & Hobbs Ltd., at a cost of £18.18/- and £11.19.6d respectively.

In August the Committee recommended that a large letter box be fixed to the inside of the Gate of the Institution for the reception of books and periodicals from the public, the work to be carried out by the Institution staff. However, the Board decided it would serve no useful purpose but arrangements were made for an appeal for reading matter for the inmates to be inserted in the local press by the Chaplain.

In November the Committee approved the suggestion of the Master that the small room on the first floor Female Receiving Ward be used as a Mess Room for the non-residential female officers and in connection therewith instructions for the provision of a small gas stove.

In January 1929 the Master reported that the slates on the roof of "D" block School House, and the Furniture Store and Stables were in a bad condition and the Clerk was instructed to bring the matter to the notice of the Works Committee.

In July one couch and two easy chairs needed replacing in the Gate Porter and Portress sitting room, instructions were given for new ones to be purchased, cost not exceeding £16. A three-piece-suite was bought for £9.9/-. Mr & Mrs Noble wrote letter of thanks to the Committee.

In September the Clerk brought to the notice of the Works Committee the matter of a provision for a Cloakroom for non-resident female Officers.

The Laundry employed many workers, paid and otherwise (inmates), and the possibility of a larger Mess Room was looked into.

In October the Master reported that the Gas Stove in the Main Kitchen was in a very bad condition and the main supply pipes were rusted and leaking. The matter was referred to the Works Committee, to be dealt with urgently.

In January 1930 the Clerk was instructed to bring to the notice of the Works Committee the question of three Sewing Machines in the Linen Room be fitted with electric motors.

That the Master submitted his half-yearly report as follows:-

LADIES AND GENTLEMEN,

I beg to submit the following report for the half-year ended 31st December, 1929.

Number of Inmates on 1st July, 1929		603
Number admitted during the half-year	1,529	
Number discharged during the half-year	1,509	
	———	
	20	20
	———	
Number of deaths during the half-year		3
		———
Number remaining on 31st December, 1929		620
		———
Highest number during the half-year		631
Lowest number during the half-year		572
Average daily number during the half-year		604
Average daily number for the corresponding period of last year		622

BAKING DEPARTMENT - During the half-year 576½ sacks of flour were made into bread, this being 12½ sacks less than the corresponding period last year. The yield averaged 99 quarterns of the sack.

SHOEMAKER'S DEPARTMENT - The number of boots repaired was 1,517. The number of boots made was 6 pairs.

TAILOR'S DEPARTMENT - The number of garments repaired was 1,658.

LAUNDRY - The number of articles washed was 832,417 as against 892,977 for the corresponding period last year.

I desire to express, on behalf of the Matron and myself, our sincere thanks to the staff for their loyal co-operation.

I remain,
Your obedient Servant,
(signed) A.E. BROWN
Master

Messrs. H C Davis & Co., were requested to provide 39 guards for the radiators in "D" and "E" Blocks and the female Receiving Wards for the sum of £67.12.6d.

In February a letter was received from Mr H Griffin, Estate Agent, on behalf of the tenants of property adjoining the Institution alleging that noise and vibration was caused by the machinery recently installed under the Engineering Reconstruction Scheme. Mr Binny, the Consulting Engineer, reported that he had given this matter his attention and the Committee are of the opinion there was no cause for complaint.

Reverend J P Redmond had applied for an Honorarium for Mrs Holley for playing the organ at the Roman Catholic Service during the past year. £2.2/- was granted.

In December 1930 an Electric Carpet Sweeper, two Perambulators, and a Hand Rubber-roller Wringing Machine were purchased, the wringing machine was for the officers' wash house.

The Sub-Committee asked for the fixing of a wooden partition with felt interlining on the west side of the clothing stores to form an office for the Matron. Work to be done by inmate labour.

The surface of the ground at the entrance of the Institution needed repair, it was a danger to motor vehicles, particularly ambulances.

ENTERTAINMENT

In this decade there were so many concerts that at times they had to be refused. Between December 1920 and December 1922 there were 18 concerts, one was by the Mandoline Orchestra.

There were 15 concerts during 1923. One was by the very popular Mandoline Orchestra again and one party wrote a letter expressing appreciation of the conditions at the Institution.

Ten aged female inmates were taken for a drive to Dorking and provided with tea by the Salvation Army.

At Christmas of that year Carol Singers gave a concert and two Attendants hired a piano at their own expense to entertain "H" Block.

In 1924 there were a total of 22 concerts. Two were for the Blind inmates. One was for them to go to Fairlight Hall, Tooting, given by the Servers of the Blind Leagues, and the other was to go to a Carol Service at Central Hall, Westminster.

The Salvation Army took 100 inmates to tea and a concert on 6/7 January 1925, the blind inmates were also included.

82 female inmates were taken to a tea at Earlsfield Baptist Hall on 21 February 1925.

In the same year there was a lot more support for the blind inmates. 14 inmates were given an excellent concert and tea at Central Hall, Westminster. Locally they were taken to Fairlight Hall, Tooting, for another concert and tea. In August ten inmates were taken to Southend by motor car, by the Braille Servers of the Blind League. Also in October 11 inmates were entertained at Mrs Doyles' residence, New Bungalow, Sylvan Avenue, Hornchurch, Essex.

There were 15 other concerts, some were given by the Salvation Army. The Earlsfield branch of Women's Co-operative Guild, The Fairlight Hall, Tooting, and The Anchor Sisterhood, Wandsworth. Some parties came from as far away as Highgate and West Norwood.

Sister Marion of Worsfield Street, Battersea, entertained 12 inmates at a time to tea.

60 female inmates were taken on 30th December to St Gregory's Hall, Earlsfield, for a tea by Father Wray, and a Mrs Gluckhurst had a tea party for the female infirm inmates.

Mrs Olney continued to entertain inmates at her home twice a year.

Reverend A J Payne and Mrs Lake entertained 130 aged inmates at the Vicarage Rooms, Battersea Square.

GIFTS

Gifts were always welcomed. The general public were often coming forward with generous items, not just once but on a regular basis. Here are samples of the gifts between May 1921 and December 1925:-

Magazines and periodicals from Mr Potterton of Ravenslea Road, Wandsworth.
Evergreens for the Wards.
New sixpences, and toys for the children of the Institution from the magazine "Truth".
Toys and flowers from Reverend A J Haggis.
Magazines from Miss Edney.
Books from Mr Bradley at Putney Library.

Papers and periodicals from Mr Varley and Mr Andrews (Guardians).
800 cigarettes were given by Mr Brown of Henning Street, Battersea.
In December 1924 there were Evergreens, toys and sixpences, artificial flowers.
Beer from Young's Brewery.
Sweets and tobacco and 10/- from the Mayor of Battersea.
A Mrs Smith donated a quantity of Walking Sticks.
In December 1925 they had Evergreens, toys and sixpences.
Beer from Young's Brewery.
Fruit and nuts from Caithlin Laundry, also dolls and flowers.

CLOTHING

In 1928 a considerable amount of out of date children's clothing had accumulated. The Committee accepted the tender of Messrs. Beavis & Co., £10.16/- for the clothing.

MEDICAL

Doctor Dodson died in March 1921. He had been the Medical Officer for 35 years. The Guardians conveyed their sympathy to his widow and family in their bereavement.

Report from the "House" Committee:-

That your Committee considered upon reference from the Board, the question of the appointment of an Assistant Medical Officer and in connection therewith applications received from Dr Topalia and Dr Saunders for the appointment. Having fully discussed the matter, your Committee gave instructions for a letter to be sent to each of the Medical Practitioners within a radius of one mile of this Institution informing them of the vacancy so as to give them the opportunity of applying for the position, should they so desire

Report from the Medical Officer for the six months ended 30th June 1921.

I have not been in medical charge of this Institution for the whole period in question but have been in close touch with it. The health of the Inmates has been satisfactory and leaves no room for comment. The class of Inmates admitted recently has slightly changed. Inmates more capable physically and mentally have been admitted, but not in appreciable numbers. The Lying-in Ward has been transferred to St James' Hospital. Since its transference one confinement, which was a sudden and urgent one, took place on 18th May.

The death of Dr Dodson removed an officer who had been, up to that time, the first one to be appointed.

(signed) C THOMAS
21st July 1921
(Dr Thomas was appointed in April 1921).

In July Dr Topalia was appointed Assistant Medical Officer with a salary of £40 a year for the Institution and £26.13s.4d for the Intermediate Schools.

In December 1921 the Committee had under consideration the question of the duties of the Assistant Medical Officer. The Clerk reported that he had interviewed the Officers concerned, but was unable to get them to agree mutually upon a list of duties. Having regard to the above, your Committee decided that the duties of the Assistant Medical Officer should be as set out hereunder, viz:-

(A) To carry out the instructions of the Medical Officer.

(B) To attend the Institution at 8.30 on two mornings each week, pass the new admissions and render any medical attention which may be necessary. (It is necessary that this rule be punctually observed, otherwise the routine of the Institution is interfered with).

(C) To be available to attend the Institution in the event of the Medical Officer or his Deputy not being available in case of emergency.

(D) To arrange for some medical man to be at hand during the holidays of the Medical Officer, in the event of the Assistant Medical Officer not being available, and vice versa.

(E) To appoint a Deputy to carry out his duties during his absence.

(F) To keep the Medical Officer and Master informed of any special case at the Institution which he may have treated during the absence of the Medical Officer.

Your Committee investigated the case of Frank Woodberry relative to his complaint that he was not examined by the Medical Officer on admission. This man was in St. James' Hospital from the 9th June to the 9th August 1923 when he was discharged by the Medical Superintendent as he was in his usual health. Woodberry's complaint of being put to hard work although suffering from a tubercular hip of very old standing was disposed of by the fact that the first work he was put to was weighing up and washing potatoes, the second weighing out butter and the third was sitting down working in the fibre shed. Both the Medical Officer and Assistant Medical Officer were in attendance'; they had seen the man at various times and were of opinion that he was able to do light work and your Committee having fully enquired into the matter are satisfied that Woodberry's complaints were groundless.

That the Clerk submitted a letter received from the Ministry of Health, transmitting copy of a communication received from Francis J Flynn, in which he complained that he was being kept at Swaffield Road Institution instead of St James' Hospital. It would appear that Flynn has a small lupus condition of the chin and neck of some 25 years standing resulting in a warty scarred state of the affected area but his general health is satisfactory. When before the Committee Flynn made complaints against everybody and everything and your Committee came to the conclusion that whatever was done for him he would still be dissatisfied and they therefore decided that no action was necessary.

That the Medical Officer submitted his half-yearly report as follows:-

Ladies and Gentlemen,

I beg to submit my report for the half-year ended 31st December 1926.

During the past six months the number of admissions among the adult class, of persons over 60 years of age was 357 and under 60 years of age 678 inmates. The latter includes 12 expectant mothers, 6 married and 6 unmarried. The number of children for the same period was 477.

The most striking feature amongst the admissions was the inclusion of 4 foundlings, 3 female and 1 male, brought into the Institution by the police.

Two deaths only occurred during the same 6 months.

The "D" Block (nursery) was immune from infectious disease, not a single case of any infectious disease occurring during the period.

The number of infants was considerably increased and consequently two extra Attendants were engaged as a temporary measure.

The Infirm Wards on the female side have kept full and there is a considerable number of feeble and infirm inmates. It might be of interest to the Guardians to know that at present there are four ladies of the ages of 91, 93, 96 and 98. One of them, aged 96 years, is remarkably well and active, with a cheery face.

In conclusion I again wish to thank the staff for their help and your Committee for their kind consideration.

I am, Ladies and Gentlemen,
Your obedient Servant,
(Signed) H.A. TOPALIA, Medical Officer"

That estimates were submitted for the supply of artificial teeth to inmates and the Committee are of the opinion that having regard to the numbers of dentures now being supplied some arrangement be made for the Board whereby dentures for all Guardians Institutions are obtained from one source.

In August 1927 the dietary for children under one year was as follows:-

To make one pint.

Milk (soured)	10 ounces
Vitroleum	1 ounce
Sugar	½ ounce
Water	To 1 pint.

There was a suggestion from the Medical Officer that the "Schick" test should be applied to the children to find out if they were susceptible to Diptheria and for immunising those found to be susceptible, but adjourned in consideration of the matter for the present.

In November 1929 there was a report on Coffins.

All coffins shall be of appropriate size construction of best English one inch Elm throughout, soundly put together with closed joints and fastened with two inch cut clasp nails punched and stopped; the exterior to be planed, top edge chamfered, smoothed and well oiled and the interior well pitched and lined with good quality white shrouding calico and provided with a pillow 9"x8". Lid to bear a brassed plate suitable to be inscribed with name, age and date of death and to be fastened with 6 x 2½ inch iron screws. Sides to be fitted with two pairs of stout brassed handles.

There was a proposal to discontinue the use of Paupers Corner in the Cemetery and also that the hearse shall carry only one body at a time. A coach shall be provided for each party of mourners. Fares of mourners to and from a cemetery shall not be paid by the undertakers.

Medical supplies shall in future come from the Chief Officer of Supplies.

MENTAL DEFICIENCY ACT

That in connection with four cases before your Committee, the Clerk submitted the following memorandum with regard to cases referred to the Ministry of Health as being suitable to be dealt with under the Mental Deficiency Act:-

The Mental Deficiency Act was passed in 1913, and the then Local Government Board (now Ministry of Health), in their circular letter of 31st March 1914, pointed out that the Guardians would still have to deal with cases chargeable to them who did not come within the proviso of that Act, but expressed the following opinion "At the same time it may be expected that the Act will bring about a gradual reduction in the number of mental defectives for whom the Poor Law Authorities will be responsible. This reduction will be effected partly by the transfer of cases under the Regulations, partly by the voluntary discharge from Poor Law Institutions of defectives who will subsequently obtain admission into the Institutions of the Local Authorities and partly by the Local Authority intercepting cases, especially cases of defective children, which would formerly have reached the Poor Law".

It might be of interest to see how the Act is being worked:-

D.S., (CP 24,61) was reported to ministry of Health in August 1920. In August 1921 the London County Council, as the "Local Authority," wrote that owing to the restriction of expenditure by the Board of Control, the Council were unable to provide institutional treatment for D.S., and the final result was that although the girl has been certified as suitable to be dealt with under the Mental Deficiency Act, expenditure stood in the way of her well being; the consequence was that the girl took her discharge from the Guardians' Institution as the officers could not detain her.

B.A.H.,(CP 6,718) This case was duly reported to the Board of Control, who on 26th February 1923 replied that as the case was not one of urgency it could not be dealt with, "the Treasury instructions to the Board having been of so imperative a character that it was and is still necessary for the Board to advise the Local Authority as to the character of the cases which could be regarded as urgent." The result is that the women is still in the Swaffield Road Institution.

A.M.H., (CP 724) This girl was reported on 3rd May 1923, as being a mental defective, and on 17th May 1923 a letter was received from the London County Council to the effect that the "Local Authority" would consider as to arranging for the admission of the girl to a certified institution, but on 13th August 1923 the Board of Control wrote that they had been informed by the London County Council that the Local Education Authority did not propose to notify the case of AMH to the Local Authority under Sec.2(") of the Act, but suggested that the Guardians should take into consideration the question of coming to an arrangement with the Local Education Authority as proposed in Sec. 59 of the Education Act,1921, as the girl was under 16. In order to safeguard the girl the Guardians dealt with her under the Lunacy Act and sent her to Darenth.

L.C.,(CP 35,112) This is a case which was reported as a mental defective, but the Authorities of the London County Council came to the opinion that she was educable and capable of attending a "Special School". As the Matron of the Intermediate School reported that the girl, who was 14 years of age, required constant care and attention (she had attended a School for Mental Defectives prior to admission) it was decided, in the girl's interests, to deal with her under the Lunacy Act, and she was transferred to a Metropolitan Asylums Board establishment.

E.W.D., (CP 60,379) This youth, who is 15 years of age, was reported on 15th December 1922 and on 5th January 1923, the London County Council wrote that they had been notified by the Board of Control that the boy appeared to be a mental defective and the "Local Authority" would consider as to arranging for his transfer to a certified institution. As nothing further was heard in the matter, the London County Council were communicated with on 27th October 1923, and the reply was that as the "Local Education Authority" did not propose to notify the case to the "Local Authority," no action could be taken, but they suggested that the matter should be again raised when the lad had reached his sixteenth birthday, which will be in August, 1924. It seems inexplicable, from the information before them, how the "Education Authority" arrived at the decision, unless it was with a view to saving expense under the Act. It will be observed that the lad is now over 15 years of age, and if it is necessary to take charge of him under the Act when he is 16, surely if anything is to be done for his benefit it ought to be done at once. Again, it seems inexplicable why the "Local Authority" cannot act without notice from the "Education Authority" as it will be noticed that the "Local Authority" had already been notified of the case by the Board of Control. This youth before admission here had been attending a School for Mental Defectives, was quite unmanageable at home, attempted on more than one occasion indecently to assault his sisters and because they resisted threatened to murder them.

It is suggested that a more suitable case could not be found for placing under the Mental Deficiency Act, and it is recommended:-

(a) That the attention of the Board of Control be again called to the case of E.W.D.

(b) That the attention of:-

(1) The Ministry of Health,

(2) The Board of Control,

(3) The Poor Law Unions Association,

(4) The London Guardians' Association,

(5) The Local Members of Parliament,

be called to the unsatisfactory working of the Mental Deficiency Act, 1913, with a view to the improvement of the same.

INTERMEDIATE SCHOOLS

The older children of the Intermediate Schools were invited by the Schools Chaplain to a party at the Wandsworth Baths and that they received for wear on that occasion 24 pairs white plimsoles with white stockings given by Mr Scroggie.

The Matron obtained from the Daily Mirror tickets for the children to go to the Pantomime at the London Hippodrome. The children were given a pair of stockings by Messrs. Harris & Co., of Oxford Street and were entertained to tea at the Strand Corner House.

Four boys were sent to the Training Ship Exmouth, one apprentice sent to a Cloth & Flannel Manufacturer, and another one to a Tailor.

In April of that year a parcel of Easter Cards was received from Miss Skeggs of Balham Park Road.

In May sweets were received from Mrs Massey (Guardian), books from Mr Mansfield, Iron Mill Mission.

In June there was a report from the Committee:-

That your Committee approved of suet pudding with fruit syrup, bread and margarine and milk pudding being supplied during the hot weather to the young children, as a substitute for the dinner consisting of stew.

Miss Stretchley of Geraldine Road sent tickets for the Zoological Gardens for six children and an attendant, they spent an enjoyable day there.

In July 32 children were taken to Epsom Downs with St Anne's Sunday School Treat they also had toys and books given to them. For the children who did not go out they had flowers and toys.

In November the Head Teacher took the eldest children for a days outing to Box Hill.

In December the Committee authorised 30/- for decorations and £5.10/- for toys. Mr Knight gifted toys and books. Miss Fisher and Mr Charrington gifted evergreens. Books from Mrs Swift, crackers and chocolates from the Guardians, dolls from Mrs Hayward, toys and books from Reverend A J Haggis. The "Truth" Magazine sent money which enabled 33 children to go to the Pantomime at The Grand Palace, Clapham Junction. The Medical Officer gifted 20 tickets for the same performance so 53 children in all attended. The Manager gave a reduction of the price of the tickets.

The Manager of Earlsfield Picture Palace, gave a reduction of the price of the tickets for the children to go to the pictures.

In February 1922 the younger children attended a Fancy Dress Party at the invitation of the Chaplain. The older girls were entertained by the "Girl Guides" at St Michael's Room, Wandsworth Common.

The Matron suggested that two of the eldest girls could assist in light duties, they could go out with the infants in the afternoons.

The Schools had a Lantern entertainment, and the "Girl Guides" gave them boxes of cakes.

The Medical Officer reported with regard to the children's dietary as follows:-

I have read your (the Clerk's) letter of 10th November, and have considered the report made by Miss Hill, the Chairman of the Intermediate School Committee, regarding the dietary.

The health of the children in the Institution is very satisfactory and the dietary adequate. Fruit and salads are served during the summer months and a good supply of green vegetables is also served throughout the year. I do not see any need to change the existing dietary.

At Easter 1922 Miss Halls and Miss Savage gave a chocolate egg and an orange to each child.

In August the Schools had an Electric Light Installation and Fire Alarms cost £100.

Mrs Swift gifted a parcel of Books.

At Christmas 1922 the children had a Lantern entertainment and were given bags of sweets, and decorations for the Christmas tree. Fifty children went to a tea for the Christmas Tree and Fairy Play and 25 children attended a Fancy Dress Dance at Wandsworth Baths. The School was gifted chocolates from Mrs Kippax.

The Women's Co-Operative Guild gifted sweets to the School.

In May 12 children were taken to Box Hill by Miss Byatt, one of the School Mistresses.

That the Matron reported that on 28th July, on the occasion of the visit of their Majesties the King and Queen to Wandsworth, all the children were arranged on a stand erected in the yard, and the infirm men and women from the Institution were accommodated in the children's dormitories and on the landings. Mrs Glanvill kindly lent a very large Union Jack and gave 72 balloons for the children. After their Majesties had passed the Schools, Mr Fowle (the Chairman of the Board), addressed the children and presented them with the 70 souvenir boxes of chocolates sent with 70 small flags by the Mayor of Wandsworth.

The Matron also reported the receipt of flowers from the Earlsfield Baptist Sunday School and toys from the Deaconess, St Mary's Mission, Garratt Lane. (The Clerk was directed to thank the givers.)

The Matron was given £10 for short excursions for the children in the summer holidays.

In November Mrs Coplestone, wife of the Bishop of Calcutta, entertained six elder girls at her home.

Also in November Mrs Fay sent a box of fireworks. The children were very excited to have their own Firework display.

In December the following was recorded in the Visitors book:-

That your Committee desire to place on record their appreciation of the services of the Matron and the Staff generally in entertaining the children at Christmas time.

The Matron reported as follows:

That the following have been received:
Lott's Bricks from Miss Widdowson, of Hammersmith.
6 dozen crackers from the Austin Confectionery Co., of Earlsfield.
5 dozen cinema toys from Mr Kippax (Guardian)
Christmas Tree decorations from Mrs Parsons (Guardian)
Christmas Tree decorations from Miss Smith Parkhurst, of Croydon
Toys and sixpences from the Editor of "Truth"
30 dressed dolls from Mrs Hayward, of Nightingale Lane.
Evergreens from Miss Fisher, of Upper Tooting.

That 20 children had been entertained at a tea party given by Mrs Massey of Lavender Gardens on 30th December 1922.

That 30 children were given a Christmas Tree tea and entertainment by Mrs Drew of Fulham on 1 January 1923.

And the Clerk was directed to thank the givers.

The following entry was made in the Visitors Book:-

My wife and myself have today visited the School. We have been impressed by the splendid state of efficiency of the School and the happy and joyous children. This is a tribute and testimony to the Matron who was so anxious to explain and show everything and we were especially glad to note the spirit of true affection between the Matron and the little young people.

(signed) HENRY JACKSON
Mayor of Wandsworth
28th December 1923

The following was also reported by the Matron:-

On 20th December 1923 the children attended the Circus at Olympia. They were provided with reserved seats and tea through the kindness of Mr Russell Pickering.

On 21st December the United Band of Hope Union gave a Lantern entertainment to the children.

On 29th December 12 girls were entertained by the St Mary's Sunday School Club, Battersea.

That Lady Norton-Griffiths sent £1 for the Matron to purchase something for the children.

In February 1924 St Michael's Girl Guides entertained 20 children to tea with games. They were given books and toys too.

Mrs Barron (Guardian) gave the children money to go to the pictures and some sweets to take with them.

On 20th March the Anchor Mission entertained 20 girls to tea and games.

And the Clerk was directed to thank the givers.

The following is a comparison of the full-time staff at this Institution:-

1903 (Certified accommodation, 103)	1924 (Certified accommodation, 101)
1 Matron 1 Head Attendant and Needlemistress 4 Attendants 1 Cook 1 Kitchenmaid 1 Housemaid 1 House Porter 4 Scrubbers	1 Matron 1 Assistant Matron 1 Head Attendant 3 Attendants 2 Assistant Attendants 1 General Assistant 1 Needlewoman 1 Cook 1 Assistant Cook 1 House Porter 2 Wardmaids 3 Domestic Helpers 1 Matron's Clerk
—— 14	—— 19

It must be borne in mind that the hours of duty having been decreased from between 60 to 70 hours to 48 hours per week, a greater number of officers is required than formerly, also that the "3 Domestic Helpers" are young girls between 14 and 16 years of age.

I have talked the matter over with the Matron, Miss Veall, and the only suggestions that appear practicable with a view to reducing expenditure without impairing efficiency are -

(1) That the offices of Head Attendant (Williams) and Relief Attendant (Blanchard) be abolished and Junior Attendants appointed instead.

(2) That the Attendants be responsible for the cleanliness of all the children's dormitories, lavatories, &c., and it will then be possible to dispense with the services of the temporary Wardmaid.

It must be remembered that provision has to be made for the care of the children 24 hours each day, and this entails a large staff. Further, the children who are too young to attend school are taken out for walks in fine weather and this occupies the time of the staff, especially in dressing and undressing the young children. The time of the staff is also taken up in the transfer of children to and from the District and other Schools, also to Hospitals and Clinics.

With regard to the suggestion as to closing part of the Establishment, this is not possible under existing arrangements. The greater portion of one block is utilised in connection with the school rooms, and as provision has to be made for the accommodation of girls up to 15, boys up to 14, and infants, and the number of each class varies every week, it will be seen that some vacant beds in each Ward must be kept in reserve.

22nd July, 1924.

(If the foregoing proposals are adopted it is estimated that a saving of about £120 per annum will be effected.)

Recommending -

That the suggestions as set out in the foregoing be adopted and that it be left to the Clerk to try and find appointments for the displaced Attendants.

That your Committee considered the following report of the Clerk relative to the question of whether any reduction can be made of the Staff:-

The present Intermediate School was opened on 12th June 1903, as the accommodation provided for children in the Workhouse was inadequate and the building was certified for 103 cases. (In 1913 the then Local Government Board - now Ministry of Health - issued an Order prohibiting children over 3 years of age being maintained in an institution for adults.)

Subsequently the accommodation was insufficient and in 1910 it was necessary to erect iron buildings on the ground opposite, which brought accommodation up to 204.

The fluctuation in the number of children in the School is remarkable:-

THE AVERAGE NUMBER	CERTIFIED ACCOMMODATION
To March 1904 was 108	103
To March 1908 was 143	103
To March 1910 was 158	204
To March 1912 was 212	204
To March 1914 was 125	204
To March 1918 was 150	204
To March 1920 was 85	192
To March 1921 was 55	192
To March 1922 was 74	*101
To March 1923 was 74	101
To March 1924 was 64	101
	*iron huts handed over for Adult Inmates

At the present time the number in this Institution is very low, viz. 50, but these figures cannot be accepted as a guide, as it is quite possible for a case of infection to arise and then for weeks no children can be sent to District or other Schools.

During 1923, the numbers ranged from 44 to 86, whilst during January to June 1924 from 36 to 65.

One does not expect that the numbers will ever reach what they were years ago, as the policy of the Guardians is rather to give Out-door relief in preference to taking children into Schools and this is evidenced by lower numbers at Anerley.

30th July 1924.

In September Mr Spicer of York Road, Wandsworth, provided conveyances for the infants to go to Wimbledon Common, he also gave them a large Scrap Book.

In October of that year butter was substituted for margarine for the children.

In December there were many gifts for the Schools. A large rocking horse, books, sweets, evergreens, gramophone records, fancy candles, fruit and money. This money enabled the children to be taken to see the play "The Windmill Man". They were also given tickets for the Zoological Gardens.

At the end of January 1925, 17 girls were entertained by the St. Michael's Girl Guides.

In July Mrs Barron (Guardian) gave 5/- which was spent on giving the children a treat on Empire Day.

Inspector Harding from Earlsfield Police donated toys to the Schools.

Mrs Quinlan of 344 Garratt Lane also donated toys to the Schools.

In October the Schools received fruit and vegetables from the Harvest Festival Celebrations from Wandsworth L.C.C.Schools and St Anne's Church gave them fruit and bread.

In December the Committee approved the sum of £6 for toys at Christmas. The children had the presents from the Christmas Tree on 31st December at 5pm.

Also at Christmas the Wandsworth Brownies donated evergreens, money (10/-), two boxes of crackers, toys, scrap book and balls.

Some 26 children were taken to the Circus at Olympia by Mr Mills and given tea, the other children had a Lantern Entertainment.

On Boxing Day 34 children went to St Anne's Vicarage, they all received a toy

The Clerk reported that he had made arrangements with the Master whereby the winter stoking at the Schools could be carried out by the staff there thus obviating the House Porter having to attend on Sundays and your Committee approved of the foregoing subject to the 5/- per week (including bonus formerly allowed to the House Porter) being distributed amongst the Stokers.

That the following entry was made in the Visitors Book:-

We have visited the Schools and have seen the children at dinner, which was nicely cooked and which they enjoyed very much. The decorations in the dining hall, day room, entrance and officers' mess room, did great credit to the staff. We were sorry to hear that the Matron had had a breakdown and hope that she will be back to her duties again soon.

(signed)	*T HARDING*	*F M GLANVILL*
	S BAKER	*J T KNOCK*

Christmas Day 1926.

Three Guardians of the Lewisham Union visited the Schools and made the following entry in the Visitors Book:-

We have today visited the Receiving Home at Swaffield Road Intermediate Schools. We were very pleased at the appearance of the children. They seemed all very happy and well. We were greatly pleased with the kitchen and the cleanliness of all utensils and tables. The dormitories too, were in good order and the beds and bedding were clean and well kept. We should like to say how kind were the Matron and her Staff.

(signed) C A HORSHAM   F A JACKSON   E L MACNAMARA

The Ministry of Health suggested that each child should have a Health Card similar to those in use by the London County Council. Having consulted the Medical Officer and Assistant Matron on the subject, the Committee did not see any good would accrue from the introduction of such cards as no reliable information is available when the children are admitted and it would only cause unnecessary clerical work for the Medical Officer and Staff.

However, the Guardians thought otherwise and approved of a record card being kept in order to show the illness of any child, such card to be sent with the child upon his or her transfer to any other Institution.

In March 1929 an entry in the Visitors Book was as follows:-

We had a most interesting tour of the Schools and found the children extraordinarily friendly and happy. Also the Kitchen Department looked cheery and bright and shone with cleanliness.

(signed) D A D RIDLEY   E H ELSWORTH

(Students from the Charity Organisation Society, Battersea Committee).

In June the Visiting Committee reported:-

(a) *They gave instructions for prices to be obtained for providing and laying new linoleum in the Assistant Matron's sitting room, the Matron's Office and one bedroom in No 2 Block.*

(b) *They authorised the purchase of eight assorted caddies for use in the kitchen.*

(c) *They authorised Mrs Read and Miss Wyatt, in conjunction with the Matron, to purchase 24 Day Cots at a cost of £7.10/-.*

In October the Committee had under consideration the question of a new refrigerator similar in size to the one in use at St James' Hospital.

DIETARY

In May 1921 the weather became very hot and the Master suggested tinned meat instead of Irish Stew.

A Special Committee was appointed to consider and accept a tender for the supply of tea. They purchased as per sample submitted by Messrs. J.F. Percival Limited @ 1/7d a pound.

Porridge was also discontinued for the hot weather, bread and margarine substituted.

In March 1922 the Medical Officer authorised butter instead of margarine for the Infirm Ward.

96lbs bread was rejected by St John's Hospital. Nothing appeared wrong with the bread on inspection, it was decided to make it into bread puddings. The inmates enjoyed this so much they requested to have it regularly one Friday each month. Upon the occasion of the next flour supply being required, each firm tendering should send in a sample sufficient to make into a loaf and that such loaves should be submitted to the Guardians before accepting any tender. The Baker to report to your Committee upon the quality of each delivery.

Potatoes were to be cooked in their skins for one month's trial.

The Medical Officer reported that the Ministry of Health had pointed out that the Dietary for the "D" Block had been operational for 20 years! A revised Dietary was approved by the Committee.

In September 1927 a Visiting Committee requested that ordinary milk and white sugar should be substituted for condensed milk and brown sugar for the inmates tea. This must have been a welcome change for the inmates.

In February 1928, for the first time, Turkey appeared in the Dietary. Unfortunately at one time it was rejected together with 45lbs of herrings.

In October the Committee considered buying a slicing machine from Messrs. Berkel & Parnell and gave instructions for prices to be obtained from various makers as well. The idea was adjourned as the Committee found that the Tooting Home had a slicing machine spare and they transferred it to the Institution.

In August 1929 the Visiting Committee noticed that the bacon was fat and the potatoes were poor at lunch time. This was drawn to the attention of the Master and corned beef was issued with the bacon. The clerk had to communicate with the Contractor with a view to Canadian bacon being supplied in future.

In December the Medical Officer reported with regard to the present system of storing milk and appointed a Sub-Committee to consider and report upon the whole question of the storage of food stuffs.

In December the Committee at last decided that the inmates could have refreshments when attending a concert. They could have ½ pint of tea and three biscuits.

In February the Sub-Committee appointed to enquire into the present system of storing food stuffs accepted the estimate of Messrs Marco Limited for one large and six small ice-chests, cost £41.2.3d. Ice was delivered once or twice a week.

On and after 1st April 1920 there would be a standard quality for certain food stuffs. The groceries - jams, bacon, eggs, cheese, lard, flour, margarine, tea, coffee would be supplied to "Council Standard".

When receiving their issue of tobacco the inmates could ask for twist or roll (which many of them preferred).

In March 1930 it was decided to have Belgian new laid eggs. It was only occasionally possible to obtain English new laid eggs of equal quality to the Belgian eggs within the 100% limit of preference. Approximately 168,000 eggs would be required in Institutions weekly.

The supply of meat would be from the Stores and Contracts Committee.

That the action taken by the Chief Officer of Supplies in arranging for the supply of milk until 30th September to Institutions under the direction of the Committee of similar character to that supplied during the period up to 1st April be approved.

A Lion electric meat mincer was purchased, cost £65.

In November the cost of Christmas Dietary Fare was increased by 3/- a head.

Cold storage capacity of 650 cubic feet had to be available as quarters of beef and mutton were to be delivered direct from Smithfield Market.

A weigh-bridge capable of dealing with loads delivered with modern transport had to be considered, cost £700.

WORK

In February 1930, Messrs. Durrell & Co., supplied 10 fathoms of board ends @ £10.10/- per fathom, this was to be chopped for firewood.

The Special Committee on Unemployment forwarded a circular dated 22nd January 1930 from the Ministry of Health urging Local Authorities to arrange that painting and other decorative work should be put in hand as far as possible during the winter months.

It was also felt desirable and urgent that more adequate arrangements should be made for the employment of able-bodied inmates. We have found that inability to keep such men well employed has an ill-effect on their morale and we consider that more workshops with varied employment should be established or alternatively that a greater quantity of work should be made available for the existing shops.

The Committee decided that window cleaning should be put out to contract, but that full use should be made of inmates to clean windows of easy access. The contract would be for six cleanings a year.

TRANSPORT - MOTOR VEHICLES

That your Committee received and adopted the following report of their Sub-Committee, consisting of Messrs. Cooper and Smith in conjunction with Mr Allen, with reference to the motor vehicles in use at the Institution:-

MORRIS MOTOR VAN - This was purchased in August 1926 at a cost of £253.5s.0d, and since then has completed 5,985 miles. The total cost of repairs has been £2.14s.0d, of which 9s.3d was in respect of the last twelve months. The Sub-Committee recommend - That the coachwork only be dealt with, as the other work is in excellent condition.

VULCAN MOTOR LORRY - This was purchased in November 1923 at a cost of £475, and since then has completed approximately 21,646 miles. The total cost of repairs from the date of purchase has amounted to £179.8s.0d, the amount during the last twelve months being £51.17s.8d.

In view of the fact that a somewhat expensive overhaul is necessary and that, whatever is done, further repairs will probably continue to be needed during the time the lorry is retained, the Sub-Committee recommend - That the Vulcan van be run for the next four or five months and that the Board then dispose of it and proceed to the purchase of a new van after the close of the present half-year.

CHAPTER 5: *Updating the Institution - 1940*

The Local Government Act 1929 made sure the Chief Officers Department was kept busy for the next five years of this decade.

REPORT OF LOCAL VISITING SUB-COMMITTEE
15TH AND 29TH January, 1931.

Swaffield Road Institution

1. **Staff** We have requested that advertisements be issued to fill the vacancy of female relief attendant at the Swaffield Road Institution.

2. We have arranged that Mr Edward Jennings, laundryman, Swaffield Road Institution, shall be engaged on light duties in the wards for a further six weeks.

3. **Inmates' Furniture - Disposal - We Recommend** - That arrangements be made for the disposal of any property stored at the Swaffield Road Institution which is not likely to be claimed by the owners or relatives. **AGREED**

4. **Inmates - Notice of Discharge - We recommend** - That P.A. (W.16028) be required to give 168 hours notice of her intention to take her discharge, in accordance with the provisions of Section 33(d) of the Poor Law Act, 1930. **AGREED**

5. **Supply of dentures, etc. - We recommend**
   (a) That authority be given for the supply of dentures in two cases. **AGREED**
   (b) That the quotation of Mr A D Mislin to supply dentures to two inmates at a cost of £4.4s., be accepted. **AGREED**

6. **Inmates' transfer - We recommend**
   (a) That P.G. (W.1334) be recommended for transfer to Hollesley Bay labour colony, H.W. (W.19119), S.J. (W.19892), W.W. (L.14043), and W.S. (L.12780) for transfer to London Industrial colony, and C.C. (W.9568) and H.C. (L.12911) for transfer to Dunton farm colony. **AGREED**
   (b) That steps be taken to effect the admission of J.F. (W.9642) and J.H. (L.22714) to Wallingford farm colony. **AGREED**

7. **Inmate's travelling expenses** - We have authorised the payment of travelling expenses incurred in permitting J.T. (W.7553) to visit his wife at the Brentwood mental hospital.

8. **Outings** - The Institutions sub-committee have asked for observations of local committees as to the adequacy of the arrangements made last year for inmates' outings etc. We recommend - That in the opinion of this local committee consideration should be given to the question of increasing the expenditure allowed for outings, etc., during the summer of 1931 to twice the amount authorised last year, to enable an additional outing to be given to the inmates of the institutions in area VII. **AGREED**

Iron Buildings - Swaffield Road Institution

9. In accordance with the reference from the local committee on 8th January 1931, we have considered further as to the origin of the iron buildings known as huts H1 and H2, and find that the buildings were erected and completed in January, 1910,

for the accommodation of children, and continued to be so used until December, 1920. From 1921 to 1929 the buildings were utilised for the accommodation of infirm inmates of the Swaffield Road Institution, and later for a short period for educational and Sunday school purposes in connection with the children's receiving home, being finally vacated in May, 1930. There are, in addition, two huts which are at present leased to the Battersea Borough Council. **We recommend -**

(a) That the foregoing information as to the past use of the iron buildings at Swaffield Road Institution be forwarded to the Institutions sub-committee in connection with their consideration of the local committee's resolution 13(4) of 11th December, 1930. **AGREED**

(b) That the Institutions sub-committee be asked to arrange, upon the expiration of the existing lease, for the iron buildings situated within the cartilage of the Swaffield Road Institution, and leased to the Battersea Borough Council for housing purposes, to be retained under the management of the Public Assistance Committee for the accommodation of inmates of the institution. **AGREED.**

Children's Receiving Home

10. **Educational Facilities - We recommend** - That the Institutions sub-committee be asked to approve the proposal that children of "in and out" parents should be so far as possible sent to an elementary school, a report as to such children being submitted at each meeting of the Visiting sub-committee. **AGREED**

11. **Entertainments, etc.,** - We have accepted with thanks the offer of the third Southfields Brownie pack to give a party to the children.

Half-yearly reports

We have had before us the half-yearly reports of the master, matrons, medical officers and chaplains of the Swaffield Road Institution, children's receiving home and home for the aged poor respectively, copies of which will be circulated to each member of the committee.

As required by Article 72(f) of the Public Assistance Order, 1930, we have to report as follows:-

12. **Swaffield Road Institution** - The period under review has been one of considerable pressure on the capacity of the institution especially as regards the number of males and infants.

The number of aged females who require constant medical or nursing attention causes much concern and we again urge that 60 of these cases be transferred to St. Benedict's or other home, as they cannot be housed in the upper floors of this institution unless lifts are installed. The medical officer considers, and we agree, that the huts are unsuitable for female infirm cases and these huts are required for the accommodation of male inmates.

We have also recommended that the huts leased to the Borough Council should revert to this institution at the end of the lease, so that better accommodation can be provided for male cases which, at present, at times of pressure, have to be accommodated in the workshops.

The painting, pointing, etc., in the wards, dining hall, chapel, master's house and staff rooms, recommended last year has not yet been begun and we would again call attention to the unsatisfactory condition arising therefrom.

The amount of office work has very largely increased, and even with the increased staff a very large amount of overtime has been necessary. This would be considerably lessened if the Council's new books conforming to the returns required by them could be immediately supplied to the institution.

The internal telephones asked for last year and not yet fitted would facilitate the work of the institution and would be especially useful in enabling the master and matron to leave the offices more frequently and inspect other parts of the institution.

The constantly-recurring cases of conjunctivitis amongst the staff attending the infants is a matter of much concern, and we feel it is necessary to close and repaint the two blocks in turn to purge them of infection.

The employment of a larger number of the inmates is most desirable and for this purpose it seems desirable (a) that the sorting room of the laundry and the alteration to the calendaring machines be put in hand as speedily as possible; (c) that mattress remaking for more institutions be taken in hand under the present skilled charge hand; (c) that the re-pointing of the boundary and internal walls be taken in hand and the master authorised to obtain the necessary hand tools and materials as and when required; (d) that the mineral water machine be replaced by a new one.

We feel that it would greatly facilitate our work if we were regularly informed as to what action the Council proposes to take on the recommendations that we make and also if the Council's engineers and architects would confer with us on the draft estimates which they prepare before they submit them to the Council.

We have pleasure in stating that the institution staff have fulfilled their duties satisfactorily.

We recommend -

(a) That the institutions sub-committee be asked to arrange for the transfer to St. Benedict's Home or other appropriate institution, of 60 aged female inmates of the Swaffield Road Institution requiring constant medical or nursing attention. **AGREED**

(b) That the iron buildings at Swaffield Road Institution be utilised solely for the accommodation of male inmates. **AGREED**

(c) That the institutions sub-committee be asked with regard to Swaffield Road Institution to arrange for:-

(1) The provision of a bathroom with two baths in "A" block.

(2) The repair of the corridor floors.

(3) The early repainting of the wards, etc., and pointing of the interior walls of the chapel and dining hall.

(4) The paving of the roads and yards.

(5) The provision of a new fire grate in, and the re-plastering of, the female officers' recreation room.

(6) The erection of a solarium glazed throughout with "vita glass," together with the installation of ultra-violet light, outside "D" block nursery.

(7) The provision of a light for the lectern in the chapel.

(8) The fitting of two additional wash basins in the nursing mothers' dormitory and two additional wash basins on the first floor of the male receiving ward, the work being executed by inmate labour. **AGREED.**

(d) That the staff sub-committee be asked to consider as to the appointment of visiting ophthalmic and dental surgeons at the Swaffield Road Institution. **AGREED.**

13. Children's receiving home, Swaffield Road - During the early part of the period under review the capacity of the home was at times crowded, due to the transfer orders not coming to hand, and, at times, to infection, but lately the orders have been more promptly received and the numbers in the home have been much reduced.

We are in agreement with the suggestion of the acting-matron that the small piece of ground in front of the home should be made up with new mould and laid out with shrubs and plants.

We are of opinion that ten small hand fire extinguishers should be supplied.

The staff have carried out their duties satisfactorily.

We recommend

(a) That arrangements be made for the ground in front of the Swaffield Road children's receiving home to be planted with shrubs and plants. **AGREED**

(b) That a door be fixed at the entrance to the boys' lavatories in the yard of block 2 at the Swaffield Road children's receiving home.

We feel that it would greatly facilitate our work if we were regularly informed as to what action the Council proposes to take on the recommendation we make and also if the Council's engineers and architects would confer with us on the draft estimates which they prepare before they submit them to the Council.

The amounts of office work has been largely increased, and we urge the new books conforming to the returns required by the Council should be immediately supplied so that unnecessary time shall not be spent on extracting information for the returns.

The staff have performed their duties to our satisfaction.

E.C. GIVEN, Chairman.

BUILDINGS

In January 1931 the Committee approved:-

16 small lockers for the non-resident officers' Mess Room

A settee and two easy chairs for the clerks' Mess and Recreation Room

That two sides of the balcony of "E" Block should be covered with "vita glass"! and the front fitted with shutters.

Early redecoration of the Master and Matron's apartments - work to be done by a Contractor.

In April the Committee requested a settee and two easy chairs, one sideboard, one table and four chairs for the Master's dining room. The sideboard was deferred.

That the Staff Sub-Committee be asked to arrange for the positions of Porter and Portress be made non-resident and that the Assistant Master and his wife be granted permission to occupy the accommodation at present allocated to the Porter and Portress.

In June it was decided that the Tennis Court should be enclosed with wire netting, cost £45.

Regular Fire Drill continued, given by Messrs. Riley & Company.

In October it was decided that the nursing accommodation should be re-organised in "D" Block. Part of it should be for "Reception" up to 20 cots. The other part for nursing mothers and their children with provision for 15 beds and 16 cots. "E" Block should be used for children up to 2 years, up to 25 cots.

In November 1931 it was decided that the Receiving Nursery kitchen should be used as a Day Room and Play Room, the coal range to be replaced by a radiator and cupboards to be built for toys etc. That the bath be replaced by a bath 15" deep and raised 16" from the ground.

The Committee recommended the installation of an all electric radio in the Dining Hall.

In January 1932 urgent attention was drawn by the Institution's Sub-Committee to the condition of the sanitary arrangements of "H" Block and that in the opinion of this Committee at least three water closets and several wash basins should be provided at the north end of the block and the small room at the north east corner of the dormitory be adapted for this purpose.

In October 1932 it was decided that steps were to be taken for the replacement of an Alter Cloth for the Chapel. Cost £16.16/-.

In March 1933 the attention of the Institution's Sub-Committee be drawn to the position of the entrance to the Master and Matron's apartments which are situated in a corridor traversed by all persons entering the female side of the building and that in the opinion of this Committee, in order to secure reasonable privacy, a partition complete with door should be erected at the end of the corridor together with a covered way extending across the yard from the wall on the outer side of the proposed partition to the adjacent corridor leading to the main building.

In June the Committee requested the laying of a Granolithic Floor in the Bread Room, (this was not sanctioned until January 1934).

Also in June an additional washing machine and hydro-extractor should be provided for the laundry to deal with the increased washing sent from St James' Hospital.

Necessary steps were taken to replace the following:

2 Hearth Rugs	1 Night Commode Chair
1 Tennis Net	4 Pairs Counter Scales
18 square yards Linoleum	1 Table
1 Carpet	6 Small Windsor Chairs

All of which had been condemned.

Expenditure on the lighting in the Nave of the Chapel, cost £37. The Pipe Organ was cleaned and overhauled, cost £26. Also the Piano and Harmonium was repaired, cost £17.

The Institution's Sub-Committee decided that where ever practicable a recognised party of inmates should be organised at each of the larger institutions to carry out cleansing and painting work under the supervision of the Master in cooperation with the

Chief Engineer and that subject to limits of the height at which inmates are to work, the inmates should deal with the cleansing and painting of all wards, corridors, rooms, etc., requiring treatment.

In January 1934 a Gladiron was to be purchased so that the staff washing should be properly finished.

The Bakery was to be enlarged to cope with increased output to supply Grove Hospital and St. Benedicts, with 590 quarterns and 300 quarterns a week respectively. Also an additional mixing pan and 150 quartern loaf tins.

In June 1934 the equipment fixed benches in the Dining Hall were deemed uncomfortable; the Committee considered replacing them with tables and chairs.

In July the Sub-Committee was asked to consider as to providing separate Day Room accommodation for all female infirm inmates and in this connection it be suggested that steps be taken to secure the allocation of the vacant hut at the institution for institutional purposes.

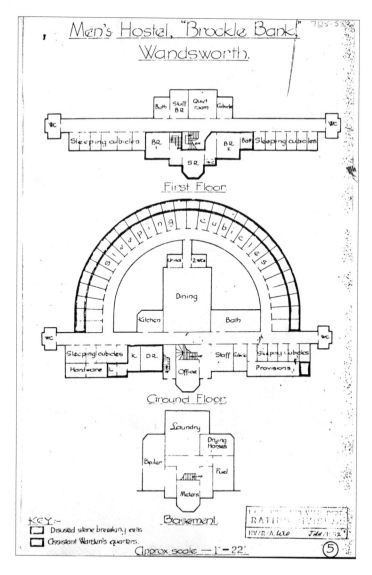

Entrance to the men's hostel, formerly the Casual Wards

The Institution had all "Lath" beds, which were now deemed uncomfortable and should be replaced by spring bedsteads. 157 were changed immediately and 337 were to be costed for the years 1935/6. They were to be changed as and when they were unfit for further use.

Tables and chairs for the Dining Hall were sanctioned for 1935/6, provision of cost.

In May 1935 for the male infirm inmates of "H3" ward, the sanitary facilities would be best improved by an installation of a stall urinal. The Chief Engineer reported that it could not be installed in existing space and that the building would have to be extended by about 8ft 6 inches, cost estimated at £145; provision in year 1935/6.

The grounds needed new lawns to be laid, due for expenditure 1936/7.

In October 1935 there was proposed work in the kitchen;

More modern equipment.

Tiling of walls.

Relaying of floor on account of its dangerous condition, to be done by Maintenance Staff.

2 more boiling pans and potato steamers.

ADMINISTRATION

The interval at which inmates could visit children maintained in other establishments was four months. The Committee decided that it was too long a time and that the interval should be one month.

The inmates were at least able to keep some money on them when they were admitted. Just 1/6d !

In April 1931 there was to be a rearrangement of hours of labour masters to meet the large number of able-bodied inmates.

The hour of rising during the summer months was to be altered to 6.45am instead of 5.45am.

In July an infirm attendant had to tender her resignation upon marriage.

It was decided that male attendants and labour masters be provided with three quarter blue coats of a washable material, these coats to be regarded as inventory stock and not emollients of the officers.

The children had to be taken to Wandsworth Common for outings as the grant for taking them out to different places was withdrawn.

In January 1932 the difficulty in obtaining non-resident female attendants and the shortage of staff at night was becoming apparent, and the Committee decided that additional staff accommodation should be provided. The Sub-Committee to be asked to arrange for the conversion of "H" Block (at present unused) into cubicles for the accommodation of about 30 female resident attendants.

In nearly two years there were 84 inmates transferred to the London Industrial Colony, where they were trained for different skills.

The Master was frequently called to the telephone in his office and it would greatly assist him if four additional telephone points were installed. This would involve an annual rental charge of £15.8/-. This idea was deemed to be expensive and was scrapped.

In 1932 several inmates were sent to the Dunton Farm Colony.

In April 1932 the opinion of the Committee thought that the "pass" system in regard to the visiting of inmates of institutions was not necessary and the proposed rules should be amended to provide:-

(1) *That butter shall be included as an article that may be brought by visitors for inmates.*

(2) *That visiting shall not ordinarily be allowed before the expiration of seven days from the date of admission*

(3) *That able-bodied inmates shall not be allowed visitors more frequently than twice a month.*

An inmate was allowed to visit her children at Dr Barnardo's Home, Barkingside, and was given her travelling expenses.

The Institution had one addition Telephone Exchange Line installed in June 1933.

The Public Assistance Committee made a rule prohibiting tradesmen from entering institutions for the purpose of selling goods among inmates.

In 1933 Miss M.M. Blanchard was appointed as Matron's General Assistant.

In June there was an outing for the inmates to Epping Forest.

In January 1935 it was decided that inmates could take a half day leave on Tuesdays, Thursdays and Saturdays.

Here is a list of the newspapers and periodicals at the time:

Daily Newspapers

News Chronicle	10	Daily Express	10
Daily Herald	10	Morning Post	10
Daily Mail	10	Daily Mirror	10
Daily Sketch	10		

Sunday Newspapers

The People	4	Sunday Express	4
Sunday Dispatch	4	Sunday Pictorial	4
News of the World	2	Sunday News	4
Reynolds	3		

Local Papers

Borough News	9	Tooting Mercury	8
South Western Star	8	South London Press	8

In October 1935 a light type of Wheel Chair was provided for an inmate.

In March 1936 quotations were to be obtained for the provision of an outing to Herne Bay, on 16th June for selected inmates.

JARROW STREET MARCHERS

The Jarrow Street marchers reached London on 5th/6th November 1936. They presented their case at Westminster and were taken to Swaffield Road Institution by coach, the designated Receiving Centre.

The Assistant Master, Mr W. I. Smith was the Receiving Officer, he was shocked at the appearance of the exhausted and footsore marchers.

They had medicals and without exception needed treatment for their poor feet. Mr Smith made sure they were well fed and rested. They all had new socks and boots given them, as the soles of their boots were worn right through and were packed with newspaper or cardboard for most of the march.

The London County Council paid for their transport back to Jarrow.

In April 1937 it was decided that Jewish inmates were allowed a whole days leave on Saturday instead of Sunday if they so desired.

It was decided that inmates may return for tea if they were on a whole days leave and go out again to return at the normal hour.

In October 1937, 200 flowering shrubs were provided for the gardens.

The Committee recommended that a number of fixed forms and 35 seats of an obsolete pattern should be replaced by 59 Garden seats and that 20 suitable canvas chairs also be supplied.

The Committee discussed the option of transferring the blind inmates to a more suitable establishment. Nothing came of it.

In February 1938, in the opinion of the Committee, the lighting over the Billiard Table should be improved.

There was a memorandum from the Institution's Sub-Committee recommending outdoor games wherever possible, and a suggestion that Clock Golf be provided.

Also in October 1937 the Institution's Sub-Committee had directed the Chief Officer to submit to them, in due course, a report as to the number of Irish Immigrants who became chargeable in Hospitals and Institutions of the Council for a period of six months.

The Committee cautioned a female inmate as to her unwillingness to work in the Institution.

In November, authority was given for the supply of a "Lingual Retainer" for a female inmate.

In December 1937 the Brother hoods and Sisterhoods provided Tea and Entertainment for 60 female inmates at the Anchor Mission, Garratt Lane.

In December it was decided that the disused wood chopping shed should be converted into a Day Room to be used as a quiet room and that the floor be covered with linoleum "B" quality.

The Committee complained about the pigeons which made a nuisance of themselves with their noise and destroying the plants in the gardens.

Keeping inmates clothes in store had become a problem so it was decided to issue the inmates with replacement items on their discharge. One such cost for this was £70.0.2d.

Request from the Chief Officer of the Public Assistance Committee for a review of work among women casuals over a six month period. They wished to be informed of the arrangements made for assisting women casuals.

The Committee cautioned an inmate for striking another inmate and the Matron transferred her to another work area.

In March 1938 the scales used in the nursery for weighing children were to be replaced.

The Annual Outing for the inmates should be held on Tuesday 14th June in the form of a visit to Littlehampton. The Mayor of Wandsworth gave 6d to each of the 183 inmates to spend.

After the report of the Sub-Committee on Irish Immigrants becoming chargeable, no further action would be taken.

It was decided that women inmates should be allowed to smoke, subject to the discretion of the Matron, as regards time and place and that there was no inconvenience to non-smokers.

It was decided that evening visiting of inmates be allowed other than able-bodied, under 60 years of age, be permitted on Tuesdays and Thursdays 6.30 - 7.30pm.

Mrs F.W. Reddis of 26 Terrapin Road, SW17, took four blind inmates to Brighton for the day.

In connection with the number of pregnant women from Ireland in 1938 who enter the Institution, it was suggested to the Institution's Sub-Committee that steps should be taken to seek legislation to enable Irish Immigrants to be repatriated.

It was decided that the hours of retiring shall be 9pm, other than sick wards, mental wards and nurseries, throughout the year.

THE POOR LAW AMENDMENT ACT 1938

An Act to authorise the payment of personal allowances to inmates of the age 65 and over of Poor Law Institutions.

The enactment relating to the relief of the Poor shall have effect as if amongst the powers conferred on Councils of Counties and County Boroughs there was included power to grant a personal allowance not exceeding 2/- a week to any person in receipt from them in a Workhouse or other Poor Law Institution, being a person aged 65 years or upwards.

This Act was interpreted by the Institution as follows:-

That from 15th August a personal allowance of 1/- a week under the above law, subject to the condition that an inmate receiving a "comforts" allowance shall be granted a personal allowance only if the value of the "comforts" allowance is less than 1/- a week and in that case the personal allowance shall be of such an amount as represents the difference between 1/- a week and the weekly amount of the "comforts" allowance. The inmate must have been capable of appreciating the allowance and be able to use it satisfactorily.

In May 1939 the Committee suggested that a Library Cupboard and a Housemaids Cupboard should be provided in the reading and writing room.

On 6th June 1939, there was an annual outing to Southend.

In July 1939 the Committee suggested that there should be a wireless set, table and set of table tennis, set of dominoes and a set of draughts and board, for the Officers' Mess.

On 3rd September, the Second World War broke out. The children from Earlsfield House (The Intermediate Schools renamed) were evacuated to the country. The only children there were from alien families.

Owing to the war the summer treat was a special tea followed by a concert.

Once again the Institution was going to lose staff that will be either called up or will volunteer to join the forces. This was going to be very different and cause the Master and Matron many difficulties. Food rationing and the constant air raids to name but two.

A new Weighbridge was purchased, it was to be placed at the entrance of the Institution in front of the Assistant Master's quarters.

Additional games were to be provided for the inmates, 8 sets of draughts and boards, 4 boxes of dominoes and 2 dart board and 2 sets of darts.

MEDICAL

In February 1931, there was a Tuberculosis Care Committee appointed.

Between April 1932 and July 1934 there were 115 pairs of spectacles provided or repaired. This would mean more inmates would be able to read the papers provided. There were also two artificial eyes supplied.

Between October 1932 and July 1934 there were 44 pairs of dentures supplied or repaired.

In July arrangements were made for an inmate to convalesce for four weeks at a cost of 19/6d a week.

Between January 1935 and July 1939 there were 115 dentures and 234 pairs of spectacles issued. Knowing that they were available encouraged inmates to demand dentures and glasses to make their lives more satisfactory.

An application for an artificial leg had to be referred to the appropriate Committee.

In December 1937 there was authority for a pair or arch supports for a male inmate and a new strap for an artificial limb of another inmate.

In November 1938 various Surgical Appliances were authorised - A Truss, a Surgical Boot, Stump Socks, a Glass Eye, an Arch and Toe Life for a foot and a Surgical Spinal Jacket.

INTERMEDIATE SCHOOLS

The Intermediate Schools were renamed "Earlsfield House" in 1930.

Two of the boys were granted travelling expenses to enable them to attend a central School and Scholarship Classes.

In January 1931 a Piano was purchased, which would have made an enjoyable difference to the children's entertainment at the Home.

In November 1932 wooden blocks were to be attached to framework of windows in rooms to which children had access, so as to limit the opening of the lower sashes to 5 inches.

In February 1933 it was decided that the children could have 2ozs of boiled sweets a week, provided that such issue shall be subject to the concurrence of the Medical Officer of the Home in the case of sick children.

In June of that year six garden seats and two garden tables were purchased for the use of the children.

In December 1936 Mr H. Wooley entertained 30 children at the Wandsworth Palace Cinema on Christmas Eve.

Newspapers and Periodicals for the Home:
1 Children's Newspaper
1 Playbox
1 Film Weekly
1 Mickey Mouse
1 Film Fun
1 Dazzler
1 Rainbow

The Second Balham & Tooting Boy Scout Group took one of the boys for a fortnight's camping holiday in August, he returned looking bronzed and fit.

The following was the Christmas Day Dietary for 1936:

Breakfast	Cereal, Cornflakes or Wheatflakes, Toast & Marmalade.
Dinner	Roast Pork, or Poultry (if supplied) Sage & Onion Stuffing, Roast & Creamed Potatoes, Brussels Sprouts and Christmas Pudding & sauce.
Tea	Savoury Sandwiches, Trifle, Jelly & Blancmange, Iced cake, Sweets, Apples, and nuts (if procurable).
Supper	Chocolate Drink with leftovers.

Two Christmas Trees were ordered and each child received a gift and an entertainer was engaged.

DIETARY

In 1930 it was decided that the inmates could have bread and margarine with marmalade twice a week, apart from the Christmas Dietary; this the first time marmalade was allowed in the day-to-day dietary. The infirm inmates could have butter in lieu of margarine upon certificates from the Medical Officer. The infirm inmates could also have boiled eggs, fruit and cake once a week. All these changes should be on different days.

In July 1931 the Committee were asked for a butter-pat machine which was agreed, and also for 16 Galvanised Cots for the nursery which was refused.

In October 1931 every male inmate was to receive 1oz Tobacco each week. Inmates engaged on disagreeable or special nature work could have up to 3ozs a week. Every married couple were to have 4ozs dried tea a week and an allowance of milk and sugar at the rate of 2½ ozs sugar and 10 fluid ozs of milk for each ounce of tea.

In June 1932 all the female inmates could have an allowance of boiled sweets. Tea time was changed from 5pm to 5.30pm.

In April 1933 at Easter, there was an issue of 2 x 2oz Hot Cross Buns for each inmate and to each Officer entitled to the emolument of one or more meals daily.

In June 1933 it was arranged that a drink of tea could be served after dinner to the aged and infirm.

In January 1934 it was decided that the time for supper to the able-bodied and healthy inmates was to be 6.45pm.

In March 1934 it was decided that the time had come to recognise that some inmates were Vegetarians. They could have ½oz margarine, 3oz peas, beans or lentils and one apple in place of meat allowance at dinner.

The Public Assistance Committee" decided that Vegetarians could have one apple or banana, 4oz stewed fruit, berries or dried fruit according to season and cost may be substituted for meat or fish extras prescribed at breakfast for inmates of Institutions.

The Committee have decided that pint cups and mugs in use at Homes for the aged poor and in sick and inform wards at Institutions shall be replaced on condemnation, by cups and saucers of rather more than ½ pint capacity but that the use of either large cup or mugs of 1¼ pint capacity shall be continued in dining halls at Institutions.

Also the sweet issue could be varied to include toffees or a 2d chocolate bar. This must have made a welcome change to the boring boiled sweets week after week.

In April 1937 the Committee decided that the period during which the additional allowance of stewed fruit for adult inmates should be changed to the six months ending 31st October, raw fruit could be issued at no extra cost.

Also in October the Master had to submit that 60lbs of beef had to be destroyed as a result of the brine turning sour.

There was to be an addition to the dietary of expectant mothers, 1 pint of milk, an apple or orange or a teaspoonful of marmite each day.

In December 1938 the new Weighbridge was installed, it measured 25ft x 8ft, it would check all deliveries.

CHAPTER 6: *The Second World War and Renovation of Buildings - 1950*

ADMINISTRATION

During a very long air raid one night, a large chunk of masonry fell through the roof and massive cold-water tank in the loft of one of the female blocks. Thousands of gallons of water flooded the top floor quarters and soaked the poor inmates in their beds. The water flooded the floor area and then rushed down the three flights of stairs until it reached the ground floor which it then flooded.

All residential staff were called to the scene where they helped the poor inmates down the stairs and into the dining hall draped in anything they could find that was dry. The kitchen was opened and hot drinks were given out to the inmates and staff. The Matron opened the stores and issued clothes for the inmates.

It took a long time to clear up the mess in the block and builders were brought in quickly to repair the roof and replace the water tank.

An expression of appreciation of the visiting Committee was conveyed to the Master and Matron and other staff for their action in dealing with the damage by enemy action and removing inmates to safety.

It was decided that inmates could recover the cost of visiting family in other Institutions or in their homes.

Mr J A Brook was initially employed as a temporary lorry driver, but by 1945 he had been there for some considerable years. A Diploma was awarded to him by the Royal Society for the Prevention of Accidents and subsequently a five year Medal and Bar was also awarded and presented to him by the Chairman of the Committee.

The Chief Officer of the Social Welfare Committee enquired as to the practicability of supplying cardigans for the use of aged men.

Victory in Europe came on 13 May 1945, but Victory in Japan didn't come until 15 August 1945 after the atom bombs were dropped on Hiroshima on 6 August and Nagasaki on 9 August. Japan capitulated then and all the newspapers had the headline "PEACE ON EARTH".

Victory Celebrations were to be made:-

1) *Inmates of Social Welfare Residential Establishments (excluding casuals, men and women lodged in emergency hostels).*

   (a) *Inmates who so desire and who are fit to go out by given leave to attend the Official Celebrations.*

   (b) *An allowance of 2/- an inmate to be granted for special fare and entertainment to take the form of a garden fete, concert and/or visit to a local cinema subsequently to see the films of the official celebrations.*

   (c) *Each adult to be given the choice of 1/- or ½ oz tobacco or 10 cigarettes in addition to the normal allowance, each child to be given 6d or a small toy.*

   (d) *Children of suitable age in receiving homes to be taken to see any entertainments arranged in a local park or the Royal Park or to participate if practicable in any organised arrangements for school children to see the celebrations in London.*

    (e) The approval of the appropriate Committee to be obtained to the special fare to be provided and the entertainments to be arranged.

2)   *Casuals in Institutions - Casuals not to be detained for work on 8 June 1946.*

3)   *General Premises under the management of the Committee to be decorated on 8 June 1946 with such flags and other decorations as may be available.*

The summer treat in 1946 was a visit to Chessington Zoo. 100 inmates went and for those who stayed behind a special tea and entertainment.

By October 1947 the Institution was having to cope with a lot of homeless families and also just mothers and children - often late at night. Children had to stay with their parents before they could find accommodation but generally the children would be transferred to a Receiving Home after a couple of days. The children's Homes were full at that time however, but children were not supposed to be kept in Institutions longer than necessary.

In May 1947 the Chief Officer of the Social Welfare Committee was considering whether wireless earphones should be supplied for the use of deaf inmates.

Inmates Personal Clothing.

    Inmates of Social Welfare Establishments possessing suitable private clothing shall wear it inside or outside the establishment, but if the clothing is unsuitable for wear in the establishment or cannot be worn by the inmate, for say six months, it shall be returned to relatives subject to the inmates consent. Visiting Committee are authorised in the case of clothing which cannot be worn by the inmates within six months or returned to relatives to decide whether it should be disposed of or taken into stock for issue to other inmates.

    In December 1947 the Institution was to have a boot finishing machine from the Fulham Road Hostel, the transfer and installation would cost £12.

    It was decided that if an inmate had an accident outside the Institution, he or she would have to refer to the Poor Man's Lawyer as the Council had no power to provide legal assistance.

    The Social Welfare (General) Committee stated that they were of the opinion that there should be more opportunities for aged men and women to mingle freely and that they would therefore be glad if the Visiting Committee would consider as to the advisability of making some of the sitting rooms common to both sexes.

    By May 1948 it was decided that the visiting of adult inmates other than expectant and nursing mothers should be permitted daily between 2 and 4pm and in the evening hours between 6 and 7.30pm.

THE NATIONAL ASSISTANCE ACT 1948

That from 5 July 1948, under the National Assistance Act 1948, the Poor Law Acts would be repealed and any Orders made by the Minister of Health under those Acts would cease to have effect and the appointment of the Social Welfare Committee would be terminated' and that it followed, therefore, that the meeting called for 2 July 1948 would be the last meeting of the Swaffield Road Institution and Earlsfield House and that it was contemplated that the new Committee to be appointed by the Council would wish to make arrangements or Visitation and Inspection of the Residential Establishments which would come under their management; but that it was not however possible to give any indication as to the form which these arrangements would take until the new Committee had met and considered the matter.

If inmates assist in the running of an Institution they should be given a small monetary recompense, it had to be of regular assistance though would not constitute employment under a contract of service. A maximum of 10/6d a week was appropriate. The recompense would be in addition to the sum which they are allowed to retain for personal requirements. The work performed should be regular and of communal benefit such as domestic duties in the kitchen and scullery, laying tables and clearing away in the dining hall, cleaning dormitories, laundry work etc.

In September 1948 it was decided that the Institutions should be called Homes. Swaffield Road was now to be called Brockle Bank, after the brook that ran through the grounds.

On 5 September 1948 the South African War Veterans Association distributed 7.6d each to 10 Veterans in the Home.

Gate checks were carried out at 12 noon on 31 July and 5pm on 14 September. On the first occasion the contents of a case of one male employee was examined.

In June 1949 an Open Day had been arranged for Wednesday 27 July, the Diamond Jubilee of the Council. The Public were to be invited to inspect between 2 and 4pm and a member of the staff should conduct small parties and explain the working of the Home.

In June the Warden and Matron, Mr & Mrs Brown, retired and Mr W I Smith, Assistant Warden was promoted to Warden at Norwood House. Mr A. M Stricklan was appointed the new Warden at Brockle Bank.

By July it was decided that the Residents were to be called at 7am in the mornings. Breakfast was to be at 7.45am, dinner 12 noon, tea at 5pm, supper at 7pm, time to retire to be fixed.

The Open Day arranged was a huge success. It was proposed to have further Open Days annually.

In October a resident who was deaf and dumb was admitted to Brockle Bank. His condition told them he had been sleeping rough. Documents he had showed that he had left home in Doncaster after trouble with his landlady. His wife was traced and she travelled all night to come and collect him and take him home. She was also deaf and dumb.

In December 1949 there were visits from the following:

Six Students from Westminster College of Commerce.

Dr Cram and Miss Calder from the Public Health Department.

Representatives from the Glasgow Corporation accompanied by Mr S K Ruck of County Hall, the Chairman also was present.

Also in December two Whist Drives were organised for the residents, prizes for which were purchased from appropriate profits of the Canteen. Total cost £2.10.4d. This innovation had been quite successful, some 40 residents, male and female, taking part.

A new Residents Committee was formed also in December meeting fortnightly and submitting suggestions etc., some of which were found reasonable and instructive.

To help large homes maintain a good library, grants were authorised. Brockle Bank was granted £22.

In March 1950 the Chaplain held a Baptism Service for seven infants. He said it was one of the nicest he remembered. His thanks was to the Matron for the general arrangements including the flowers.

In May it was proposed to hold a Billiard and Snooker Tournament. The Committee were asked to authorise expenditure from the Canteen Profits to the value of £1 for prizes, 1st prize 7.6d and the runner up 2/6d, for each Tournament.

Handicrafts were also encouraged. The women took to it quicker than the men, but lampshades and basket work seemed to interest the men. It all helped to pass the time and create an interest for them.

At the Open Day on 2 August 1950, the Mayor and Mayoress visited the Home and from a letter received later were more than pleased that they made the visit. The local Press was well represented. Opportunity was taken of displaying some of the work done by residents in connection with handicrafts. Most of the work displayed as sold, the proceeds being paid to the Council's Treasurer.

Mr Ruck of County Hall had made two visits to the Home accompanied by parties of American and Canadian visitors. Also a party of students from the University of London visited the Home on 14 August, this being arranged by the Chief Officer.

In October Budgerigars, cage and stand were purchased for one of the female wards, they were a popular interest with the old ladies, so much so that another cage, stand and Budgerigars were bought for another ward.

Mary Price, who had been a maid for the previous Assistant Master, was transferred to the Matron as her maid, being paid 5/- a week.

By December 1950 there were 270 male residents, 246 female residents and 71 children. These figures included Homeless Families of 31 women and 71 children.

The Warden reported:-

A Tea Party was arranged for a resident, Miss Ellen Martin, who attained the age of 100 years of age on 10 October 1950. The Chairman and various members of the Committee were able to visit on this occasion. A very good tea, including Birthday Cake, was provided, all of Miss Martin's fellow residents in her ward joining in. The press were well represented and Miss Martin received congratulatory telegrams from their Majesties the King & Queen and the Chairman of the National Assistance Board.

In December two Assistant Commissioners from Ceylon visited the Home. They were accompanied by Mr Plant from County Hall.

At Christmas time carols were sung and gifts included a Christmas tree, beer (from Young's Brewery), toys, books, dolls houses and cakes. The number of toys received enabled the staff to make up a parcel for each child together with some fruit on their beds for Christmas morning.

There was a Tea Party for the Homeless Family Children organised by the Matron which included a Punch & Judy Show and a conjuror. The Chairman of the Committee took the role of Father Christmas with an outfit loaned by Arding & Hobbs of Clapham Junction.

Parties from the Southfields Baptist Church and the Church of Ascension, Balham, sang carols in the wards on the 21st and 23rd December 1949. The Mayor of Wandsworth visited on Christmas Day. Young & Co., Rams Brewery gave 4 x 18 gallon barrels of beer and an excellent entertainment was provided by Mr F. Early of 3 Freshwater Close, Tooting.

The issue of tobacco, cigarettes and sweets was to be increased as follows:-

Men   1oz tobacco or 20 cigarettes, or 4oz of sweets

Women   4oz of sweets, or 20 cigarettes.

But if anyone's conduct was unsatisfactory whole or part of the ration could be withheld!

A Tropical Fish tank was purchased for one of the Day Rooms in "C" Block. It cost £20 from Canteen funds. It was much appreciated by the residents.

DIETARY

In September 1943 the War Dietary included these instructions:-

Eggs, 1 shell egg or equivalent of dried egg once a week.

Sweet puddings, to be served each day.

Bread to be discontinued at dinner, but allowed when giving soup, stews, or "Hotchpotch" (stew or kind of Mutton Broth with vegetables).

Potatoes, 5 ozs potato cake or scone or baked potato served at tea once a week in lieu of bread.

Fried potato instead of bread at breakfast or baked potato occasionally for supper in place of biscuit.

In September 1946 the Prime Minister made an appeal to avoid waste of bread and use potato as a substitute.

In 1948 the following Christmas Fare was proposed:

Breakfast: Eggs, bread, butter and marmalade, tea.

Dinner: Roast Pork, baked potatoes, sprouts, Christmas Pudding, beer or mineral water.

Tea: Salad and sardines, bread and butter, tinned fruit, tea.

Supper: Cocoa and biscuits.

A professional concert party will be hired and small gifts of tobacco, cigarettes, apples, oranges and toys will be made to residents.

In 1949 the cost of the Christmas Fare (over and above the normal dietary):

Food	*£10. 0.0d*
Decorations and plants	*£20. 0.0d*
Concert party	*£12.12.0d*
Small gifts	*£50. 0.0d*
	£92.12.0d

There was to be a review of cash, tobacco and sweets to residents.

a)   *Cash. To increase the cash allowance to 2/- a week for women. No change in cash allowance to aged men receiving tobacco issue but to non-smokers of 2/- a week and a ration of sweets.*

b)   *Tobacco allowance.*

   (1) Increase of standard allowance to tobacco from ½ oz to 1oz a week.

(2) *Women smokers under 65 years of age to be allowed 10 cigarettes a week instead of sweets, at the discretion of the head of establishment and subject to periodical review by the Visiting Committee.*

c) *Sweet allowance.*

(1) *To increase the limit of expenditure from 2½d to 4d a head, a week. This would permit the issue of the present full ration (3½ ozs of chocolate or boiled sweets and also allow a wider selection, including toffee.)*

It was decided that an early morning cup of tea could be served for aged people.

BUILDINGS

The Medical Officer had once again shown his extreme concern in the overcrowding of the Receiving Ward with many including new-born babies sleeping on the floor.

In February 1945 the Visiting Committee reported on the Institution Buildings:-

We are deeply concerned (after examining the records of heat in different parts of the establishment) with the condition of the buildings, are of the opinion that immediate attention should be paid to the lining of the roofs and the heating apparatus in the two bathrooms and the Matron's stores and wish it to be noted that sickness, through lack of heat, is having considerable effect on the usual efficiency and happiness of the staff, so characteristic of this Institution.

That enquiries be made as to the future use of the bowling green and the possibility of it's reinstatement, or cultivation as a lawn with flower beds.

Expenditure would be £200, so it was deferred for the time being.

Steps should be taken to replace the lining of the roofs of the dining hall and general store, damaged by enemy action.

Approval was given to the use of a portion of the vacant site on the western side of the Institution by the Supplies Department for the temporary parking of surplus Civil Defence vehicles during the period between their collection from Civil Defence Services and their disposal on the understanding that no responsibility for the custody of such vehicles fall on the Master or the staff of the Institution.

That approval in principle be given to the use of the piece of ground at the South East corner of the Institution, except that portion which contains staff tennis court, grass plot and greenhouse, for the erection by the Council of Emergency Factory made houses, on the understanding that a fence be erected between the Emergency Houses and the Institution shall be un-climbable and of such construction as to prevent inmates of the Institution being overlooked.

This proved too problematical and was eventually rejected in favour of the Earlsfield House having the area for a playground later on.

In February 1946 the Bell that was in the Belfry at the Institution which was damaged by enemy action in the early part of the war and subsequently demolished was used to summon inmates to meals and to Chapel, has resulted in many of the old people being late for meals during the summer months when they were out in the grounds. While on the other hand a large number of them wait in the corridors adjacent to the dining hall rather than be late and their presence has caused congestion there. It is not practicable to restore the Bell until the Belfry has been rebuilt but, we understand that the Chief Engineer has advised that at an estimated cost of £20 a standard fire bell (weighing about 23lbs) could be hung from the gable end of the Dining Hall where it could be rung from the kitchen.

That subject to the Ministry of Health and Finance Committee approval the sum of £20 be sanctioned in respect of the installation of a bell at the gable end of the Dining Hall complete with the necessary brackets and gear and with an asbestos hood, the work to include making good the hole in the roof and flashing.

The decision of the Social Welfare (General) Sub-Committee to re-open the Nursery with 20 cots would cost £855. The Committee expressed their disagreement with the proposal in that it involves a revival of the arrangement, which they consider undesirable, for accommodating children in a general Institution. The opening of the nursery in May is part of a plan to re-establish nurseries in London following the ending of the Government Evacuation Scheme. Before the war there was a nursery for 57 infants with 32 cots in the main building and 25 cots in "E" block, a detached building. It was proposed that the part of the nursery which was in the main building shall continue to serve its war time purpose, accommodation for infirm women. After repairs of air-raid damage have been effected and additional equipment has been installed, "E" block will make a very suitable unit for 20-25 infants, whose mothers, in some cases, will be accommodated in the Institution. There is an urgent need for nurseries in London, but under present conditions it is not possible to proceed with new building and all suitable existing buildings must be brought into use.

In the interests of aged inmates it was decided to provide handrails on stairs and in corridors.

In October 1947 the heating system needed an overhaul, it should be cleaned thoroughly before the onset of winter.

The kitchen floor needed retiling in July 1948, the estimated cost was £350 and was put on the special work list to be considered for execution during the period 1948/9.

That to provide a playground for the children from Earlsfield House, an area of approximately 2000 square yards on a site at the South East corner of the Institution be fenced, paved and drained at an estimated cost of £950 of which £910 would be recoverable from the War Damage Commission; and that the work be considered for inclusion in the programme of works for 1948/9. This was deferred as the Children's Bill was about to become Law.

The Sub-Committee put forward a proposal for a Canteen. Tea was still rationed in 1948, but drinks such as minerals, Bovril, Oxo and Horlicks could be available. It could also sell tobacco, cigarettes, sweets, stationery and haberdashery. The only available accommodation was the furniture store measuring 40' x 26' equipped already with electric lighting and low grade heating. Redecoration and supplementation of both lighting and heating would be required and a sink with hot and cold water supply and a gas ring or hot water boiler. These works could be provided for in the draft maintenance estimate for 1949/50.

Report by the Chief Officer of Welfare, regarding the repair of the Chapel Windows:

1) *For the permanent reinstatement of the windows including the stained glass and for restoring them to pre-war condition, £925.*

2) *For taking out the existing defective leaded lights and replacing with new leaded lights and clear glass with small rectangular or diamond shaped panes, including*

the repair of two windows over the altar and the renewal of the centre one in clear or tinted glass, £270.

3) *As in 2 above but with obscure (i.e., fluted) glass for ordinary windows, £390.*

The cost of the work would be recoverable from the War Damage Commission and it is estimated that there is sufficient margin within the current maintenance votes to enable the work to be put in hand.

By March 1949 the Chief Officer had other thoughts regarding the estimates for the Chapel. He obtained new estimates!

Reinstatement of stained figure centre panel altar window, £175.

Two side windows, £14.10/- a pair.

Four windows to return walls, £28.

In 1949 it was decided that the canteen would not now be in the old Furniture Store. It was too big and too cold, or the new building in the courtyard between Blocks "C" and "D" (women's section). Arrangements were made for the construction of a small canteen shop in the dining hall and the work was in progress. The necessary timber had been found by breaking up and using some obsolete and surplus items of furniture from other establishments.

In June 1949 there was insufficient room for the Homeless Families, women and children were still sleeping on the floor of the Receiving Ward and children two to a bed.

In October 1949 the Welfare Committee decided that as the first part of a five year scheme of improvement, furnishings shall be supplied to Brockle Bank. The sitting rooms were provided with Windsor Armchairs with cushions; some upholstered easy chairs, fireside chairs and settees and extending foot rests are suggested for infirm residents. The provision of occasional tables, more pictures, rugs and net curtains in the sitting room would provide a more homely atmosphere there. Small tables to replace the long tables are proposed to bring the seating in the dining hall in line with other establishments.

Curtains should be provided for those dormitories which have none at present and new counterpanes are needed. There was insufficient room at the moment for each resident to have a bedside locker but a few lockers were suggested for use by old people when they were confined to bed. The estimated cost of all these items was £1440.

Items authorised:-	
Bedchairs	*6*
Bedside lockers	*18*
Bedspreads	*144*
Curtain material (yards)	*500*
Lloyd Loom Chairs	*16*
Pictures	*12*
Hearth Rugs with non-slip backing	*12*
Rexine Settees, cushions to match	*5*
Tables, small for dining room	*40*
Coffee Tables	*6*
Occasional Tables	*16*
Upholstered Chairs	*40*

In May 1950 the Warden purchased 12 small Palms for Ward and Dining Hall decoration. Cost £5.2/-, paid from Canteen profits.

After all the fuss regarding opening Nurseries, not to mention the cost, the Nursery was closed. It was to have constructional alterations and would be utilised as a Male Infirm Ward holding some 15 beds. The fact that it was on ground level must have influenced the decision.

MEDICAL

By June 1941 the number of inmates applying for dentures, spectacles and surgical appliances totalled 115 in one fortnight.

On 26 December 1949 a child of an Indian Homeless Family was transferred by the Medical Officer to the Grove Hospital as a suspected Typhoid Fever case, he having information that this family had disembarked from the "SS MOOLTAN". The Medical Officer's diagnosis was confirmed and the Home was placed in quarantine until 16 January 1950. The family was removed by the Wandsworth Borough Council on 2 January to a prefabricated house in Putney for isolation purposes.

In the Medical Officer's report of March 1950 he stated that the numbers of Homeless Families now numbered 82 and still some of them were sleeping on the floor.

The Medical Officer was very concerned for the chronic sick in the wards. There were no places for them in hospitals. He needed a wash-basin in each ward and a small sick bay for residents that were dying. The beds were only a chair apart and it was distressing for residents to see their fellow residents dying, there being no room for screens.

OUTINGS

On 27th June 14 male and female residents were entertained by Lady Liardet and the Chiddingfold Women's Institute. The party travelled by coach and came home laden with flowers, fruit and eggs. A suitable letter of appreciation has been sent. This form of outing is as you are aware, an innovation for this home and I cannot speak too highly of the manner in which the ladies put themselves out to ensure that all participants had a good time.

On 19 July a further party of residents went to Rydis Hill Women's Institute, Guildford. This outing was in every way comparable with the above, all concerned having a thoroughly enjoyable afternoon.

An afternoon coach tour was arranged for a mixed coach load of residents accompanied by two officers who were taken for an afternoon tour of Surrey on 9 June. It was a lovely afternoon and the trip was greatly appreciated. The coach left at 2pm and returned about 5.30pm having made a half-hour stop for light refreshments. The cost of £16.15/- had been met from Canteen profits as authorised by the Committee.

A further tour has been arranged for the afternoon of 26 July, total cost including a cup of tea £5.5/-.

As proposed, 120 residents went on the annual outing to Littlehampton on 23 June 1950. The day was fine and all enjoyed the ride and tea which was provided for them. The party left at noon and returned at 9.30pm. Those residents not taking part on the outing had a special tea provided.

In August the last of the series of three Women's Institute Outings took place. A party of 30 residents were entertained to lunch and tea by the Women's Institute at Caterham.

The afternoon followed very much those of previous outings, all participants having a thoroughly enjoyable time. I hope, and have every reason to believe, that similar opportunities will be afforded the residents next year.

Two afternoon coach trips as authorised with stops for tea were arranged. These short trips are quite enjoyed by the residents, endeavours are made to include some of the old people who, for various reasons, seldom leave the home.

In October 30 children from the homeless families were taken to Chessington Zoo by the Matron. It cost £7 for transport, entrance to circus and refreshments paid for by Canteen profits. All the children were well behaved and enjoyed themselves.

Thirty old people went to Olympia Circus paying for themselves out of earnings.

In October 1948 The Anchor Mission took four female residents by Motor Coach to Oxford for a day's outing.

The Outing for 1949 was to Littlehampton for 115 residents. Residents not taking part had a special tea of salmon and egg followed with fruit salad and blancmange. They also had a concert in the evening.

In February 1950 three coaches of residents, some 80 old people in number, visited Wimbledon Theatre to see a Pantomime, the residents paying their own expenses. The Matron had arranged a small savings club some weeks prior to the visit.

The summer outing in 1950 was once again to Littlehampton. They left at noon and arrived back in the evening. Cost £17., excluding coach hire.

EARLSFIELD HOUSE

Earlsfield House (the Intermediate Schools) was re-opened on 1 October 1945, as a receiving home for children between the ages of 3 and 16 years, coming into the Council's Care.

In May 1946 the Reverend P M Gedge conducted an outing for a party of children from Earlsfield House to Kew Gardens.

The boys were unruly in their behaviour and created great difficulties for the staff who were responsible for them. One boy had to be referred to the Juvenile Court, Lambeth, which sent him to a Remand Home and subsequently to a Residential School.

Pocket money had been authorised for children in Receiving Homes by the Social Welfare committee:

Age Group	Allowance
3 - 5	Occasional allowance at discretion of Head of Establishment
5 - 8	1d a week
8 - 11	2d a week
11 - 14	3d a week
14 - 16	6d a week

By October it had been increased to:

Age Group	Allowance
3 - 4	1d a week
5 - 8	2d a week
8 - 11	3d a week
11 - 14	1/-
14 - 16	2/- a week

The pocket money was withheld during the week ending 27 November 1948 to the children in groups 5 - 14 years for disruptive misbehaviour.

In December 1948 the Wandsworth Rotary Club and Inner Wheel supplied gifts for the Christmas Tree for all the children. They also received many gifts from the Guides and Brownies of Wandsworth District, all their gifts were new and good quality.

CHAPTER 7: *Residential Home Status - 1960*

ADMINISTRATION

Three loud speakers were installed in the Dining Hall; they were to be used in connection with Cinematograph Shows. These greatly improved the sound reproduction.

It was suggested that a television set would be good for the Home. £80 was to be set aside for the purchase.

In March 1951 a temporary Porter was apprehended by police outside the Home. He was found to have a 7lb tin of jam belonging to the Council. He was charged with larceny. He appeared at the South Western Magistrates Court and fined £1. His employment was terminated by the Council.

Three French Social Workers, one Colonial Welfare Officer, two Swedish students from the London School of Economics and the Welfare Officer of the Fountain Hospital visited the Home.

It was decided that Homeless families were to be chargeable and husbands were to pay charges. If they were behind with their charges and if after two weeks nothing was paid, the husband was to be notified that the wife and children would be evicted and legal proceedings would be taken against him. It was hoped to recover costs. Subsequently eight families were evicted for rent arrears.

In September the Television set was purchased and installed. It attracted small audiences at first.

After the National Assistance Act 1948 the residents were expected to pay for accommodation at a standard rate fixed by the Council, 21/- a week they kept 5/- for personal requirements.

Miss Ellen Martin was 101 in October once again she had a Tea Party with the Mayor and Mayoress in attendance, and flowers etc, and Mr. Adams M.P. and his wife.

In January1952 the staff had their Annual Staff Dance held in the Dining Hall.

Also in January the Home had a visit from Miss Fox from the Ministry of Health.

Members of the Battersea Telephone Exchange gifted sweets, fruit and cigarettes to the residents, personal visits were made by the members for the distribution of these gifts.

So many handicraft items had been made in the January that a Sale of Work was held and as most of the items were sold, it was a profitable afternoon.

Members of the Intercession Fellowship visited the Infirm Wards on 19 January distributing small gifts to the residents.

Mr. Filer of 24 Burntwood Lane visited the Home on the 24 February and provided tea for the residents in "C" 26 Ward.

Following the sad news of the death of His Late Majesty George VI a memorial Service was held in the Chapel at the Home on the day of the Funeral, to which I am pleased to report some 200 or more Officers and residents attended.

In a report by the Chief Officer of the Welfare Department, it was stated that the Bakery at the Home was providing bread for Brockle Bank and six other establishments. There were only two staff Bakers. Taking into account expenditure on wage rewards to residents in the bakery, materials, (including fuel) cartage, rent, repairs, cleaning, electricity and insurance the estimated cost of a 3½ lb loaf baked there was 1/4d as against the charge of 1/1.½ d for bread supplied under contract. It was recommended that the bakery be closed and the two staff be offered suitable alternative positions.

By May 1952 the number of Homeless families were down to nine mothers and 26 children.

Mr. Doran aged 69, resident, was entitled to receive Maundy Money from Her Majesty and attended Westminster Abbey on Friday 10 April 1952.

On 14 March Dr Ibrahims a Sudanese Doctor visited the Home, he was accompanied by Mr. Reeve from County Hall.

It was decided that the Open Day in 1953 would take place on 26 August.

In an effort to keep the Bakery open there was a discussion as to whether the bakers could divide their time between bread, slab cake, buns and pastries. The only problem was that new equipment would be needed.

A party of Nurses visited the Home from St Thomas' Hospital. They also had a visit from a Social Science Student from Germany accompanied by a Practical Worker from the Social Science Department of the School of Economics.

The Matron reported:-

At the wish of the Chief Officer an elementary course of training for subordinate staff has been introduced and commenced here. The course will consist of lectures and demonstrations to staff employed here during the past year and new entrants as soon after engagement as practicable. The Warden gave his first Lecture on 27 June on Welfare Administration to 12 members of his staff. A class of six were given a lecture on Hygiene and demonstration of bed-making etc., by me on 2 July. Further training may be discussed and planned. It is hoped that we may by these courses be able in future to find suitable staff for vacancies in smaller Homes.

On the Open Day in August they had over 150 visitors including representatives from the British Red Cross, Women's Voluntary Services, Family Welfare Association and National Assistance Board. A band was hired, the £15 cost taken from the Canteen Fund. The Mayor of Wandsworth was there and in the company of the Chairman attended the Sale of Work of Handicrafts. Tea was served to 184 people at a charge of 6d per head.

In August of that year Miss Ellen Martin died peacefully just before the Open Day on 23rd, at the age of 101 years.

A collection was made by staff and residents for the Lynmouth and Lynton Disaster Fund. It totalled £15.5/-.

In November the Warden reported that many gifts of fruit and vegetables from various schools and Church organisations from their Harvest Festival Celebrations.

Planning had begun for the Queens Coronation Celebrations, the residents were to have a special tea:-

Ham and bread and butter, fruit salad, jellies and ice-cream.

Extra's 1 pint of beer or mineral water.

½.oz tobacco or 10 cigarettes.

4ozs sweets and biscuits for the women.

A concert for the evening, and three coaches to be hired for a three-hour tour to see Street Decorations.

The Chalet is a section of the Home that had been altered from existing buildings in the grounds. These units comprised 72 infirm beds and by March 1953, 62 beds were occupied.

The source of admission had in the main been dealt with by Homes Division. The friends and relations of many new admissions have registered their appreciation of facilities available. The new residents have an average age of 80 years and many are suffering from varying degrees of blindness and other incapacity with the result that falls are frequent. They require very close attention and supervision and staffing problems are great.

A resident in Ward "C6"died and had £1.12.4d in her purse. A relative requested that it be spent on residents for a treat. They all had strawberries and cream for tea.

Herbert Vaughan, a resident, wanted to donate £300 which was part of a legacy received by him. The Chief Officer sent a Repetitive Officer of the Council to interview him prior to the gift being accepted.

In September the Matron reported that a resident aged 37 who was deaf and dumb would remain at the home until suitable accommodation was found for her. The deaf and dumb foundation had her case in hand.

Mr. Donohoe the Gate Porter died in tragic circumstances taking his life on 18th October. A floral tribute was sent by the staff and representatives went to the funeral.

In October there were 12 members from the German Educational Reconstruction who visited the Home. Also the Home had a visit from Mrs. Armstrong from British Ghiana accompanied by the Chairman of the Committee.

All homeless families were finally removed from Brockle Bank on 4 September 1953. It was proposed to use the three rooms formerly occupied by the families to provide a small detached self-contained unit of 16 beds (in two rooms) and a sitting room for suitably healthy women. The fourth room, previously a Doctors room, would be a reception unit for new admissions (women) and their friends/relatives when they first arrive at the Home and to be suitably furnished for this purpose.

With provision of the small unit for healthy women it was proposed to take the opportunity to make a corresponding reduction in the number of healthy women's beds on the second (top) floor of "C" Block to relieve overcrowding.

The annual Staff Dance would be held on 8th January 1954. A request was made for a licensed bar.

Local church choirs and other bodies were encouraged to give carol visits etc., in the days preceding the Christmas Festival.

On 19 December a band performance was given in the Dining Hall, this being arranged by Mr. Eastleigh of the British Imperial Band. This performance was the first of its kind to be held at Brockle Bank and was very much appreciated. Tea was supplied to the members of the Band after the performance.

There was not an Open Day if 1953, no reason was given.

As part of the Refurbishment Plans a report by the Chief Officer stated that the expenditure for 1954-55 was to be £2780, which was available for internal cleaning and painting. Thereafter it was agreed that large Homes should be redecorated every ten years, with washing, painting, whitening ceilings every five years, except for certain accommodation affected by regulations under the Factories and Food and Drugs Act which has to be washed down and distempered at more frequent intervals.

On 21 January 1954 Mrs. Freundt wife of the Peruvian Ambassador with the Chairman visited Brockle Bank, and on 3 March there was also a visit from Mr. Mehamed Zabidin, a Colonial Service Officer from Malaya.

One of the residents in the Chalet unit requested a "Home Perm", permission was granted and her niece visited and gave her the necessary attention - result- quite nice. The Matron expected to have further requests!

Mr. T.H.E.Clark from the County Hall visited the Home with Mr. Phillips from the Ministry of Health on 28 April.

In connection with the appointment of Reverend Shells as Chaplain to Brockle Bank, on 26 April the Bishop of Kingston attended the service for the purpose of installing the Reverend Shells as chaplain. Several members of the staff and residents attended also the Chairman. The Reverend Shells arranged for his Choir from St Anne's Church with other Church Officers to attend. Tea was supplied to the members of the choir and other Church Officers.

Talking Books were ordered for the blind residents in the Chalet and "C6" ward. Sockets would have had to be installed to facilitate their use.

The purchase of a Trolley Shop for residents unable to visit the Canteen was made, it was expected that the Trolley Shop would visit the wards twice a week.

Open Day was held on 9 June 1954. A sale of work was combined with the arrangement. A very high attendance of visitors was recorded, between 250-280. The Mayor and Mayoress of Wandsworth and several members of many organisations. An Orchestral performance was arranged in the Dining Hall. Tea was supplied at a nominal charge.

Nine members of the Mitcham Labour Party visited the Home on the 12 August and were taken on a conducted tour by the Warden and Matron.

£30 was authorised by the Chairman for the purchase of an electric record player for use of the residents in the Chalet. The residents were to provide the records, according to their tastes.

The chairman authorised the purchase of one radio receiver for use in "E" Block, this was in addition to the two in use elsewhere. This type of receiver was found to be eminently suitable for use in the small units of this Home. The Committee authorised the cost of £15 to be met from the "Vaughan" bequest.

The staff, on leaving the Home, were still subject to regular searches.

"C6" ward had been decorated and it was thought that a small tropical fish tank would brighten the appearance of the ward. The ward was the only one without either a tropical fish tank or budgerigars and the installation of this item would be appreciated. The cost was estimated to be £12.4.9d.

On 12 July the Home had a visit from Mrs. Basjab an Indonesian from County Hall.

In the Chalets the individual teapot system had been set up. It had proved so successful that it was proposed to operate it in the main Dining Hall and in "C6" ward.

The Talking Books, which were arranged for the benefit of the blind residents, was not very popular. They were returned to the Royal National Institute for the Blind.

The Warden in his report stated that the number of residents had dropped to a total of 460 compared to 494 at the last Committee meeting.

A Whist Drive was arranged by the Matron for the residents of the Chalet. Prizes were given to the value of 11/6d.

The new Church, built at ground level for the residents, was consecrated by the Bishop of Kingston, assisted by Reverend Shells on 1 December 1955. The Chairman, one of the Committee and the Chief Officer and Deputy of the Welfare Department attended. Many residents and Officers of the Home also attended the service and tea was served for the visitors.

A resident, Mr. Charles Reid, aged 80, died in tragic circumstances on 22 November 1955. He was found on the railway line near Streatham Common Station. The inquest found there was insufficient evidence as to how Mr. Reid actually got on to the railway line and in consequence an open verdict was returned by the Jury.

The Home was visited on 22 December by Mr. Hughes Young MP, making a tour of the wards, speaking to many members of the staff and residents.

Mr. Tylers, the Mattress maker, retired on 23 November 1955

FOOD AND DRUGS ACT 1955

FOOD HYGIENE REGULATIONS 1955

Report (6.2.56) by the Chief Officer of the Welfare Department.

1) *In exercise of the powers conferred by the Food and Drugs Act, 1955, the Minister of Agriculture, fisheries and Food and the Minister of Health have made the Food Hygiene Regulations, 1955, which mostly came into operation on 1st January 1956. The operation of certain of the regulations which may require alterations to premises or substantial changes in existing practices is made subject to a delay of six months.*

2) *The regulations lay down requirements in respect of the cleanliness of food premises and of apparatus and equipment; the hygienic handling of food; the cleanliness of persons engaged in the handling of food and of their clothing, and the action to be taken where they suffer from, or are carriers of certain infections; the construction, repair and maintenance of food premises and the facilities to be provided; and the temperature at which certain foods that are particularly liable to transmit disease are to be kept in food premises.*

3) *The interpretation of "food premises" means any premises on or from which there is carried on any food business, which includes the undertaking of a canteen, club or institution, whether carried on for profit or not, and any undertaking or activity carried on by a local authority.*

4) *The enforcement of the provisions of these regulations is the responsibility of the local authority, defined as the council of the borough, urban district or rural district and in London, the council of the metropolitan borough in which the premises are situated.*

5   *So far as welfare establishments are concerned, existing conditions and practices broadly conform to the regulations although some minor measures may require to be taken at some premises. Heads of all welfare establishments at which food is handled have been advised of the regulations and asked to ensure that they are complied with.*

C.S.PETHERAM.

A Mrs. Hood, who was physically handicapped and attended the handicrafts session during the week, was known to be alone for Christmas. A bed was made available for her in the Chalet and she stayed for a couple of nights. Mrs. Hood was extremely grateful and thanked everyone for their kindness to her.

To get sufficient residents to partake of the annual outings was becoming increasingly difficult. It was suggested that in 1956 the Council's annual treat should consist of a treat within the Home, possibly coupled with an Open Day and sale of work. The hire of a Band with perhaps an artist or two could be included and the supplying of a special tea. The Open Day was to be 19 June 1956. The Band was to be the Band of H. M. Scots Guards.

A report from the Welfare Committee on Hot Water Bottles.

Stocks of hot water bottles were available in many large Homes. In most Homes they were mainly filled by staff. Many residents were comforted by the presence of a hot water bottle, but as the heating of large Homes had been much improved, they were not strictly necessary. There had been a case where a cover had been removed by a resident and, in consequence, had suffered a burn on her leg. However it was decided to leave the provision of hot water bottles to the Warden's and Matron's general direction of the Visiting Committee.

Report by the Chief Officer of the Welfare Department on waking and washing of the more infirm residents:

Rule 5 of the Committee provides that:-

1) *Residents shall not be requested to rise before 7 a.m., but it was mentioned that many of them are roused long before that hour.*

2) *Although it was necessary to rouse certain residents e.g. diabetics, for injections and incontinent cases, for their own benefit and in the interests of other occupants of the ward, sometimes as early as 4.30 a.m., there was no general rousing of an entire ward at such an early hour. Some of those who are awakened prefer to get up but others, after being given the necessary attention, go off to sleep until the normal hour of rising.*

3) *Chronic sick residents who are incontinent may similarly be awakened once or twice during the night - the usual times are around 2-4 a.m. in order to be cleaned, but they sleep between times and have breakfast in bed and even those who are able to get up for a few hours seldom leave their beds before 10 a.m.*

4) *Residents who need no special attention are never woken by staff before the normal hour but many of the aged and infirm residents who make it a practise to retire very early naturally wake early and prefer to get up. Cases were mentioned by the Wardens and Matrons of aged residents who on their own initiative mainly in the summer months, are regularly up washed, dressed and taking a stroll in the grounds of the Home or in the adjoining street, long before 6 a.m.*

5) *In order that some of the infirm residents unable to wash and dress themselves may be ready for breakfast by 8 a.m., it is necessary for the staff to start helping them sometime before 7 a.m., but in most of these cases, because they have retired so early the night before, the old people are awake and anxious to be up and about as soon as the staff are able to help them wash and dress. The spirit,*

if not in every case the letter, of the Committee's rule if therefore being observed and it is a matter for Visiting Sub-Committees to ensure that this essentially local aspect of administration; is adapted to suit the convenience and welfare of the old people.

A magnifying glass was purchased for the T.V. set in an "A" Block day-room.

In May 1956 there were several visitors to the Home. A Miss Buhrmann a Public Health Student Nurse from Holland, Miss Michael-ides a Cypriot National taking a Colonial course. Also a Doctor Felix Brummer, Under Secretary Social Welfare Officer, from South Africa.

As well as the services in the new Church in the grounds, the Chaplain takes Communion to many residents in the Wards.

PLAY HUT - *A play hut owned by the Corporation and used as an adjunct to Earlsfield House Children's Home sands on a site adjoining the GLC's Wandsworth Hostel in Swaffield Road. This hut is used by the children in care at Earlsfield House almost exclusively during Sunday afternoons, evenings, weekends and at holiday periods.*

The Wandsworth Borough Pre-School Playgroups Association, an organization which provides nursery facilities for children aged from 3 - 5 years, has recently approached the Council with a request for the use of the hut on weekday mornings during school term times when normally it is not in use by the Corporation. Its reasons for making this approach are that there is an acute need for playgroup facilities in the area, particularly for children living in the Corporation's nearby Henry Prince Housing Estate, and there is no alternative or suitable accommodation available in which the playgroup can be established.

We consider that the establishment of the playgroup in the area would be most useful and should have the Corporation's full support, particularly as it may well have the affect of a quasi-preventative measure under the Children and Young Person Act 1963. We therefore propose that subject to certain safeguarding conditions to the issue of necessary consents and to the payment of a nominal rental the organization be granted the use of the hut in question.

WE RECOMMEND - That the Wandsworth Borough Pre-School Playgroup Association be granted the use of the play hut referred to on weekday mornings during normal school term times and that the Corporation's officers be authorized, in consultation with our Chairman, to settle the conditions and terms governing such use.

In October 1957 the Matron reported that she was having trouble with several women who caused disturbances when under the influence of drink. They were all over 70 years of age!

A Harvest Thanksgiving Service was held in the new Church. Thirty residents took tea in the Vicarage at St Anne's in the afternoon and attended the Parish Church for Service in the evening.

In December 1957 the Medical officer reported that during a whole week the whole of "B" Block had been evacuated in preparation for a large modernisation scheme, designed to provide a lift to all floors with smaller bed-wards, dining-rooms etc, on each floor.

In February 1958 the cost of accommodation for residents was 32/6d a week and they had 10/- a week for their personal needs. The Welfare Committee had decided that they would make representations to the Ministry of Health with a view to the issue of new Regulations increasing the minimum charge for residents in Part III accommodation from 32/6d to 40/- a week and to support similar representations already made by the County Councils Association and the Association of Municipal Corporations.

Four Fish tanks needed dismantling, reconstituting, and restocking with fish - cost of the work would be defrayed from the "Vaughan Bequest". Ward "C6" did not have a Budgerigar so the Warden purchased one complete with cage and stand from the Canteen Profits, cost £3.15.9d

The Warden reported a visit of 15 Students, this being arranged by the National Old Peoples Welfare Council, the persons concerned coming from various County Councils in England being part of a course they were taking.

The Home had no special arrangement with the borough library service. The Warden had to discuss with the Librarian the possibility of making such an arrangement. Books were available to the residents in the Canteen and there was a Trolley service to the wards. New books were purchased from Canteen funds.

In September 1958 a resident was married to a Mr. Stone a resident of Southern Grove. The reception was held in the Chalet and the catering cost £7.10.6d organised by the Matron. The couple were found accommodation at Ashmead, a new purpose built Council Home.

In November the residents numbered 399, 80 men and 319 women.

On December 4 the Handicraft Sale was held amongst the staff and residents, totalling £55.19.6d, the best sale on record.

A wheelchair resident lost her purse in the street just before Christmas. She was depending on this money to take her out for a two-week's Christmas leave. The Warden obtained authority from the Chief Officer to advance her the sum of £4 from the Welfare Fund as a temporary loan. This was repaid when she received her arrears of National Assistance due to her whilst not in residence.

Three 21inch screen TVs were purchased for "B" Block, one for each floor, cost to be defrayed from Canteen profits.

On 27 December the Warden was requested to collect a "lot of cakes" from Marks and Spencer. With his assistant they took two cars which Marks and Spencer literally filled with cakes. He had sufficient to give Earlsfield House Children's Home quite a quantity leaving him sufficient to make a least three issues to the residents.

In January 1959 a Welfare Officer was appointed for Brockle Bank. Mrs. Eccles was previously employed in the Homes Division, County Hall.

A resident was found hanged in an outside toilet. At the inquest it transpired that he had attempted to take his life some years ago.

The Matron reported that a number of residents had been admitted for "Holiday periods".

The Warden reported that all the work in connection with the recent parliamentary election was carried out satisfactorily. This involved quite a volume of clerical work for which he wished to record his appreciation to members of his clerical staff and the Welfare Officer. Visits to the establishment were made by representatives from the Labour, Conservative, and Liberal parties.

In October there were three visitors. Mr. Vaughan C.B.E. and Mrs. Vaughan, a Consul General from Buenos Aires and Mr. A C Maby, Deputy General Consul from New York.

Following the modernisation of "B" Block, part of the tar-paved yard was relayed with planted areas and lawns. It was proposed to extend this treatment to the rest of the yard at a cost estimated by the Chief Officer of the Parks Department at approximately £234. Further provision was also made for the planting between "D" and "E" Blocks. The cost was approximately £210.

Following authority from the Chairman it was decided to give small gifts of cigarettes, tobacco or chocolate to residents of wards known not to be receiving any Christmas gifts. Costs from the Canteen profits.

Christmas Festivities 1959 passed off as usual with all the residents enjoying themselves. The usual gifts were received e.g. Beer from Young's Brewery and carol singers doing the round of the wards.

The Tuesday Club made their usual gifts to "D" and "E" wards.

Following the appeal made by the Red Cross in connection with the Agadir Disaster, staff and residents were given the opportunity to subscribe towards the fund and the Warden had pleasure in reporting that £13.7/- had been forwarded to the Red Cross.

It was decided to modernise "C" Block and the residents were transferred to other homes.

The number of daily papers etc., supplied to the Home were halved as the numbers of residents had decreased.

In May 1960 the Brigadier R. M. Williams D.S.O, Secretary of the Royal Hospital and Home for Incurables at Richmond, visited. Also in July Mrs. Pearl Siston from the Department of Public Welfare, Toronto visited the Home.

Gifts of several Bibles were distributed around the wards, made by Mr. D. Hills of the Gideon Society.

For the first time the 1960 Christmas Lunch featured roast turkey and the Beer from Young's Brewery came in bottles instead of barrels.

It was recorded that one of the very elderly male residents was 98 years old.

By October 1960 the modernisation of "A" block had been completed.

BUILDINGS

By May 1950 the Nursery unit was eventually closed. The Medical Officer reported:-

Whilst the necessity for refurbishment for re-organisation is of course recognised, one cannot refrain from expressing a sentimental regret at having had to part company with these infants and babies, many of whom we have had practically since birth and whose day-by-day progress it has been a great pleasure to watch. The unit was an excellent one and I venture to believe was instrumental in giving these unfortunate children a sound and healthy start in life amidst happy surroundings"

Three wards have been redecorated and furnished with curtains and the resulting bright and cherry atmosphere cannot but have a beneficial effect on the mentality of the residents. The provision of a wash basin in "H 3" ward and of cot-beds in "H 3" and "C 26" wards is much appreciated. Finally the gardening staff are to be congratulated on the delightful display of flowers in the grounds - the wealth of colour which has met the eye on entering the gates has been a joy to behold.

Further improvements to Furnishings for 1950/51.

Air rings	*12*
Back rests	*12*
Bedspreads	*144*
Lloyd Loom chairs	*12*
Net curtaining - yards	*100*
Food trolleys-3 tiers	*8*
Library bookcase	*1*
Lockers small nested	*50*
Mirrors frameless	*6*
Settees Rexine	*4*
Tables-occasional	*12*
Wardrobe cupboards	*6*
Dining tables	*50*
	Cost £1144.5/-

There was a discussion on the proposal of the Canteen being transferred to the Furniture store. However, the cost would be £360, the furniture store had been empty for a long time and would need decorating as well as the need for fixtures and fittings.

The long awaited "Sick Bay" had at last been opened, there enough beds for 12 residents.

In July 1951 the large kitchen had been completely retiled and refitted.

In March 1952 further refurbishing programme had been agreed;-

Curtain Material	*300 yards*
Bedside Lockers	*110*
Fireside chairs, Rexine	*50*
Wing-armchairs, tapestry covered	*12*
Material for chair backs	*72 yards*
Armchairs club type Rexine	*18*
Settees with 2 cushions	*6*
" " tapestry	*6*
Cushion covers	*12*
Settees with 2 cushions, Rexine	*6*
Occasional tables	*6*
Dining room chairs, "Windsor"	*60*
" " "Warite tops"	*15*
Wall plaques	*6*
Smokers companion sets (oak)	*24*
Chromium art pots	*6*
Condiment sets (plastic)	*100*
Chairs tubular stacking	*30*

The Dray and Mascot of Young's Brewery

In September 1952 the staff requested that the heating be improved during the winter months. Even the Trade unions brought up the subject in regard to the Mattress Shop. To improve the heating in the Mattress Shop, Barber Shop, General store, Laundry, and Packing Room would cost £812 a year. Would the Committee authorise the Engineers suggestions?

A report from the visiting Committee:-

In August 1955 the previous open corridors on the male and female side have now been half bricked and glazed, translating a very draughty corridor into a warm lounge with seats and the female one has window boxes and net curtains which make it very like a sitting room, and the appreciation of this is shown by the number of residents who sit there and are now able to shop in comfort from the trolley.

It was proposed to purchase a Washing Up Machine, the staff looked forward with keen anticipation, but would the cost be sanctioned?

In April 1958 the Matron reported that many residents were appreciative of handrails fitted in the toilets.

By May 1959 the "B" Block modernisation had been completed and was occupied immediately.

In September, there was a report from the visiting committee:-

In order to increase the accommodation for the infirm male residents, a scheme was proposed in consultation with the Chief Engineer for converting the ground floor of "A" block into a self-contained open ward unit for infirm men. The 2 main rooms on this floor are at present allocated as sitting rooms but are no longer required for this purpose. If the Scheme is accepted one room could become a bedroom for 16 persons with toilet and lavatory facilities, with 2 units opening off it and the other a sitting/dining room with its own kitchenette/dining room. The unplastered wall would be plastered and the whole unit decorated and lighting would be brought up to good standard. The total cost exclusive of any equipment required was estimated at £2300.

On completion the Scheme would provide 16 additional beds for very infirm and semi chronic sick men and would be valuable supplement to the accommodation in "B" Block.

DIETARY

Christmas Day 1953

Breakfast	Ham, Eggs, Bread and Butter, Tea.
Dinner	Roast Pork, Potatoes, Parsnips, Sprouts, Apple Sauce, Onion Stuffing and Christmas Pudding and Custard.
Tea	Bread and Butter, Jam, Iced Cake, Tea.
Supper	Cheese and Biscuits, Margarine, Coffee.

Extras included, Beer/Minerals, ½oz Tobacco or 10 Cigarettes for men, and 4ozs Sweets and Biscuits, for women. An apple and an orange for both men and women.

The women in "C6" ward had ½lb grapes instead of an apple or orange.

Boxing Day

Breakfast	Egg, Bread and Butter, Marmalade, Tea.
Dinner	Roast Beef, Potatoes, Cabbage, Mince Tart, Custard, Tea.
Tea	Bread and Margarine, Jam, Fruit Jelly, Tea.
Supper	Sausage Rolls, and Coffee.

Cost £158

In October 1954 there were several gifts of fruit received from local schools and Churches following their Harvest Festivals.

In May 1955 the Medical Officer reported that a system of diet sheets had been established for the residents to conform with their requirements. These were of necessity rather rigidly defined but it had proved possible now to arrange for a choice of food and dishes to be made available for bed cases not on a strict diet.

Marks and Spencer gifted several dozen cakes for the Home.

In 1957 the Medical Officer reported that there had been an increase in the weekly allowance for food for the residents, which had made possible a more generous, varied and interesting diet.

In October 1958 there was a gift of fruit from St Michael's Church, Apple Pies from Mark's and Spencer's, Cakes and Chocolate from the Salvation Army.

ENTERTAINMENT

Two whist drives were to be held, one during August and one in September. The residents really enjoyed these, they would be eagerly anticipated. £1 for each occasion would be allocated for prizes and refreshments from the Canteen profits.

There were four Concerts during November and December 1953. They were given by:-

      The Primrose Party,
      The Regal Concert Party,
      The Whimsical Party,
      The Embassy Party, all were paid for from Canteen funds.

A small concert was given in May 1954 by the Darby and Joan Club in the Day Room of "C" Block. This concert party consisted in the main of singing old songs etc, to which the residents were invited to join in. This new form of entertainment proved very successful among the residents that attended.

In November 1954 the Matron organised another Whist Drive, which was always a popular event.

Prior to Christmas 1954 the children from Broadwater Junior Schools Choir and Orchestra, in company with their Headmaster, visited the Home giving an entertainment in the dining hall. This was much appreciated by the old people. I have sent a suitable letter of acknowledgement to the Headmaster who made the arrangements.

The Warden reported:-

On 20th November there an excellent concert party known as All Change for Happiness. It was an outstanding concert consisting mainly of children's acts, colourful in costume, it appealed to the residents. A fee of £5.- was charged and I should be grateful if authority could be given for this to be defrayed from Canteen profits. Having regard to the type of concert, I re-engaged it for a second appearance in "C 6" Day Room and Chalet for 8th January 1955.

In March 1956 three concerts were organised:-

      The Lutton Concert Party,
      The Darby and Joan Concert Party,
      The Primrose Concert Party.

Following the Chairman's authority the Warden made a tentative arrangement for the attendance of a Hungarian Gipsy Orchestra. The Orchestra was accommodated as refugees in St George's in the East Hospital. The proposed fee would be £10, plus the cost of hiring a coach. The event took place on 8th March 1957 and was greatly enjoyed.

It was becoming more and more difficult to encourage residents to attend concert parties in the dining hall. It was very suitable there as the dining hall had a stage one end of the hall. However the Warden proposed to engage 3 or 4 musicians who would tour the building giving musical selection to the ward units leaving the residents to please themselves as to whether they preferred T.V. or radio during the evening.

The attendance of the Travelling Musicians from ward to ward was very successful.

In October there was a request from the members of the Women's Institute at Chiddingfold to visit the Home. As they had for many years entertained the residents, the Warden was pleased to arrange the visit, which took place on 22 October 1958. Eight visitors arrived making a complete tour of the Establishment. The tour was conducted by the Matron and they were provided with refreshments afterwards.

GIFTS

A small radio set was received for the residents from Mr. Barnes of Magdalin Road, Wandsworth.

A gift of a combined T.V. and Radio set was received from Mr. Dumbrell of 39 Stephendale Road, Fulham. Mr. Dumbrell stated that the tube of the television required replacement. If the Committee agree I propose to arrange for the Chief Engineer's Department to check and overhaul the set replacing any defective components cost of this could be defrayed from Canteen funds.

In March 1956 a gift of a handmade Tapestry Prayer Desk Kneeler was received from Mrs. Deer. When the Prayer Desk has been cleaned and repolished this kneeler will be permanently attached to the Prayer Desk. The gift was acknowledged by the Chief Officer.

In April there were gifts of sweets and chocolates for the wards "D and E" from Miss Astley of the Tuesday Club.

In September there was a gift of a wheel chair from Mrs. Gray of 51 Langfield Street, Wandsworth.

Marks and Spencer donated several dozen cakes in May, June and July, 1958

HOLIDAYS

A great deal of time and effort was spent on arranging holidays for the residents. Some of the holidays were at Guest Houses others were to Council Holiday Homes.

The Warden and Matron made some arrangements but others were made by the Chief Officer.

In October 1950 twelve residents had 2 weeks holiday at the Council's Home at "Kenwolde", it was arranged by the Chief Officer. It was understood that all the residents had a very enjoyable time and appreciated the change.

Later that month arrangements were made for a male resident to go to Bournemouth and a female resident to Leigh-on-Sea for 2 weeks.

The Homeless families were encouraged to go to the hop fields for the season, 6 families left the Home for this purpose. It was not long before 4 families were back because of the living conditions!

In May 1953 the Matron arranged that 4 women residents should take advantage of the holidays offered to old age pensioners by the Brighton Corporation. They would visit for one week's holiday at the end of the month at their own expense.

Also in May 5 residents took advantage of the Eastbourne Holiday Home and stayed for one week, and 2 other residents stayed at Ramsgate and Newhaven respectively also for one week.

Frederick Judd went to Worthing arranged by the Infantile Paralysis Fellowship following instructions received from the Chief Officer. Ambulance transport to and from Victoria Station was arranged as well as the supply of the return railway ticket.

It was arranged that a number of residents were to go to the Council's Home at Broadstairs:-

8 went for one week on 13th May,
7   "   "   15th July,
7   "   "   23rd September.

In May 1954 information was received from the Chief Officer that vacancies were available for paralysed residents to partake of an annual holiday at Tankerton, in September two residents went to Tankerton for a week's holiday.

The Chief Officer made arrangements for four male and four female residents to have a weeks holiday at the Council's small Home at Broadstairs.

In 1955 a resident went on a 14-day holiday from 28 May to Worthing by arrangement with the Infantile Paralysis Fellowship, the Council being responsible for the cost of one week.

A blind resident went for two weeks holiday from the 18 May to a Blind Home at Worthing

Five female residents went on leave to Leigh-on-Sea for one week during the month of June.

Between June and the end of August, 30 residents went on holiday to Leigh-on - Sea, Herne Bay, and Broadstairs, for one week.

One crippled resident went to Tankerton for a week in July and four residents went to Eastbourne, these holidays were arranged by the Council.

In 1957 during April and May 30 residents went to Carlton Lodge Broadstairs, a Private Hotel in Hastings and two cripples went to Tankerton.

In 1958 twenty-four residents between May and October went to Bognor, Bournemouth, Tankerton, Clacton, Broadstairs and Eastbourne, all the holidays were arranged by the Chief Officer.

In 1959 from July to September 18 residents went on holiday to Tankerton and Carlton Lodge, Broadstairs.

Further holidays arranged during 1959 were to Lawn Villa Guest House, Herne Bay, 15 residents, Carlton Lodge, Broadstairs, seven residents and Greyfriars, Herne Bay, eight residents.

In June 1960 seven residents went to Lawn Villa, Herne Bay, for one week and three crippled residents were taken also to Herne Bay under the auspices of the National Association of the Paralysed.

On the 27 June eight residents, all infirm, three being wheelchair cases were taken for two weeks holiday to Herne Bay accompanied by two members of staff. This was an experiment it being the first time infirm residents had the facility of going on holiday. Their infirmity, of course demanded being accompanied by staff. The Warden and Matron visited the Home prior to the holiday being organised and were quite satisfied with the conditions they saw.

MEDICAL

In October 1950 the Medical Officer reported:-

There is an ageing population in the Home with quite a number in their 90's. Thirteen aged men in "H3" ward had Dysentery, after the strictest isolation and disinfection all made a complete recovery and no spread of disease. Some 20 chronic sick have died and they now number 17. The problem of Homeless Families remains as before.

In 1953 the proposed Dental Clinic operated from 29 April. To begin with the Dentist visited fortnightly.

Arrangements being made for an Eye Clinic that will use the same facilities as the Dental Clinic, will be for the benefit for the older residents who find it difficult to attend an outside Optician.

The Medical Officer reported that it was very noticeable of late that the old folk that are now admitted, both male and female are of a much more infirm type than formerly. This has resulted in a great strain being thrown on our ground floor accommodation which is now proving inadequate.

The Homeless families were now reduced to four, the Medical Officer welcomed the policy of complete evacuation.

He also welcomed the trips to Women's Institutes and other short trips for the more infirm residents which inevitably relieve the monotony of Institutional life and have a very valuable tonic effect both physically and psychologically.

In November the Doctor reported that it was most noticeable in the increased numbers residents with malignant disease, many of them inoperable by reason of their advanced age. In these cases efforts are mainly to keep the patients comfortable and free from as much pain as possible.

There was to be an additional Chiropody Service authorised by the Chief Officer, a three-hour session each Monday. It was well attended and it was agreed that the demand for foot treatment by the many old people in the Home was now fully met.

Subsequent to the reporting of 3 male residents being removed to hospital and their condition diagnosed as T.B., arrangements were made for all male residents and staff in contact with the removed residents, to be mass X-rayed with the X-ray Van and equipment attending the Home.

In October 1954 there was a visit from Doctor Piedrola from Spain a member of the World Health Organisation.

In November 1954 all the women Residents and staff were mass X-rayed. The results of the Mass X-ray showed that further 4 residents were found to be suffering from T.B. Two were sent to hospital but the other two were being treated in a separate ward their ages being 92 and 65 years, they slept and ate in their ward together and their crockery was kept separate from those of other residents. The results of the Mass X- ray of the female residents proved no one had T.B.

In March 1955 the Medical Officer reported that there were 34 deaths during the winter due to the extreme weather conditions. This was the highest figure since he was appointed in 1948 and four more than during the Influenza epidemic in 1951. Their average age was 78 years. There had been one more case of T.B. admitted. He hoped to arrange for further Mass X-ray examinations of residents and staff.

Report from the Medical Officer:-

It is proposed in future to alter the procedure in the case of those residents whose mental condition necessitates their removal to Tooting Bec Hospital. In the past application has been made to the Hospital and the relatives informed after admission. Following upon representations that have been made, it is now proposed to inform the next -of-kin that the removal to Tooting Bec has become necessary and invite observations. Should permission be refused, then the responsibility will rest with them to make alternative arrangements, but it is felt that this preliminary notification to the relatives should be made.

In September 1956 the Medical Officer and the Warden made a recommendation to the Engineer's Division with a view to the installation of Ventilator Fans for ward "C6". Bearing in mind that the residents in this ward are all bedridden and for the most part incontinent and also that it is obligatory on the staff to man the ward throughout the night as well as the day, this provision would appear to be an urgent necessity.

In January a modern sluice was installed in ward "C6" and much appreciated by the staff, as was anticipated the residents have frequent use of commodes and bedpans.

In May 1957 the Medical Officer felt that great benefit would result from the services of a Physiotherapist. If these were available, he felt that some of our residents who are at present bedridden might be mobilised and others who are threatening to become bedridden might be kept ambulant. To begin with she might attend for 2 or 3 sessions per week though in view of the increasing age and infirmity of our residents, she may well be usefully employed for up to 5 sessions per week.

In April the Medical Officer reported that out of 23 recent deaths, the average age had gone up to 83 years. Six of those were over 90 years old.

In July 1959 there was an Influenza epidemic, in 2 months there had been 53 deaths, 20 directly attributable to Influenza.

In September 1959 the Matron reported that a young women aged 44 years old was admitted who suffered from Epilepsy. She was badly disfigured by the loss of an eye and her hair was stated to have suffered by fire. She was a constant source of worry to the old folk.

In May 1960 there were more arrangements for Mass X-ray following an application to the Local Authorities by the Medical Officer.

OUTINGS

In March 1951 Brockle Bank was allocated 10 tickets for the L.C.C. staff Pantomime, eight children went with two mothers the fare of 7/8d was paid for from Canteen funds.

The Annual outing for 1951 was to Margate, on 22 June, 130 residents went and the Margate Corporation Catering Department provided tea for the residents at 2/6d per head, the cost defrayed from Canteen profits.

In July the Matron took a small party of old people to the Tower of London by Riverbus, they had an enjoyable time and returned late afternoon.

During August and September there were four outings to Women's Institutes, they visited Cranleigh, Kennington, Kent, Reigate, and Abinger Hamer.

In the school holidays, the Homeless families were sent off to a park after dinner with a packed tea plus 3d a person for the purchase of beverages. Most days between 50-60 (mothers with children) left the Home after 1 p.m. not returning before 6p.m.

On 1 October 1951 10 residents visited the Play House Theatre for the recording of Henry Halls Guest Night.

A Children's party invitation was received from the Battersea Labour Party to send 12 children to a Christmas Tea and Concert, two mothers went with them.

In February 1952 the Putney and British Legion organised a party for the Homeless children. They were escorted by some of the mothers.

In May 1952 the Warden reported that he had 5 invitations from Women's Institutes, the cost of transport would be defrayed from Canteen profits. He had also received an invitation for a number of residents to visit the home of Sir Edward Bligh at Swanley.

There was a proposal to take four Coaches to Worthing, with some 120 residents during June. They would have a packed lunch and tea was arranged on arrival as usual. The day was fine and warm and everyone had a most enjoyable day.

In July 10 residents were invited to a B.B.C. performance of "All Star Bill" at the Aeolian Hall- this was much appreciated by the residents taking part.

In September 30 residents with the Warden and Matron visited Sir Edward Bligh's home at Swanley. Everyone had a delightful afternoon.

In January 1953 a party of 10 residents attended the Playhouse Theatre for the performance of "Henry Hall's Night House"

In 1953 10 seats were allocated to Brockle Bank to see the Royal River Pageant, this was greatly enjoyed.

During July and August 1953 there were five visits to Women's Institutes. They came from Chelsfield, Chiddingfold, Shermanbury, Weybridge, and Barnes Green. All these outings were up to the usual high standard as given by the Women's Institutes, and all residents taking park had a most enjoyable time.

Three afternoon outings were arranged to take the more infirm residents for a two-hour round trip. Cost per trip was £5. Refreshments to be provided cost £1 payable from Canteen funds.

In November 1953 arrangements were made to take a party of residents to the Wimbledon Theatre to see a pantomime.

On December 15, 15 women attended St Paul's Hall for a concert and tea organised by Miss Rosetta Kemp. On the same day a party of women attended the Anchor Mission for a tea party.

The Warden received 70 tickets for the Harringay Circus presented by the Animal Health Trust, two coaches were hired. A visit was also made to the Ice Show at the Empress Hall, the residents paid for themselves.

The annual outings to Littlehampton took place on 4th and 11th June, two coaches were hired for each occasion.

In March 1955 arrangements were being made for the summer outing. They were to take 2 coaches of Male residents to Goodwood, taking lunch and tea. Also 3 coaches to go to Littlehampton taking lunch and tea as usual arranged there. Those not going on the outing, had a special tea consisting of Ham, Tomatoes, Fruit Jelly and Ice-cream.

It was anticipated that the cost of the above arranged would exceed the amount allowed e.g. the difference being made up from Canteen profits.

There were two Women's Institute outings in 1955 one to Chelsfield and the other to Sheppey, Kent. They were usually half-day outings but the one for Sheppey was a whole day's outing taking a packed lunch, leaving the Home at 10.30 am.

On the afternoon of 21 May a Mr. Murley of the Northcote Road Baptist Church Young People's Society Christian Endeavour, arranged for a party of 32 residents to have a tour of Surrey. He provided the coach and tea and biscuits were purchased for the residents during the afternoon. The cost amounting to 8/- which was defrayed from Canteen profits.

On 24th June a three-hour tour of Surrey was arranged for the more infirm residents. The cost of transport was £3.10/-. Light refreshments during the afternoon cost 15/-.

In 1955 Father Callan, the Roman Catholic Priest arranged a full day's coach outing for 27 residents to Littlehampton on 16 June. A packed lunch was taken from the

Home. In order to reduce the cost as far as possible for Father Callan the Warden arranged for the Coach to be supplied via the Chief Officer of Supplies. Father Callan refunding the cost.

On a day the visiting committee were at the home they were just in time to see the return of infirm residents who had been on a three-hour tour of Surrey. They reported:-

The unloading of this was an illustration of the help and co-operation of their fellow residents, the staff, Matron and equipment. The cheerful, good humoured and responsible care lavished on them was a lesson to any onlooker.

The Reverend Shells invited a party of residents to his Harvest Festival tea at St Anne's Church on 9 October. Transport was required to convey the residents to and from the Church.

The Matron arranged for a party of residents to attend an Ice Show at Earls Court in December.

St John's Ambulance Brigade donated 20 tickets for the entrance to tea and entertainment at Wandsworth Town Hall, it took place on 7 January 1956.

The Earlsfield Congregational Church Social Club invited 70 residents to a tea and entertainment in the Congregational Hall. Transport was arranged from the Home and the expenditure met from the Canteen profits.

In May 1956 a coach load of more infirm residents were taken on a coach tour through Windsor, Ascot and Virginia Water. They were entertained by the Matron of Kenwolde to tea.

On 13 June a similar tour through Cobham, Newlands Corner, Leatherhead and Epsom was also arranged. Tea and Biscuits were provided at Newlands Corner.

Between June and August there were four outings to Women's Institutes. They went to Chelsfield, Chiddingfold, Holmwood and Canterbury. The day they went to Canterbury it was made a full day's outing, the morning being spent at Herne Bay with a packed lunch.

The Committee Chairman arranged five-day trips for the residents, those of the infirm type, or those performing useful work in the establishment. Cost to be defrayed from Canteen profits. They had:-

A full day trip to Brighton, plus cost of tea.

A three-hour tour of Kent.

Another full day trip to Brighton plus the cost of a meat tea.

An afternoon trip to Ide Hill.

A three-hour tour of Surrey.

In August the Chief Officer gave permission and the chairman agreed to give £10 from the Canteen profits to Earlsfield House for the Warden to take a party of 40 children to West Wittering. All the children had a thoroughly enjoyable day.

In 1957 the Warden was making tentative arrangements to take 20 residents to spend the day at Brighton taking a packed lunch, and tea being provided by the Aquarium Restaurant. By the time June arrived, there were 86 residents who wanted to go to Brighton, with six staff! They had a fish tea in the Aquarium Restaurant.

In August the Reverend Shells arranged a visit for 30 residents to Church House at Caterham.

In July there was another invitation to the Women's Institute at Lancing. It was decided to make it a full day's outing going to Brighton in the morning with a packed lunch. Two more invitations arrived, one for the Women's Institute at Chiddingfold and another to Dorking.

An invitation was received via the Church of England Chaplain for a visit of some 30 residents to the Young Wives Guild at Ardleigh, Colchester. A packed lunch was taken and tea was provided by the Young Wives Guild. Matron was in charge of the outing and all the residents had an enjoyable time, the cost of the coach could have been paid by the Guild, but as the residents were so well entertained it was considered that the cost should be taken from the Canteen profits.

In January 1959 seventeen residents were escorted to the Palace Theatre for an afternoon's entertainment, the tickets were provided. Records do not show what the show was titled.

In July 1959 there was another invitation to the Women's Institute, 32 residents took part. They went to Brighton in the morning with a packed lunch, the cost of the coach was £5.17.6d and biscuits bought cost 8/9d defrayed from Canteen profits.

In September some 32 residents were taken to Eastbourne. They had a packed lunch and then went on to Wannock Gardens for tea. Each resident was given 2/6d from Canteen funds for them to purchase their own tea. The new idea of allowing residents to choose their own tea was most successful.

In September 1959 the more infirm residents were taken for a half day's outing to Newlands Corner, Surrey. Cups of tea and biscuits were provided, the coach cost £4.5/- and the tea £1.

In January 1960 there were 11 blind residents accommodated. It was suggested that they visit a club of the Metropolitan Society of the Blind. Only one resident was found willing to go. Arrangements were made for him to go to the Social club at Caius College Mission Hall, York Road. He had an enjoyable afternoon and the Society agreed to collect him on a regular weekly basis.

The annual outing for 1960 was to Eastbourne, 64 residents went. A packed lunch was taken and a ham tea was provided at Wannock Gardens. A special tea was provided for the remaining residents.

The Reverend Shells arranged an outing to Ardley where the residents were entertained to lunch and tea by a personal friend of his.

The Women's Institutes continued to support the Home and entertain the residents, so kindly, it was a much-appreciated support by the Warden and Matron. Year on year the invitations arrived. In 1960 they had three invitations, to Chelsfield, Lancing and Chiddingfold.

On 19 November invitations were received for residents to attend Billy Smarts Circus at Clapham Common. Thirty-five residents went the cost of the coach was £3.- paid from the Canteen profits.

There was information from the Chief Officer that members from the I.T.V. Company that attended the Home on 8 December in connection with a filmed documentary entitled "Searchlight". Eleven technicians arrived and spent 4 hours filming externally and internally, the latter being of "C" and "B" blocks. This was subsequently shown on television on 22nd December. The producer paid £5 to the Welfare Fund.

On 12 December there was a performance by the West Croydon Orchestra that a coach load of residents attended. It was obviously much appreciated. Cost of transport from Canteen funds.

The WVS took 34 residents to a Christmas dinner at Wandsworth Town Hall. This was a new departure and the residents had an enjoyable time.

Mr. Hughes Young M.P. visited the Home on 21 December making a tour of the wards and extending Christmas greetings to the residents.

The Warden reported that an outing for 22 ex-service men was arranged by the British Legion City London Branch. It was for a full day on the river, a Steamer hired and lunch and tea was given on board. Music was supplied and all the residents had an enjoyable day.

In October the Reverend Shells arranged for 30 residents to be taken to St Anne's Church for a Harvest Festival Tea.

CHAPTER 8: *The Closing Years - 1972*

In 1960 the London County Council was replaced by the Greater London Council.

The Greater London Council started assessing the cost of maintaining the larger Homes, pro rata to the number of residents they housed. In a few short years changes would be made. The large Homes stood on a lot of land and as the modern approach to Residential Homes was "smaller units" and irrespective of the amount of money spent on the modernisation, the large Homes days were numbered.

BUILDINGS

The scheme for converting the ground floor of "A" Block into a self-contained unit for very infirm men was approved. The two main rooms on the floor are no longer required as sitting rooms and one will provide sleeping accommodation for 16 residents with toilet facilities off it. The other will be converted into a sitting/dining room, with it's own kitchenette/duty room.

March 1961. Provision of new quarters for the Assistant Matron had been made. They were to be sited over the new Church of England Chapel and will comprise of a living room, 2 bedrooms, kitchen and bath room. New linoleum to be fitted throughout and completely redecorated. Cost of work would be £1243.

There was to be provision of a new toilet in "D" Block Solarium. The Chief Engineer had prepared a scheme which provided for the construction of a unit containing two separate W. C.' s each of which will be fitted with sliding doors to admit wheel chair cases and a separate hand washbasin. The estimated cost of the work would be £990, which includes water, heating and electrical services, new drains, a tiled dado to all walls and quarry tiles for the floor.

Improvement to the main Provision Store.

The Chief Engineer prepared a scheme for the main Provision Store, which provides for the replacement of the existing wall, shelving and cupboards with adjustable metal shelving, the provision of a new service counter, the formation of a new door opening between the store and Butchers Shop and re-siting of a radiator. The worn flooring in the store would be replaced with a hardwood boarded floor and the room redecorated.

In 1962 it was reported that the modernisation and enlargement of the Rehabilitation Centre was complete and was occupied. The Centre should be in full use by the Physical Handicap Department of the Council.

The redecoration and rewiring of "D" Block was completed and 44 women residents were transferred from Ladywell Lodge, in order that a building programme could be commenced at that establishment. The transfer was for a period of approximately six months.

The Warden reported: -

I have to inform the Committee that arrangements have been made for holding a weekly club for the blind residents of Brockle Bank and Milton Close. This will be held in the dining hall on Tuesday afternoons. Arrangements will be made by the Metropolitan Society of the Blind for entertainment in the way of Musicians or Singers and we supply the tea and biscuits. The afternoon is under the supervision of a lady named Mrs Lawson who is attached to the Metropolitan Society of the Blind.

It was decided that the wards should be given names. The Matron came up with the idea that all the names of the wards should make up the name "Brockle Bank" with their initial letters. "D" block was to be named Bankside, "A" Block Ashdene and "E" Block Beechwood. As the wards were all having alterations so they would have their new name on completion.

There were additional extras for the completed wards: -

The Reconstitution of a fish tank, including new heater, pump and fish	£17.0.6d
3 bird-cage stands	£5.0.0
Christmas Tree lights	£1.7.6
" " bulbs	£2.12.0
" " extras	£3.8.0
Decorations	£-.13.8
Extras	£25.6.8
Flowers	£1.0.0
Artificial flowers	£3.13.0
Records	£1.14.0
Billiard Ball	£-.1.6

The Warden reported: -

I am pleased to report that the programme of cleaning and painting for the year ending 1962 which included a considerable amount of plastering, has now been completed. As far as possible all walls, corridors etc., that were previously painted brickwork have now been dealt with and I think that the improvements by this work are very obvious. Several visitors have commented upon the brightness of the corridors etc.

I understand that steps are now being taken to improve the two top floors of "A" Block. This I understand will follow much the same lines as "C" Block. Initial steps are also being taken to provide the extra day room accommodation in the Chalet, this I am sure the Committee well know is a much desired improvement.

I have been requested by the Chief Officer to submit a list of furniture that I require to bring "D", "E", and "F" Blocks as far as possible up to the standard of modernised Blocks, including carpets, bedroom equipment, etc. This list has now been submitted and now awaits a visit from an Officer from County Hall to go into details. All were agreed and the furnishings duly arrived.

The estimate for Brockle Bank modernisation of Heating and Hot Water systems would come to £31,700, a residual amount of £650 would be met from the Council.

Further recommended painting works using directly employed labour amounted to £2500, and Day Room improvement was estimated at £1000, also using directly employed labour.

Further work to be carried out by directly employed labour was: -

Interior decorations and repairs to	"C" Block	£ 300
" " "	"D" block	£ 475
Works to cold water services in	"G" Block	£ 600
Repairs to roofs and brickwork		£3000

In 1966 in accord with the requirements of the London Fire Brigade, the fire alarm system at the Chalet needs to be extended. Five additional call points and three additional fire bells are required and because of the nature of the work we have arranged for it to be carried out with directly employed labour in accordance with the Director of Building Works, the estimate for the work was £170.10/-.

In September 1967 a considerable amount of lead had been stolen from the roof of buildings by persons unknown. During the theft slates were damaged and an order was given to the Director of Building works to replace the stolen lead on these buildings which are to continue in use with "Nuralite" at an estimated cost of £700. As in the case generally with Corporation Properties these buildings were not insured against the risk and there is no provision in the budget for this expenditure.

We recommend that the emergency action to effect repairs to the buildings be approved and confirmed.

The following three tenders had been received in response to invitations to selected contractors for supplying and laying of linotiles on the floor of the Rehabilitation Centre.

Contractor	Tender
Universal Parquetry Ltd, Wimbledon	£201. 2/-
Ajax Flooring Co Ltd, Battersea	£206.13/-
Englewood Ltd, New Malden	£245.10/-

We recommend that the tender of Universal Parquetry for £201.2/- be accepted.

In January 1967 the two 36" Hydro Extractors used in the laundry recently broke down as a result of water entering their motors from a blocked outlet. Accordingly authority has been obtained under the provisions of Standing Order 39 for the Borough Architect to place an order with Thomas Broadbent and Sons Ltd. In accordance with their estimate £206 for the supply ex-works, of two service exchange stators and their fitting to the motors of the Hydro Extractors concerned.

ROAD REPAIRS

The authority of the Council has been given in pursuance of the provisions of standing order 39 for the Borough Engineer to execute at an estimated cost of £200 for urgently needed repairs to the services roadway at Brockle Bank which had been damaged partly through the heavy use of transport conveying people to the Rehabilitation Centre.

GIFTS

At Christmas 1961 each resident received a small gift (from Canteen funds), the women had either handkerchiefs, talcum powder, necklace, etc., and for the men pipes, tobacco pouches, wallets or cigarettes, total cost £28.6.10d.

Gifts for the residents of "D" Block from the members of the Tuesday Club and presents for the women residents in "B" 2 Block from members of the Inner Wheel.

The WVS. entertained the "Darby and Joan Club" to a Christmas Dinner at the Town Hall, transport cost was provided from the Canteen Funds £2.15/-

The Warden reported: -

A master and pupils from Spencer Park School visited me on 22nd December and handed me a cheque for £17.10/- to be spent on Christmas Fare for the residents. I was able to provide each resident with a glass of Sherry before dinner on Christmas Day.

I have also received a cheque for £7.10/- from the Baltic Exchange of the British Legion. It was stipulated that this money was to be spent on Ex-Service Men and enabled me to provide cigarettes for all the men within this category. Gifts of cigarettes and tobacco were also received from Putney Primary School; the children distributed these gifts themselves to the men of "A" and "B" Blocks.

A further gift of £5 from the students of Olivia House, Garratt Green School, requesting that this be spent on an outing for some of the "old ladies". A trip to Runnymede was arranged and 2 or 3 girls were invited to go with them, the Head Mistress giving her permission.

Following the usual procedure of previous years the member of Zion church visited all wards on 21st January for the purpose of distributing presents to the residents.

The Home was still receiving gifts at frequent intervals of pastries and cakes from Marks and Spencer.

In 1962 they received gifts of fruit and sweets from local Schools and churches in connection with their Harvest Festivals.

Gifts for the residents of Kenwood were received from the Tuesday Club and gifts were also received from Wandsworth Inner wheel for the residents of Rosedean. Two South African War Veterans received 10/- each from the South African War Veteran's Association.

The Warden reported: -

An amount of £30 was received from the Baltic Exchange Branch of the British Legion; this was distributed to ex-service men and allowed me to give a cash gift of 6/6d to each man. This year I also received from the schoolboys of Spencer Park School a Christmas tree together with a cheque for £60. From this sum I purchased for all residents on Christmas Day, Sherry costing £15.15/- and as there was a considerable amount left I purchased more Sherry for New Years Day. I made a present of sweets for the women and cigarettes for the men at a total cost of £35.13.3d. The total in excess was £7.3.3d which was paid for by Canteen Funds.

On Christmas Eve two small children called into my office and presented me with an amount of 8/- in coppers, this being the result of carol singing and they wished it to be spent on the "old ladies". A special letter of acknowledgement was sent.

In 1963 the usual gift was received from the Young's Brewery, the Tuesday Club the British Legion and the boys from Spencer Park School (donating a cheque for £50) for the purchase of Sherry, Sweets and cigarettes. The Sherry was bought from the Forrester's Arms and they also donated 20 bottles of Sherry for the residents!

In 1964 the Warden reported: -

I can report to the Committee that I am continuing to receive gifts of cake and fruit from Marks and Spencer. These are distributed amongst the wards and I am quite sure are appreciated by the residents particularly the pastries, which are a type not normally included in the dietary."

The Christmas Day dietary was as usual including the beer and presents given to all the residents. They all enjoyed their day. Cash gifts included: -

£15 from the Baltic Exchange Branch of the British legion.

£50 from the boys of Spencer Park.

£10 from Reverend Ockwell of the Ascension Vicarage, S.W.12. This exclusively for the children of Nightingale Square, Homeless children.

£16.4/- was paid for the Sherry for the residents.

£28.15.8d for cigarettes for the male residents.

£9.7.10d for toys for the children at Nightingale Square.

£1.7.6. For Sherry for the Christmas Party of the Blind Club.

£1.6.11d for refreshments for the Blind Club.

£2.18/- for Tree lights."

ENTERTAINMENT

In January 1962 a Party of Southfield Methodist Scouts gave a concert to the residents of the Chalet.

In October 1963 a Mrs Brooks of Park Gate Youth Club, brought a party of young people to give a concert to the residents of the Chalet. This was quite a change and from what I saw the residents quite appreciated their visit.

A special Christmas Tea was organised for the Blind Club, on 18 December, with three bottles of Sherry cost £1.13/-.

After Christmas five members of the Remo Band gave two concerts, making a tour of the wards, total cost £10. The wards had several visits of Carol Singers as well.

HOLIDAYS

In 1961 the following holidays were arranged: -

5th May to the 19th May, 9 men and 11 women to Cliftonville.

13th May to the 27th May, 5men and 2 women to Broadstairs.

13th May to 27th May, 3 women to Folkestone.

8th July to 15th July, 9 women to Herne Bay.

12th August to 19th August, 9 women to Herne bay.

In connection with the holidays to Herne Bay, this was again following the practice that was implemented last year where the residents were of an infirm type and were accompanied for the period by members of the staff who would not otherwise be able to partake of a summer holiday. This year twice the number of residents are participating in this establishment, Matron having already made arrangements for members of staff, two on each occasion, to accompany the party.

The holidays continued likewise year after year. Encouraging as many of the residents to participate as possible. The residents were becoming more frail and it was difficult to persuade some of them to take advantage of these holidays.

OUTINGS

In 1961 twelve residents were entertained by Rediform Television Sports Club at a party at Unity House.

The summer treat that year was a trip to Eastbourne. Seventy residents went in two coaches, they had the usual packed lunch and tea was provided at Wannock Gardens.

In May and June there were the usual outings to Women's Institutes to Chelsfield, Lancing, Chiddingfold and Ardley.

There was the usual invitation from the City of London's Branch of the British Legion for the Ex-service men to go on the River all day trip. This was a much appreciated trip and was eagerly looked forward to.

Brockle Bank had a 40 seat reservation at the Scala Theatre for a performance of "Brigadoon" from the City of London Branch of the British legion who also arranged transport to and from the Home.

Also from the British Legion, Baltic Exchange Branch, there was an invitation for 20 Ex-service men to attend an Annual Reunion in November. It took place at the Baltic Exchange and took the form of a cabaret with refreshments.

Three residents accompanied by one member of staff attended a Thanksgiving Service at Southwark Cathedral on 11th October. The member of staff was authorised to buy tea and return home by taxi.

In January 1962 a party of 30 residents went to a Pantomime at Wimbledon Theatre, these tickets were donated by the Wandsworth Rotary club. Transport was arranged and refreshments were given in the Theatre.

Also in January the Reverend Shells entertained a party of 25 residents to tea and a concert at St Anne's Church.

In February a party of 20 residents were entertained by St John's Ambulance Cadets to tea followed by a concert, at the Headquarters of the Wandsworth Branch.

In May June and July the residents had their usual outings to the Women's Institutes. These Institutes gave their loyal support each year and the visits were eagerly awaited by the residents.

The steamer trip that the British Legion arranged each year was organised by a Mr Roberts. This year he took some photographs and sent them to the home for the men who went on the trip.

In October the Reverend Shells invited a party of residents to take part in their Harvest Festival Tea. A coach was hired at a cost of £3, this to be met from Canteen funds.

In November a party of 68 residents plus two members of staff, went to see Billy Smarts Circus at Clapham Common, the seats were free. Transport was hired at a cost of £2.10/- this to be met from the Canteen funds.

The Warden reported: -

In Christmas Eve I was given tickets for 20 seats for the Lyric Theatre Hammersmith, transport arranged by the donor. 18 residents and 2 staff attended the performance.

Records do not show the name of the donor.

Twenty-four members of the Darby and Joan Club attended a Christmas Dinner at Wandsworth Town Hall arranged by the W.V.S. Transport was paid for by Canteen funds.

In January 1963 thirty -five residents went to see the Pantomime at the Croydon Theatre arranged by the Wandsworth Old People's Welfare committee costing £10.15/-

By arrangement with the Chief Officer, 15 seats were allocated to Brockle Bank for the Fortune Theatre on 4th July for the afternoon performance. Records do not show what the performance was called.

In April 12 residents attended a concert at Wandsworth Town Hall arranged by the Mayor of Wentworth, tickets were sent from the Wandsworth Old People's Welfare Committee, no charge was made for the tickets.

The Matron reported that with the expected outing to the Women's Institute to Chelsfield in May, it would be for the ninth year running.

There were three outings during July and August, one half-day outing to Newlands Corner, a full day to Brighton with a packed lunch and they were given 2/6d for their tea, they enjoyed choosing their own tea, and a half-day to Runnymede.

The usual invitation was received for the 12 residents for the River trip, from the British Legion and the summer treat trip was to Eastbourne, they had a Ham salad tea at Wannock Gardens.

In October 25 residents went to see a play at the Adelphi Theatre and in November 10 residents went to Billy Smart's Circus, the ticket cost 2/- and the fare was 1/6 to Clapham Common.

The Chief Officer arranged for 30 seats to be donated to Brockle Bank for the Richmond Theatre. Transport was paid for by Canteen funds.

Thirty residents from the "Over 60 Club" were entertained by the W.V.S. on 18th December to a Christmas Dinner and party at Wandsworth Municipal Buildings. Transport paid for from the Canteen funds.

There was a special tea for the blind residents and those from Milton Close, they celebrated with three bottles of Sherry, paid for from the Canteen funds.

Fourteen tickets were donated for the residents to attend the Wimbledon Theatre in January 1964; the arrangements were made by the Wandsworth Rotary Club.

Five "Maghorays" were purchased for the partially sighted residents, cost £3.1.11d.

Following an invitation from Redifon Ltd, Wandsworth, eight residents participated in a day's outing to Margate in September 1964. They were given 8/- each for spending money which was issued from the Canteen funds.

The Matron reported in January 1965: -

Today a party of 19 residents have gone to the Wimbledon Theatre to see a Pantomime. It was extremely difficult to find this small number fit enough to travel. The infirmity and senility of the recently admitted residents has increased over the past months.

ADMINISTRATION

In February 1961 the Home had a visit from Dr Egan from the Public Health Department. There were also 2 students visiting from Birmingham University arranged by the Wandsworth Family Welfare Association, where they were completing a course on Social Welfare.

The Warden and Matron made visits to Supplies Department and Templeton's to choose curtains and carpets for the modernisation of "C" Block.

The Wandsworth Mayor and his wife visited the Home on the 20 March; they spent the whole afternoon going round all the Departments.

On 10 May six visitors from the C.A.B. and the Family Welfare Association were accompanied by Miss Marster on a tour of the Home.

In May Dr Derapisz visited the Home, he was the Medical Rehabilitation Officer from Israel.

It was decided that "C" Block should have three TV sets one for each floor. One other set was bought from Canteen funds.

In September 1961 there were just 341 residents in the Home.

On 30 August Mr Hobbs visited the Home. He was a Director of Queen Victoria Homes, Sydney Australia.

In September the Mass X-ray unit was to visit again for 222 residents to be X-rayed.

On 31 January 1962 Mr Hoshino, a Japanese Social Worker visited the Home, he was from the London School of Economics.

In February the Matron had 7 women trainees (for attendants) arranged through the Old People's Welfare Council.

In June 1962 the Minister of Health accompanied by the Chairman of the Welfare Committee, the Chief Officer, Mr Hughes Young, M.P. and Mr Milree, Principal Regional Officer, Ministry of Health, visited the Home. A tour was made of the building principally of the Modernised sections, including the Handicapped Centre.

Lord Amulrye accompanied by Mr Hutton from the Welfare Department, and three Medical Officers had a tour of the Home.

On 18 July the Open Day was a huge success with the Mayor and Mayoress attending. 250/300 visitors attended, seven staff conducted tours round the establishment. A Band was engaged to play in the grounds which in no small measure added to the occasion. The cost of the Band was 25 Guineas paid for from Canteen Funds.

The Warden reported the suicide of a resident on Tuesday 4 September1962, the resident being Mrs Elizabeth Ray, aged 88 years in "C 2" ward. This resident at a time unknown, placed a plastic bag over her head and was found dead by a member of the night staff. The usual routine of reporting at once to the police was followed resulting in the immediate attendance of the police surgeon. An inquest was held on 6 September, the coroner's verdict being: -

"Asphyxiated by smothering with a plastic bag."

It was decided to purchase three garden tables with sun umbrella's for use in the new gardens of "C" Block, cost £30 paid for from Canteen funds.

In October 1962 Mr Crowley from the Institute of Social Work Birmingham Welfare Department visited the Home also there were 10 pupils (nurses) from St. Benedicts Hospital who visited the Home.

One travelling book trolley was purchased for use in connection with Library Books received on loan from Wandsworth Central Library. The cost £21.5/- was met from Canteen funds.

At Christmas time in 1962 the Warden hoped to engage 2 or 3 musicians to tour the wards.

The winter of 1962/3 was a severe one regarding weather, with smog and heavy snow storms. The Medical Officer reported 49 deaths.

Luxborough Lodge another large Home, was to close. Nineteen residents came to Brockle Bank. This was the first of the exercises, of which the Warden anticipated in the foreseeable future, all in connection with the total evacuation of Luxborough Lodge.

In September 1963 five Swedish Social Workers visited the Home. Also the Vice President of Government Benevolent Association, Columbo, toured the Home.

Eleven healthy men and women were transferred to a new small Home recently opened at Ladywell, this Home now being known as Willowmere. A further nine residents were transferred to Fulham Road in connection with the Luxborough Lodge closure.

The Warden reported: -

Doctor D.H.Alexander resigned on 31st March 1964. I should like to record my appreciation of the interest that he has shown in the old people during his term of office. The many calls that have been made on his services have always been met with instant response and he has dealt with many matters that has made administration in this establishment more efficient for his attention.

The Handicapped Centre was to be used by the Multiple Sclerosis Society once a month every fourth Wednesday evening.

The Warden reported: -

I can report to the committee that the work in connection with the extension to the Chalet is proceeding and I am quite sure that when finally completed it will be a considerable improvement. I understand that I am to be allowed carpets for the extension also a carpet for the existing large lounge.

Improvements due during the year 1964. Improvements to the Optician's Room, a Hoist to be fitted to first floor "D" Block for food, a Ramp from "C" Block to the Matron's Stores, and Cupboards to be fitted under the stairs in "D" Block.

The Warden reported that the clothing given away to male residents would be replaced by new stock cost £119.0.4d. A large majority of the clothing was for residents being transferred to small Homes.

The Warden reported: -

I am happy to report to the Committee that Dr Welbourne has been appointed visiting Medical Officer here at Brockle Bank. The Committee will of course know that Dr Welbourne was Dr Alexander's partner for many years and in that capacity regularly visited the Home as visiting Medical Officer and was well known by all the old people and members of the staff. I think I am right in saying that everybody was appreciative of the appointment.

I have been notified by the Chief Officer of the opening of two small Homes in the Greenwich and Lewisham districts and have been asked to submit 25 names for transfers.

Report from Dr Welbourne: -

It was interesting to look back at the old reports to see how far we have advanced since that time from the rather depressing conditions of a very old building to the very comfortable furnishing and bright modern décor of the Home at the present time, which must contribute so much to the morale of the residents. We have recently been considering the number of residents who might benefit from the service of a Physiotherapist and found that there is a large number who would benefit from skilled and regular exercise in walking.

Twenty -six residents were transferred to other Homes during the summer of 1964.

In July 1964 a visit was made on the Matron's invitation to several members of the Women's Institute at Lancing. They were entertained to tea and had a tour of the Home.

Two Social Science Students from Amsterdam visited the Home on August 4 1964.

In 1965 31 residents were transferred to other Homes.

The Warden reported: -

I have to report that I have purchased from Supplies Department on 4 occasions oranges and bananas for all the residents. I am not yet in receipt of a charge note for this fruit but when it is received it is proposed to defray the cost from Canteen profits.

The Matron reported:-

That the degree of infirmity was becoming very acute among the residents. The situation is coped with under great difficulties due to the type of staff that she was able to recruit.

Estimate for the year 1965/6 of Brockle Bank Home for old people.

Contributions by Residents etc.	*£81,250*
Maintenance Payments by other Local Authorities	*45,730*
Payment for Meals etc,	*1,045*
Canteen Sales	*1,800*
Industry Sales (laundry)	*12,390*
Other Income	*140*
	=======
	£142,355
	=======

Estimated cost for the Brockle Bank Rehabilitation Centre.

Wages	*£260*
Fuel Gas etc,	*90*
Equipment	*300*
Rates	*50*
Provisions	*550*
Miscellaneous Expenses	*25*
	=====
	£1,275
	=====

£1 million Social Development Plan

Wandsworth Council Plan by 1972 completely to demolish Brockle Bank the former "Workhouse" in Swaffield Road and build on the site a comprehensive £1 million Social Development Plan with a community day centre for old people, children's home, health and physically handicapped centre, central kitchen for the meals on wheels service, central laundry for all the borough's homes, some housing and a small open space.

To deal with problems which overlap between one committee and another, the Council has formed a co-ordinating committee which has, in effect, instructed the borough architect to draw up a plan along these lines after each committee has submitted to him their requirements.

Most of the site, however, will be used by the Welfare Committee because it is under their control.

Alderman John Parker, chairman of the Welfare Committee, emphasized that the borough architect may not be able to get all the council's requirements on the site. In his opinion and without expert advice, he thought the cost might amount to £1 million.

WRONG TYPE OF PLACE

He told Wandsworth Ratepayers' Association on Monday that the Council had found Brockle Bank was not the right type of place to house old people, who should be living in small, all-purpose homes with accommodation for about fifty. At present Brockle Bank housed 460 people, of which 130 places had been set aside for Hammersmith Council, which met a proportional share of the outgoings.

It was intended gradually to demolish Brockle Bank by 1972 and a very large site would be left because there was at present a lot of wasted space. The Council planned to use the whole space to advantage and members of the Welfare, Health, Children's and Housing Committees were endeavouring to tackle the problem of how best to use it.

7th May 1965.
Wandsworth Borough News.

Brocklebank Health Centre in Garratt Lane

Earlsfield House, formerly The Intermediate Schools

PROPOSED REDEVELOPMENT - 4 November 1966

The buildings forming the Corporation's old people's welfare establishment known as "Brocklebank" at Swaffield Road, Earlsfield, are now approaching the end of their useful life and it is approved Council policy to replace them by building new homes for old people on alternative sites. The proposed closure of the establishment will provide the Council with an opportunity to plan for the comprehensive redevelopment of the Brocklebank site for the social services generally and charged as we are with the duty of co-ordinating these services we have therefore given our attention to the subject.

The principal group of buildings at Brocklebank consists of seven large institutional blocks used as a home for some 472 old people, the majority of whom are infirm, together with ancillary office and storage accommodation. There is also a boiler house and laundry which not only caters for the laundry requirements of this and a number of other Corporation establishments, but provides a service for some other London Borough Councils, the recently built residential home for blind people called "Milton Close" and an old hostel building for men which, unlike the rest of the property in the Brocklebank complex in the Corporation's ownership, became vested in the Greater London Council when reorganisation came into effect in April 1965.

The northern boundary of Brocklebank fronts on to Swaffield Road and the property is bounded on the east by 2-storeyed terraced housing in Brocklebank Road, on the south by further terraced housing in Wilna Road adjoined by some temporary bungalow sites in the GLCs ownership, and on the west by terraced housing and a builder's yard in Atheldene Road. All this housing was built at the turn of the century and whilst its structural condition is reasonable, having regard to its age, the houses in Wilna and Atheldene Roads in particular are outmoded with limited amenity space to the front and rear. Further to the west lies a pocket of property sandwiched between Atheldene Road and Garratt Lane; more terraced housing; the Anchor Mission, with local shops on either side fronting the main road, together with some miscellaneous commercial premises at the rear.

Accordingly, we propose that, in planning the redevelopment of Brocklebank, the Council should seek to extend the site westwards to Garratt Lane and southwards to Wilna Road taking in the four TLC temporary bungalow sites at the junction of Atheldene Road, Wilma Road and Winfrith Road and closing the northern stretch of Atheldene Road and a portion of Wilna Road. The Corporation owns three houses in Atheldene Road and although negotiations have commenced for the purchase of a few others, it is unlikely that all the properties needed can be acquired by private treaty and, with the multiplicity of interests involved, it will clearly be necessary to seek powers of compulsory purchase. The GLC has already agreed to the transfer of the temporary bungalow sites to the Corporation; and we understand from informal discussions between the officers of the two authorities that the site of the men's hostel could be included in the redevelopment scheme, provided satisfactory arrangements can be made to locate a new hostel elsewhere on the site, or even in the rear vicinity.

We also propose that the enlarged site, which will be some 17½ acres in extent, be redeveloped by the provision of: -

Two 50-bed old people's homes;
a day centre for the elderly;
a centre for the physically handicapped to replace the present centre at
Brocklebank;
a health clinic and school treatment centre to meet the needs of the school and
maternity services in the area;
a day nursery;
an industrial training centre for the mental health service;
an alternative site for the GLC's men's hostel;
a number of shops; and
as much general housing as the remainder of the site will allow.

We at first considered the inclusion in the redevelopment scheme of a large central kitchen for the meals-on-wheels service, but there are no particular reasons which dictate that this user should be located here and it could with equal advantage be sited elsewhere in the locality and within an area zoned specifically for industry. Similarly, it will be necessary to replace the existing laundry at Brocklebank, but we have agreed that this should be located in an area zoned for industry and we report upon this matter separately.

The Borough Architect has submitted to us a preliminary sketch layout to illustrate how it would be possible to provide on the enlarged Brocklebank site for the various establishments to which we have referred. Generally, this allows for the retention of Milton Close, the residential home for the blind, the provision of the industrial training centre near to the site of the existing men's hostel, and the location on the Garratt Lane frontage of a small shopping complex and health clinic, the new hostel for men, and a centre for physically handicapped all forming something of a buffer between the main road and the main residential content of the scheme. The phasing and completion of the development is initially dependent on the provision of alternative premises for the present users of Brocklebank, but we hope that, subject to the Council being enabled to acquire the additional lands needed to implement the scheme, Brocklebank as it exists today will have finally closed down by 1972. The Welfare Committee have already approved the general requirements of the two old people's homes which will comprise the first phase of the scheme and work has commenced on the preparation of detailed plans. The detailed planning of other buildings will be left to the other user committees concerned and full reports, including a financial appraisal and the priority which we suggest the various projected establishments be afforded in the Council's general development programme, will be submitted to the Council in due course. In the meantime,

WE RECOMMEND -

(a) that the proposed redevelopment in the manner we have outlined, of the site of the "Brocklebank" welfare establishment, enlarged by the acquisition of certain additional lands, be approved; and

(b) that an order be made under Part V of the Housing Act 1957 for the compulsory purchase of the following properties -

Atheldene Road	Nos. 48/48A: 54/54A-72/72A: 74: 76/76A-96/96A: 100/100A-118/118A and 120 (even)
	Nos. 95-171 (odd)
Brocklebank Road	No.88
Garratt Lane	Nos. 231-255 (including yard and premises at rear): 263 and 273 (Anchor Mission Hall) to 305 (odd)
Wilna Road	Nos. 2-78: 102/102A-110/110A (even)
Wilna Yard	"The Cottage" and land occupied by garages.

and more particularly shewn within a red verge on the map marked "London Borough of Wandsworth (Atheldene Road) Compulsory Purchase Order 1966" and that the Town Clerk be instructed to submit such order to the Minister of Housing and Local Government for confirmation.

Par.2. Central Laundry. As reported in the preceding paragraph early plans need to be made to replace the existing laundry if the redevelopment of Brocklebank is to proceed with expedition.

When the Council took over Brocklebank in April 1965, the laundry was running at a capacity of almost 18,500 articles per week, of which almost 12,000 were for other London boroughs. This position has largely continued but, with the increasing difficulty of obtaining suitable private laundries to undertake other laundry work for the Council, the Supplies Officer has arranged for the Brocklebank laundry to do work for other welfare and children's establishments. The laundry has a capacity to handle the present volume of work but most of the plant is old and there are risks of major breakdowns.

The officers have examined the total amount of laundry work which is likely to be required by the Corporation in 1975. We have accepted their conclusion that the laundry work for all Council services and establishments in the Borough (welfare, children, health, baths, etc.) and for the large children's home at Beechholme, Banstead (the estimated total of all these is to be about 38,000 articles per week) could best be undertaken at a central laundry operated by the Corporation; and that it would continue to be more advantageous for the children's and welfare establishments at Woking, Crawley and Broadstairs, and probably Cobham, to continue to be undertaken by local contract laundries We also consider that any new central laundry built by the Council should include, on grounds of efficient working, a small disinfecting and personal cleansing station. Such additional facility will be required if and when the complex of baths and other buildings at Latchmere (which includes a disinfecting station) are to be demolished.

An industrial establishment of this nature ought to be located in an area specifically zoned for the purpose. We have in mind an industrially zoned site in Kimber Road, part of which is already owned by the Corporation and held for housing purposes, but before making recommendations to the Council as to the extent of the site required, we have decided to seek specialist advice on the briefing requirements, layout, equipment, and organisation of a central laundry. In the meantime,

WE RECOMMEND -

(a) That the proposed establishment on a site in Kimber Road of a central laundry to meet the Corporation's own requirements for this service, including a disinfecting station, be approved in principle, subject to further detailed investigation;

(b) that the action we have taken in appointing L.A.Edwards & Partners to advise on laundry requirements, at fees in accordance with the appropriate professional scale, be approved and confirmed; and

(c) that the development and management of the proposed central laundry establishment be placed within the terms of reference of the Baths, Cemeteries and Parks Committee and that its management be made the responsibility of the General Baths Superintendent.

BROCKLE BANK SCHEME PUBLIC ENQUIRY

Last November, Wandsworth Council approved outline proposals for the closure of it's welfare establishment, Brockle Bank, Swaffield Road, Earlsfield, the acquisition of some properties in Wilna Road, Atheldene Road, and Garratt Lane, and the clearance and redevelopment of the whole site by the erection of new housing and ancillary social service establishments.

The Council made a compulsory purchase order under Part V of the Housing Act 1957 for the additional properties which it needs for the scheme. These consist of terraced houses, some local shops, the Anchor Mission premises and some miscellaneous premises between Garratt Lane and Atheldene Road.

The Order was submitted to the Minister of Housing and Local Government for confirmation; and the Minister has now announced that, following objections received, he has arranged for a Public Local Inquiry to be held by his inspector Mr R.St.G. Whelan, at Municipal Buildings, on Tuesday, October 31st at 10.30 a.m.

1966.
Wandsworth Borough News

The Annual cost of running the service for the blind Braille Library books was £10. for Brockle Bank. Welfare Authorities contribute at the rate of £3. per reader, with 115 residents registered blind people in the borough the cost of continuing this grant was estimated to be £345 in the current financial year.

The South East Regional Association for the Deaf which also received from the L.C.C., has among its objects the promotion of the welfare of all persons suffering from defective hearing. The Association applied for an annual grant towards its management expenses and has suggested a subscription at the rate of 6d per 1000 of the population. This would amount to £8.5/-.

The Warden reported: -

The Orpheus Payers a Battersea Dramatic Society, presented a performance of "Sailor Beware" at the Battersea Town Hall on Weds 16th June 1965 for the elderly and handicapped people of the borough and we agreed to meet certain expenses in connection with the show, up to a limit of £25.

The Battersea and Wandsworth Metropolitan Borough councils had a contract with Henry Smith (Battersea) Ltd for carrying out funerals and these contracts are continuing in force for the time being pending a review later in the year. Meanwhile the contractor has applied for the scale of charges, which has been in force since 1958, to be revised as set out below. (The present rates are in parenthesis):-

Age of deceased person	Charge for Coffin	Charge for Hearse or Limousine For child
Still born	£1.10/- (17/6)	£2.- (£1.-)
Under 1 month	£1.18.6. (1.12.6.)	£2.- (£2)
1 month to under 5 years	£4.11.6. (3.17.6.)	£3.12.6. (£3.0.6.)
5 and under 10 years	£6.4.0. (£5.5.6.)	£4.18.6. (£4.1.6.)
10 years and over as:- As adult	£8.16.6. (£7.16/-)	£5.13/- (£4.13/-)
Prior removal to private chapel, when required		£1.19.6. (£1.12.6.)
Conveyance for Mourners		£2.15/- (£2.5/-)

We recommend :- That the revised scale of charges requested by the contractor be approved and adopted.

WELFARE COMMITTEE
Estimates for the Year ending 31st March 1966

	EXPENDITURE	1965-66 ESTIMATE		INCOME	1965-66 ESTIMATE	
	Brocklebank large home for old people			Brocklebank large home for old people		
1	Salaries & wages	141,560		Contributions by Residents, &c	81,250	
2	Superannuation	1,700		Maintenance Payments by other Local Authorities	45,730	
3	Repairs & Maintenance	17,790		Payments for Meals, &c.	1,045	
4	Specified Works	3,500		Canteen Sales	1,800	
5	Fuel	11,000		Industry Sales (Laundry)	12,390	
6	Gas, Electricity & Water	6,700		Other Income	140	
7	Furniture, Equipment & Materials	7,210				
8	Rates	5,000				
9	Provisions	28,500				
10	Clothing & Uniforms	5,825				
11	Laundry	1,500				
12	Hired Services	300				
13	Transport & Travelling Expenses	600				
14	Telephones, Miscellaneous Expenses	400				
15	Canteen Stocks	1,750				
16	Christmas Extras	500				
17	Flowers & Garden	600				
18	Funerals	400				
19	Haircutting, Chiropody	450				
20	Handicrafts	150				
21	Holidays	910				
22	Newspapers	360				
23	Outings & Entertainments	500				
24	Rewards	700				
25	Sweets	600				
26	Tobacco	2,000				
27	Sundries	200				
28	Loan Charges	5,980				
		TOTAL	246,685		TOTAL	142,355

The laundry had an annual turnover of approximately 981,000 articles, 547,000 of which are from eight other London Boroughs from the National Assistance Board (Camberwell Reception Centre and from the G.L.C. Wandsworth Hostel). The laundry charges were last reviewed by the L.C.C. in December 1964 and were based on the average costs known at that time for its large laundries in London. The costs at Brockle Bank were known to be higher than average, partly because of external cartage costs and we have approved in the charges from £2.1.8. To the known rate of £2.5.10d per 100 articles as from 1 April 1965. The estimated additional income in the current financial year would be £1,100.

Arrangements were approved for accommodation and facilities at Brockle Bank Rehabilitation Centre to be made available free of charge on Saturday afternoons for a weekly meeting of a club for blind people. The club organizer Mr C.H.Juden of 67 Rogers Road, Tooting has had considerable experience of running such clubs and we feel sure this club will meet and be of benefit to blind people in the Borough.

The Christmas Party for the blind and physically handicapped people in the borough will be held in 5 or 6 separate venues including the Rehabilitation Centre at Brockle Bank. It was for a traditional meal and entertainment and was not expected to cost more than a £1 a head.

Wandsworth Old Folks Trust - As a matter of urgency we have approved a grant of £900, the amount provided in the budget, to the Wandsworth Old Folks Trust to meet expenses in respect of their holiday scheme for elderly people.

November 1965 Christmas Festivities - The Committee were pleased to report that that they had approved arrangements for Christmas Festivities at the Corporation's old peoples Homes. The Homes will be suitably decorated and Christmas Trees will be provided; entertainments had been organised and special menus prepared for both Christmas Day and Boxing Day. The old people for whom the Corporation is responsible in establishments administered by voluntary societies or other local authorities will also enjoy extra fare. The estimated cost was £875 equivalent to approximately £1 per person.

The Handicrafts Exhibition January 1966 -The Committee were pleased to report that in the annual Handicrafts Exhibition recently arranged by the Central Council for the Disabled, which was open to handicapped persons throughout the country, 10 items were submitted made by handicapped residents of the borough who attend the Centre at Brockle Bank and 4 certificates of merit, together with a small cash prize were awarded for articles gaining more than 80% of the possible marks.

Bed Control Service April 1967 - Since the reorganisation of London Government in April 1965 a bed control service has operated for inter-borough mutual aid so that, in cases of emergency, old persons in need of care can be admitted without delay to certain welfare homes situated throughout the London area. This service is operated by the London Borough of Camden and under its provisions, persons normally resident in one borough may be accommodated as a matter of urgency in a home in another borough.

This service operates entirely separately from the "sharing arrangements" for the accommodation of old persons of Brockle Bank which exists between the Council and the London Borough of Hammersmith in consequence of the London Government Act 1963.

When it was inaugurated it was envisaged that the bed control service could continue until April 1967 when its working would be reviewed by a Working Party of the London Boroughs' Association in the light of the then existing situation and needs. This initial period has now almost expired and accordingly the Council has been asked for its observations on the need for he continuation of the service.

We have therefore reviewed the work of the service having regard to Wandsworth's known existing and possible future needs for emergency accommodation. We find that although advantage was taken of these facilities to secure the urgent accommodation of Wandsworth residents, the need to make demands on the service has slackened in recent months.

The re-arrangement of accommodation at Brockle Bank which has been brought about by the decanting of old people into another home recently opened within the borough will further improve these conditions and as a result we believe that in future Wandsworth would have had little or no call to use the bed control service.

In addition to this aspect we are mindful of the fact that the accommodation of "Wandsworth" residents in need of care and attention is the Council's direct responsibility under the National Assistance Act 1948 and that this being so it would accept that it has the prime duty to make its own provisions for borough residents. Coupled with this is our belief that it is not always in the best interests of an old person to be accommodated in a home in another borough away from his family and friends.

For these reasons we have come to the conclusion that the continuance of the bed control service is unnecessary and propose that Wandsworth should not continue to use it beyond the 1st April 1967.

WE RECOMMEND - That the London Boroughs' Association be informed that the Council does not consider that the bed control service should continue to operate beyond 1st April 1967 and that as from that date Wandsworth will not participate in this arrangement.

Mr Sticklan, the Warden, retired in July 1967.

July 1967. The Scheme for the Replacement of Brockle Bank as an old people's Home was proceeding and with the retirement of the resident Matron and Warden there, we have arrangements of their deputies, the residents assistant Matron and Assistant Warden to undertake the duties of the principal posts. They will hold these temporary posts in an acting capacity at existing salaries, but with a special responsibility allowance of £200 in each case, the post of Assistant Warden being deleted now in view of the steps being taken to close the home.

The Council was acquiring from the Greater London Council a site in Atheldene Road which has hitherto been occupied by temporary bungalows, for redeveloping as an old people's Home as part of the Brockle Bank Redevelopment Scheme. It is necessary to protect the site with fencing and the following two tenders have been received in response to invitations extended to 4 specialist contractors for the erection of approximately 500 yards of 7ft corrugated iron fencing.

Modern Rustics Co Ltd, Mitcham	*£1533.-*
Verdale Fencing Co Ltd, S.E.16	*£1899.-*

The cost of the work, which the Borough Architect estimated at £1500, will form part of the capital cost of the redevelopment and we have asked the Finance Committee to submit an estimate.

We recommend that the tender of £1533 of Modern Rustics Co Ltd, for this work be accepted.

Swimming Pool, May 1967 - Some years ago the former LCC purchased small plastic swimming pool and filtration plant and installed it on land in Swaffield Road for use by children from the nearby Earlsfield House Children's home. Now, due mainly to the fact that the children at the home prefer to use the nearby public swimming bath, little or no use is being made of this pool and it is therefore surplus to requirements.

Although advertised for sale only one offer for the pool and equipment was received and that came from Anerley School for maladjusted boys who, due to lack of funds, could only proffer the sum of £50 and undertake the removal of the pool and the reinstatement of the land afterwards.

This school accommodates 40 boys aged from 9 - 15 years who for some time have been endeavouring to provide a pool by their own communal efforts. Through lack of outside support the momentum of these efforts has slackened and the headmaster, anxious that the project shall not fail has applied to purchase the surplus pool with the only monies available.

As we know that the Council would wish to support the boys' endeavours we suggest that it would be a generous gesture to promote by offering the school the pool and equipment free of charge provided that clearance and site reinstatement is carried out under the direction of and to the satisfaction of, the Council's officers. Therefore on the understanding that no liability whatsoever devolves upon the Council.

WE RECOMMEND - That the pool and ancillary filtration plant surplus to the requirements of the Council's Earlsfield House children's home be offered, free of charge, to Anerley School subject to compliance with the aforementioned conditions.

Health Centre - The Minister of Health on 21st April 1967 issued Circular 7/67which gave advice and guidance to local health authorities on the provision of health clinics. This Circular also referred to the upsurge of interest in the provision of comprehensive health centres, which are premises established in accordance with Section 21 of the National Health Service Act 1946, to provide local authority health services plus facilities for Executive Council services, namely, the general medical practitioners, and the dental and pharmaceutical services.

Where a local authority provides accommodation in one of its health centres for the use of general practitioners, it is the approved Ministry arrangement for the accommodation to be leased on economic terms to the Executive Council of the National Health Service who in turn make it available to general practitioners.

We are of the view that where the Council is satisfied that there is a genuine desire of doctors to practise in one of the Corporation's local health centres it should provide wherever appropriate suitable accommodation and facilities for them to do so.

After protracted negotiation, the Corporation has been notified by the Inner London Executive Council that two partnerships (one of four doctors and one of two doctors) and two further doctors practising independently would practise from the proposed local health centre which is to be provided in the Brocklebank scheme. In the circumstances,

WE RECOMMEND - That the specification for the proposed Brocklebank Health Centre be extended to include six consulting rooms and ancillary facilities for general practitioners provided that the Inner London Executive Council gives a formal undertaking to take a lease, on terms to be agreed, for a period of not less than 21 years.

By September 1967 it was proposed that there would be 234 dwellings on the Brockle Bank site, which was amended to 227 later on.

Report of the Consulting Engineer - January 1968.

Although work on the housing element of the Brockle Bank Scheme is not scheduled to start until 1970 the first stage in the redevelopment of this site, comprising of a 50 bed residential old peoples Home for the Welfare Service, is due to commence next year.

The Borough Architect considers that the point has therefore been reached in the planning of the overall scheme for the appointment of a Consulting Engineer to deal with soil investigation and advise on foundations.

Action Taken *- In accordance with the authority delegated to him by the Council, the Town Clerk is now in the process of purchasing the following interests in properties required for approved redevelopment schemes upon the terms recently agreed on its behalf by either the District Valuer or Messrs J R Eve & Son, that is, for a total sum of "275,778 plus the vendors' legal costs and surveyors fees (wherever applicable): -*

Property (and scheme concerned) **Brocklebank Scheme, Earlsfield**	Interest
62/62A Atheldene Road	*Freehold*
32 and 71-77 (odd) Atheldene Road	*Freehold*
19 & 21 and 80-88 (even) Wilna Road	*Freehold*
43-51 (odd) Winfrith Road	*Freehold*
84 Atheldene Road	*Freehold*
86 Atheldene Road	*Freehold*
110/110A Atheldene Road	*Freehold*
101-107 (odd) Atheldene Road	*Freehold*

Action Taken *- In accordance with the authority delegated to him by the Council, the Town Clerk is now in the process of purchasing the following interests in properties required for approved redevelopment schemes upon the terms recently agreed on its behalf by either the District Valuer or Messrs J R Eve & Son, that is, for a total sum of £182,250, plus the vendors' legal costs and surveyors' fees (wherever applicable): -*

Property (and scheme concerned) **Brocklebank Scheme, Earlsfield**	Interest
54, 56, 58, 64-70 (even) Atheldene Road	*Freehold*
60/60A Atheldene Road	*Freehold*
86A Atheldene Road	*Freehold*
95/99 (odd) Atheldene Road	*Freehold*

117, 119 and 121 Atheldene Road	*Freehold*
137-143 and 149-159 (odd) Atheldene Road	*Freehold*
88 Brocklebank Road and 12-16 (even)	*Freehold*
Wilna Road	*Freehold*
283-289 (odd) Garratt Lane	*Freehold*
293 Garratt Lane	*Freehold*

Brocklebank (No.1) Home, 26 February 1968 - *Part of the Brocklebank site, formerly occupied by 'A' block and having an area of 0.75 acres, has been set aside for the erection of a new 51 bed old people's home and we have now had before us sketch designs prepared by the Borough Architect for this development.*

The vacant site is situated at the south-eastern corner of the Brocklebank complex and is at present bounded to the east by the rear gardens and properties in Brocklebank Road, to the south by the gardens and property in Wilna Road, and to the west by buildings which will form part of the existing large old people's home. Eventually the home to be built on the site will form an integral part of the overall development of the Brocklebank site and in due course will be surrounded by predominantly 2-storey housing development.

The home will, in the main, be a two and three-storey brick-built flat roofed structure of a roughly cross shaped design and its eternal elevations will be designed complimentary to those of the housing redevelopment and will be finished in coloured facing bricks. The home will provide forty-three single bedrooms and four double bedrooms, accommodation for a matron, her assistant and other staff, four communal living rooms, together with an entrance hall, cloakrooms, communal dining room, kitchen, toilets, bathrooms, laundry rooms, utility and store rooms.

The residential accommodation for old people will be provided in the two 2-storey wings. A single storey wing will contain a dining room and kitchen and this wing will be directly linked with the 3-storey section providing circulating space, staff quarters and the additional ancillary services necessary to support the residents. The basic components of the residential wings will be four small suites each with one double bedroom and ten to twelve single bedrooms, a communal sitting-room, casual sitting-out space for the old people and usual toilet and bathroom facilities.

The area immediately surrounding the home will be landscaped and the main garden space which the old people will be able to enjoy will be concentrated on the southern side of the home. Garages and parking space, the garden store and refuse rooms will be located on the other side of the home. A service road will lead to the single storey wing containing the dining room and kitchen facilities and will also serve the garage and parking space and refuse storage.

The fittings and equipment installed in the home will be to the Council's usual high standard and will be selected with the needs of the old people in mind. Rooms will be heated individually by means of manually controlled radiators and it was intended that the source of this heating should be a central boiler-house designed ultimately to serve the whole of the redevelopment scheme. However we propose that this principle should be given further thought and we have therefore given the architect the necessary instructions upon the matter in so far as it concerns the old people's home.

Brocklebank (Stage 1 - Phase 1) Site, Earlsfield - Detailed Scheme -We have examined the detailed scheme for the redevelopment of the Brocklebank (Stage 1 - Phase 1) site, SW18 (Earlsfield) which has been prepared by the Director of Development.

This detailed scheme, which accords with the outline scheme for the whole site already approved by us, deals with the first part of the site available for housing redevelopment. This part is situated in the northern corner of the larger site. It is vacant land, about two acres in extent, which is already in the ownership of the Corporation. This first phase is included in the approved housing building programme and building works are planned to commence in June 1971.

It is proposed to erect 42 one-bedroom flats in three 3-storey groups and 14 three and four bedroomed 2-storey houses, in the following proportions: -

Type of Dwelling	Total
1-bedroom flat (2 persons)	42
3-bedroom house (5 persons)	12
4-bedroom house (6 persons)	2
Grand Total	56 dwellings

The blocks of flats will be built on the eastern part of this section of the site and the houses in two terraced rows will be erected to the west. The main vehicular and pedestrian access to the redevelopment will be by means of a new service road leading from Swaffield Road and pedestrian access to all dwellings will be segregated from vehicular traffic. All the dwellings will be constructed in load bearing brickwork on normal concrete strip foundations. Elevations will be of an attractively textured light coloured facing brick and the houses will have pitched tiled roofs. The internal planning, fixtures and fittings in all these dwellings will be to the Corporation's usual high standard. Space heating will be by means of gas warm air heaters and domestic hot water will be supplied by electric immersion heaters. There will be ample storage space and refuse disposal will be by means of individual containers.

All the houses will have individual rear gardens and the remainder of the surrounds will be pleasantly landscaped, with the considerable number of mature trees on site being retained. There will also be a play area and adequate facilities will be provided for car parking by means of garages and open parking bays.

The total costs of all these works, including site acquisition costs, staff salaries, professional fees and all other incidental expenditure, is estimated to amount to £336,160.

The Planning Committee have concurred and we have asked the Finance Committee to submit a covering estimate.

WE RECOMMEND - That the detailed proposals we have described for the redevelopment of the Brocklebank (Stage 1 - Phase 1) site be approved.

Petition - A petition signed by twenty-four occupiers of properties in the locality of the Brocklebank site, SW18 (Earlsfield) was presented by Councillor Ballantine to the Council at its last meeting.

The petition complained about the condition of that part of the site already demolished and claimed that, for a year or two, residents have had to put up with the dumping of filth and the vandalism which the site has encouraged. It stated that the filth remained a breeding place for rats and was a menace to public health, and demanded that immediate action should be taken to remedy this state of affairs. In addition, the petition strongly protested at the manner in which demolition works were being carried out and the dangerous condition of the pathway due to debris and damage to the pavement. It pointed out that the pathway leading from Atheldene Road to Wilna Road was a source of danger and suggested that the existing fence be replaced with chain-link fencing so that persons using the pathway could be seen from the adjoining roads.

After carefully considering reports by the officers on the problems associated with the demolition of properties and the clearance of redevelopment sites, we have come to the conclusion that, unfortunately, it is not possible to secure the clearance of a site as large as this without some undesirable disturbance in the locality. The work involved inevitably gives rise to a certain amount of dust and untidiness, and there are difficulties preventing effective action against the offenders concerned in unlawful dumping.

The petitioners have been informed of this but have also been assured (a) that the officers will redouble their efforts to prevent the dumping of rubbish on this site and will give special attention to street cleansing in the area; (b) that houses awaiting demolition will be kept secured in an attempt to prevent vandalism; (c) that the Medical Officer of Health will continue to keep the site under surveillance to ensure that the conditions do not give rise to rat infestation or to any other public health nuisance; and (d) that the existing fencing to the pathway leading from Atheldene Road to Wilna Road will be replaced with chain-link fencing, where necessary, to ensure that persons using the pathway can be seen from either Atheldene Road or Wilna Road.

Brocklebank (No.2 Home) Sketch Designs - The Housing Committee are reporting upon the overall proposals for the redevelopment of the Brocklebank site (Earlsfield) by the construction of low rise housing and a number of social service establishments. Among the latter are two 51-bed old people's homes. One of these is nearing completion and we have now had before us sketch designs for the other home prepared by the Director of Development.

The site reserved for this second old people's home is about an acre and lies on the south side of the development site and straddles a part of Wilna Road, which is to be closed. It is bounded on the east by Winfrith Road, on the west by Atheldene Road, on the north and south by the residential properties in Atheldene and Winfrith Roads. Those on the northern boundary are to be demolished to make way for new houses included in the second phase of the housing element of this redevelopment scheme.

The home will be a 2 and 3 storey brick-built, flat roofed structure planned roughly in the shape of a cross with its external elevations finished in light brown stock bricks. The home will contain forty-three single bedrooms and four double bedrooms, accommodation for a matron, her assistant and other staff, four communal sitting rooms together with an entrance hall, cloakrooms, communal dining room, kitchen, toilets, bathrooms, laundry rooms, utility and store rooms.

The residential accommodation for old people will be provided in the two 2-storey wings. A single storey wing will contain a dining room and kitchen and this wing will be directly linked with the 3-storey section providing circulating space, staff quarters and the additional ancillary services necessary to support the residents. The basic components of the residential wings will be four small suites each with one double bedroom and ten to twelve single bedrooms, a communal sitting room, casual sitting-out space for the old people and the usual toilet and bathroom facilities.

The area immediately surrounding the home will be suitably landscaped, grassed and planted with trees and shrubs. Parking space, the garden store and refuse rooms will be located on the eastern side of the home. A service road will lead to the single storey wing containing the dining room and kitchen facilities and will also serve the garage and parking space and refuse storage.

The fittings and equipment to be installed in the home will be to the Council's usual high standard and will be selected with the needs of the future residents in mind.

The question of heating for all buildings in the Brocklebank complex, including this home, is to be the subject of a future report by the Director of Development.

Brocklebank Site, Earlsfield, Anchor Mission - In October 1968, we reported that the Minister of Housing and Local Government had decided to confirm with modification the Council's Atheldene Road Order, which included the premises of the Anchor Mission, 273 Garratt Lane.

We have now had an opportunity of considering whether the compulsory powers granted to the Council to purchase this property should, in fact, be invoked. In order to meet objections of the owners at the public local Inquiry into the making of this Order, the Council gave an undertaking that, if the existing Mission Hall premises were required for the Council's Brocklebank Scheme, other accommodation for the Mission would be provided within the scheme; and the Minister, in confirming this Order, agreed that this should be done. Whilst no compensation has yet been negotiated, the District Valuer is in no doubt that the costs of relocation would be very substantial; and the Borough Architect is of the view that he could design a scheme of redevelopment with the exclusion of the Mission. Our Chairman has met representatives of the Mission and they are happy for their premises to be left undisturbed.

In all these circumstances, we have decided that the Council should not operate its Order powers in relation to these Mission premises. We have, however, agreed to bear in mind the request of the Mission's representatives that, in planning the new estate, the Council should try and afford some means of vehicular access to the rear of the Mission premises;' and that persons using the Mission should be permitted to use any spare parking space that may eventually be provided nearby on the new estate.

WE RECOMMEND - That the action we have taken in this matter be approved and confirmed.

Redevelopment of part of Brockle Bank site as a Home for 51 people, development and erection including fees and salaries was estimated at £150,000,

Furniture and Furnishings equipment not included   £9,200.-
Demolition Works.

The four following tenders have been received in response to invitations extended to four specialist contractors for the work of demolishing buildings at Brockle Bank.

Contractor	Tender
J.E.Walkley Ltd	£ 485.-
T.A.King Ltd	£ 492.10/-
R.Ashton and Sons (Stoke Newington Ltd)	£ 944.-
Charles Griffiths Ltd	£1173.-

We recommend that the tender of J.E.Walkley Ltd for £485.- the lowest received for this work be accepted.

In January 1969 the Wandsworth Hostel (Casual Wards) to be included in the demolition of Brockle Bank.

A further rise in laundry prices took the price of an item to 10 ½.d.

By March 1970 a substantial part of Brockle Bank was closed.

By May 1970 the first of the new 51 bed old people's Homes, which are to be provided as part of the Brockle Bank Redevelopment Scheme, was nearing completion. It was hoped to commence work on the second Home in March 1971.

***Brocklebank Site, Earlsfield - Outline Scheme - May 1970** - We have examined an outline scheme prepared by the Director of Development illustrating his proposals for the comprehensive redevelopment of the Brocklebank site, SW18 (Earlsfield).*

In 1966, the Council agreed that Brocklebank, the large institutional building, situated in Swaffield Road and formerly owned by the LCC, should be replaced by more modern and smaller homes; and that the site, together with adjoining land, should be redeveloped comprehensively. The target date given for the closing down of Brocklebank was 1972 and considerable progress has already been made to achieve this. The Council then decided that provision should be made in the redevelopment for a number of social service establishments, plus as much general housing as the remainder of the site would permit. It was also accepted that the existing home for the blind, Milton Close, and the children's home, Earlsfield House, should be retained and incorporated within the redevelopment.

The entire site is about 16½ acres in extent and is situated on the eastern side of Garratt Lane and is generally bounded by Brocklebank Road, Swaffield Road and Wilna Road. It includes Brocklebank; the site of the former GLC Wandsworth hostel; Earlsfield House and Milton Close; terraced properties in Atheldene Road and Wilna Road; sites originally occupied by GLC temporary bungalows, also in Wilna Road; and a number of commercial and shop premises in Garratt Lane. The majority of this site is already owned by the Council and possession of the remainder is readily available by virtue of a confirmed and operative compulsory purchase order made under Part V of the Housing Act 1957 or, as in the case of the temporary bungalow sites, by arrangement with the GLC.

The Director of Development's outline scheme envisages the redevelopment of this site to provide a wide range of Council services. In accordance with the wish of the Council to commence redevelopment on this site as quickly as possible, an old people's 51-bed residential home is already under construction on the extreme eastern boundary and is due for completion by November this year; and the building of a second home is planned to be commenced in 1971 on the southern part of the site. Both homes are integral to the decanting from Brocklebank, which is to be replaced.

The other social service establishments to be provided in this scheme are as follows: -

(a) a combined training centre for mentally and physically handicapped persons, incorporating a day centre for old people (catering in all for approximately 270 persons daily), to be sited at the junction of Garratt Lane with Wilna Road;

(b) a comprehensive health centre to serve a population of 20,000 to 30,000 people, plus a school treatment centre and facilities for six medical practitioners (with an allowance for a possible extension at a later date for a further two practitioners), to be erected on the Garratt Lane frontage on the northern side of the Anchor Mission; and

(c) a 50-place day nursery to replace the existing prefabricated day nursery at Summerley Street, to be located at the rear of the combined training centre.

The housing element of the scheme comprises the erection of 222 dwellings in 2 and 3-storey blocks (of which two units will be specially designed for occupation by disabled persons). Over half of the dwellings will be 2-storey houses and all of them will be designed to the Corporation's usual high standards. In addition, a small parade of shops, with residential accommodation on two floors above, will be erected on the Garratt Lane frontage.

Garratt Lane is very heavily trafficked and carries a large volume of commercial vehicles'; the western side of Garratt Lane is, in fact, zoned for industrial use. It is, for this reason, that the residential element in the scheme will be sited as far removed as possible from this busy main road in order that environmental conditions can be made reasonably satisfactory. Most of the social service establishments and the shops will be sited along the Garratt Lane frontage to form a "buffer area" between the road and the residential accommodation, thus achieving two purposes. First, they will be easily accessible to those using public transport. Secondly, they will be used only during the daytime when traffic noises are more easily acceptable; and they will act as a barrier to prevent traffic and probable industrial noise from troubling the housing tenants and those in the residential homes for the blind and elderly, to the rear of the site.

Approval to the acceptance of a tender for the incorporation in the Garratt Lane Depot of a new central laundry was given by the Council in October 1969 and this work should be completed by August this year. This will then allow the existing establishment on the Brocklebank site to be demolished. The existing boiler-house on the site will need to be retained until all the occupants of Brocklebank have been transferred and until new arrangements have been made for providing heating and hot water to the old people's home in course of construction on the site, and also for Milton Close. A new central boiler house is proposed to be provided near to the Garratt Lane frontage and this will supply space heating and hot water to Milton Close, the new combined training centre, the health centre, the day nursery and possibly to both old people's homes.

The scheme will involve the closure of that part of Atheldene Road running from Earlsfield House in Swaffield Road to a point just south of its junction with Wilna Road and a small part of Wilna Road between Winfrith and Atheldene Roads. Originally, provision was also made in the layout for the closure of that part of Swaffield Road extending along the frontage of Earlsfield House. Consultations have recently taken place on this proposal with the GLC which has indicated that this scheme should not include any part of the highway of Swaffield Road; that this road should remain open at its junction with Garratt Lane; and that no action should be taken that would prejudice the future installation of traffic signals at the intersection. However, the GLC suggest that the scheme should be cast so that a closure at some time in the future is not precluded when improvements to the road system in the area allow this to be done.

Whilst the GLC's objection to the closure of this part of Swaffield Road at the present time is regretted, this requirement has been accepted. With the concurrence of the Social Services Committee and the Planning Committee, we have now approved this outline scheme and have instructed the Director of Development to proceed, without further delay, to prepare a detailed sketch scheme, supported by estimates of costs.

WE RECOMMEND: -

(a) That the action taken in this matter be approved and confirmed;

(b) that a formal application be made to the Minister of Transport for the closure of specified parts of Atheldene Road and Wilna Road; and

(c) that Mr W S Scott, B.Eng., C.Eng., F.I.C.E., F.I.Mun.E., M.I.Struct.E., M.I.M.E., be appointed, upon the recognised terms and conditions, as structural engineer for this scheme.

In assigning names to these two Homes we are of the opinion that it would be most appropriate to recognise the work of two persons closely connected with the immediate community. We therefore propose that the first Home be named Sticklan Close in appreciation of the services of Mr Sticklan M.B.E. who was Warden of Brockle Bank for a period of 18 years, until his retirement in July 1967. We also propose that the second Home be named Sherwood Lodge in token of the voluntary social work among the elderly undertaken for many years by Mrs Margaret B. Sherwood, a member of the Wandsworth Metropolitan Borough Council and former Alderman of the Borough.

In July 1970 the different posts in the new home were considered.

Designation	No of posts	Grade
Matron	1	6
Deputy Matron	1	3
Senior Attendant male or female	1	£17,18/- or £15.6.6.p.w.
Attendant Male	2	£17.3/- p.w.
Attendant Female	8	£14.11.6.p.w.
Cook in charge	1	£17.13/- or £14.0.6.p.w.
General porter 20 hours a week	1	£16.- p.w.
Domestic Assistants	5	£12.3.6.p.w.
Visiting Medical Officer	1	£65.- per annum.

By 25 June 1970 the second old people's Home had started to be built, capital outlay £150.446 including professional fees, staff salaries, furniture and fittings.

By July 1970 at Brockle Bank (stage 1 phase 1) site erection of 56 dwellings costing £247,345.

Building tenders

The following five tenders have recently been obtained in response to an invitation to see selected contractors for the erection upon a fixed price basis, of 12 two storey houses and 42 flats in 3 storey groups: -

Contractor	Tender
L. W. Whitehead Ltd, Lambeth	*£232,015*
C.J.Howard and Son (builders and contractors) Ltd	
Chatham,	*£237,160*
J & J Dean (Contracts) Ltd, Ilford	*£255,473*
Thomas McInerney and Sons Ltd, Croxley Green	*£264,748*
Groudace Ltd, Chatham	*£302,798*

The Director of Development's comparable estimate of the cost of this work amounted to £240,000 and upon his recommendation, we now propose the acceptance of the lowest tender: -

L & W.Whitehead Ltd	*£232.015.*

July 1971 for the Year 1972
Brockle Bank (Stage II - Final Stage) no of dwellings expected 151

A number of these dwellings have been rephrased and carried over from the 1971 programme because of difficulties in planning site of a new social service establishment.

16th September 1971

Brocklebank Site, Wandsworth

Combined Training Centre/Day Centre - The director of Development has submitted to us his detailed sketch scheme for the erection of a combined training centre for the mentally and physically handicapped and a day centre for the elderly on the Brocklebank site, SW18 (Earlsfield).

The site of this combined establishment of approximately 0.539 hectare (1.33 acres), is on the western side of the Brocklebank redevelopment site. It is bounded to the north by the Anchor Mission, to the west by Garratt Lane and to the south by the western end of Wilna Road. The boundary to the east will be formed by a new estate road linking Swaffield Road with the remaining section of Atheldene Road. This site is level and is covered by mostly empty residential properties on the Atheldene Road and Wilna Road frontages and empty residential and shop premises on the Garratt Lane frontage, all of which are soon to be demolished.

The combined centre will cater for 120 mentally handicapped adults, 90 physically handicapped, and 60 elderly people. It will comprise an L-shaped block of 1- and 2-storeys. The 2-storey part will contain workshops, craft rooms, offices, lounges, and rooms for teaching and recreation, linked by a central entrance hall with the single storey block which will contain the dining hall and kitchen. The building will be constructed with a reinforced concrete frame and non-load bearing brick and block panel walls, set on isolated reinforced concrete pad foundations. The roof will be flat; and the external brickwork elevations will be of buff modular bricks with the concrete parapet walls having a natural aggregate finish. It is hoped to commence building work on this project in August 1972.

The main accommodation for the mentally handicapped will be on the first floor of the 2-storey block and that for the physically handicapped will be on the ground floor with some shared accommodation on both floors. Access to the first floor will be by means of a large lift capable of taking several wheelchairs and there will also be a separate goods lift which could be used in the case of emergency. All the main workshops and craft rooms will have a northern aspect to avoid the discomfort from excessive solar heating associated with large glazed areas in summer months. The lounges for the elderly which form part of the day centre accommodation will be on the ground floor, and the training rooms and offices will have a south or west aspect. The dining hall, with windows facing north, east and south, will have a stage with a ramped access, together with special dressing rooms and toilet facilities that will enable it to be used by the physically handicapped. The hall will also be available for evening activities. The adjoining kitchen will supply 300 meals a day for the person using the training centre and the day centre, and also additional meals for the meals on wheels service. Separate toilet facilities will be provided at each floor level and these have been so positioned as to help isolate the more noisy workshop areas from the rest of the building. A caretaker's flat on the second floor level will have an independent access by means of an adjoining secondary escape staircase.

A gas-fired boiler will provide space heating for the whole centre by means of radiators and convectors; and it will also provide hot water, but that to be used by the mentally handicapped will be pre-mixed and controlled to ensure delivery at a safe temperature.

There will be a paved and fenced ball games area and a small garden for cultivation by the mentally handicapped to the north of the centre and a sitting-out area in the south-west corner. The remaining open space area will be landscaped with grass, shrubs and small trees.

The main pedestrian access to the centre will be from Garratt Lane but there will be secondary entrances on the northern and eastern sides of the building which will link with the proposed housing estate footpath system. Vehicular access will be by means of a large courtyard with its entrance at the rear of Atheldene Road. The courtyard will be used for goods deliveries and the meals on wheels service and it will also have four covered bays linked to the main entrance for coaches providing transport for the handicapped. In addition, eleven open car parking spaces will be provided and there will also be some space for vehicles used by disabled persons.

It is estimated that the total cost of the project, including site acquisition costs, staff salaries, professional fees, furnishings, and all other incidental expenditure will amount to just over £535,000.

Capital Estimates (shown to the nearest £1,000)

Est. No	Purpose	Previous Estimate	Current Estimate	Key Sector	Free of Government control	Locally determined schemes quota			
						1971/72	1972/73	1973/74	1974/75
CH63	Social Services Committee Brocklebank Combined Centre: Site Development Furniture and Equipment Fees Salaries	64,000 275,000 20,000 15,000 18,000 ——— 392,000	64,000 398,000 21,000 24,000 28,000 ——— 535,000	398,000 24,000	64,000 19,000	9.000			
CH64	Brocklebank Day Nursery: Site Development Furniture and Equipment Fees Salaries	15,000 37,000 2,000 3,000 4,000 ——— 61,000	15,000 54,000 3,000 4,000 5,000 ——— 82,000	54,000 4,000 3,000	15,000	2,000	3,000		
CH65	Borough Services Committee Land transferred from GLC to LBW Chalmers Street Latchmere Grove	——— ———	33,000 16,000 ——— 49,000		33,000 16,000				

Demolition Works, December 1971.

We have approved acceptance of the tender (£8,890) submitted by H. Smith & Co., (Orpington) Ltd the lowest obtained from 6 specialist contractors - for the demolition upon a fixed price basis of a further 51 properties, the sites of which are acquired for the Redevelopment of the Brockle Bank site, S.W.18.

The Finance Committee have been asked to submit the necessary concerning estimate.

1972 Brockle Bank Day Nurseries.

The following 4 tenders have recently been obtained in response to an invitation to seven selected contractors for the erection upon a fixed-price basis, of a 60 place day nursery: -

Contractor	Tender
C. Ash and Son Ltd, Clapham	*£66,870*
Joseph Cartwright Ltd, Mitcham	*£90,040*
J. Garrett and Son, Balham	*£92,616*
Edward Dyke (Greenwich) Ltd, Greenwich	*£95.428*

The director of Development's comparable estimate of this cost of this work is £65,350.

We now propose to accept the lowest tender; the contractors concerned have undertaken to complete all the works involved within a period of fifty weeks and this is considered reasonable.

In June 1972 the different posts in the second new Home, Sherwood Lodge, which was due to open in December 1972 were considered: -

Designation	No of posts	Grade
Superintendent	1	Range 6 (3-7)
Deputy	1	Scale 4
Clerical Assistant	1 (half time)	CL ½
Senior Attendant	1	
Care Assistants	10	
Cook in Charge	1	
Domestic Assistants	5	
General Porter	1 (half time)	
Visiting Medical Officer	1 (part time)	

24th February 1972

Health Centre

Brocklebank Site - We are pleased to report that the Director of Development has submitted to us his detailed sketch scheme for a third comprehensive health centre in Wandsworth; and that this centre is to be built as part of the Brocklebank redevelopment scheme, SW18 (Earlsfield).

The site for this establishment which is in the process of being cleared, has an area of 0.309 hectare (0.765 acre), and is situated next to the Anchor Mission Hall between Garratt Lane and Atheldene Road, just south of Swaffield Road.

Although it is a somewhat larger establishment than those proposed to be built in Balham and Battersea upon which we reported in detail to the Council in November and December last, the construction, planning, layout and facilities provided are basically the same, having been designed to accommodate Council health services, school health services and general medical practitioner suites.

The building, roughly oblong in shape, will be generally of one-storey construction, with practically all of the services at ground floor level. Internally, it will be planned around a central core comprising the waiting and health education areas, reception, administration and accommodation for audiology and speech therapy. This central core will be bounded by corridors giving access to all the rooms on the periphery of the building. The main points of difference from the other two establishments are the increased number of general practitioner suites (six) compared with Balham (five) and Battersea (four), and the provision of accommodation for audiology and speech therapy. Also, because of the larger size of this establishment, accommodation will be included for a resident caretaker' this accommodation will be situated at first floor level immediately above the school dental wing.

Externally, such minor variations of treatment as are proposed have been necessitated solely because of the different location. For this reason, the building will have a flat roof and the facing brickwork will match the character of the proposed redevelopment adjoining.

The public pedestrian approach to the main entrance, which will be set well back from the road, will be from Garratt Lane, where provision will be made for a bus lay-by. The staff entrance and the entrance to the caretaker's flat will be on the south side of the building. Parking facilities will be provided at the rear of the building for the public and on the south side of the building, behind the Anchor Mission for the staff, with vehicular access from Atheldene Road.

On the assumption that building work will commence in April 1973, it is estimated that the total cost of this project, including site acquisition costs, staff salaries, professional fees, furnishing and all other incidental expenditure, will amount to just over £222,000.

We have approved this detailed scheme and the Planning Committee have concurred.

We attach high priority to this project and we have therefore asked the Finance Committee to consider it accordingly in relation to the Council's development budget as a whole.

WE RECOMMEND - That the action we have taken in this matter be approved and confirmed.

13 April 1972

Brocklebank Site, Earlsfield

Stage II - Detailed Scheme. WE have examined the detailed sketch scheme prepared by the Director of Development for the redevelopment of Stage II of the housing element of the Brocklebank site, SW18 (Earlsfield).

The bulk of the land comprising the overall Brocklebank site is held by the Council under the National Assistance Act 1948, the Children's Act 1948 and the Housing Act 1957. The Stage II housing site itself consists of land which is already owned by the Corporation under these powers of where possession is available either under a confirmed and operative compulsory purchase order made by the Council or by arrangement with the GLC. Originally, redevelopment of this particular stage was due to have commenced this year but, because of delays in decanting from the existing Brocklebank Institution and the lengthy period which will then be required for demolition of that building, it is unlikely that redevelopment will commence before April 1973.

The overall site, which has an area of 6,68 hectares (6.5 acres), is situated on the eastern side of Garratt Lane and is generally bounded by Brocklebank Road, Swaffield Road and Wilna Road. In December 1969, the Council approved the comprehensive redevelopment of the whole site and agreed that the following social service establishments and new housing should be provided there:-

(a) a combined training centre for mentally and physically handicapped persons, incorporating a day centre for 50 elderly people;

(b) a comprehensive health centre, including a school treatment centre and facilities for a number of local medical practitioners;

(c) a 50-place day nursery (together with a special unit for 9 handicapped children);

(d) two 51-bed residential homes for old people;

(e) 222 dwellings in 2- and 3-storey blocks (of which 2 units were to be specifically designed for occupation by handicapped persons); and

(f)   a small parade of shops with residential accommodation above.

Since then, a number of modifications have necessarily been made to the originally approved layout, the main one being the provision of a children's home as part of the scheme to replace "Beechholme" which will result in the reduction from 222 to 207 of the total number of dwellings to be provided at this site. One of the old people's homes (Stricklan Lodge") has already been built and is now occupied and at present the second home is under construction. Work on the day nursery is programmed to start in Jun 1972, on the combined training centre in December 1972 and on the comprehensive health centre in April 1973. The building of the children's home was programmed to start in January 1972 but has been delayed due to difficulties in obtaining planning permission from the redevelopment of "Beechholme". Stage I of the housing element of this scheme, which comprises 56 dwellings, is also under construction and these detailed proposals relate to the remainder of the site which is available for housing development. These proposals are generally in accord with the approved outline scheme.

The Stage II housing site, which has a net area of 2.47 hectares (6.09 acres), comprises the greater part of the land occupied by the existing Brocklebank Institution to the rear of privately-owned properties in Brocklebank Road and Wilna Road; together with the sites of some of the former residential properties on the eastern side of Atheldene Road; two isolated cleared temporary bungalow sites and the former sites of some houses and shops near the junction of Garratt Lane and Swaffield Road.

The Director of Development's detailed scheme for the site proposes the erection of 92 three-bedroom and 14 four-bedroom 2-storey houses, 38 one-bedroom flats in two 3-storey blocks which will also incorporate 2 three-bedroom flats for the handicapped, together with a 2-storey block comprising 5 lock-up shops and 5 two-bedroom flats above - making a total of 151 new dwellings. Most of the 2-storey houses will be grouped in short terraces around the centre of the site with the 3-storey blocks of flats located on the southern and western boundaries of this development. The 2-storey block of shops with flats above will be located on the Garratt Lane frontage between Swaffield Road and the new comprehensive health centre. All the new housing will be of load bearing brick wall construction and it is anticipated that the buildings will have normal concrete strip foundations. The houses will have pitched roofs covered with blue/grey interlocking tiles and the remaining blocks of dwellings will have flat roofs. Elevations will probably be in a light buff coloured facing brick.

Space heating will be by means of individual warm air electric heating units with domestic hot water supplied by immersion heaters. Refuse disposal will be by means of individual bins and ample storage space will be provided for each dwelling. The houses will be equipped with separate clothes posts in the rear gardens and communal clothes drying rooms will be provided in the blocks, supplemented by a small number of external clothes posts, for use by the tenants of the flats.

Adequate facilities will be provided in the overall housing estate for car parking and initially one small site will be required by the London Electricity Board for a transformer chamber. Another site for a transformer chamber has been provisionally reserved in case it should be needed to increase electricity supplies to the new development in this area.

A large ball games area for older children will be formed near the western boundary of the new estate and two spaces containing play equipment for younger children will be located in courts formed by the terraces of houses. Each house will have an enclosed rear garden and the remaining areas not occupied by other buildings, roads, footpaths, parking and play areas will be pleasantly landscaped with trees and plants, and turfed or paved. The scheme, which has been formulated to allow maximum pedestrian/vehicular segregation, involves the stopping-up of part of Atheldene Road and the necessary authority for this closure has already been obtained.

The total cost of all the works involved in this second stage, including site acquisition costs, professional fees, staff salaries and all other incidental expenditure, is estimated to amount to £1,505,500.

We have asked the officers to examine the possibility of restricting the use of certain of the pedestrian accessways which will serve the new housing estate so as to ensure privacy for the tenants who will occupy the dwellings close to these footpaths. In addition, we have given instructions for a number of minor modifications to be incorporated in the design and layout of a small number of the ground floor dwellings so that, if the need should arise at any time when they are vacant, these units would also be suitable for occupation by handicapped people. Our attention has particularly been drawn to the estimated charge of £70 per dwelling which the South Eastern Gas Board will require for installing merely a gas point for a cooker in each kitchen. We feel that this charge is excessive and, by 10 votes to 9, we have given instructions for gas points to be omitted from all the dwellings in this scheme. Electric points will, of course, be installed in the kitchens so as to provide tenants with means of cooking.

The Planning Committee have concurred and we have asked the Finance Committee to submit the necessary budget variation.

WE RECOMMEND - That the revised detailed scheme we have described for the redevelopment of the Brocklebank (Stage II - Final Stage) site be approved.

23rd November 1972

Brocklebank Site, Earlsfield.

Combined Training Centre/Day Centre. The following tenders have recently been obtained in response to an invitation to five selected contractors for the erection, upon a fixed-price basis, of a combined training centre for the mentally and physically handicapped - incorporating a day centre for old people, on part of the Brocklebank Site, SW18 (Earlsfield); together with an estimate submitted by the Director of Building Works in competition:-

	Tender/Estimate £
Director of Building Works	510,000
L & W Whitehead Ltd., Clapham	533,924
F G Minter & Co., Ltd., Putney	546,962
Keith Andrew & Co. (London) Ltd., Westminster	548,320
Crudens Ltd., Stanmore	553,430
W J Simms, Son & Cooke Ltd., Croydon	559,469

The Director of development's comparable estimate for the cost of these works amounted to £550,000.

We now propose that the estimate submitted by the Director of Building Works be approved; the Director has undertaken to complete all the works involved within a period of 96 weeks and this is considered reasonable.

A detailed analysis of the Director of Building Work's estimate is now being prepared for discussion with the Department of Health and Social Security before a revised costs limit for the project can be agreed. The Department may, however, require the Council to make savings in the scheme. To avoid any delay in the commencement of the works, we have authorised our Chairman, Vice-Chairman, together with a member of the minority party, to approve any necessary savings and adjustments, which will in no way prejudice the standard of planning and design, in order to meet the Department's requirements.

We have asked the Finance Committee to submit the necessary budget variation, and

WE RECOMMEND - That the estimate (510,000) of the Director of Building Works for these works be approved.

Day Nursery - The following further tenders have also recently been obtained in response to an invitation to five selected contractors for the erection, upon a fixed-price basis, of a 60-place day nursery on another part of this site, together with an estimate submitted by the Director of Building Works in competition:-

	Tender/Estimate £
L & W Whitehead Ltd., Clapham	95,346
F G Minter & Co. Ltd. Putney	99,926
Keith Andrew & CO. (London) Ltd., Westminster	99,940
W J Simms, Son and Cooke, Ltd., Croydon	104,653
Director of Building Works	105,000
Crudens Ltd., Stanmore	105,100

The Director of Development's comparable estimate of the cost of these works amounted to £95,000.

We now propose the acceptance of the lowest tender; the contractors concerned have undertaken to complete all the works involved within a period of 52 weeks and this is considered reasonable.

A detailed tender analysis is now being prepared for discussion with the Department before a revised costs limit for this project can be agreed. Here again, the Department may require the Council to make savings in the scheme. To avoid any delay in the commencement of the works, we have authorised our Chairman, Vice-Chairman, together with a member of the minority party, to approve any necessary savings and adjustments, which will in no way prejudice the standard of planning and design, in order to meet the Department's requirements.

In May this year, the Council authorised the acceptance of a tender for the erection of this day nursery, but the successful contractor withdrew. Fresh tenders were then invited but, due to the withdrawal of the lowest tender and the excessive cost of the next lowest tender, we recently decided to invite further tenders.

We have asked the Finance Committee to submit the necessary budget variation, and

WE RECOMMEND - That the tender (95,346) of L & W Whitehead Ltd., for these works be accepted.

A visit to the site in 2004 showed that the two units, namely Sticklan Close and Sherwood Court are no longer in existence.

CHAPTER 9: *My Memories*

I was 11 months old when we moved into Swaffield Road Institution; my father took the post of Assistant Master in May 1935.

I grew up accepting our living conditions as quite normal. Friends and relations thought otherwise and always asked to stay the night, being able then to brag that they had "slept in the workhouse" afterwards. Although Swaffield Road had been designated as an Institution in 1915 it was still referred to as "The Workhouse" by people locally and was still run on a daily basis very much the same as when it was a "Workhouse"

As I grew up I gradually learned the names of the staff. Our quarters were opposite the Gate House and were situated either side of the main gates. Apart from the Gate House Keepers an inmate also worked there. His surname was Morgan and Morgan he liked to be called. He was a very polite dapper little man and knew all the names of the staff. Visitors would be taken by him to the relative member of staff they had come to visit and he also knew all the wards and where they were situated. He tried to persuade me to say his name and when very young could only manage "Orgi", later it became "Gorgi" and "Gorgi" it remained to the day we left the institution!

The Gate House had a little female tabby cat. Originally it was a stray, it was fed and so stayed and helped to keep the mice down. Sometimes my mother would give me some scraps of food for her and I liked to take them to her. She had several lots of kittens, I used to love going in to see them. Unfortunately when the kittens were two days old the Gate Keeper would drown them in a pail of water. When he told me I was very upset, and would not speak to him for a long time. That little cat would go around calling for her kittens for days. My mother, who was an animal lover, was horrified, and eventually persuaded my father to have the poor little cat spayed. She even offered to pay for the operation herself, but my father put the cost through the "expenses".

By the time I was four years old I would sometimes do the "rounds of the institution" with my father. I was told to be good, so I dare not say a word unless I was spoken to and just tucked my hand in his and off we would go. All the staff knew me of course and they would offer me a sweet. I would not take one until my father said yes, if I had a sweet in every department we went to I would not have eaten my lunch.

I was fascinated by the laundry, although I did not like the wet floor. There were lots of large machines working. The machine I liked the best was the "Calender". It was a long machine with lots of heated revolving rollers. Two women would feed the machine from one end (after the item had been pulled straight) and slowly it would disappear between the rollers, guided by tapes threaded through the rollers to come out the other end with two women taking the ironed item folding it up and putting it into the linen basket. I liked to see the item disappear into the machine and try to follow it along saying to myself, "it goes over there and under there " all along the machine until it came out the other end. All the items that were washed in the laundry had the name of the establishment that it belonged to stitched in red on the corner, which when folded had to be on the outside.

The Linen Room was a favourite of mine. It smelt so lovely and clean with a wooden floor that was highly polished and I used to slide on it. It was run by three lovely women officers and two inmates who did all the work on the treadle machines. The officers names were Miss Smith, Miss Blanchard and Miss Longman. They were very good with me and let me hide in one of the linen trolleys, putting linen over me so I could not be seen. Then when one of them returned to the Linen Room they would pretend they did not know where I was and come to find me, so that I could say "Boo" to them.

I was very interested in the Mattress Shop. All the mattresses were hand made with "horse hair" and very hard. They were made in a "bed frame", all single size of course. The mattress maker was very skilled and would show me how he could put the little round pieces of leather on the mattress as he pushed his threader to the other side, hooking the back piece of leather to the top side. Years later my father said that the Mattress Shop was always a source of interest to visitors.

Our lounge was in the round windowed room beside the gates, looking down the approach road. At night wooden rounded shutters were put up against the windows. These shutters had long metal spikes that went through the window frame into the lounge and attached to the window frame inside were pieces of chain with a flat piece of metal that was put into the eye of the metal spikes. This was always my job each evening to secure the shutters. These shutters were necessary because sometimes men would try to get into the hostel (previously Casual Wards) which had the entrance in the approach road after it was closed and if they could not get in would come to the Institution Gates and cause trouble. Often they were drunk, and would have to be taken away by the police. If they were not drunk they could sometimes be allowed into the Institution. The Gate House also had the same shutters. The pedestrian gate had a window in it so that the Gate Keeper could see who was outside at night. The pedestrian gate had a fixed light over it not a swinging one.

My parents bedroom

Reception ward

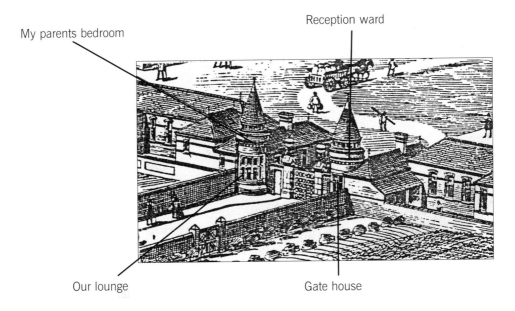

Our lounge

Gate house

We had a "maid", she was one of the inmates. Her name was Mary Price, she was a very sweet gentle soul. My mother told me when I was older that "she did not have a living soul in the world". Mary would come over to our quarters after she had her breakfast and help my mother clear away after our breakfast. She would do anything my mother needed help with during the morning and then go to the dining hall for lunch.

After lunch she would return and spend the rest of the day with us returning to her ward in the evening. My mother always gave her supper, some of what we would have, eating it in the kitchen. Now and again my mother would buy her kippers for a special treat, she liked to have bread and butter with them. I can remember watching her sit down at the large table ready to start her supper.

It was a very sad day for Mary when we had to move away during the Second World War as my father joined the Royal Air Force. His post was kept open for him, and when we returned - so did Mary. The next time we moved, some years later, it was for good. We did not see Mary again. We were informed when she died. It was a sad day for us.

I had a large toy cupboard in the room where the stairs were. Each November I had to turn it out and put to one side the toys I did not play with any more. I was a very lucky girl and always had lots of toys. The toys I did not play with were taken to a man named Terry who ran an Off-Licence in Garratt Lane. He collected toys from families who were customers in his shop and gave them out to all the very poor families locally each Christmas. Needless to say there were plenty of very poor families around Garratt Lane. Terry did this for a great many years and it was a gesture that was appreciated by both the families who gave as well as the families who received.

The men's hostel was run by a Mr Doran. He was married and I used to call his wife Auntie Doran. I would go to stay with them if my parents were going out and would be back late. They had a lovely garden with masses of Hollyhocks all round the walls. There was a side gate that led to the back of the building. Through this were all the indoor stone task cells. I used to run round there and try to climb in one of them. They had a rounded roof of brick and I used to shout into them to get an echo back. They did tell me what these cells were for but as a young child I did not understand. Only later did I realise the significance of the Guernsey Spalls still on the floor of the cells.

George Creasey was the Baker when we were at Swaffield Road. He was tall and very jolly and an excellent baker. He lived locally and his wife ran a sweet-shop. The loaves of white bread weighed 4lbs, so we always had half a loaf; this was for my father as my mother and me would only eat brown bread, we bought it from a local shop.

Mr John Roe was the Store Keeper who would bring us our order from the stores. If the stores did not stock the item my mother requested she had to buy it locally. My mother became great friends with Mr Roe and his wife, which lasted many years, even after we left Swaffield Road.

During the Second World War the hall in our quarters was "shored-up" with large timber and mattresses were put down on the floor. We slept there for some time until my father joined the Royal Air Force. I remember the telephone was in the hall, and it would ring for my father to attend to a problem in the Institution. The night the wards were flooded, my mother went to help as well and I was left to sleep on my own. We would also use the hall in the day-time during an air-raid, I used to take some toys with me, and my mother, Mary and me would sit there until the "all clear" sounded.

The institution had quite a lot of visitors. There would be the regular Visiting Committees as well as Officers from County Hall, Foreign Doctors, and Health Officials. After the usual tour of the Institution these people would have to be entertained. Mr & Mrs Brown (the Master & Matron) would do some of the entertaining, but my parents seemed to do most of it. My mother would serve freshly baked scones and butter with coffee or tea in the mornings and freshly made cakes and tea for the afternoon. I always wanted to be involved if I was at home at the time and remember being allowed to offer the plates of scones and little cakes to the visitors. I was told not to speak until spoken to, but I was quite happy in my little chair listening and watching the visitors. As I grew older I can remember helping my mother set out the tea tray and put the doilies on the plate for the scones & cakes.

One day when I was about 12 years old my parents were out and only Mary was with me. The Visiting Committee called one afternoon. I invited them in and realised that I would have to entertain them on my own if my parents did not come back in time. There were not any scones or cakes available, my mother was not expecting anyone obviously, but there were plenty of biscuits. I laid the tea tray, made the tea or coffee and served it up. Helping my mother and being observant during the previous years paid off.

Apparently the Visiting Committee told my father later that they were very well entertained and he could be proud of me.

A little way up from the gates was the main building housing the Chapel, Long Committee Room, Master's Office, General Office and Assistant Master's Office; this then led on to the Dining Hall and beyond that to the main stores and kitchens.

The front entrance of this building was "grand", with curved arches over the top of a covered porch. The sides were open so that you could see the shrubs either side and the flooring had red stone tiles. I loved this entrance and would go inside and close the door and then open it and walk across the tiles and down the steps feeling very important. Sometimes I would go there to play ball, I don't know what people thought of me at those times but no one complained about me.

As a family we enjoyed having a tennis court for staff use. Both my parents played tennis with friends regularly. When older, with a school friend who was staying with me, we would play tennis on our own.

Apart from four years of the Second World War, I spent most of my first 15 years growing up in Swaffield Road Institution. I feel privileged to have experienced a very important era of social history.

By early 1972 the last of the residents had been moved from Brockle Bank and it was finally closed down for the last remaining buildings to be demolished.

Unfortunately the buildings were pulled down with few photographs having been taken of the most important aspect of the establishment, for perpetuity. I can remember them very well but cannot reproduce them; this I find very frustrating. I would like to think that my parents would be pleased that I have written this book so that the memory of Swaffield Road would not be lost in the annals of time.

CHAPTER 10: *Postscript*

On examination of the Brocklebank site I could not find any commemorative plaque or paving stone. However, I did find a name plate saying "Brocklebank Estate".

I contacted Wandsworth Town Hall who put me in touch with Paul McCue, Deputy Director of Leisure and Amenity Services. He was very helpful and understanding and suggested designing a Blue Plaque. He contacted Christopher Buss, Director of Housing and between them they drew up and produced a blue plaque which was installed on site in April 2005.

On 29 April 2005 we had a photo-shoot with the Wandsworth Borough News. Paul McCue came together with Brian Reilly who represented the Housing department to record the Blue Plaque's installation. I was able to thank them once again for their cooperation in my quest for recognition of Brocklebank's existence.

The Site of the

Wandsworth and Clapham
Union Workhouse

(Swaffield Road Workhouse)

Later renamed Brocklebank

1886 - 1972

W.B.N. & Deadline Pik

Opal Gibson, Brian Reilly and Paul McCue on the Brocklebank Estate with the
Blue Plaque in situ